NEUROPSYCHOLOGY OF LEFT-HANDEDNESS

ERRATA

NEUROPSYCHOLOGY OF LEFT-HANDEDNESS
Edited by Jeannine Herron

In the chapter by Helen Shaner Schevill, beginning on page 331, Figures 1 and 2 are reversed. The figure appearing on page 337 should appear on page 335. The figure on page 335 should appear on page 337. The legends appear correctly.

PERSPECTIVES IN
NEUROLINGUISTICS and PSYCHOLINGUISTICS

Harry A. Whitaker, Series Editor
DEPARTMENT OF PSYCHOLOGY
THE UNIVERSITY OF ROCHESTER
ROCHESTER, NEW YORK

HAIGANOOSH WHITAKER and HARRY A. WHITAKER (Eds.).
Studies in Neurolinguistics, Volumes 1, 2, and 3

NORMAN J. LASS (Ed.). Contemporary Issues in Experimental Phonetics

JASON W. BROWN. Mind, Brain, and Consciousness: The Neuropsychology of Cognition

SIDNEY J. SEGALOWITZ and FREDERIC A. GRUBER (Eds.). Language Development and Neurological Theory

SUSAN CURTISS. Genie: A Psycholinguistic Study of a Modern-Day "Wild Child"

JOHN MACNAMARA (Ed.). Language Learning and Thought

I. M. SCHLESINGER and LILA NAMIR (Eds.). Sign Language of the Deaf: Psychological, Linguistic, and Sociological Perspectives

WILLIAM C. RITCHIE (Ed.). Second Language Acquisition Research: Issues and Implications

PATRICIA SIPLE (Ed.). Understanding Language through Sign Language Research

MARTIN L. ALBERT and LORAINE K. OBLER. The Bilingual Brain: Neurophysiological and Neurolinguistic Aspects of Bilingualism

HAIGANOOSH WHITAKER and HARRY A. WHITAKER (Eds.). Studies in Neurolinguistics, Volume 4

TALMY GIVON. On Understanding Grammar

CHARLES J. FILLMORE, DANIEL KEMPLER and WILLIAM S-Y. WANG (Eds.). Individual Differences in Language Ability and Language Behavior

JEANNINE HERRON (Ed.). Neuropsychology of Left-Handedness

FRANCOIS BOLLER and MAUREEN DENNIS (Eds.). Auditory Comprehension: Clinical and Experimental Studies with the Token Test

In preparation

R. W. RIEBER (Ed.). Language Development and Aphasia in Children: New Essays and a Translation of "Kindersprache und Aphasie" by Emil Fröschels

NEUROPSYCHOLOGY OF LEFT-HANDEDNESS

Edited by

JEANNINE HERRON

Langley Porter Institute
University of California, San Francisco
San Francisco, California

ACADEMIC PRESS

A Subsidiary of Harcourt Brace Jovanovich, Publishers

New York   London   Toronto   Sydney   San Francisco

ACADEMIC PRESS, INC.
111 Fifth Avenue, New York, New York 10003

United Kingdom Edition published by
ACADEMIC PRESS, INC. (LONDON) LTD.
24/28 Oval Road, London NW1 7DX

Library of Congress Cataloging in Publication Data
Main entry under title:

Neuropsychology of left–handedness.

(Perspectives in neurolinguistics and psycholinguis–
tics)
Includes bibliographies and index.
1. Left– and right–handedness. 2. Neuropsychology.
I. Herron, Jeannine. [DNLM: 1. Laterality.
2. Neurophysiology. WL335 N494]
QP385.N45   612'.76   79–23854
ISBN 0–12–343150–6

PRINTED IN THE UNITED STATES OF AMERICA

80 81 82 83   9 8 7 6 5 4 3 2 1

Contents

I

WHENCE SINISTRALITY?

1

Left-Handedness: Early Theories, Facts, and Fancies   3

LAUREN JULIUS HARRIS

13
Cognitive Deficit and Left-Handedness: A Cautionary Note 281

JAMES M. SWANSON, MARCEL KINSBOURNE, AND JOSEPH M. HORN

14
Age-Related Changes in Cognitive Abilities and Hemispheric Specialization 293

KATHERINE M. KOCEL

15
Which Hand Is the "Eye" of the Blind?—A New Look at an Old Question 303

LAUREN JULIUS HARRIS

16
Tactile Learning, Handedness, and Reading Disability

HELEN SHANER SCHEVILL

List of Contributors

Numbers in parentheses indicate the pages on which the authors' contributions begin.

CHARLES E. BOKLAGE (115), Department of Microbiology, East Carolina University Medical School, Greenville, North Carolina 27834

MICHAEL C. CORBALLIS (159), Department of Psychology, University of Auckland, Auckland, New Zealand

DIANA DEUTSCH (263), Department of Psychology, University of California, San Diego, La Jolla, California 92101

RUBEN C. GUR (199, 211), Department of Psychology, University of Pennsylvania, Philadelphia, Pennsylvania 19174

RAQUEL E. GUR (211), Department of Psychiatry, University of Pennsylvania, Philadelphia, Pennsylvania 19174

LAUREN JULIUS HARRIS (3, 303), Department of Psychology, Michigan State University, East Lansing, Michigan 48824

JEANNINE HERRON (233), Langley Porter Institute, University of California, San Francisco, San Francisco, California 94143

JOSEPH M. HORN (281), Department of Psychiatry, University of Texas at Austin, Austin, Texas 98112

MARCEL KINSBOURNE (177, 281), The Hospital for Sick Children, Toronto, Ontario, Canada M5G 1X8

KATHERINE M. KOCEL (293), Department of Psychology, University of Hawaii, Honolulu, Hawaii 96822

JERRE LEVY (199), Department of Behavioral Sciences, University of Chicago, Chicago, Illinois 60637

CAROLYN J. MEBERT* (273), Department of Psychology, Boston University, Boston, Massachusetts 02215

GEORGE F. MICHEL (273), Department of Psychiatric Research, Children's Hospital Medical Center, Boston, Massachusetts 02215

PAUL SATZ (189), Department of Psychology, University of Victoria, Victoria, British Columbia, Canada V8W 2Y2

HELEN SHANER SCHEVILL (331), Graduate School of Education, University of Pennsylvania, Philadelphia, Pennsylvania 19174

ALAN SEARLEMAN† (139), Department of Psychology, State University of New York at Stony Brook, Stony Brook, New York 11794

SALLY P. SPRINGER (139), Department of Psychology, State University of New York at Stony Brook, Stony Brook, New York 11794

JAMES M. SWANSON (281), The Hospital for Sick Children, Toronto, Ontario, Canada M5G 1X8

SANDRA F. WITELSON (79), Department of Psychiatry, Chedoke-McMaster Hospital, McMaster University, Hamilton, Ontario, Canada L8N 3L6

*Present address: Department of Psychology, University of New Hampshire, Durham, New Hampshire 03824

†Present address: Department of Psychology, St. Lawrence University, Canton, New York 13617

Preface

Derided, chided — the offending hand smacked with a ruler, even tied behind the back. Shamed and blamed, left-handers have suffered vicious assaults. Despite this history, left-handers did not quietly wither away. They survived. Why? Because, as this book shows, they do not choose their preference; they follow a neurological imperative.

This neurological imperative is the subject of this book. What is unique about the brain organization of left-handers? Where does it come from? How does it vary among left-handers, and how is it expressed in terms of ability or personality? Research on left-handedness has snowballed in recent years because of the surge of interest in the specialties of the two cerebral hemispheres. This volume serves to bring together representative studies and reviews by the foremost investigators in this field.

The book is introduced with a witty and scholarly chapter that takes the reader historically through some of the more colorful theories of left-handedness. This introduction lays the groundwork for the newer data on left-handedness presented in later chapters. In the first section other authors probe current ideas about the origins of left-handedness: possible genetic mechanisms, the manner in which asymmetries may occur during the first cell cleavages following fertilization, handedness of twins, and the possibility that some left-handedness may be due to environmental (even pathological) influences.

Quite early in the book the neurological imperative appears: Hand preference is linked to the functional organization of the two hemispheres of the brain. The brain's activity is aimed toward behavior; to study its organization is to take into account the asymmetric components of the entire sensory–cognitive–motor loop: from the environment back to the environment.

In the second section several chapters are devoted to investigations of asymmetric hemisphere specialization in right- and left-handers. A variety of research methods are presented, and different groups of left-handers are identified and examined separately: male and female, strong left-preferrers and ambidexters, familial and nonfamilial left-handers, and those who prefer an "inverted" position for writing as opposed to a "noninverted" position.

As the brain has been probed in more detail in the last two decades, we find the list of asymmetries growing remarkably. There are structural asymmetries, functional asymmetries (sensory, motor, and cognitive), and even biochemical asymmetries. How are asymmetric patterns of organization developed? What is the relationship of hemisphere asymmetries to eye, foot, hand, or ear preference? Does a particular pattern produce "talent"—musical, mathematical, or artistic genius? (It does not take too much wondering to be curious why Michelangelo, Leonardo da Vinci, Holbein, Picasso, and Escher were all left-handed.) Or are left-handers really "gauche"? Matters of skill and achievement are considered in the final section.

These are the kinds of questions that concern researchers in the brain sciences today. The study of left-handedness serves a vital role in this research because it is frequently through the exceptions that we understand the rule. Left-handers provide a population that varies in brain asymmetry, and by examining different groups of left-handers and asking the same questions about each one, investigators are learning much about brain organization.

Although the subjects of these investigations are left-handers, the real questions being asked are not just about left-handedness per se, but about how the human brain functions.

This book is dedicated to left-handers. At last their unique attributes are seen in the light of modern research, research that is supplying some of the most important clues to help answer our most probing questions into the mysteries of the human brain.

I would like to acknowledge the assistance and encouragement of my colleagues David Galin, Jack Johnstone, and Robert Ornstein, and of my right-hand (and right-handed) man (and husband), Matt.

I

WHENCE SINISTRALITY?

1

Left-Handedness:
Early Theories,
Facts, and Fancies[1]

LAUREN JULIUS HARRIS

The left hand has nothing to do with conducting. Its proper place is in the waistcoat pocket, from which it should emerge to restrain, or to make some minor gesture—for which in any case a scarcely perceptible glance should suffice.

—RICHARD STRAUSS
quoted by Schonberg, 1967, p. 237

The left-handed are precious; they take places which are inconvenient for the rest.

JEAN VALJEAN
in Victor Hugo's *Les Miserables*

I have not adequate knowledge derived from experience to warrant me in expressing an opinion as to the best means of dealing with left-handed pupils.

A. B. POLAND
School Superintendent
Newark, New Jersey (McMullin, 1914)

[1] This chapter is an expanded version of a paper presented at a symposium, *The Sinistral Mind*, March 3-4, 1977, San Francisco, Calif., and at a conference, *Left-handedness, Brain Organization, and Learning*, March 5-6, 1977, University of California, Berkeley. The section on "Ambidextral Culture" was presented, in different form, in papers at the Annual Meetings of the Midwest Psychological Association (Harris, 1978) and the International Neuropsychology Society (Harris, 1979).

I am grateful to the staff of the Science Library and the Inter-Library Loan Office of Michigan State University for their help. Preparation of this paper was supported, in part, by an All-University grant from Michigan State University.

3

The stranger greets thy hand with proffered left?
Accept not: 'tis of loyalty bereft.
Left-handed friends are underhanded foes;
True openness a swordless right hand shows.

—HARVEY
Sheep in Wolves' Clothing, (Burt, 1937, p. 314).

His name is Babe Ruth. He is built like a bale of cotton and
pitches lefthanded for the Boston Red Sox. All lefthanders are
peculiar and Babe is no exception, because he can also bat.

—ANON. NEW YORK SPORTSWRITER
quoted by Creamer, 1974, p. 108.

INTRODUCTION

"Cack-handed, bang-handed, wacky-handed, gammy, keggy, scrammy, skiffly, skivvery, watty, coochy, schoochy, scroochy, quiffy, bawky, cowey, cowley, hawky, garpawed, kay-pawed, and cow-pawed"—the British have proved themselves true adepts at the sport of naming left-handers, and these are a few of the terms they have coined. No surprise that nearly all are ugly in tone (e.g., cack-handed from "cack," meaning excrement).[2]

Left-handers, being exceptions to the rule of right-handedness, have provoked more than mean-spirited names; like many minorities, they also have inspired enmity, suspicion, and the reputation for lacking practically every human virtue and skill. For instance, their supposed deficiency in finer muscular coordination inspired the late British educational psychologist, Cyril Burt, to rhapsodize: "They squint, they stammer, they shuffle and shamble, they flounder about like seals out of water. Awkward in the house, and clumsy in their games, they are fumblers and bunglers at whatever they do . . . [1937, p. 287]."

Proportionately more left-handers than right-handers also have been said to be psychoneurotic, epileptic, stutterers, reading-disabled, mentally retarded, mirror-writers, poor in penmanship, deficient in spatial or artistic

---

[2] These and other terms were collected by Samuel Orton and reported by Michael Barsley, an estimable philo-left-hander, in his book, *Left-handed Man in a Right-handed World* (1970, pp. 157–158). Orton also listed "southpaw"—the only name likely to be familiar to North Americans. The term is believed to have arisen from the position of the arm of a left-handed pitcher in an old baseball park in Chicago. In this park, when the left-handed pitcher faced west, with the setting sun behind him, his pitching arm was on the south side of his body. "Southpaw" is not a term of opprobrium, but still, the minority was singled out. Right-handed pitchers, after all, are not called "northpaws."

sense, stubborn, resistful of authority, inclined to lives of crime and moral dissolution, dirty, and homosexual or bisexual. Little wonder that they also have been deemed unlucky. As Quarles warned, "If left-hand fortune gives thee left-hand chance, be wisely patient [quoted in Burt, 1937]."

In part redress, a smaller number of scientists and other writers have said positive, or at least neutral, things about left-handers—that proportionately more of them than right-handers are twins, male, artistic, athletic, and even intellectually superior. Burt himself, in the same passage quoted above, went on to say that "Among bright and imaginative children of an emotional disposition, left-handedness is far from rare; and biographers report many eminent persons, of high ability and unquestioned skill, as having been left-handed [1937, p. 287]." Burt offered the even then overworked examples of DaVinci and Michelangelo, but added Michelangelo's contemporary, Sebastiano del Piombo. Largely, though, the negative characterizations have won the day. As a leading nineteenth-century German anatomist said, "That a few great men, such as Leonardo da Vinci, were left-handed, does not neutralize the prevalent belief—in all ages—that left-handedness implies a sub-standard subject [Von Bardeleben in Anon., 1914, p. 312]."

Why left-handedness? Why this peculiar exception to majority rule? There have been nearly as many different theories about "sinistrality" as there are supposed facts about the phenomenon itself—and the theories, or the evidence supporting them, have come from an astonishing variety of disciplines (e.g., paleontology, genetics, education, psychoanalysis, criminology, speech pathology, neurology, art history, and developmental psychology). Everyone seems to have had something to say.

In this chapter, I shall review several of the early theories—with few exceptions, those proposed before the 1920s. I believe an historical reconstruction is both intrinsically valuable and, through providing a context, helpful in fostering our appreciation of current research. If I am not very much mistaken, we shall see, in our current work and theories, vestiges of many of the old ideas. Because of limitations of space, I shall have to sacrifice some detail of presentation of the early views, though I have tried to give enough detail, particularly through frequent but brief quotations from original papers, to impart some of the "flavor" of the early theorists and their work.[3]

[3] Through the 1940s many writers published brief summaries of then extant theories of handedness, sometimes as introductions to new experiments (e.g., Beeley, 1919; Blau, 1946; Cuff, 1928; Parsons, 1924; Schiller, 1936; L. G. Smith, 1917). Each summary, however, depended heavily on secondary citations of earlier summaries, and where secondary citations were not given, one has the uneasy feeling that the original paper was never consulted anyhow. The basic theoretical positions usually were maintained by this process, but important shadings were lost, misstatements of facts were inadvertently made, a vast number of im-

The explanations of handedness can be divided roughly into several major categories. Some stressed structural asymmetries of the human body, with left-handedness resulting from a reversal of the usual design; others emphasized cultural conditioning, or learning; and still others identified hereditary mechanisms. For the most part, these kinds of explanations saw left-handedness simply as a statistically rare exception to the norm and attached no special characterization to left-handers. Another class of explanation, though often containing elements of one or more of the first three, went further and identified left-handedness as a pathological condition of the brain or personality, therefore associated with various undesirable traits, like those listed earlier.

HOW MANY LEFT-HANDERS?

> *Boys crown'd the beakers high*
> *With wine delicious, and from right to left*
> *Distributing the cups, served ev'ry guest*
>
> —HOMER
> *The Iliad,* trans. by Cowper

Many early theories—like those today—were sensitive to the question of the numerical rarity of left-handedness, or the commonness of right-handedness, and there were several attempts to determine whether right-handedness was always the norm, in every culture and every time. If it were, and in roughly the same proportion, it was argued that this would indicate that the critical influence was biological. In contrast, if the proportion of right-handedness could be shown to have varied systematically with social and technological developments thought to be potentially critical for the determination of hand use (e.g., development of writing, tools, and

---

portant authors and publications (not to mention certain other theories) were omitted, and, above all, a kind of standardized, assemblyline review was the result.

One can sympathize with the dependence on secondary sources. Many nineteenth- and early twentieth-century writers were casual about providing full references, sometimes omitting journal volume numbers, page references, book and journal titles, and even the author's first initial. I therefore have tried to read (or, in the case of the German papers, to consult for the purpose of checking tables and figures) every paper in its original form. Unless otherwise noted, translations and paraphrases are my own. Whenever I could not consult the original paper, I have given the secondary and primary citations. Where I have had to use secondary citations, in nearly every case I have been able to avoid using reviews like those cited above in favor of publications that were contemporary to the original papers.

For all this, there may well remain mistakes or questionable interpretations in my review. Where I am not completely sure of my grounds will be evident in my use of appropriate qualifying terms. I welcome further information from readers on whatever points of evidence or interpretation they can provide.

weapons), then socialization or culture would be implicated as the critical influence. Early investigators therefore tried to infer the incidence of right- and left-handedness from a variety of historical records and artifacts.

With respect to the modern era, that is, since the Old Testament, there was near consensus that right handedness had always been the norm. The Bible itself was often cited as evidence, and it was an illustrious English physician and writer, Sir Thomas Browne (1605–1682), who appears to have been the first to make biblical reference. In 1646, in a work entitled *Pseudodoxia Epidemica,* Browne wrote that "almost all Nations have used this [right] hand and ascribed a preheminence thereto . . . [p. 186]." Here he quoted from Genesis:

> and when Joseph saw that his father laid his right hand upon the head of Ephraim, it displeased him, and he held up his fathers hand to remove it from Ephraims head unto Manasses head, and Joseph said not so my father, for this is thy first borne, put thy right hand upon his head . . . [Browne, 1646, chap. V, p. 186].

After Browne, biblical references in demonstration of the early preeminence of the right hand became standard. Perhaps the neuropsychologically most revealing of these is the beautiful passage from Psalms 137: 1–6:

> How shall we sing the Lord's song in a strange land? If I forget thee, O Jerusalem, let my right hand forget her cunning.
>
> If I do not remember thee, let my tongue cleave to the roof of my mouth.

Is there, here, an awareness of the link between aphasia and right-sided hemiplegia?

Many early writers also used the Old Testament to estimate the exact number of left-handers. The reference to the Benjamite tribe in Judges, chapter 20, verse 15 is mentioned in dozens of early papers. In the King James version we read, "And the children of Benjamin were numbered at that time out of the cities twenty and six thousand men that drew sword. . . . Among all this people there were seven hundred chosen men left-handed; every one could sling stones at an hair breadth, and not miss."[4] Sir Daniel Wilson, President of University College, Toronto, and,

[4] The Hebrew word for "left" or "left-handed" is not actually used. Instead there is the phrase "itter yad yemino," literally, "men who were inferior, or restricted, in the use of their right hand." The sense of this phrase has been rendered variously in different translations, sometimes as "left-handed," sometimes in the sense of bidextrous (could sling stones as well with either hand). The Anchor Bible translates the critical passage as, "from all this people were seven hundred elite soldiers, each restricted in his right hand; and each one could sling a stone at the hair without missing! [Judges, 1969, p. 281]," but also characterizes the Benjamites as "ambidextrous," not as left-handed, which seems inconsistent with the rendering "restricted in his right hand."

in his day, an important and widely quoted authority on handedness, took note that 700 is 2.7% of 26,000, and commented, "Nearly the same relative number, viz., two per cent, is assigned by Professor Hyrtl, of Vienna, as the proportion of left-handed persons at the present day, as determined from observations made by him in one of the most civilized centres of modern Europe [Wilson, 1885–1886, p. 127]." (Hyrtl, whom we shall meet again, was the author of an influential theory of handedness.)

Thomas Browne also mentioned the 700 left-handed Benjamites, but got the number wrong, or was ill-served by his printer: "nor should we wonder at seven thousand in one Army, as wee reade concerning the Benjamites [Browne, 1646, p. 187]."

To this consensus about the handedness of the ancient Hebrews, there was at least one demurral—by Adolf Erlenmeyer (1822–1877), a distinguished German neurologist. Erlenmeyer is described, in a letter to the *British Medical Journal* (Anon., 1883), as having asserted that the ancient Hebrews were a *left*-handed people on the grounds that Hebrew, like other Semitic languages, is written from right to left, whereas "Most of the Aryan peoples . . . write from the left to the right . . . [p. 1161]." Thus the Talmudic prescription for use of the *right* hand for special prayers and inscriptions was interpreted by Erlenmeyer as evidence that the normal way would have been left-handed. The theory does not seem to have found many advocates.[5]

In further support of the statistical normality of *right*-handedness, other literary sources than the Bible were mentioned. Again, Thomas Browne:

> That the Greeks and Romans made use hereof, beside the testimony of divers Authors, is evident from their customs of discumbency at their meales, which was upon their left side, for so their right hand was free, and ready for all service . . . nor was this only in use with divers Nations of men, but was the custome of whole Nations of women, as is deduceable from the Amazones in the amputation of their right breast, whereby they had the freer use of their bow: all of which doe declare a naturall preheminency and preferment of the one unto motion before the other . . . [Browne, 1646, p. 18].

Writers also drew evidence from art. Hollis (1875, pp. 263–264) presented many examples, including the false door of the tomb of Teta, at

[5] The theory itself is presented in Erlenmeyer (1879). Erlenmeyer's reasoning is, of course, tendentious inasmuch as modern Hebrew is also written right-to-left, and Israelis are not a left-handed people. Ancient Hebrew, furthermore, was chiseled, scratched, or incised in stone, not written—a method, it might be argued, granted Erlenmeyer's logic, that would have encouraged right-to-left direction by a *right*-handed majority inasmuch as the hand holding the stone steady (i.e., the left hand) thereby would not obscure the work. In any case, direction of script seems to be an unreliable index of handedness in any fundamental sense, the pre-eminence of left–right scripts being instead the result of a combination of historical, economic, and religious factors unrelated to laterality (see Hewes, 1949).

Gizeh (2200 B.C.), showing carved stone figures holding the right hand across the breast in an attitude of supplication, while the left hand hangs by the side; the bas-reliefs of the ancient Assyrians showing soldiers always using the right hand for the more important manipulations with the sword and other weapons; depictions of battles indicating the prevalence of right-handedness (e.g., British Museum carvings illustrating the battle between Assur-Bani-Pal and the Susians); a fragment of the bas-relief of the great temple Angkor Wat in Cambodia, illustrating the great epic, Ramayana, and showing the warriors holding their weapons in the right hand.

The question of handedness in the modern age apparently answered, attention focused on the prehistoric period, which Sir Daniel Wilson (1885–1886) viewed as a sterner test:

> If, far behind oldest historic periods, in the prehistoric dawn, it can be shown that man appears to have manifested the same preference for the right hand which we know him to have done throughout the historic period, it will no longer be possible to question that it has its origin in some obscure organic source [p. 129].

Now the historical record was tools, weapons, and cave drawings, but this time, no agreement seems to have been reached. Wilson saw predominant right-handedness from his and others' studies of biases in the construction of flints and other tools, and argued that arrow-making doubtless was a craft "pursued by specially skilled workmen; for considerable dexterity is needed in striking the flakes from the flint core, and fashioning them into the nicely-finished edged tools and weapons to be seen in many museums [Wilson, 1885, p. 124]."

Wilson also mentioned the drawing and carvings of the cavemen of Europe's Mammoth and Reindeer periods. From the direction of profiles represented in the drawings, as well as from the hands in which tools or weapons were shown to be held, he found what he thought was confirming evidence of predominant right-handedness. The profiles were typically left-facing, which Wilson argued would reflect right-hand use. This interpretation is not unreasonable (cf. Burt, 1937, p. 351).

Careful not to assert that the proportion of right-handedness in stone-age man was the same as in "civilized" people, Brinton (1896) states that Wilson in a later work (1891, pp. 165–166) "rejected the opinion . . . that savage races and primitive men present greater evidences of left and both-handedness than modern, civilized people [Brinton, 1896, p. 175]." But other evidence pointed in just this direction. For example, Gabriel de Mortillet (1890) studied 354 stone scrapers from various sites in France and Switzerland, all of the double-edged variety and hand held because they were not set into a haft or hilt. Of these, 52 were of a mixed or intermediate type, 105 were made for the right hand, and 197 for the left, leading Mortillet to conclude that during this prehistoric period, left-handers were far more abundant than in the current day (Mortillet, 1890, p. 580). Later Brinton (1896) studied the stone implements, blades of arrows, and spearheads of aboriginal North American Indians, found a third to be left-handed work, and concluded that "the aboriginal race of North America was either left-handed or ambidextrous to a greater degree than the peoples of modern Europe [p. 180]."

The aforementioned studies were of Stone Age tools and weapons. The work of the anthropologist Paul Sarasin (1918), however, suggested that there had been an important transition to right-hand preference during the Bronze Age that followed, a transition shown not only in the effects of wear on the cutting edge of tools, but in the methods of manufacturing the sickle for predominant right-hand use. In his discussion of this work Blau (1946) proposed several reasons for the change: the metal tools were more complicated, better suited for one hand, and had to be specially fashioned for such use. In this, however, Blau recognized the impress of cultural convention, not physiology:

> In other words, the inventor or maker could decide the side of usage, whereas the user had little choice. Such a tool became a valuable possession, not too easily replaced, and was handed down from generation to generation along with its dictates as to side of usage [p. 61].

On the other hand, one could as well imagine that for the first time the tool maker saw sufficient reason to build his tools to match the already existing hand preference of his kinsmen.[6]

Thus, the historical record was blemished with sufficient inconsistencies, or permitted enough different interpretations, to preclude any simple choice between culture and biology as the fundamental agent. The authors of the various historical studies instead frequently invoked combinations of several then-prevailing physiological and cultural explanations named earlier. We turn, now, to an examination of these theories.

EARLY THEORIES

> *Sir,—Can any of your correspondents tell me where I can get any real information on this matter? Of course, I have read all that has been brought forward, but it has not helped me at all.*

[6] Recently, Coren and Porac (1977) reported a survey of more than 5000 years of art works depicting unimanual tool or weapon usage that disclosed 93% right-hand usage, and no systematic trends across time, history, or geographic region. But from their report, it cannot be determined whether and to what extent their earliest (and smallest) sample, 39 art pieces dated pre-3000 B.C., covers the transition from Stone Age to Bronze Age periods. It would de-

I will instance my own family. My mother was a splendid pianist, left-handed for choice; my father entirely right-handed. I am able, fortunately for myself as a surgeon, to use both hands equally well; that is to say, I can dissect, etc., as well with my left hand as with my right. My eldest child, a girl, has a desire to use the left hand, but has been made to use the right. My second child, a girl, also has a predisposition for the left hand; the third child, a great powerful boy, is utterly left-handed, but has been taught to use his right; the fourth, a girl, is absolutely left-handed, and is at present rather too young to educate. . . . I am sure there must be some reason for this condition, but, according to my reading, I have not convinced myself with any satisfactory explanation. . . ."

from "F.R.S.,"
—Letter to Editor of the British Medical Journal, 1885.

Structural Asymmetry

In the middle to late 1800s, a number of eminent scientists explained handedness as the product of certain naturally occurring lateral asymmetrical arrangements of the internal organs of the body, such as the heart and liver. Consequently, where there was reversal of the normal visceral pattern, reverse-handedness (i.e., left-handedness) was declared the result. The first fully documented cases of "situs inversus totalis" were reported in 1650 by Riolanus, and in 1660 by Morand. The latter report, according to Gould and Pyle (1956, p. 291), was the more celebrated, becoming the subject of much discussion in European medical circles. As I have seen neither report, I cannot say whether the question of handedness was raised. But it was raised in a still later paper. In 1788, Matthew Baillie published a description, in *Philosophical Transactions of the Royal Society of London*, of congenital dextrocardia with complete situs inversus viscerum in a 40-year-old man: "a complete transposition of the abdominal viscera, each of them preserving its proper relative situation to the others [p. 487]." The man, however, was right-handed:

The person seems to have used his right hand in preference to his left, as is usually the case, which was readily discovered by the greater bulk and hardness of that hand, as well as the greater fleshiness of the arm [p. 487].

And Baillie was unsurprised, dismissing any idea that a shift in handedness should accompany the shift in visceral position:

It was not indeed to be expected he should be left handed. . . . The person, while alive, was not conscious of any uncommon situation of his heart; and his

---

pend on the geographic region because the beginning of the Bronze Age varied with regions (e.g., before 3000 B. C. in Greece, but not until c. 1800 B. C. in China. See the *Encyclopedia Britannica*, 1974, p. 254).

brother has his heart pointing to the left side as in ordinary cases. Indeed, there was little reason to expect that we should meet with any thing particular in the account of his life. His health could not be affected by such a change of situation of his viscera; nor could there arise from it any peculiar symptoms of disease. Still less could there be any connection between such a change and his dispositions, or external actions. He might have known that his heart was directed towards the right side; but if we consider how little every person, especially those of the lower class, are attentive to circumstances not very palpable, it was scarcely to be expected he should know of it [Baillie, 1788, p. 487].

In light of Baillie's considerable reputation—he was a pioneer pathologist, physician to St. George's Hospital, and a Fellow of the Royal College of Physicians—one might suppose that the visceral asymmetry explanation of left-handedness would find few new advocates. But the idea apparently was too attractive to give up. Eighty years later, Baillie's report seems to have been forgotten (if it was known at all), and the situs inversus theory took on new expression.

Dynamic Balance

In 1862, what was to become a well-known and much discussed version of the "visceral" theory was advanced by Andrew Buchanan, Professor of Physiology in the University of Glasgow, in an address to the Philosophical Society of Glasgow (1862a,b). For Buchanan, the major contributing factor was an asymmetry in the lungs, and in the position and great weight of the liver.

The right lung is more capacious than the left, having three lobes, while the left has only two, and it receives more air on inspiration. . . . In consequence, the right side of the chest bulges out more than the left on inspiration, as is manifest to the eye; and the lower ribs, as they recede from the middle plane, carry with them the liver. . . . Now, the liver being the heaviest organ of the body, weighing nearly 4 lbs. avoirdupois, to whichever side it swings, it will incline the common centre of gravity in the same direction. The combined effect, therefore, of greater expansion of the right side of the chest, and the motion of the liver, is to shift the position of the centre of gravity of the body obliquely backward and to the right, and probably also somewhat downward [1862b, pp. 152–153].

The result was a shift of balance to the left side, leaving the right leg—and right arm—freer for action. Thus, for left-handers,

There are men born, who may grow up and enjoy perfect health, in whom the position of all the thoracic and abdominal viscera is reversed. . . . Now individuals so constituted must use their left limbs most effectively from a mechanical necessity, just as other men use their right [Buchanan, 1862b, p. 167].[7]

Buchanan had relied exclusively, in his analysis, on independent demonstrations by Borelli and Weber (no references given) on dead bodies whose center of gravity they determined by poising a table on the edge of a triangular prism, placing the body on the table, and then shifting the body upward and downward until equilibrium was produced. Both demonstrations, Buchanan observed, permitted determination of the transverse plane in which the center of gravity is placed, but not whether the center was situated in the mesial plane or to one side. Buchanan's analysis of handedness therefore was hypothetical—a limitation he freely acknowledged—"in the absence of direct experiment we must have recourse to general reasoning (1862b, p. 151)."

This "general reasoning" the next year inspired a reply by another anatomist, John Struthers, a Fellow of the Royal College of Surgeons and a lecturer on Anatomy in the Edinburgh School of Medicine. Struthers (1863a) damned Buchanan's report with faint praise, calling it "most interesting and philosophical," and questioned the anatomical facts on which the theory depended.

The question which meets us at the threshold of Dr. Buchanan's theory, is whether the foundation on which he has rested it is correct; and even granting a likelihood that the descent of the diaphragm will disturb a supposed equipoise of the viscera, it is in vain to expect the acceptance of a theory the starting point of which is involved in doubt [p. 1087].

Struthers himself deigned to provide the "starting point"—summaries of exacting and detailed measurements of the viscera, including the liver, spleen, pancreas, stomach, kidneys, lungs, heart, and intestines. In the end, however, Buchanan was vindicated; Struthers concluded that the body actually is "considerably heavier on the right side than on the left [the actual difference being 15 oz.], with the consequent position of the centre of gravity to the right side of the middle line . . . [Struthers, 1863a, p. 1104]." Unlike Buchanan, Struthers did not draw a strong inference from his findings, confining himself to the general remark that the asymmetry "cannot but exert an influence on the attitudes and movements of the body and limbs, and on the muscles concerned in them [1863a, p. 1104]." (There followed a somewhat testy but always polite dispute between the two men

[7] In 1844, a French surgeon, Henri-Marie-Joseph Desruelles, had made a similar proposal, although for Desruelles the critical factor producing disequilibrium was what he claimed to be the leftward curving of the spinal column. Buchanan probably knew nothing of the earlier paper. It is mentioned in a later review by Péré, who says that it "won few supporters" and "seems to have passed unknown" (1900, p. 52). The judgment evidently was correct.

on the distinction between anatomical symmetry and "equipoise"; and, more important, on who had provided the best documentation of the asymmetry [Buchanan, 1863; Struthers, 1863b, 1877]).

Other studies followed quickly. Harting (1869) reported that the bones on the right side are heavier; Bischoff (1863), Gaupp (1889), and Theile (1884) agreed (all cited in Moorhead, 1902, p. 400), and Theile found that the right arm of a newborn child weighed 4 percent more than the left. However, combining the results of 11 cases from Gaupp's and Theile's reports, "it is found that . . . the right arm was the heavier in three, the left three, and that complete equality existed in six [sic] cases [Moorhead, 1902, p. 400]."

Struthers (1863a) had, in fact, measured the organs only of adults and children from 2 to 3 years of age. In the case of the fetus, however, he supposed that the large size of the left lobe of the liver equalized the weight of that side with the right. Moorhead (1902), using viscera hardened in formalin (an improvement over the method available to Struthers), confirmed the earlier findings.

> From the fifth month of foetal life onwards the centre of gravity of the body is placed to the right side of the mesial plane, the . . . viscera on this side representing 52.6 percent of the total weight. . . . The child therefore enters upon its extra-uterine existence with a marked right-sided bias [Moorhead, 1902, p. 403].

In their enthusiasm to quantify the asymmetry between the two sides of the body, few anatomists—not Buchanan, Struthers, nor Moorhead in the papers cited here—even speculated about how visceral asymmetry could have been created in the first place. This question was more in the province of the embryologists, and according to Pye-Smith (1871, p. 142), an explanation was first advanced by von Baer (1828) and afterwards adopted by Förster, in his treatise on "Malformations."[8] Von Baer believed that the condition was traceable to the position of the yolk-sac in the embryo. When it lies to the right, the viscera become transposed, and left-handedness results.

In addition to the original observations on which the theory was founded, Pye-Smith (1871) reported confirmation "by cases in which the right-hand one of two embryos, with a single umbilical cord and vesicle between them, had transposed viscera [p. 142]."

Criticisms of the visceral asymmetry theory were frequent and unsparing. Handedness was not found to be consistently associated with the direction of the asymmetry; "situs inversus" was far less frequent than the in-

---

[8] "Förster" is not identified but, presumably, is A. Foerster (1865).

cidence of left-handedness itself; and, as Baillie had pointed out in 1788, and as many said later (e.g., Pye-Smith, 1871; Shaw, 1877–1878), even the rare individuals having situs inversus were not invariably left-handed. Pye-Smith (1871) thought the occasional association of visceral transposition and left-handedness "a mere coincidence [p. 141]," then rubbing in the point: "Indeed, by an examination of the chest in left-handed persons it may be readily seen that most of them at least have their hearts in the right [i.e., the left] place [p. 141]."

Blood Supply

A different version of the structural asymmetry theory emphasized asymmetries not of all the viscera, but of blood supply and of the related arteries and veins. Credit here—and, indeed, credit for the very idea of a relationship between "situs inversus totalis" and left-handedness—perhaps belongs to an Italian savant by the name of Ludovico Ricchieri (1450–1520), also known as Lodovicus Caelius Rhodoginus. Rhodoginus believed that ambidexterity, not right-handedness, was the norm. Thomas Browne (1646) summarized his views as follows:

> Men, saith he, are Ambidexters, and use both hands alike, when the heat of the heart doth plentifully disperse into the left side, and that of the liver into the right, and the spleen be also much dilated; but men are left handed when ever it happeneth that the heart and liver are seated on the left side, or when the liver is on the right side, yet so obducted and covered with thick skins, that it cannot diffuse its virtue into the right . . . [p. 188].[9]

Browne rejected Rhodoginus' theory for two reasons: The first was statistical, and anticipated the criticism of the nineteenth century physicians mentioned earlier.

> and as for the seate of the heart and Liver in one side whereby men become left handed, it happeneth too rarely to countenance an effect so common; for the seat of the liver on the left side is very monstrous, and scarce at all to be met with in the observations of Physitians [Browne, 1646, p. 188].

The second was on narrower anatomical grounds:

> Others not considering ambidextrous and left-handed men, doe totally submit unto the efficacy of the liver, which though it be seated on the right side, yet by

[9] Browne did not identify the publication in which Rhodoginus presented his theory. A likely source is his monumental 1516 work, *Sicuti Antiquarum Lectionum Commentarios.* I am grateful to Professor Frank L. Huntley, of the Department of English Language and Literature, University of Michigan, for bibliographic help.

the subclavian division doth equidistantly communicate its activity unto either
arme, nor will it salve the doubts of observation, and many use the left, in
whom that part is strongest [Browne, 1646, p. 188].

Presumably Browne meant that the blood from the liver, after flowing to
the heart, would be dispersed *equally* to either arm through the left and
right subclavian arteries—those short parts of arteries originating under the
clavicle and continuous with the axillary arteries extending to the arms.[10]

Another early blood supply theory was advanced by Gabriello
Fallopio, or Fallopius (1523–1562), Vesalius' most famous student, who
first described the ducts that bear his name. Of him, Thomas Browne
wrote:

Fallopius is of another conceit [as to the explanation of handedness], deducing
the reason from the Azygos or *vena fine pari*, a large and considerable veine
arising out of the cava or hallow veine, before it enters the right ventricle of the
heart, and placed onely in the right side . . . [1646, p. 188].[11]

Browne was unimpressed with this reasoning too and continued:

but neither is this perswasory, for the Azygos communicates no branches unto
the armes or legs on either side, but disperseth into the ribs on both, and in its
descent doth furnish the left Emulgent with one veyne, and the first veyne of
the loynes on the right side with another; which manner of derivation doth not
conferre a peculiar addition unto either [1646, p. 188].

In the early 19th century, blood supply theories were still being pressed,

[10] Browne's objection to Rhodoginus' theory is puzzling. Because Rhodoginus was writing
more than a century before William Harvey's *Exercitatio anatomica de motu cordis et
sanguinis in animalibus* (1628), it is to be expected that his analysis would reflect Galen's views
on the role of the liver in the manufacture of blood (note the reference to the dispersal of
"heat" from the liver). Browne, however, was Harvey's close contemporary, and, according to
Oppenheimer (1947), "quick to appreciate the implications of Harvey's contribution . . . [p.
18]." One wonders, then, why he did not criticize Rhodoginus on more fundamental grounds.
Perhaps Browne thought it prudent to be cautious in this instance. As Whitteridge (1964)
reminds us, Harvey's work was slow to win acceptance so long as the church embraced Galen.
Although Protestant England, in Harvey's time, was less strict than Rome, the College of
Physicians kept strict watch on what was taught by its Fellows, "and anyone propounding
theories contrary to the teaching of Galen was liable to be fined [Whitteridge, 1964, p. XXXI]."
[11] The azygos vein actually originates on both sides, but after an embryological stage, part
of the left azygos vein obliterates, leaving what is called the hemi-azygos, while the right
azygos remains, the result being that the blood now flows into the superior vena cava more efficiently. Though Browne was unenthusiastic about any such physiological difference as an explanation of handedness—as we see in the text—the word "conceit" in the passage quoted
probably was meant in the original sense of "conception" or "notion."

but now the anatomical reasoning was somewhat more sophisticated. What appears to have been a vigorously debated theory is alluded to by Sir Charles Bell, in his seminal book, *The hand: Its Mechanism and Vital Endowments as Evincing Design* (1833):

> In speaking of the arteries which go to the hand, it may be expected that we should touch on a subject, which has been formerly a good deal discussed, whether the properties of the right hand, in comparison with those of the left, depend on the course of the arteries to it. It is affirmed that the trunk of the artery going to the right arm, passes off from the heart so as to admit the blood directly and more forcibly into the small vessels of the arm [pp. 123–124].

The reference again was to the subclavian arteries, but now to an asymmetry in *their* origin—a feature not considered by Thomas Browne in his criticism of Rhodoginus' theory, nearly 200 years before. The right subclavian artery arises off the brachiocephalic trunk (innominate artery) and is closer to the heart by about 1 in. The left subclavian artery arises later, though directly off the aorta. The implication, presumably, was that the blood in the right subclavian artery, being closer to the heart, would be under greater pressure, thus providing more blood to the right side of the body.

Bell, no less than Thomas Browne, was unconvinced that blood supply explained handedness.

> This is assigning a cause which is unequal to the effect, and presenting, altogether, too confined a view of the subject: it is a participation in the common error of seeking in the mechanism the cause of phenomena which have a deeper source [Bell, 1833, pp. 123–124].

Bell was not more explicit than this, through evidently he saw as a limitation of the theory the fact that "the property [handedness] does not depend on the peculiar distribution of the arteries of the arm—but the preference is given to the right foot, as well as to the right hand [Bell, 1833, p. 125]."

Notwithstanding Bell's negative views, the "subclavian artery" theory found yet another advocate in the 1860's in Josef Hyrtl (1810–1894). Judging from the frequency of citation, Hyrtl's views were seriously listened to. He was, after all, the acknowledged founder of topographic anatomy, a pioneer cardio-vascular researcher, and for 30 years holder of the chair of anatomy at the University of Vienna (Willius & Dry, 1948, p. 150). The theory was outlined in his classic *Handbuch der Topographischen Anatomie* (1860). Hyrtl was specific about the circumstances giving rise to left-handedness:

> There occurs an anomaly in the origin of the vessels from the arch in which the right subclavian is given off after the left. This . . . occurs twice in one hun-

dred cases. This . . . agrees tolerably with Malgaigne's observations on the frequency of left-handedness. If the right subclavian arises after the left, we have,
in regard to pressure, the reverse of what occurs in the normal arrangement.
The left extremity will be stronger, and consequently used in preference to the
right [Hyrtl, 1860, p. 291; quoted in translation by Dwight, 1870, pp.
535–536].

But even Josef Hyrtl's authority proved insufficient. For example, Dwight
(1870), without citing Charles Bell's 1833 work, dismissed the theory for
the same reason—that it accounted only for lateral differences in development of the arm, when in fact "the abdominal aorta divides into the iliacs a
very little to the left of the median line, so that any difference in the supply
of blood for the legs would be in favor of the left [Dwight, 1870, p. 537]."
Hyrtl was roundly criticized, too, on the basis of the same cold, statistical
evidence used against his predecessors.[12]
    More than anything else, the subclavian theory may have died as it was
increasingly recognized that the critical organs were not the hands at all.
They were the hemispheres of the brain, which, after all, controlled hand
movements. Let us consider the developments that led to this shift in focus.

Handedness, Brain Specialization, and
the Question of "Crossed Aphasia"

    The critical intellectual event that underlay the shift in focus to the brain
was the proposal of a relationship between right-handedness and localization of speech in the left cerebral hemisphere. This relationship is taken for
granted today (though much refined and qualified in light of new evidence
of both left- and right-hemisphere language functions and levels of processing). However, in the 1860s, the "localization" hypothesis, though "in the
air," was not yet clearly conceived. Then, beginning in 1861, several things
happened. In August, Paul Broca (1827–1880), already a distinguished
neurosurgeon, anatomist, and physical anthropologist, presented a soon-
to-be-famous paper to the Anatomical Society of Paris. In that paper,
Broca presented his findings on the aphasic patient called "Tan" (so called
because this was the only articulate sound he could make), and, from the
postmortem examination, identified an area in the posterior part of the
third frontal convolution of the left hemisphere (i.e., the frontal operculum
just anterior to the motor-face area) as the site of the lesion producing Tan's
aphasia. (Broca's term was "aphemia," meaning articulate language, or

[12] Less clear is whether there was any challenge to Hyrtl's basic statistic—that the left
subclavian arises first in about 2 in 100 cases. In any case, his estimate probably overestimates
the actual incidence by a factor of 10 (see Grant, 1972, Fig. 446.4).

speech.) A second report followed in 1863, this time of eight aphasic patients, all again with lesions in the left third frontal convolution.

Broca's reports stirred tremendous interest—one admirer called Broca's
work the *"ne plus ultra* of pathological topography [Bateman, 1868, p.
523]," though it by no means was taken as having resolved the question of
the relationship between side of lesion and speech disturbance. Broca
himself, in the 1863 paper, confessed his reluctance to draw a conclusion.
Furthermore, Broca had not yet said anything of handedness, save a passing comment, in his 1861 paper, on Tan's inability to write because of
paralysis in his right hand. The question of handedness was to await (and
here I must turn to Riese's 1947 account) a discussion by Bouillaud on April
4, 1865, at the meeting of the Imperial Academy of Medicine. Bouillaud,
not satisfied with a fellow scientist's categorical refusal to admit two different functions for two symmetrical organs,

> recalled the difference in performance made by the right and the left hand and
> the distinction between right- and left-handedness, the latter believed by him to
> be exceptional. Would it not be conceivable that we were left-handed as to cer-
> tain acts, e.g., language? These words indeed marked the birthday of the doc-
> trine of left cerebral dominance, since for the first time speech was linked with
> handedness [Riess, 1947, p. 331].

Broca himself apparently did not consider the question of handedness per
se until a few months later—on June 15, 1865, in an address to the Anthropological Society of Paris. Then he was specific: Just as, in the case of
right-handers, the left hemisphere directs the movements of writing, drawing, and other fine movements, so do we speak with the left hemisphere
("nous parlons avec l'hémisphere gauche," 1865, p. 383). Moreover, it is a
habit carried from earliest infancy. (One may suppose that Broca was influenced by Bouillaud's statements two months earlier, though they are not
mentioned in Broca's 1865 paper.)[13]

[13] In 1865, the question of Broca's priority in specifically identifying the left third frontal
convolution as the seat of articulate speech was challenged by Gustav Dax on behalf of his late
father, Marc Dax, who, according to the son, had presented the same thesis in a paper given at
a medical congress in Montpellier in 1836. The father's paper and Gustav Dax's communication were published together in 1865. A vigorous controversy ensued, an account of which has
been given by Joynt and Benton (1964; see also Hécaen & Dubois, 1969, pp. 95–107). Evidently, Marc Dax had indeed made his observations prior to Broca, but, as Joynt and Benton
conclude, there is no evidence that he made them known to the world except through distribution of his findings to a few colleagues rather than before the medical congress, as his son had
asserted. Broca himself (1865) said that he had searched in "all the 1836 journals and could find
no trace of the Dax memoir." At Broca's request, persons in attendance at the meeting were in-
terviewed; none could recall any such presentation. Indeed, "the question of language was not
mentioned [Broca, 1865, pp. 379–380]." What is clear, in any case, is that Dax, unlike Broca,
neither mentioned handedness nor did he link hand preference to hemispheric localization of
speech. Here, Broca's priority has not been questioned.

If right-handers spoke from the left hemisphere, what of left-handers? Broca used the very fact of their existence to buttress his physiological theory. Against the argument of others that handedness is a product of imitation and education, Broca said there are circumstances that must preclude these factors from consideration. Everywhere there are some individuals who, despite all efforts and perseverance, remain left-handed. For them, therefore, one must admit the existence of an inverse organic predisposition ("existence d'une predisposition organique inverse") against which imitation and even education cannot prevail [Broca, 1865, p. 382]. Thus, whereas most people are naturally left-brained, or "left-handers of the brain," left-handers are right-brained ("nous dirons que la plupart des hommes sont naturellement gauchers du cerveau; et que par exception quelques-uns d'entre eux, ceux qu'on appelle gauchers, sont au contraire droitiers du cerveau [Broca, 1865, p. 383].")

The existence of a small number of individuals who "speak with the right hemisphere" also explained, Broca went on to say, the exceptional cases in which aphemia (aphasia) resulted from a lesion of the right hemisphere (Broca, 1865, p. 386). There were, indeed, several such cases reported. Ogle (1868) described several individuals with left-hemiplegia and speech loss whose postmortem examinations revealed right-sided brain injury. He did not, however, identify the subjects' handedness. J. Hughlings Jackson, the pioneer British neurologist, mentioned a patient whose handedness was known, and whose symptoms seemed to fit Broca's rule. The man said he was left-handed, and he showed "hemiplegia of the *left* side" with "considerable defect of speech" (Jackson, 1866, p. 210; emphasis in original).

There were almost from the start, however, a certain number of reports that did not fit Broca's rule. These were the cases of so-called *crossed aphasia*—aphasia associated with a cerebral lesion on the *same* side as the preferred hand. This outcome was most common in left-handers and was found only rarely in right-handers. Jackson himself later (1868) mentioned several such "exceptions to the common rule [p. 457]." Perhaps the best-known early account of crossed aphasia was by Bramwell. Among other cases, Bramwell (1899) described a 59-year-old woman "left-handed since the age of 17 years in consequence of an injury received at that time to the right hand . . . [p. 1477]," and who, at age 57 became aphasic and completely hemiplegic on the left side. Postmortem examination revealed a tumor in the right hemisphere, and no lesion on the left side.

Such exceptions to Broca's rule, however, were seen mostly *as* exceptions. Jackson, for example, concluded, "So far, then, the facts are few, seemingly contradictory, and only supplied by clinical inquiry," and then added the reasonable suggestion, "we must not forget that both sides of the brain may be damaged when there is permanent paralysis of but one side of the body [1868, p. 457]." Less reasonable, but regretably more influential, was Bramwell's analysis. Speaking of the 59-year-old woman, Bramwell attributed the anomalous finding to the act of writing with the right hand.

> This case would seem to show that, even at the age of 17 years the "leading" or "driving" speech-centres, in a right-handed person, may—I do not, of course, say that they will always—or will usually, if the patient becomes left-handed in consequence of disuse of the right hand, be transferred from the left to the right hemisphere [Bramwell, 1899, p. 1477].

Bramwell himself may have been writing under the influence of the English neurologist Thomas Buzzard (1882), who believed that stimulation of the left hand, either through active use or by the application of "encircling blisters," would, through afferent impulses, develop the corresponding convolution in the right hemisphere. Buzzard based a kind of exercise therapy on this assumption (see 1882, Lecture XXIV, pp. 427–441).

Broca's rule that left-handers are neurological mirror-images of right-handers was slow to lose its force. It was stated unqualifiedly, for instance, by Cunningham nearly 40 years later: "Left-handed people therefore speak from the right brain [1902, p. 287]." According to Hécaen and Sauguet (1971, p. 19), not until the appearance of a study by Chesher (1936) were the crossed aphasics no longer presented as constituting simple exceptions. Instead, the organization of the representation of language in left-handers "could be considered as being different from that in right-handed subjects," and the possibility was raised that in left-handers, cerebral representation was "divided more equally between the two hemispheres. . . [Hécaen & Sauguet, 1971, p. 17]."

Blood Supply to Brain

With respect to early theories about handedness, the paucity of clinical data on aphasia in left-handers was unfortunate because such data might have been a brake on continued variations on the visceral asymmetry theories. The revelations of Broca's work instead merely shifted the focus of then-prevailing theories from the extremities to the brain. Hyrtl's sub clavian artery theory thus could be changed into a theory about asymmetries in carotid artery blood supply to the cerebral hemispheres, and indeed, this is what happened in the 1860s. It was hypothesized that right-handers were right-handers (and spoke from the left brain) because the left hemisphere was more generously supplied with blood, and that the reverse situation held for left-handers. This shift in emphasis from arm to brain brought with it another kind of shift, one apparently unrecognized by any critics of that time. Where the subclavian theory supposed the right subclavian's position to be more favorable to the right arm because the right subclavian arises closer to the heart, the carotid theory supposed the position of the left carotid to be more favorable to the left hemisphere because, like the left subclavian artery, it arises directly from the aortic arch, whereas the right carotid, like the right subclavian, is only a branch off the brachiocephalic trunk (innominate artery).

Among the advocates of some form of hemisphere blood supply theory were leading lights of the scientific establishment, including Armand de Fleury (1865), John Ogle (1871), and later Fritz Lueddeckens (1900), and the Italian criminologist, Cesare Lombroso (1903). Broca himself (1877) discussed this idea in great detail, summarizing de Fluery's, Ogle's, and his own work. He concluded that the mode of origin of the two carotids may exercise "une certaine influence" on the division of labor between the two hemispheres, but "non pas une influence décisive [Broca, 1877, p. 526]." Broca's reason echoed the earlier criticisms of visceral asymmetry theories: If, as had been argued, individuals with visceral reversal are ordinarily left-handers, it was certain that in the vast majority of cases, left-handers are exempt from this rare anomaly. And with respect to the origin of the aortic vessels, Broca said that left handers are obviously not different from right-handers (Broca, 1877, p. 526). A related assumption was that the left carotid artery was usually larger in circumference than the right (e.g., de Fleury, 1865; Ogle, 1871), providing yet another reason for superior blood supply to the left hemisphere, though the opposite assertion was made as well (Bennecke, 1878; cited by Carmon, Harishanu, Lowinger, & Lavy, 1972).

Generally, all of the various theories about vascularization differences began to be discounted in the face of new anatomical evidence. Particularly critical was the realization that, by the presence of the anterior communicating artery, which connects the two cerebral arteries of the brain and forms part of the Circle of Willis, the cerebral blood supply becomes pooled, thus equalizing the blood supply (and pressure) to both hemispheres. This implication was mentioned at least as early as 1898 (Kellogg, p. 358) and frequently thereafter in general reviews and by critics of blood-supply theories (e.g., Beeley, 1919, p. 391; Crichton-Browne, 1907, p. 643; Huber, 1910, p. 261). It also was demonstrated that there were no appreciable and consistent differences in the size of the carotid arteries. Cunningham (1902) took wax casts of the carotid arteries as they entered the cranium and compared the total area of the left carotids with the total area of the right. In 24 crania, there were considerable differences in size, sometimes favoring one side, sometimes the other, but the overall difference was negligible.[14] Crichton-Browne reported corroborating evidence from measurements of the diameter of rings cut from the internal carotid arteries (Crichton-Browne, 1907, p. 643).

Brain Weight

Inasmuch as it was believed that the left hemisphere was better vascularized than the right, it was argued that the left hemisphere was heavier, larger, or denser as a result, though as the vascularization explanation became suspect, interest in brain structure seems to have taken on its own momentum. The period of the 1860s through the 1890s saw a flurry of reports that were to figure importantly in theories of the physical basis of handedness.

Two of the most influential papers were by the English physician, Robert Boyd, and the anatomist, H. Charlton Bastien. In 1861, Boyd, then a physician to the Somerset County (England) Lunatic Asylum, reported, from examinations of nearly 200 brains, "that almost invariably the weight of the left [hemisphere] exceeded that of the right by at least the eighth of an ounce [p. 261]." Boyd's professional affiliation notwithstanding, the specimens in this instance were not of lunatics but of men and women "among the poor of the parish of St. Marylebone [Boyd, 1861, p. 260]." Later, in 1866, Bastien, then an assistant medical officer at the State Asylum in Broadmoor, reported on the specific gravity of the gray matter of the hemispheres. In measurements of 27 brains (of sane adults) Bastien found, for the frontal, parietal, and occipital regions, respectively, greater density on the left side in 7, 12, and 9 brains; greater density on the right side in 1, 2, and 4 brains; and equal density in 19, 13, and 14 brains. The actual average differences, however, were extremely small, though favoring the left side. Nevertheless, Bastien saw his results as being consistent with Boyd's earlier report (Bastien, 1866, p. 496).

More than balancing the reports of greater weight on the left side were reports of just the reverse. Wagner (1862) weighed 18 brains, finding the right hemisphere heavier in 10, the left in 6, and no differences in the remaining 2. The over-all difference, however, favored the right by 1 gram

---

[14] Within limits, the significance of differences in arterial size would be negligible anyhow because in a smaller-diameter artery blood would flow under *greater* pressure, resulting in greater diffusion pressure in the capillaries. As for the subclavian arteries, any differences in their point of origin should have no effect. What the anatomists of Hyrtl's day apparently did not know, or neglected to consider, was that the aorta and the subclavian arteries themselves expand on systoly (contraction of the ventricles) and constrict afterwards in order to dampen pulsing and equalize blood pressure and flow throughout the arterial system.

(427 versus 426 grams).[15] Thurnam (1866) weighed many more brains (470) and obtained results in the same direction as Wagner. Braune made still another comparison, finding the right hemisphere heavier in 52 brains, the left in 34, and both equal in one case (cited without date [probably Braune, 1891] in Cunningham, 1902, p. 289).

Broca himself evidently did not become directly involved in the question of the weight of the hemispheres until 1875, when he made a brief report to the Anthropological Society of Paris. At this time, he remarked that he had been making such measurements since 1861 and had so far compiled weights on 440 brains but had not had time to analyze these data. Finally, at the instigation of a doctoral candidate, he selected 37 brains from the 440 and presented their measurements at the 1875 meeting. The specimens were from adult male patients from the hospitals at Bicêtre and Saint-Antoine. In weight of the entire hemisphere, the differences, in fact, favored the right side, by less than 1.5 grams in each sample. Broca did not mention these differences in his spoken remarks (they are shown only in a table). Instead, and understandably, he confined his comments to the weights of the frontal lobes alone. Here, the difference was larger and in a direction consistent with his views. The left frontal lobes averaged 3.5 and 4.5 grams heavier in the Bicêtre and Saint Antoine groups, respectively. In the discussion that followed, recorded by a secretary of the Society (Assezat, 1875), Broca was asked (by Aubertin) whether he concluded that the difference was the result of a difference in the third frontal convolution. Broca was disposed to this view but was reluctant to make a strong statement in light of the difficulty in surgically isolating the third convolution.

A disagreement followed about the reliability of the differences Broca had found. Delasiauve mentioned having found no differences, and Lunior remarked that the number of observations (referring perhaps not only to Broca's but to all studies) was insufficient to permit any general conclusions. Curiously, Broca did not identify the handedness of the 37 individuals; nor was he asked.

It must be said that not all the authors of the various reports seemed much interested in the implications of their findings for theories of handedness. Boyd (1861), for example, though emphasizing the lateral differences in weight of the hemispheres, made no mention of the handedness of the individuals whose hemispheres were measured. This is understandable, since Boyd's major aim was to publish tables of all the human organs "with a hope that they may aid in forming a standard of the weight of the

---

[15] Different weights for a series of 18 brains weighed by Wagner (1864) are given in Von Bonin (1962, p. 2), in this instance, 570.5 grams for the right hemisphere, 569.8 grams for the left.

human organs from early infancy to old age [Boyd, 1861, p. 241]." To this end, he included tables of weights of all the abdominal viscera, the lungs and heart, along with the average height and weight of the entire body. Similarly, Bastien's (1866) major aim was to provide tables of the specific densities of brain regions. Both Boyd and Bastien, as well as Thurnam (1866), also provided comparisons of organs according to certain characteristics of the individuals from whom the specimens were taken (e.g., sanity versus insanity; social position and education; reason for death; sex; age).

Some of the original investigators themselves evidently were not even very concerned about the discrepant findings—understandable, again, because lateral comparisons were not their main interest. They also were aware of the methodological problems involved as others were not. Thurnam (1866), for instance, wrote:

> Though the results obtained by me do not confirm Dr. Boyd's observations, I do not wish to be understood as saying that they refute them. A nice, and at times difficult, section is requisite to ascertain the weight of one hemisphere, as compared with that of the other; and in dividing, it may be, a softened great commissure, it is difficult to cut always in the exact median line [Thurnam, 1866, pp. 3–4].

Thurnam specifically disclaimed "any pretensions to minute accuracy (1866, p. 4)." Later, Cunningham (1902) echoed these views, "An accurate determination of the relative weights of the two cerebral hemispheres is no easy matter, as many factors may contribute to vitiate the result [p. 289]." These cautions counted for little. One or another of the brain weight studies or Bastien's paper was mentioned in virtually every paper on handedness published during this period and for many years afterwards, the data being either accepted or challenged according to the writer's own position. For instance, one physician, defending Broca against a criticism of his view that the left hemisphere was heavier, cited Boyd's measurements as having "settled this point conclusively [Wyeth, 1880, p. 130]." Little by little, however, enthusiasm for such gross indexes as brain weight or density as explanations of handedness weakened as it finally was realized that the differences were too small and the methods of weighing too inexact.[16]

---

[16] Whether all the original investigators themselves later became engaged in the debate as to the physical basis of handedness, I am not prepared to say because I have not yet examined very many of their papers subsequent to the original reports cited in the text. People like Broca who were leaders in theoretical and empirical research on handedness and cerebral specialization did, of course, participate in this debate. But others, like Boyd, seem not to have; at least they are not specifically named in later reports as having advocated one view or another.

Bastien, three years later (after he was M.D., F.R.S., and Professor of Pathological Anatomy in University College, London), did take up the question of the localization of

Brain Convolutions

In addition to weight and specific density, the basis for the left cerebral hemisphere's superiority was believed to lie in the richness and complexity of its convolutions—what Cunningham (1902) called "the convolutionary plea." The author of this developmental hypothesis was the distinguished anatomist Pierre Gratiolet (1815–1865), who in his *Anatomie comparée du système nerveux* (Gratiolet & Leurat, 1839), had proposed that in the growth of the brain, the convolutions of the left hemisphere form earlier than those of the right. Broca (1865) saw the implication: "One therefore understands why, from the first moments of life, the child shows a preference for the limbs having, at that time, the more complete innervation, why, in other words, he becomes right-handed [p. 383]."

Broca, himself, according to Bateman (1869), examined 40 brains and concluded, in Bateman's words, that the convolutions "are notably more numerous in the left frontal lobe than in the right, and that the converse condition exists in the occipital lobes, where the right is richer in convolutions than the left" [Bateman, 1869, p. 380; Broca reference not identified].[17] It was but another small step to argue that these characteristics were reversed in the brains of left-handers (e.g., Ogle, 1871).

The developmental part of Gratiolet's hypothesis—that the convolutions form earlier on the left side than the right—appears to have been controversial from the outset. For instance, Bateman cited the objection by the eminent naturalist Carl Vogt, "an equal authority [Bateman, 1869, p. 383]," and added, in a nice display of chauvinism, that "this is an extremely interesting and important question about which very few are in a position to give a valid opinion, and I regret I can quote no British authority in

cerebral function—but with great skepticism: "Even Perception, Intellect, Emotion, and Volition are all so intimately associated with one another in our ordinary mental processes, that as it seems to me, if we were ever to attempt anything like a definite mapping out of the territories of these—allotting a special province for each . . . in the cerebral hemispheres—we should fall into a grevious error [Bastien, 1869, p. 456]." As for lateral differences, Bastien makes only a passing reference to brain convolutions ("There has risen a very slight though still perceptible want of symmetry between the convolutions of the two hemispheres") and no mention at all of his work on specific density (1869, p. 455).

[17] Bateman's (1869) discussion of Broca's report alluded to yet another reason to question the meaning of a comparison of the two hemispheres in *total weight*. Noting Broca's demonstration that the difference of weight between the hemispheres is "scarcely appreciable" (here Bateman cited Boyd's report of the figure of one eighth of an ounce), "yet the frontal lobe is perceptibly heavier than the right," Bateman then concluded, "There would seem, therefore, to be a sort of compensation between the weights of the two frontal and the two occipital lobes, as we have already seen that the right occipital lobe is richer in convolutions and therefore presumably heavier than the left [1869, p. 380]."

reference to it [Bateman, 1869, p. 383]." Cunningham, in commenting later on certain of the anatomical theories of handedness, announced his scepticism of the "convolutionary" hypothesis, citing Ecker's (1868) failure to find any developmental differences, and adding that Gratiolet had never expressed himself with any confidence on the question in the first place.

Differences in Fissure Length

While most attention was on such gross measures as the weight of the cerebral hemispheres, interest began to turn to finer structures, in particular, certain details of the fissures. Here, in contrast with the brain weight measures, some rather substantial and reliable differences were found. For instance, in 1884, Eberstaller reported that the Sylvian fissure in the adult brain was longer on the left than on the right—58.2 mm versus 51.8 mm (cited in von Bonin, 1962, p. 5). Later, Cunningham (1892) demonstrated anatomical differences between the left and right Sylvian fissures in the fetal human brain, as well as in the brain of the gorilla, chimpanzee, and orangutan. Cunningham did not actually measure the length of the fissure but reported instead that the posterior end of the left fissure was more depressed than the right and concluded that the entire region of cortical surface bounded below by the Sylvian fissure (i.e., the region of the planum temporale, part of Wernicke's area) therefore was more extensive on the left side.

Despite the strength of this evidence, its significance was not widely recognized at the time; at least these reports are rarely cited in the literature on handedness through the 1920s. In Cunningham's case, the reason seems clear: he disavowed the relevance of his own discovery.

> That this [greater depression of the left Sylvian fissure] is in any way associated with right-handedness, or even with the localization of the active speech centre in the left cerebral hemisphere, I am not prepared to urge, because the same condition is also a characteristic of the ape. This it is true would offer no impediment to the acceptance of this explanation by those who believe that the ape is right-handed, but, as I have already stated, I cannot persuade myself that the ape possesses any superior power in either arm . . . [Cunningham, 1902, p. 293].

Cunningham was confident, nonetheless, that a structural explanation would be found, commenting that his inquiry "has been conducted up to the present along wrong lines, and I do not doubt that the problem will ultimately be satisfactorily explained [Cunningham, 1902, p. 293]."

Higher Incidence of Diseases and Deformities on Left Side

Whatever physiological reason for handedness was accepted—blood supply, cerebral weight, convolutional complexity—it was widely reported, by the mid-1800s, that a great variety of diseases and congenital defects appeared more frequently on the left side of the body whereas the right side showed more vigorous growth. These reports were seen as further evidence of the superiority of the right side and of the left cerebral hemisphere.

In one of the earliest reports, Armand Trousseau, a pioneer cardiologist, reported that the incidence of neuralgia was of such prevalance on the left side that for the 3 years during which he kept notes, he did not observe a single example of it on the right side of the chest when real neuralgia was carefully distinguished from pleurodynia, pleuritic stitches, and hepatic colic (Trousseau, 1868, p. 668; cited in Ireland, 1881, p. 213). A major review by G. Stanley Hall and E. M. Hartwell (1884) gave over 40 other (for the most part, undocumented) examples consistent with Trousseau's report. Among diseases these examples included fever and resulting weakness, pneumonia, cancer, and epilepsy; and among the deformities or deficiencies those of the lung, kidney, eye, and ear were included.[18] Also cited were reports of superior right-sided growth of the teeth, hair and beard, and nails; and superior production by the right parotid gland ("secretes the most saliva"), and female breast ("observed to have the best and richest milk, and to be preferred by infants"). A few years later, Allen (1888) offered still other examples, including a report by Donaldson (no reference) that in humans the wart on the nasio-labial groove is much more frequent on the left side.

Ocular Dominance

At least by the 1880s, notice began to be taken of yet another asymmetry, and the seed was planted for still another theory of handedness. An intimation appeared in two brief letters to *Nature* from Joseph Le Conte (1884a).

> In pointing with the finger, whether of the right or left hand, with both eyes open, it is the right-eye image of the finger (the left in position) that I range

---

[18] Hall and Hartwell also noted that for "conflicting or contrasting sounds, the impression made on the right auditory nerve is more likely to prevail [1884, p. 94]." Is this actually a description of what we today would call a "right-ear advantage" in a dichotic listening experiment? Unfortunately, the authors provided no documentation, though they went on to say, "Even taste and smell, according to Valentin, present phenomena analogous to rivalry between their two lateral moieties when different tastes or odours are simultaneously applied to each; but there was no differentiation, no record of preference for right or left [1884, p. 94]."

with the object. In the case of two or three left-handed persons on whom I have made observations, I have found, on the contrary, it is the right-eye image that they neglect, and the left-eye image that they use in pointing [p. 452].

In 1897, Jules van Biervliet made a much stronger declaration—that in both right- and left-handedness, the asymmetries of hand skill extended to *all* the senses—kinesthesis, vision, audition, and touch—and that the margin of superiority was precisely one-ninth (p. 366). It was only another small step for a physician, George M. Gould (1908), to declare that the eye, and not the brain, was the organ underlying handedness.

I have measured 20,000 or 30,000 [eyeballs], and no one was perfect in shape. It is a poor and makeshift mechanism even apart from its morphology (p. 56). . . . If now the right eye is more defective, more ametropic, if its vision is poorer, more difficult, or more painful than that of the left, the left eye must be chosen to govern hand-action, and so, of course, the left hand will become habitually the more chosen, the more expert, and the more educated, for the special task, and soon the child is seen to be left-handed. Fight it all, tie the left hand behind the back, beat it, shame the child? No so; the cause, the faulty right eye, will remain uncorrected and unthought of by all such absurdities and cruelties [p. 58].

It remained for H. C. Stevens (1908) to relate visual acuity specifically to hemisphere specialization. Supposing as "fairly well-established" that right-handedness is "due to some as yet unknown ascendence of the left hemisphere of the brain [p. 272]," he developed an ingenious device to test the subjective size of objects in each hemifield of the eyes. In a majority of right-handed subjects, a disk appearing in the right hemifield was judged larger than a disk appearing in the left hemifield, and the reverse was found in a majority of left-handed subjects. Therefore,

Objects situated in the right half of vision of a left-hemisphered infant would, by appearing larger, attract its attention. . . . Eye movements would, probably, lead to head movements, and head movements to arm movements. Just the reverse of this would happen with a right-hemisphered infant [Stevens, 1908, p. 273; Stevens & Ducasse, 1912].

As an explanation of handedness, the various ocular dominance theories did not fare well. Ballard (1911–1912) was perhaps the first to note what he called a "fatal objection"—that among people born blind, a group of whom he himself studied, "the proportion of dextrals and sinistrals is about the same as among sighted people [p. 305]." What is more, among the sighted, the eyedness–handedness relationships claimed were not confirmed. The most destructive report, judging from the frequency of citation in post-1930 papers, was by Woo and Pearson (1927), who made an exhaustive examination of the records of nearly 7000 men first examined by Francis Galton. The result was

> no evidence whatsoever of even a correlation between ocular and manual lateralities, to say nothing of a master eye determining which is the master hand. Our data are wholly opposed to the theory of absolute laterality [1927, p. 181; emphasis in original].

Interest in the relationship between eyedness and handedness nevertheless has continued unabated. For one thing, Woo and Pearson's own study was justifiably criticized by Burt (1937, p. 272), among others, on the grounds that their hand dynamometer measure is mostly a test of strength, whereas handedness more properly is defined in terms of capacity for skilled movement.

Arm Length

The structural asymmetry theory of handedness was to see yet another variation. This was the "arm length" theory according to which the size of the humerus indicated right- or left-handedness. According to G. E. Smith (1925b, p. 1107), this problem was first raised for consideration by Arnold in 1845 (no reference given), following which an extensive literature developed that was summarized by Ernest Gaupp in 1909 (a,b). Gaupp concluded that the excess in length of the left or right arm was usually associated with left- and right-handedness, respectively. The difference, furthermore, was assumed to become manifest only in the course of postembryonic life, since the arms are equal in length at birth.

Smith, a Fellow of the Royal Society who was associated with University College, London, was himself a proponent of the arm length theory and specifically invoked it in 1925 in support of a controversial interpretation then being made of yet another asymmetry. The occasion for Smith's communication was a report in March of that same year (see Smith, 1925a) exciting widespread attention as well as incredulity, that a fossilized skull found in London was that of a left-handed woman. The inference of left-handedness had been made on the basis of a large lunate sulcus (i.e., a crescent-shaped furrow) found on the *right* posterior side of the skull in an area corresponding to the visual cortex. Smith recalled that earlier, he and Wood Jones (Smith, 1908) studied the significance of such an asymmetry of the brain case, "accepting as the criterion of right- and left-handedness respectively the observation whether the right or the left humerus was the longer and stronger. In the cranium I found that the asymmetrical impressions upon the occipital bone were reversed in those cases where the left humerus was longer and more robust than the right [Smith, 1925b, p. 1107; Smith, 1908]." Meanwhile, Jones, who had been studying the skeletons of the inhabitants of Nubia (an ancient kingdom in the Nile Valley of southern Egypt and northern Sudan), correlated his observations with measurements of living Egyptians. The results confirmed the interpretation of the use of humerus length as an indication of handedness (W. Jones, 1910; cited in Smith, 1925b).

Despite his ambitious claims, Smith's name seems not to have been associated, historically, with the "arm length" theory. Judging from the frequency of citation from papers, including brief reviews, published through the 1940s (e.g., Beeley, 1919; Blau, 1946; Schiller, 1936; L. G. Smith, 1917), that distinction has gone instead to W. Franklin Jones, a South Dakota professor of education, who was the author of what was called the "ulna plus" theory (1915, 1917).

Jones' purpose was frankly practical. His concern was for the left-hander, the "one child who has been an apparent stumbling-block in education [W. F. Jones, 1915, p. 959]." Jones' plan was to devise tests to distinguish and classify individuals into three groups: pure right-handers (individuals right-handed both by birth and by adoption, i.e., actual use); pure left-handers; and "transfers"—individuals born right- or left-handed who have adopted the use of the other arm. The aim was to develop with these groups "such tests for hand and arm skill as will enable us to say whether or not the left-hander should be transferred or made over into a right-hander [Jones, 1915, p. 959]."

Where earlier investigators had relied on bone length alone, Jones added measures of musculature, reasoning that the bone measures, especially the length of the "ulna plus" (length of the ulna, plus the hand to middle knuckle, chosen because it was more easily determined than the length of the ulna alone), would reveal "born" handedness; and muscle measures (relaxed and contracted forearm and biceps circumference) would mark the hand actually used more. From measurements on 10,000 individuals, ranging in age from newborns to centenarians, Jones found 96% right-handed, and 4% left-handed, and among the latter group, 77% were "transfers." A later test of several hundred school children disclosed strong correlations between handedness, as measured by these tests, and hand differences in a rate-of-tapping test.

Psychologists, educators, and the popular science press took notice (e.g., *Scientific American*, 1918), evidently impressed with the simple educational formula implicit in Jones' work—teach the child to use the arm having the longer ulna. Alas, new reports soon appeared saying that the method did not work. Beeley (1918, 1919) took measurements of 123 kindergarten and first grade children and obtained handedness distributions far deviant from the known facts (i.e., 46% right-handed, 40% left-handed, and 14% doubtful or ambidextrous). The actual handedness, as measured conventionally, was 94% right-handed, 3% left-handed, and 3% doubtful or ambidextrous. Beeley concluded by questioning whether native handedness could be determined at any age by bone measurements (Beeley, 1918, p. 12), and this appears to have been the last, or at least the strongest, word on this question.

Positional Asymmetry

Orientation of Infant during Birth

Some years before researchers began comparing the lengths of the arms, the weights and specific densities of the two hemispheres, or the acuity of the eyes, the French physiologist Joseph Achille Comte had taken note of still a different asymmetry, which he believed to be the key to handedness. In 1828, Comte reported a study of birth positions in 20,539 cases, a number of which he himself had observed as a surgical intern at the Maternité de Paris. Of this total, 19,810 (or 96%) were vertex presentations, meaning that the vertex (area bounded by the anterior and posterior fontanelles and by the parietal eminences) appears first, and enters the pelvic brim with the sagittal suture in or near one of the oblique diameters, with the occiput anterior or posterior. (This is the same proportion found today; Holmes, 1969).

Comte explained the greater frequency of vertex presentations by emphasizing the shape of the uterus and the shape and greater weight of the infant's head, both of which act to make the vertex presentation the safest and easiest ("la plus naturelle et la plus favorable pour l'heureuse issue de l'accouchement"; Comte, 1828, p. 35). This explanation agrees, by and large, with contemporary views. The important difference, however, was in the orientation of the head in the vertex presentation. Of the 19,810 vertex presentations, 17,226 were in what today is called the first occipito-anterior position, and only 2153 were in the "second position"— again proportions consistent with current figures. In the first, or "left," position, the occiput (i.e., the back of the child's head) is opposite the mother's left iliopectineal eminence, the forehead toward the right sacroiliac joint. In the second, or "right," position, the occiput is opposite the mother's right iliopectineal eminence, the forehead towards the mother's left sacroiliac joint. The ratio of first position births to the total in Comte's survey was thus approximately 9:1, which is the same ratio, he observed, existing between right-handers and left-handers in the population: ". . . dans le monde on recontre la mème proportion (à peu de chose près) entre les gauchers et les droitiers . . . [Comte, 1828, p. 41]."

Comte then proposed that each birth position was a clue to the infant's intrauterine position. At least this would be so from about the fifth month on because earlier the fetus has no fixed position because of its small size. However, from about the fourth to fifth month, when the fetus has become much larger, Comte assumed that it would be required to stay in the same position (Comte put this too strongly, but at least the likelihood of position changes would be expected to diminish in the last trimester.)

The first birth position thus implies that, in utero, the infant's left arm would have been against the mother's back (the lumbar region) and the right arm against the mother's abdomen. The result of the resistance of the mother's posterior part, in contrast to the yielding quality of her abdomen, Comte argued, creates a continuous compression that would be bound to delay the flow of arterial blood; to impair the return of venous blood; and therefore to slow and lessen development ("l'influence nerveuse"), by diminishing the vital energy ("l'energie vitale") of these parts. These infants therefore become right-handed, and by the same reasoning, infants born in the second position become left-handed.

Comte acknowledged the need to establish whether the similarity in ratios between birth positions and adult handedness was more than coincidental, but here, he seems to have abandoned numbers for an impressionistic description—that, in the case of "some children," their mothers' reports of the movements of their children's arms (ages of children at time of observation are unspecified) were consistent with the children's intrauterine position ("l'activité plus grande des mouvements de leurs bras m'a paru coïncider avec les rapports qu'ils avaient eus dans le sein de leur mère, . . . [Comte, 1828, p. 41].")

Judging from Comte's own account, his 1828 paper was well-received. We read, in Comte's later book (1842), that it was praised by the Academy of Sciences, publicized by Professor Magendie, who was editor of the *Journal de Physiologie*, and finally corroborated in later research carried out both in England and Germany:

> j'y suis peut être autorisé par les suffrages élevés qui accueillirent, à l'Académie des Sciences, mes *Recherches anatomico-physiologiques relatives à la prédominance du bras droit sur le bras gauche*, par l'honorable publicité que M. le professor Magendie voulut bien leur donner alors, et par la confirmation qu'elles ont reçue, depuis, en Angleterre et en Allemagne [Comte, 1842, p. 18].

None of this seems to have mattered, however, to the community of European scientists carrying out research on handedness over the next 90 years. At least I have as yet found only two citations of Comte's work in review papers (von Bardeleben, 1909, pp. 28–29; Macnaughton-Jones, 1914, p. 22). Of course, as we have seen already, Comte was unable to demonstrate that the infants born in the first and second birth position did indeed become right- and left-handed, respectively, and instead could cite only the reports of an unspecified number of mothers as to the handedness of their children. Perhaps for this reason, the ultimately small role played by his theory is understandable, although comparable methodological shortcomings proved no obstacle to serious and frequent consideration of other theories (e.g., the sub-clavian artery theory).

The birth-presentation theory, if not Comte's own work, nevertheless appeared again at least three times. One instance was described by Walter Roth in a 1903 report on superstition, magic, and medicine of the aboriginal peoples of North Queensland, Australia. According to Roth, the people of the Tully River "say, that at actual birth, according as the child presents its face to the left or to the right [presumably meaning to the mother's left or right], so will it be left- or right-handed throughout life [p. 25]." A correspondent who mentioned Roth's report in a letter to *Science* called the aboriginals' belief "a clear instance of 'scientific reasoning,' " showing that "attempts of primitive people to explain biological or physiological facts are not always of a purely mythic order [Chamberlain, 1903, p. 788]."

In 1929, Comte's theory was re-stated, in its essential form, by an American psychologist, F. A. Moss, who said that he was "cooperating in an investigation which should establish the truth or falsity of this hypothesis [p. 137]." I have not found any subsequent report. However, Moss' hypothesis later was mentioned by Overstreet, who provided her own test by correlating handedness and eyedness with the birth presentation positions of 85 subjects. The resulting correlations "clustered around zero [Overstreet, 1938, p. 520]." Furthermore, birth presentation was an unreliable index of prenatal position because more than half of the infants "altered their positions" within the 24 hours preceding birth. Overstreet (1938) concluded that birth presentation and prenatal position "probably have little, if any, effect upon subsequent laterality [p. 520]."[19]

In Utero Position and Twinning

In 1932, the role of utero position was raised again, this time with respect to the greater incidence of left-handedness in twins than in singletons. The first report of this difference usually is credited to Weitz (1925; cited in Wilson & Jones, 1932), Dahlberg (1926), and Newman (1928). In these in-

[19] Whether this conclusion can be trusted is impossible to say. The 1938 paper is only an abstract and does not describe the laterality index used (certain measures of eyedness are poorly correlated with handedness) or the subjects' ages when tested. In any case, Overstreet's paper is not the last word on the birth presentation theory. Recently, the idea has been proposed yet again, this time in an impressive empirical study that suggests an association between birth position and later handedness through the influence of prenatal postural orienta-

stances, the greater incidence was in monozygotic (MZ) twins primarily (e.g., in Newman's study, 12% left-handers among 100 MZ compared to 6% among an equal number of dizygotic (DZ) twins. Newman, earlier (1923), had proposed three different methods by which MZ twins originate: (a) division of a blastoderm into two separate blastoderms, each of which develops an embryo; (b) double gastrulation on a single blastoderm; and (c) longitudinal fission of a single embryonic axis (late in gastrulation), producing bilateral halves that regenerate and produce separate embryos. This third method, according to Newman (1928), produced reversed twins who tend to reverse asymmetry in handedness, hair whorl, and other unilateral characteristics. Wilson and Jones (1932), however, used handedness criteria somewhat different from Newman's, and found an equal raised incidence of left-handedness among both MZ and DZ twins. This finding, they proposed, could be laid to fetal position.

> Twins of either type are much more crowded, and foetal movements more restricted than among the single born . . . the [single-born] foetus usually lies with its long axis more or less parallel to that of the mother and with its head downward . . . In twins, the position is much more varied: They may both lie with their long axes either parallel or at right angles to that of the mother; the two heads may be together or . . . opposite. . . . Since twins of both types undergo the crowding and other changes of position due to the "abnormal" conditions accompanying twinning in man the effect would tend to be similar on the two classes of twins . . . [Wilson & Jones, 1932, p. 569].

Unlike Comte (1828), the authors, however, were "not prepared to enter into a detailed discussion of the relation of foetal position to the phenomena of handedness, but the possibility of such a relationship seems to deserve consideration [Wilson & Jones, 1932, p. 569]."

HEREDITY

> *I maintain that there is such a principle as* hereditary predisposition *to left-handedness in many cases, where no educational process, at least during childhood, will be of any avail.*
> *As a proof . . . I have only to refer to my own family, where the eldest son for three generations at least has been left-handed—viz., my paternal grandfather, my father, and myself; . . . I have been told that my left hand was strapped up for weeks at a time when a child, in order to overcome the natural or hereditary tendency; and I can well remember feats of caligraphy which I accomplished in my earlier school days, which were entirely written with the left hand!* [Lithgow, 1870, p. 660].

---

tions on neonatal head position preference (Michel & Goodwin, 1979; see also Coryell & Michel, 1978).

While the eye and brain measurements were being carried out, speculation began as to the possible genetic bases of handedness. Many, like the
writer quoted above, were sure that handedness was hereditary (e.g.,
von Bardeleben, 1909; Merkel, 1904; Weber, 1904; cited in Beeley, 1919;
Wilson, 1891), whereas others explicitly denied this (e.g., Gould, 1908).
Charles Darwin himself had addressed the question, using his own child
as example.

> When 77 days old, he took the sucking bottle (with which he was partly fed) in
> his right hand, whether he was held on the left or right arm of his nurse, and he
> would not take it in his left hand until a week later although I tried to make
> him do so; so that the right hand was a week in advance of the left. Yet this in-
> fant afterwards proved to be left-handed, the tendency being no doubt in-
> herited—his grandfather, mother, and a brother having been or being left-
> handed [Darwin, 1877, p. 287].

Only a few systematic genetic investigations were made in the early
years. One of the first may have been by William Ogle (1871), who found
that among 2000 individuals, 85 (4.5%) were left-handed, of whom 12 had
a left-handed parent, and 27 more knew of left-handed relatives. Later,
H. E. Jordan, of the University of Virginia, studied the family histories of
more than 2700 university students and public school pupils. Jordan (1911)
called the evidence "conclusive . . . that left-handedness is hereditary [p.
122]," but would go no further:

> In what way or by what principle this inheritance acts remains
> obscure. . . . The writer does not delude himself—nor does he wish to leave
> the impression of attempting to mislead his readers in this matter—that left-
> handedness even appears (on the basis of the limited data presented) to follow
> Mendelian principles of inheritance [Jordan, 1911, p. 122, 123].

Many new family surveys followed, with much clearer results, in particular results showing double left-handed matings giving complete left-
handed fraternities (Jordan, 1914), and when Jordan wrote again on left-
handedness in the magazine *Good Health* (1922), he was sure of his
ground:

> Left-handedness is hereditary, and follows very closely the Mendelian law of
> inheritance. [Left-handedness] conducts itself in heredity in general as a
> Mendelian recessive character. When a left-handed individual marries a right-
> handed individual, the children [from such a marriage] are all right-handed,
> due to the fact that right-handedness dominates in heredity. When such
> "hybrid" right-handed offspring intermarry, however, the children are right-
> handed and left-handed approximately in the proportion of three to one. When

left-handed individuals intermarry, the children all show a bias toward left-handedness [p. 381].[20]

Another systematic investigation was carried out by Francis Ramaley, of the University of Colorado. Ramaley studied the incidence of left-handedness among 610 parents and 1130 children, and came to the same conclusion as Jordan had: Left-handedness was a Mendelian recessive, and "probably exists in about one sixth of the population [1913, p. 738]." Ramaley further suggested that the three Mendelian types of individuals exist in "some such proportion as 9 homozygous right-handed; 12 heterozygous right-handed: 4 left-handed [1913, p. 738]."

The strict recessive model ran into difficulty because it predicted that left-handed couples would always produce left-handed children, and they did not. Jordan (1914) proposed that the exceptions might be forgiven "when allowance is made for occasional imperfection of dominance or slight degrees of bias [1914, p. 76]," or because it later was learned "that the 'left-handed' parents were only slightly so, and that they wrote with the right hand [1914, p. 77]." Ramaley likewise found that in his 305 families, only two were reported as having both parents left-handed, yet one child was right-handed. Ramaley commented, in extenuation of this result, "Of course, it is possible that one of the parents was by nature right-handed. Possibly some heterozygous [simplex] persons may easily learn to use the left hand [p. 735]."

Lending further support to a genetic theory were reports of left-handed families. Two remarkable cases were described by Aimé Péré (1900, pp. 71–72), an intern in the Medical School of the University of Toulouse. In one family, the husband and wife, both left-handed, produced 5 children, 4 of whom were left-handed. There also were 3 left-handed cousins. In the second family, a right-handed father and a left-handed mother produced 14 children, all left-handed. The father's brother also was left-handed and had 5 left-handed children. The mother's 5 siblings were left-handed, as was her father. These reports were widely cited as evidence that handedness was inherited (e.g., Cunningham, 1902, p. 280), but in the case of the second family, in which one parent was right-handed, the outcome was inconsistent with a recessive model—a point brought out by at least one critic, R. H. Compton, a British plant geneticist who did work on stereo-isomeric forms of seedling in barley and who later became interested in human handedness. Compton mentioned the Péré reports as evidence "in strong contrast to Jordan's hypothesis of the dominance of right-handedness, and

---

[20] Jordan also acknowledged what today is recognized as a necessary distinction among degrees of handedness, which he linked to the ease of change through training. He also accepted the blood supply theory supposing that degrees of variation in the asymmetrical cerebral blood supply paralleled functional degrees of manual efficiency (Jordan, 1922, pp. 381–382).

suggesting the reverse assumption [Compton, 1911–1912, p. 68; see also 1910]."

Jordan himself mentioned Péré's report only later (1922) and, without reference to Compton, put a different face on the seemingly inconsistent facts.

> The father was said to have been right-handed, but he had a left-handed brother who had five left-handed children. In view of the family history, it seems probable that the father was a mild left-handed individual trained to be right-handed [Jordan, 1922, p. 381].

Cultural Conditioning Theories

Marshalled against the various "nativist" theorists were the "nurturists." Convinced that handedness was not a product of visceral position, blood supply, heredity, or any other physiological factor, they laid emphasis on social conditioning and practice. One of these theorists, in the seventeenth century, was Thomas Browne. Indeed, he called the fourth book of his *Pseudodoxia Epidemica* an examination "of many popular and received tenents concerning man, which examined, prove false or dubious," and the "naturalness" of right-handedness was one of the "tenents" he strove to deny. Having dispatched the physiological theories of Rhodoginus and Fallopio, Browne concluded that in adults, dextral pre-eminence is the result of social institution.

Like the biologic explanations, the "learning" theories assumed several different forms. Thomas Browne was content with only a vague appeal: "It is most reasonable for uniformity and sundry respective uses that man should apply himself to the constant use of one arm (Browne, 1646, p. 186)."[21] Later explanations were more explicit, if not necessarily more convincing.

How Infants Are Carried

Beginning perhaps about the 1880s, reference began to be made to the role played by the position in which the child was held by its mother or nurse. In two sentences, the first clear, the second cryptic, Hall and Hart-

---

[21] Though not addressing himself specifically to Browne, Buchanan, writing in 1862, made an insightful reply to this argument:

> If the use of the right hand were a mere conventional arrangement founded on utility and expediency, and inculcated by precept and practice on a docile and obedient posterity, it would have varied like every other human institution left to voluntary control. Love of change, fancied utility, the spirit of opposition and mere caprice would, in every age of the world, have rendered the use of the one hand as common as the use of the other. If the barbarians who tattoo their faces, compress their skulls, distort their feet, and otherwise mutilate and disfigure the human frame, are, nevertheless, all of them, just as

well (1884) described the supposed practice and its effects. "Nurses carry children on their own right arm, leaving the child's right arm a freer field of motion. They hug them on the right side, disturbing the equilibrium of blood-pressure. [Hall & Hartwell, 1884, p. 101]."

Not to discount anatomical facts altogether, an American physician even suggested that the origin of the holding practice rested in visceral asymmetry:

> The mother when she has given birth to her child, usually assumes position, lying on the right side. She does this because it is the most restful position, because her liver, the largest of her viscera after the womb is emptied, lies on the right side. Lying on her right side she naturally takes the babe to her bosom and places it in the most natural and restful position for herself and the infant . . . on her right arm with its left arm confined against her breast [Hughes, 1890, p. 147].

The process, of course, would continue into the next generation as the child grew, sleeping by preference on its own right side, and repeating the right-sided holding practice with its own child.

As immediate problem with the "infant-holding" theory of handedness, as many sober observers brought out, was that the actual practice was not to carry in the right arm at all, but rather in the left—a fact that, as one physician stated, implied a quite different outcome.

> I have been surprised . . . that the proportion of left-handed children was not greater. A right-handed mother or nurse holding an infant to the breast, or carrying it when it is not nursing, will almost inevitably carry the child on the left arm. In this position its right arm for a considerable portion of the first year of its extra-uterine existence, is pressed helplessly between its body and that of its attendant, while the left arm is free to be used [Wyeth, 1880, p. 129].

Andrew Buchanan (1862) likewise noted that burdens—whether a heavy trunk, baskets of eggs or vegetables, or infants—are typically carried on the *left* side and, indeed, called carrying or supporting burdens "the special function of the left side [p. 162]," invoking his "balance" theory to explain the phenomenon.[22] Later, Cyril Burt satisfied himself on this point through

---

unanimous as civilized nations in the preference of the right hand over the left, we may rest assured that it is not a mere matter of choice on their part, which hand they ought to prefer [p. 142].

[22] The equilibrium of the body is better maintained by carrying it [the weight] on the left side; for the centre of gravity being upon the opposite side, less inclination of the body to that side is required when the weight is appended to the left; and there is, therefore, less interference with the natural play of the limbs in walking: whereas if the weight be appended to the right by the side of the liver, the body must be thrown very much to the opposite side to keep the equilibrium stable, and the motion of the limbs will be proportionally constrained [Buchanan, 1862, p. 163].

personal observation of 100 instances, finding the child being carried on the right arm in only 27 cases, on the left in 73 (Burt, 1937, p. 299).[23] Burt also reported a preference for the left arm, though by a weaker margin, in artistic depictions of the Madonna and Child.

Warfare Shield Theory

If cultural theories of handedness could not deny the fact of structural asymmetry, they could argue that handedness represented a conscious accommodation or reaction to this physiological state. Perhaps the best-known version of this explanation of handedness is the so-called "warfare shield" theory of the Scottish essayist and historian, Thomas Carlyle (1795-1881). Carlyle's inspiration was the failure of his own right hand from palsy when he was 75 years old. Moved to speculate about right-handedness, he outlined the theory in his journal in a few laconic passages.

> Why that particular hand was chosen is a question not to be settled, not worth asking except as a kind of riddle; probably arose in fighting; most important to protect your heart and its adjacencies, and to carry the shield in that hand [15 June, 1871; quoted in Froude, 1898, pp. 347-348].[24]

Supporters of the warfare shield theory adduced further evidence through etymology, pointing out that "sem'ol," the Hebrew word for left, means "that which is concealed or covered," and the Cymric (the branch of the

---

[23] More recently, Uhrbrock (1973) examined 1110 pictures and pieces of sculpture of the Madonna and Child and found the Child to be on the Madonna's left in 596 representations, on the right in 425, and centered in 89. I have found a far stronger asymmetry in a smaller sample—172, 58, and 15 for left, right, and center, respectively (de Kalb, 1969; Marienbild in Rheinland und Westfalen, 1968).

Several writers (e.g., Ingalls, 1928, p. 309; Schiller, 1936, pp. 694-697) attributed the infant carrying theory to Plato. Schiller (1936) named the *Dialogue* (Jowett translation) on education between an Athenian stranger and Cleinias, a Cretan. There is no such evidence. In the *Dialogue*, the Athenian remarks that "the right and left hand are supposed to be by nature differently suited for our various uses of them; whereas no difference is found in the use of the feet and lower limbs; but in the use of the hands we are, as it were, maimed by the folly of nurses and mothers; for although our several limbs are by nature balanced, we create a difference in them by bad habits [*Dialogues*, Vol. 4, Jowett, 1953, p. 361]." The Athenian, however, is not specific as to the nature of these "bad habits." In the A. E. Taylor translation (1961), there likewise is no reference to the carrying position of the infant.

[24] Carlyle must share credit for this idea with P. H. Pye-Smith, who in the same year wrote:

If a hundred of our ambidextrous ancestors made the step in civilization of inventing a shield, we may suppose that half would carry it on the right arm and fight with the left, the other half on the left and fight with the right. The latter would certainly, in the long run, escape mortal wounds better than the former, and thus a race of men who fought with the right hand would gradually be developed by a process of natural selection [Pye-Smith, 1871, p. 145].

Celtic languages, including Welsh, Breton, and Cornish) word for left, "asw", comes from "aswy"—shield (Frisch, 1968, p. 33).

The theory proved to be an easy target for critics. Parsons (1924), for instance, pointed out that the shield was undoubtedly invented well after the first club and javelin, so that the use of these weapons alone "would certainly have induced one-handedness, and might even have developed general righthandedness, since in single combat, the only sort of warfare known in prehistoric times, right handed warriors could most directly attack their adversaries on the heart side of the body [Parsons, 1924, p. 65]." A more fundamental objection was that the heart is displaced to the left by so small a margin, that, as an earlier critic recognized, "it must be denied, in the name of anatomy, that there is more than a very slight difference in the danger of wounds between the two sides [Dwight, quoted in Jackson, 1905, p. 51]." The same critic then administered what should have been the coup de grace:

> Even if the premise were correct, there is no evidence that primitive tribes advanced against each other like pasteboard soldiers. On the contrary, there is every reason to think that they often attacked their enemies from the side, or even from behind. That spears and arrows pierced the foeman [foes in battle] from right to left, and from left to right, and at every angle of obliquity, is beyond question. . . . But even if we admit the theory, how are we to account for left-handed men? Why were they not killed off? Were they wicked and perverse people who refused to listen to the good prehistoric surgeon-general, when he told them to carry the shield on the left, and who, through some lapse of justice, escaped their deserts? [Dwight, quoted in Jackson, 1905, p. 51].

Studies of Human Infants

However dramatic were the theories about shields or the handling practices of mothers and nurses, they do not appear to have been seriously considered by the scientific establishment of the time—at most, they received passing mention. Far more relevant were studies, beginning in the late nineteenth century, of the actual hand preference of the human infant. If handedness was culturally imposed, as the nurturists believed, the young infant should show no preference.

Infants and children in fact had long been seen as a source of critical information one way or the other. Thomas Browne was perhaps among the first to appeal to the evidence of the young to support his "nurturist" views.

> That there is also in men a naturall prepotency in the right we cannot with constancy affirme, if we make observation in children, who permitted the freedom of bothe do oftimes confine unto the left, and are not without great difficulty restrained from it, and therefore this prevalency is either uncertainly placed in the laterality, or custome determines its indifference [1646, p. 186].

Slow to act, it was more than two centuries before psychologists followed with empirical studies. Charles Darwin (1877), as we saw earlier, had observed his own child, and had concluded that the infant's eventual left-handedness must reflect hereditary control. G. Stanley Hall (1891) later reported observations on two infants (his own?), finding in both that there were "several months of decided left-handedness, when with a tempting object on the table exactly in front and both hands released at the same instant, the left would nearly always grasp the object, and yet distinct right-handedness was developed later in both [Hall, 1891, p. 131]." However, Hall drew no conclusions from these observations.

The best known report, judging from the frequency of citation, was by James Mark Baldwin (1890), then at the University of Toronto and later, the distinguished Professor of Philosophy and Psychology at the Johns Hopkins University. Stimulated by Wilson's (1886) discussion of handedness to which I referred earlier (pp. 8–9), Baldwin began what appears to have been the first genuinely experimental investigation, the subject of which was his own daughter. Certain details of procedure, omitted from the 1890 report but added in a later paper (1894), fully reveal the hardheaded and perhaps hardhearted experimentalist:

> Certain precautions were carefully enforced. She was never carried about in arms at all—never walked with when crying or sleepless (a ruinous and needless habit to cultivate in an infant); she was frequently turned over in her sleep; she was not allowed to balance herself on her feet until a later period than that covered by the experiments [Baldwin, 1894, p. 607].

Then over the course of the first year of life, Baldwin elicited reaching by presenting various objects before the infant, and in unsymmetrical directions. Of 2187 such tests, the baby reached with her right hand 577 times, the left hand 568 times, and both hands the rest of the time. These were all occasions, however, when no violent muscular exertions were made. By placing objects just beyond her reach, Baldwin elicited "very hard straining . . . with all the signs of physical effort [1894, p. 608]," and under these circumstances, by the seventh and eight month, "a distinct preference for the right hand . . . became noticeable [1890, p. 247]." Baldwin concluded that "righthandedness had accordingly developed under pressure of muscular effort [1890, p. 247]." Finally, presumably with Andrew Buchanan's balance theory in mind, Baldwin added that because his daughter had not yet learned to stand or creep, the development of one hand more than the other could not have been the result of differences in weight between the two longitudinal halves of the body.

Apparently no other studies followed for more than 15 years, although the relevance of such investigations was acutely perceived. Cunningham, (1902) was able to cite only Baldwin's report, saying that "it is a matter of regret . . . that this ready means of investigation has not been more fully taken advantage of [p. 280]." Then, beginning in 1906, several new reports began to appear (e.g., Dearborn, 1910; Major, 1906; Nice, 1918; Shinn, 1914; Woolley, 1910). Major's child (1906) shifted from left- and right-hand preference to no preference. Between 12 and 15 months, left-hand preference seemed to have become established, at which time left-hand use was actively discouraged. Whether or not as a result of the active discouragement of left-hand use, by the second year the right hand again was preferred. Major thought that the results did not permit clear choice between training and native endowment as the basis of handedness.

Like Baldwin (1890), Helen Woolley (1910) took pains not to encourage hand preference in her son, and found that he reached uniformly with his right hand by 7 months but only, as Baldwin had found, for far distances, where effort was called for. Woolley (1910) concluded that "right-handed-ness must be a normal part of physiological development, not a phenome-non explicable by training [pp. 40–41].

One of the remarkable aspects of Woolley's report is how it seemed to support but then more convincingly undermined the "mother holding" theory. At 8 months, Woolley's daughter began waving when she was taken out for a ride: "In taking her out to her cab, the nurse always carried her on the left arm, leaving the child's left hand free, and as a result she learned to wave 'Bye-Bye' with the left hand (Woolley, 1910, p. 39)." Subsequently, if the left hand was held, the child refused to wave but did so as soon as the hand was released. Later she began to use either the left hand or both hands in waving, but never the right hand alone. "Then gradually she began using the right hand occasionally, and by fifteen months, she had ceased using the left hand, and waved habitually with the right [Woolley, 1910, p. 39]." The early left-handed waving thus was anomalous, and "long before her right-handedness had conquered habit in the matter of waving 'Bye-Bye,' it was perfectly evident in other activities [Woolley, 1910, p. 39].

Baldwin, Woolley, and the other early researchers were familiar with the neuropsychological literature, in particular with the possibility that speech and right-hand movements would be associated in development because of the close proximity of the controlling cortical areas. In Baldwin's case, as his daughter was not yet making distinct articulate sounds when right-hand preference first appeared, he concluded that "right- or left-handedness may develop while the motor speech centre is not yet functioning [Baldwin, 1890, p. 247]." Woolley, however, saw a closer association: "The period when the tests first show a preponderating use of the right hand . . . (the

middle of the seventh month), is just the one when the child began to bab-
ble syllables [1910, p. 41]."

In Baldwin's, Woolley's, and several other biographical reports, early
periods of apparent left-hand use were found, but were dismissed as insignificant in light of the eventual right-hand preference that developed.
The psychologist, Max Meyer, however, recognized a significant
developmental pattern.

> If the left cerebral hemisphere, which serves such complex functions as speech,
> reaches maturity, so to speak, only during the second year, it appears plausible
> to assume that during the first months of life hand movements are
> predominantly controlled by the right hemisphere which serves simpler func-
> tions and probably matures at an earlier time. General left-handedness in in-
> fancy would be the consequence as naturally as general right-handedness in
> adult life [Meyer, 1913, p. 53]; 1911].

The earliest studies of infant hand preference generally were seen, then,
as upholding some sort of physiological explanation of handedness. In the
1920s, however, the theoretical ground shifted under the influence of John
B. Watson, the father of "behaviorism," who by this time had emerged as a
dominant figure in American psychology and as the best-known, if controversial, spokesman for child psychology. Watson (1924a,b, 1925) conducted an extended series of studies of handedness in infants. His studies included measurements of left and right body structures such as the width of
the palm and wrist and length of the forearm, recording how long the baby
could suspend himself with each hand, and recording the total number of
movements by attaching each hand, by means of a thread, to two pivoted
writing levers mounted in nearly frictionless bearings, so that each hand
movement was translated into a tracing on a smoked drum. No asymmetries were evident. With children between 125 days and 1 year of age,
Watson also tested for reaching for a piece of candy. These results showed
no uniformity in hand used; sometimes the right hand was extended,
sometimes the left. The conclusion seemed obvious.

> Our whole group of results in handedness leads us to believe that there is no
> fixed differentiation of response in either hand until social usage begins to
> establish handedness. Society soon thereafter steps in and says, "Thou shalt use
> thy right hand." Pressure promptly begins. "Shake hands with your right hand,
> Willy." We hold the infant so that it will wave "bye-bye" with the right hand.
> We *force it to eat with the right hand. This in itself is a potent enough condi-
> tioning factor to account for handedness* [Watson, 1924 a, p. 101; emphasis in
> original].

But why is society right-handed in the first place? Watson was scram-
bling here. Having failed even to mention any of the more conventional

physiological explanations and having ignored Baldwin's, Woolley's, and other earlier reports, Watson tried the unconventional: He considered intrauterine position ("The extent to which slight differences in the intrauterine position . . . may possibly later influence or even determine right and left handedness . . . is not known"); added the ingredient of visceral asymmetry ("the liver is on the right side in about 80% of the observed cases"); considered the implications ("Whether this large organ may swing the foetus slightly so that the right side is constantly under less restraint than the left is not known. If this is true the infant with the liver on the right side should be right-handed from birth"); rejected them ("My records on hundreds of infants prove that this is not the case, [Watson, 1924a, p. 89]"); and then fell back lamely on—of all thing—the warfare shield theory.

> It was easy enough for our most primitive ancestors to *learn* that the men who carried their shields with the left hand and jabbed with or hurled their spears with the right were the ones who more often came back bearing their shields rather than being borne on them. . . . If there is any truth in this it is easy enough to see why our primitive ancestors began to teach their young to be righthanded [Watson, 1924a, p. 102].

Then why left-handers? Watson hedged again, at one moment calling left-handers "those hardy souls who have resisted social pressure [1924a, p. 102]," and at another confessing that the answer to the question "why we have 5% of out and out left-handers and from 10–15% who are mixtures . . . is not known [1924a, p. 102]."

AMBIDEXTRAL CULTURE

> *Six thousand years of lop-armed, lop-legged savages, some barbarous, some civilized, have not created a single lop-legged, lop-armed child, and never will. Every child is even and either handed till some grown fool interferes and mutilates it.*
>
> —Charles Reade
> 2 March, 1878, p. 175

A sidelight to the debate on the origins of handedness was a curious educational movement beginning late in the nineteenth century, first in England, then America. I want to digress to consider this development, as it will shed light on some of the themes we have been discussing. The movement was for what came to be known as "ambidextral culture," and the promoters, understandably, were those who disputed the "naturalness" of right-hand preference, or, if they accepted the possibility, they deplored the social and practical ramifications, and urged training of both hands equally.

Plato perhaps was a forebear of this movement. In the *Dialogues*, the Athenian speaks to the Cretan of the folly of the Athenian custom of unimanual training:

> The custom of the Scythians proves our error: for they not only hold the bow from them with the left hand and draw the arrow to them with their right, but use either hand for both purposes. And there are many similar examples in charioteering and other things, from which we may learn that those who make the left side weaker than the right act contrary to nature [Jowett, 1953, p. 361].

In armed combat, Plato saw special merit in ambidexterity:

> For as he who is perfectly skilled in the Pancratium or boxing or wrestling is not unable to fight from his left side, and does not limp and draggle in confusion when his opponent makes him change his position, so in heavy-armed fighting, and in all other things, if I am not mistaken, the like holds—he who has these double powers of attack and defence might not in any case to leave them either unused or untrained, if he can help [Jowett, 1953, p. 362].

In France in 1780, Jean-Jacques Rousseau declared his ambidextral sentiments in *Émile*, his philosophical romance and treatise on child rearing.

> The only habit the child should be allowed to contract is that of having no habits; let him be carried on either arm, let him be accustomed to offer either hand, to use one or other indifferently . . . [1911, p. 30].

In Britain, a significant and controversial early advocate was Charles Reade, a widely celebrated author of what he called "novels with a purpose" in which he attacked the evils of Victorian Society. He was, in the words of one admirer, "champion of the lunatic and the gaol-bird, and of other helpless and inferior members of the human race [Lindsay, 1904, p. 129]." Reade argued for ambidextral training in *The Coming Man*, a series of didactic and barbed letters to the editor of the *Daily Telegraph* (1878).[25] Something of Reade's evangelical style is conveyed in his first letter:

> In a word, Sir, I believe that "THE COMING MAN" is the "EITHER-HANDED MAN"—that is to say, neither "right-handed" nor "left-handed," but a man rescued in time from parroted mothers, cuckoo nurses, and starling nursing-maids, with their pagan nursery rhymes and their pagan prejudices against the left hand; in short, a man as perfect in his limbs as his Creator intended [Reade, 19 Jan. 1878, p. 51].

[25] The 1878 date is to *Harper's Weekly*, an American publication, where the letters also appeared. I have not seen the *Daily Telegraph* letters.

Of the medical evidence showing physiological bases for laterality, Reade was simply contemptuous, eagerly—and with superb confidence—recounting the numerous inconsistencies in the clinical literature (there were many for the picking), setting the physiologists' own arguments against each other (professional rivalries to be exploited), calling the most illustrious anatomists of the day "brainless dissectors of the brain [23 March, 1878, p. 234]," and dismissing Broca's theories, in particular, as "chimerical [23 March, 1878, p. 234]."[26]

Reade's letters attracted much attention and were frequently mentioned in the lay and medical press. His appeal, however, failed to create a popular movement for ambidextral training. A later admirer wrote, "for although there was a vigorous correspondence, the subject was dropped as suddenly and completely as if it had been the most trivial and contemptible nonsense that ever dribbled from the fingers of the feeblest penny-a-liner [Jackson, 1905, pp. 140–141[." This admirer was John Jackson, also a layman, under whose guiding hands Charles Reade's ideas finally became practice. Jackson was the author of several books on handwriting and was the originator of the "system of upright penmanship," that is, writing without a slant. Jackson's ideas had been germinating through the 1890's and culminated in the founding in 1903 of the Ambidextral Culture Society in Great Britain whose goals he described in a long tract published in 1905 entitled *Ambidexterity or Two-Handedness and Two-Brainedness: An Argument for Natural Development and Rational Education.*

By 1907, all the signs of an educational craze were evident. In that year, a physician, Sir. J. Crighton-Browne, a Fellow of the Royal Society, commented,

> We have now an Ambidextral Culture Society; big books upon ambidexterity have been published, pamphlets and leaflets dealing with it are being circulated, schools are trying to attract pupils by advertising that they give ambidextral training, of course with unparalleled educational successes; and in the most renowned of all our schools the thin edge of the wedge has been introduced, for it has been ordained, we are told, that at Eton the boys who for their transgressions are called upon to write lines, are henceforth to do so with the left hand [1907, p. 624].

---

[26] That a layman should have been so bold as to presume to know better than the leading scientists, that he should criticize them in the most mocking terms, and that other laymen, not to mention educators and scientists themselves, should have listened respectfully and quoted his remarks, may seem remarkable today. But in Reade's time, the scientific establishment was not universally held in high regard, and quite vicious attacks in the press were common. Not too many years earlier, for instance, the *John Bull Examiner* had described the 1835 meeting of the British Association for the Advancement of Science as "a whole lot of glaring humbug [1835; quoted in Goodfield, 1977, p. 581]."

What kind of people were attracted to ambidextral culture? Crighton-Browne went on to say,

> In this present movement . . . I fancy I detect the old taint of faddism. Some of those who promote it are addicted to vegetarianism, hatlessness, or anti-vaccination, and other abberant forms of belief; but it must be allowed that beyond that it has the support of a large number of highly educated, intelligent and reasonable people, and of some men of light and leading [Crighton-Browne, 1907, p. 624].

Of those acolytes "addicted" to vegetarianism, anti-vaccination, but especially hatlessness, further comment perhaps is unnecessary. But what of "men of light and leading"? Crighton-Browne was speaking not of country doctors unconnected to the great teaching hospitals and relatively unschooled in scientific research, but of his own colleagues—eminent physicians and physiologists. Among the 50-member committee of the Ambidextral Culture Society was a great shining of medical and academic medals. It was these men's views that provided the engine for Jackson's movement.

Many physicians and surgeons reasonably claimed real advantages to ambidexterity in their medical practices, which they recited in numerous and sober testimonials published in *The Lancet* and other medical journals. For instance, Sir James Sawyer, a Fellow of the Royal College of Physicians and Consulting Physician to the Queen's Hospital, Birmingham, wrote to the *British Medical Journal:*

> I desire to join in recommending the general culture and adoption of ambidexterity . . . In our own manifold profession ambidexterity is a great equipment. In laryngoscopy, in ophthalmoscopy, in palpation, in percussion, and in examinations *per vias naturales* it is useful . . . [Sawyer, 1900, p. 1302].

Advantages for the national defense were seen as well. Jackson numbered among his strongest supporters Major General, later Lord R. S. S. Baden-Powell, who formally endorsed Jackson's society and wrote the introduction to Jackson's book. Like Plato, Baden-Powell looked at the question of either-handedness through soldierly eyes:

> I do not consider a man is a thoroughly trained soldier unless he can mount equally well on either side of his horse, use the sword, pistol, and lance, equally well with both hands, and shoot off the left shoulder as rapidly and accurately as from the right [quoted in Jackson, 1905, p. XII].

Baden-Powell's introduction was signed twice, once with each hand. Baden-Powell, it will be recalled, founded the Boy Scouts, whose custom it remains to shake hands left-handed.

The aforementioned, of course, were trivial advantages insofar as neuropsychological issues were concerned. For Jackson, the most ambitious benefit was the enhancement—even doubling—of mental power on the assumption that training the two hands equally would equally train the two hemispheres of the brain. And now for Jackson, the writings of two mid-nineteenth-century physicians became critical—Henry Holland and particularly Arthur Ladbroke Wigan. Both men had been inspired by the same kind of psychological phenomena, especially, as Holland later put it, reports of *"double consciousness; where the mind passes by alternation from one state to another, each having the perception of external impressions and appropriate trains of thought, but not linked together by the ordinary gradations, or by mutual memory [1852, p. 187]."* But whereas Holland (1840) limited himself to a rough sketch, "On the brain as a double organ," Wigan developed an elaborate theory (1844). Wigan outlined his theory in 20 propositions, the most important for John Jackson probably being the first two: "That each cerebrum is a distinct and perfect whole as an organ of thought"; and "That a separate and distinct process of thinking or ratiocination may be carried on in each cerebrum simultaneously [1844, p. 26]."

If two brains means two minds, and if one brain alone is sufficient for the full performance of the mental functions (Wigan's view), it was an obvious step to suppose that man's "double brain" was under-used, a shortcoming that Jackson was determined to correct. Jackson's goal was no less than

to so train our school children that . . . each hand shall be absolutely independent of the other in the production of ANY KIND OF WORK whatever; that, if required, one hand shall be writing an original letter, and the other hand shall be playing the piano; one hand shall be engaged in writing, . . . the other in making a pen-and-ink sketch . . . with no diminution in the power of concentration when only one hand may be employed . . . [Jackson, 1905, p. 225].[27]

Of all the promised benefits of ambidextral training, perhaps the most dramatic was that it would prevent, or ameliorate, the effects of unilateral brain injury resulting in aphasia and hemiplegia. A physician, W. A. Hollis, writing in the *Journal of Anatomy and Physiology,* cited such notables as Samuel Johnson and Jonathan Swift as having suffered from aphasia in their last years.

---

[27] Separate simultaneous use of the two brains on different tasks actually would have been inconsistent with Wigan's 18th proposition—that the object of education should be "to make both cerebra carry on the same train of thought together . . . [1844, p. 29]." Little wonder this proposition was not quoted in Jackson's book.

Such cases as these . . . show how active energetic brains break down by over-
work, or rather by ill-balanced work. It is perhaps too much to say, that none
of these attacks would have taken place had the patients allowed each side of
their brains to participate equally in their work, but speaking with some reser-
vation, I believe it is probable that the disease would have been indefinitely
postponed had their education been other than "lopsided". . . . The time has
arrived when our posterity must utilize to the utmost every cubic line of brain-
substance, and this can only be done by a system of education which will en-
force an equal prominence to both sides of the brain in all intellectual operations [Hollis, 1875, p. 271].

One might suppose that supporters of ambidextral culture would have
opposed left-handedness just as much as right-handedness. In principle,
they did, though they managed to enlist left-handedness in further support
of their physiological arguments. Two recognized characteristics of left-
handers were critical—that they did not use their left hand so consistently
as right-handers used the right, and that, compared with right-handers,
they were reported to be less likely to suffer aphasic symptoms after
cerebral insult. The lesson was unmistakable.

[L]eft-handed or ambidextrous people . . . by education or custom, are
strongly influenced to use the right hand largely, hence working the left as well
as the right hemisphere. These diseases [aphasias and agraphias] are often
successfully treated by compelling the patient to use his non-preferred hand and
thus bring the latent force of the accompanying brain into play. Aphasia, according to one estimate, is, in fourteen out of fifteen cases, a disease of the left
brain. This is decidedly an argument for the cultivation of both hands [Smith,
1917, pp. 29–30], summarizing the views of a physician, H. Macnaughton-
Jones (1914)].[28]

Finally, advocates saw particular support for their views in reports that appeared at least as early as the 1870's suggesting that in cases of left-
hemisphere injury, the younger the patient, the better the prognosis for the
development or recovery of speech (e.g., Brown-Séquard, 1877, p. 68). The
accepted interpretation was that differentiation between the hemispheres
for speech was less nearly complete in children than in adults, and that,
therefore, children had a greater chance for education of the rudimentary
motor speech center of the right hemisphere (e.g., Stedman, cited in Lindsay, 1904, p. 133). The moral: Begin the education of *both* hemispheres
early in each child's life, and reduce the likelihood of debilitating unilateral
cerebral injury.

The ambidextral movement did not escape criticism. For example,

[28] Macnaughton-Jones, a strong partisan of ambidextral training, was himself referring to
the work of a Dr. Manfred Fraenkel. Like Buzzard (1882), whom we mentioned earlier in our
discussion of "crossed aphasia," Fraenkel evidently used exercise therapy in patients with
Broca's aphasia (see Kipiani, 1912, p. 159).

Crighton-Browne inveighed against ambidextral training; first, because it would be unsuccessful—handedness being congenital, innate, and rooted in brain physiology—and second, because it would be dangerous.

> Pushed towards that consummation which its ardent apostles tell us is so devoutly to be wished for, when the two hands will be able to write on two different subjects at the same time, it must involve the enormous enlargment of our already over-grown lunatic asylums. Right-handedness is woven in the brain; to change the pattern you must unravel its tissues. My own conviction is that, as regards right-handedness, our best policy is to let well alone and to stick to dexterity and the bend sinister [1907, p. 652].

Eventually, in the face of many other criticisms (not all of them quite so dramatic as Crighton-Browne's) and because of its own inflated claims, the ambidextral culture movement dies out as an educational force. A reprise of sorts, however, is in the making among some of today's educators, who are envisioning benefits that nearly match those promised earlier (Harris, 1978, 1979).

LEFT-HANDEDNESS AS PATHOLOGICAL

So far we have seen left-handedness explained as a rare reversal of whatever conditions were believed to underlie right-handedness, and for the most part, no special characterization of the personality or intellect of the "reversed" individual had been implied. Many scientists, however, though accepting one or another of the physiological or social theories, went further and declared left-handedness to be a manifestation of pathology—of the brain, the personality, or both. I must confess that in certain respects I find the "pathology" theories to be the most interesting because they tried to account for the many supposed peculiarities of sinistrality listed earlier—at least the negative characteristics.

To some extent the advocates of the pathology view practiced a kind of Manichaeanism whereby "right" becomes synonymous with perfection and goodness, and "left" becomes the symbol of evil and impurity. This dual symbolism, with only a few prominent exceptions such as China (Granet, 1973), is universal and is expressed both in language and social custom. The linguistic examples by now are familiar to followers of the literature on sinistrality. Of course, there is the word "sinistral" itself, with its etymological connection to "sinister." In German, "links" (the old German is "lenka") has a pronounced pejorative sense (as in "linkisch" meaning clumsy); the French "gauche" means both left and clumsy (the word comes from the old French "guenchir," meaning to make a detour, to bend), and "sinistre" has the same meaning as the English sinister as well as meaning "a catastrophe"; in Italian "mancino" not only means a left-handed man but has the connotation of "thief." From the European languages to the African is a long linguistic step, but there too, left has negative connotations. In the Bantu languages, for instance, the name for left often implies inferiority or bad luck (Werner, 1904).

As for social custom, not all, to be sure, are so drastic as an African tribal practice wherein "If a child should seem to be naturally left-handed the people pour boiling water into a hole in the earth, and place the child's left hand in the hole, ramming the earth down around it; by this means the left hand becomes so scalded that the child is bound to use the right hand [Kidd, 1906, p. 296; quoted in Wieschhoff, 1973, p. 71]." However, in Europe, as recently as the early 1900s, it yet could be said, "One of the signs which distinguish a well-brought-up child is that its left hand has become incapable of any independent action [Hertz, 1973, p. 5]."

There are, of course, many Biblical references to the auspicious right hand, and the inauspicious left, and Biblical quotations were as common in the nineteenth century literature on handedness as they are today. Perhaps the most quoted was the parable of the sheep and the goats, from the Book of Matthew: On the day of the last judgment, "he shall separate [all nations] one from another, as a shepherd divideth his sheep from the goats; and he shall set the sheep on his right hand, but the goats on the left. . . . Then shall the King say unto them on his right hand, Come, ye blessed of my Father, inherit the Kingdom prepared for you from the foundation of the world. . . . Then shall he say also unto them on the left hand, Depart from me, ye cursed, into everlasting fire, prepared for the devil and his angels [Matthew 25:31–36]."

In Jewish writings, a similar distinction between left and right was held. The angel Michael, on the right, favors Israel more than does Gabriel, who is on the left. Samuel (from "sem'ol", meaning "left") is on the left, outside, as the antagonist of Israel. The "yezer-tov" (the reification of the inclination or instinct toward good) is on the right side of every person, and the "yezer ha-ra" (inclination toward wickedness) is on the left. And in Ecclesiastes, we read, "A wise man's heart is at his right hand; but a fool's heart at his left." The *Jewish Encyclopedia* (1925) gives many more examples.

Given such a poisonous cultural climate, it is understandable that scientific theories eventually should have arisen that specifically related left-handedness to criminality and antisocial behavior. For example, the statements of Jordan (1911) and other geneticists that left-handedness was a recessive trait were seized upon by those eager to prove the degeneracy of left-handedness. The author of a 1913 story in *McClure's Magazine* was willing to go far beyond the tentative, highly qualified conclusions in Jordan's 1911 paper:

The curious thing about the inheritance of left-handedness . . . is that it closely resembles the inheritance of two other peculiarities which are also dependent on brain structure—namely, mental ability and moral excellence. A sound and capable stock, like a right-handed one, breeds true generation after generation. Then something slips a cog, and there appears a left-handed child, a black sheep, or an imbecile. An imbecile or scapegrace parent married to a normal spouse may have half his children like himself. Two weak-minded, criminal, or degenerate parents always have all their children bad [Brewster, 1913, p. 183].

The most dramatic and influential figure among the "pathology" theorists was the Italian criminologist Cesare Lombroso. In 1903 he reported that among 1029 "operatives and soldiers" he found 4% left-handers among men and 5–8% in women. Among lunatics, the proportions were not much different. But in criminals, the "quota of left-handedness was found more than tripled in men, thirteen percent, and nearly quintupled in women, Twenty-two percent [Lombroso, 1903, p. 440]." Moreover, "some particular kinds of criminals . . . for example, swindlers, offered me again a much higher proportion, thirty-three percent, while murderers and ravishers give less—from nine percent to ten percent [Lombroso, 1913, p. 440]." Lombroso explained his findings with anatomical data. Lombroso himself "studied forty-four heads of criminals in my museum at Turin, and I find asymmetry very prevalent in the right lobe in forty-one percent, and the left in twenty percent [Lombroso, 1903, p. 444]." All theses figures he contrasted with other evidence that, in individuals, the greater development is on the left side (e.g., Bastien, 1866). Lombroso concluded that "this is a new characteristic, which connects criminals with savages, and differentiates them from sane people as well as lunatics [1903, p. 440]," so that in criminals, the right lobe "predominates very much more often than in normal persons. While the healthy man thinks and feels with the left lobe, the abnormal wills, and feels more with the right—thinks 'crooked', as the popular proverb has it [1903, p. 443]." In ending his paper, Lombroso noted that long before he had reached his own conclusions, "the people in the provinces of Emilia, Lombardy, and Tuscany had already declared the same when they framed and used the saying, 'He is left-handed', to express the idea that a person is untrustworthy [Lombroso, 1903 p. 444]."

Lombroso's (1903) views were widely quoted, and in the next few years, several confirming reports appeared. Audenino (1907) and Lattes (1907) summarized research indicating more frequent left-handedness among criminals, degenerates, prostitutes, and epileptics. To this list, L. G. Smith (1917) added delinquents, finding among children in American "industrial schools," 11% left-handedness for boys and 6.5% for girls. She concluded, "This seems to agree with the old idea of wickedness accompanying left-handedness [1917, p. 32]"—a remarkable conclusion given that the proportions are within the normal range.

A particularly insidious effect of Lombroso's theory was how it lent itself to racist views—views that found wide public expression. For instance, in the same *McClure's Magazine* article quoted previously, the writer reported Lombroso's statistics, adding that sinistrality is also "slightly more common in the lower strata of society than in the higher, among negroes than among white persons, and among savages than among civilized races [Brewster, 1913, pp. 179–180]." The sex-related differences Lombroso reported were the only stumbling block: "Oddly enough, women, who on the whole are decidedly more civilized than men and less criminal, are said to be nearly twice as likely as men to be left-handed [Brewster, 1913, p. 180]," but the author grandly dismissed this finding as having "probably no significance [p. 180]." Ironically, Lombroso's data on sex-related differences are unrepresentative; most other surveys of that time (like those today) reported proportionately *fewer* left-handers among females than males.

Two Kinds of Left-Handers

Several early writers, though they cited Lombroso's and others' reports, also made a critical distinction between two kinds of left-handedness. For example, the geneticist H. E. Jordan said that left-handedness "is not necessarily a stigma of inferiority," and distinguished the anomalous left-handers described by Lombroso from the "pure" uncomplicated type of left-handedness, "which constitutes the bulk of the left-handed population," and which, "instead of being regarded as something inherently derogatory, . . . deserves appreciation and understanding [Jordan, 1922, p. 379]."

Brain Injury

The distinction was drawn more clearly, and in anticipation of contemporary thinking (Satz, 1972) by Lattes (1907), who named two kinds of left-handedness: (a) the atavistic, or constitutional type, resulting from an inversion of normal cerebral asymmetry; and (b) the pathologic type, manifested after a left cerebral lesion, which is the type predominating in epileptics and delinquents (cited in Jordan, 1911, p. 24). A similar distinction was even recognized later by Brewster (1913), the *McClure's Magazine* writer quoted earlier, whose comment also reflected the then growing understanding of the relationship between *age* of left-brain injury and the severity and duration of speech delay or disruption.

An adult brain, wrecked on the educated [i.e., left] side by accident or disease, commonly never learns to do its work on the other; the victim remains crippled for the rest of his days. But a child in whom the thinking area on either side is still uncultivated, hurt on one side, can usually start over again with the other. A shift of this sort carries the body with it, and the child, instead of being permanently disabled, becomes left-handed. . . . There are, therefore, two sorts of left handers. The one are perfectly normal persons with an inborn aptitude for doing their talking from Broca's area on the right side. . . . The other sort of left-handers were naturally left-brained, had something the matter with the thinking side, and had to learn to think with the other [Brewster, 1913, p. 179]."[29]

Personality Theory

Two later and very influential proponents of the pathological view of left-handedness were the psychoanalyst Abram Blau and the educational psychologist Cyril Burt, whose characterization of the squinting, stammering, shuffling, and shambling left-hander we quoted earlier. Burt also distinguished congenital left-handedness from what he called the "temperamental type" and called the latter stubborn and willful.

At times he is visibly of an assertive type, domineering, overbearing, and openly rebellious against all the dictates of authority. But more often his aggressive tendencies are concealed or repressed; and the child belongs to a class well known to practicing psychiatrists and familiarly dubbed by them "obstinate introverts" . . . the dogged adherence to a perverse way of writing symbolizes, as it were, a secret desire to defy all conventions [Burt, 1937, p. 317].

As for left-handed girls, they

often possess a strong, self-willed, and almost masculine disposition: by many little tell-tale symptoms, besides the clumsy management of their hands—by their careless dress, their ungainly walk, their tomboy tricks and mannerisms—they mutely display a private scorn for the canons of feminine grace and elegance [Burt, 1937, p. 317].

Abram Blau (1946) went on in still darker terms. Left-handedness was "not only . . . a neurotic symptom but . . . one of the signs of an infantile

[29] Lombroso himself acknowledged, perhaps grudgingly, exceptions to his view:

There are in the world left-handed people who are anything but lunatics and idiots [and even less criminals] [since] the workings of the brain which influence the movements [i.e., handedness per se] are quite different from those which act on the sensibilities, and so it may easily be that the first predominates over the last. . . . The presence of a single heriditary trait in an individual [i.e., left-handedness] does not at all mean that all his organism is in a state of arrested development or of inferiority . . . such traces of lunacy or criminality [i.e., left-handedness], until associated with other symptoms, such as exaggerated cranium asymmetry, hallucinations, etc. mean nothing. . . . I do not dream at all of saying that all left-handed people are wicked, but that left-handedness, united to many other traits, may contribute to form one of the worst characters among the human species [1903, p. 444].

psychoneurosis [Blau, 1946, p. 115]." The problem was that Blau's own survey of 369 left-handed 9–12-year-old school children disclosed no reliable difference in the "negativistic reactions of these children" compared with right-handers. Blau was undaunted: "Negativism is a very common childhood reaction that may manifest itself in a number of ways and is not specific to sinistrals [Blau, 1946, p. 115]."

One might suppose that if left-handedness were merely a symptom of neurosis, it would disappear after successful therapy. Of course it did not. A 9-year-old left-handed boy whom Blau called "stubborn, disobedient, unhappy, fearful, and insecure" is said to have "responded well and improved under child guidance treatment [p. 114]," though he continued to use his left hand. Blau again had an answer.

The symptom of sinistrality soon becomes ingrained in the constitution in the course of the normal maturation of the brain. Later, even if there is an amelioration of the disturbing emotional situation and of the neurosis, sinistrality still remains as tacit evidence of the early developmental disturbance, very much like an archaeological fossil [Blau, 1946, p. 115].

Masculine–Feminine—Dual Classification

The left hand was not only bad, it was female, whereas the right was male. This symbology, too, has been culturally ubiquitous (see Needham, 1973). For instance, the pairs right and left, male and female appear in the Pythagorean Table of Opposites, given by Aristotle at *Metaph* (Lloyd, 1973, p. 171). The symbology is mentioned also in Aristotle's *Problemata:*

Why is it that if a hole is pierced in the left ear, it generally closes up more quickly than in the right ear? It is for this reason that women call the right ear the 'male' and the left the 'female'. Is it because the left parts of the body are moister and hotter, and such things close up very quickly? This is why green plants grow together again; and why wounds close up more readily in the young than in the old. That the parts on the left side of the body are moister is shown by the fact that they are softer and, generally speaking, partake rather of feminine characteristics [Forster, 1927, Book XXXII, chpt. 7, p. 961a].

Another example, for a drastic change in time and place, is the Wulwanga tribe in early twentieth century Australia. In this tribe

two sticks are used to mark the beat during ceremonies; one is called the man and is held in the right hand, while the other, the woman, is held in the left. Naturally, it is always the "man" which strikes and the "woman" which receives the blows; the right which acts, the left which submits [Hertz, 1973, p. 14, reporting the findings of Eylmann, 1909].

Right and left also figured in beliefs about the determination of sex. In the Zohar, Eve represented the left side of Adam. Later, when creation was by more conventional means, it was believed that males were conceived when the father's seed came from his right testicle, females from the left, an explanation usually attributed to Anaxagoras (500?–428 B.C.; see Lloyd, 1973, pp. 171–172).

Galen echoed the Anaxagorean idea in his own anatomical writings, but stressed the added role of heat. Because the spermatic and ovarian artery and vein going to the right male and female testes [i.e., the ovaries] and to the right side of the uterus arise directly from the aorta and vena cava below the level of the renal vessels, they "carry blood already relieved of its serious residues by the kidneys and hence warmer," whereas the vessels on the left side "arise from the renal vessels going to the left kidney [note the anatomical accuracy here] and so are still laden with serious residues." Thus the blood conveyed in these vessels is colder, and the result is to make the right male and female testes and the right side of the uterus much warmer than the left. "It follows that male and female semen originating from the right testes and reaching the right side of the uterus will be hotter and will give rise to males and that females will be engendered on the left [May, 1968, Vol. I, p. 57; See also Siegel, 1968, pp. 224–230; and Siegel, 1973, pp. 123–124.]"

Still later, William Harvey cited but rejected Anaxagoras' theory in his *Prelectiones anatomie universalis* (Lectures on the whole of anatomy, 1616; Witteridge, 1964).[30]

Left-Handedness and Homosexuality

All such beliefs that related the directions left and right to sex and to human value or quality contained the ingredients necessary for associating left-handedness with deviations from conventional sexuality, especially homosexuality. The connection is implicit in language itself. In Australia, for instance, a slang term for left-hander is "molly-dooker," derived from "molly," "an effeminate man," and "dukes," the slang word for hands, as in "put up your dukes (Barsley, 1966, p. 46)." In the United States and Britain, a heterosexual is "straight," that is, "right" in the sense of straight or true, whereas in Britain, homosexuals sometimes are called "bent."

---

[30] In rejecting Anaxogoras' theory, Harvey cited Aristotle, who, though he believed that the blood of the right side and the right side itself were more perfected than on the left, specifically denied that the child's sex was thereby influenced. Aristotle's reason, presumably, came from his belief that the testicles played no role in fecundating the sperm. Aristotle therefore also denied the related belief that if a man copulates with the right or left testis tied up, the result is female or male offspring, respectively (Whitteridge, 1964, p. 194; footnote # 5 to W. Harvey, *Anatomical Lectures*).

In the West, the left-handedness–homosexuality nexus was expounded by certain early psychoanalysts, prominently Wilhelm Stekel and Wilhelm Fliess. In Stekel's *Die Sprache des Traumes* (1911), we read,

> The right-hand path always signifies the way to righteousness, the left-hand path the path to crime. Thus the left may signify homosexuality, incest, and perversion, while the right signifies marriage, relations with a prostitute, etc. The meaning is always determined by the individual moral standpoint of the dreamer [p. 466; quoted in Freud, 1938, p. 374].

Still more extreme was Fliess (1858–1928), a Berlin physician and biologist and, through the turn of the century, Sigmund Freud's closest friend (Kris; in Bonaparte, Freud, & Kris, 1954, p. 4). In an 1897 pamphlet, Fliess outlined a theory of bisexuality that included the proposal that each body half contained both kinds of sex organs. Fliess later extended the theory to include bilateralism. The reference to left-handedness appears in his principal work, *Der Ablauf des Lebens* ("The Course of Life"), first published in 1906.

> Where lefthandedness is present, the character pertaining to the opposite sex seems more pronounced. This sentence is not only invariably correct, but its converse is also true: Where a woman resembles a man, or a man resembles a woman, we find the emphasis on the left side of the body. Once we know this we have the diviner's rod for the discovery of left-handedness. The diagnosis is always correct [2nd ed., 1923, quoted in English by Fritsch, 1968, p. 133].

Fliess (1923) also envisioned a direct association between sexual disturbance and criminality.

> Since degeneracy consists in a displacement of the male and female qualities, we can understand why so many left-handed people are involved in prostitution and criminal activities—which are very much the same thing—but we also understand how many threads can drag a person down from the artist's way of life to this first stage of dissipation [quoted in English by Fritsch, 1968, p. 133].

Freud himself was cool to such speculations. In *The Interpretation of Dreams* (1938), the only mention of left and right came when he quoted the passage by Stekel above, prefaced by a comment on Stekel's "lack of critical reflection, and his tendency to generalize at all costs [making] his interpretations doubtful or inapplicable [Freud, 1938, p. 374]." As for Fliess' theory, Freud rejected the physiology, and was largely unsympathetic to the rest:

> I am still unable to accept your interpretation of left-handedness. . . . I seized eagerly on your notion of bisexuality, which I regard as the most significant for

my subject since that of defense . . . I object only to the identification of bisexuality and bilateralism which you demand . . . [letter to Fliess, 4 Jan., 1898; quoted in Bonaparte *et al.*, 1954, p. 242].[31]

Artistic Temperament

Perhaps related to the proposed association between left-handedness and homosexuality there was a belief that left-handers (like the stereotype of the homosexual) were more emotional, artistic, and sensitive to beauty than right-handers are. The most famous examples are Michelangelo and Leonardo, both probably homosexual and left-handed. In Michelangelo's painting on the ceiling of the Sistine Chapel, we see Adam lying on the ground, with outstretched left hand, receiving the touch of life from God. Has Michelangelo intended to depict Adam—his perfect man—as left-handed? Whether yes or no, Michelangelo had no choice: If God were to give life through His right hand (the auspicious hand), and if both torsos were to face the viewer, and finally if neither God's arm nor Adam's were to cross and thus obscure the view of their bodies, God must present His right hand from the right side, to Adam's outstretched left hand. As for Leonardo, Freud did not mention Leonardo's left-handedness in his psychoanalytic study (1948), but in a letter to Fliess, he suggested him in possible support of Fliess' theory of bisexualism and bilateralism: "Leonardo, of whom no love affair is recorded, was perhaps the most famous case of left-handedness. Can you use him? [Freud, 9 Oct., 1898; quoted in Bonaparte *et al.*, 1954, p. 268]."

Speculations about left-handedness and artistic ability were not only an

---

[31] More recently, the psychoanalytic view of left-handedness has been extended to the question of left-handed *writing*, whether by the left-hander or by the right-hander who uses his left hand (Thass-Thienemann, 1955). It is ironic that in light of Freud's criticism of Stekel and Fliess, the basis for this analysis was first outlined by Freud himself in his essay, *The Problem of Anxiety* (1936). Here Freud was concerned to explain certain neurotic inhibitions in writing ("scriptus interruptions"), which Freud believed originated not from writing as such, but from writing, "which consists in allowing a fluid to flow out from a tube upon a piece of white paper," which has acquired "the symbolic meaning of coitus." Then, "writing . . . will be abstained from, because it is as though forbidden sexual behavior were thereby indulged in [Freud, 1936, p. 15]." The link in the meaning of writing and sexual intercourse is strengthened, according to Thass-Thienemann (1955), through etymology; for example, written lines are called "furrows," meaning "something turned over"; the pen "plows" the paper; and so forth (p. 240).

The meaning of *left*-handed writing should now be apparent (allowing for the limitation that the entire analysis applies rather more to males than to females). In light of the negative connotations of "left" and "left hand," left-hand writing appears as a symbolic gesture motivated, if not stimulated, by fantasies which are forgotten, repressed, and repudiated by the speech community; nevertheless these fantasies exist, and here and there in some words they loom up to the manifest surface of language [Thass-Thienemann, 1955, p. 260].

invention of the psychoanalytic era. Some years before, Daniel Wilson (1885–1886) saw the same possibility in paleolithic cave drawings:

> The horses from La Madelaine; . . . the horse from Creswell Crags; the ibex, with legs in the air; and, above all, the remarkably spirited drawing of the reindeer grazing, from Thayngen in the Kesserloch . . . , suggestive of an actual study from nature;—all appear to be left-handed drawings [pp. 141–142].

Wilson admitted that the number of examples was too small to be conclusive, "but so far as it goes, it suggests a much larger percentage of left-handed draftsmen than is to be looked for on the assumption that right-handedness is the normal condition of man [p. 142]."

Cognitive Deficiencies

Of all the evidence brought forth as proof that left-handedness was pathological, the most widely known were reports of a greater incidence of left-handedness among people, especially children, with various cognitive or motor deficiencies. For example, in the early decades of the twentieth century, there were many surveys and clinical investigations published in both professional and lay journals that found left-handedness to be common in stutterers. Forced use of the right hand reportedly exacerbated the condition (e.g., Nice, 1915). Ballard (1911–1912) reported that stuttering was four times more frequent among "dextro-sinistrals" (his term for congenital left-handers who conformed with social custom in writing with the right hand) than among other children (p. 299). Reversal of hand use, accordingly, was said to relieve the condition (Claiborne, 1917).[32]

Ballard (1911–1912) outlined a tentative neurological explanation, emphasizing the "intimate functional connexion of the writing centre with the system of word centres, and particularly with the speaking centre . . . it is conceivable that the dominant speech area is either robbed of some of its energy, or that some sort of competition takes place which tends to disorganize its function [p. 308]." A similar idea was expressed more confidently by a later writer:

> A certain number of native left-handed may acquire the ability to use the right hand for certain routine functions such as writing. But such acquirement forces the child to use a less well-developed portion of the brain for these activities,

[32] In the 1930s, writers began to name Lewis Carroll as a *converted* left-hander because he stammered. He did stammer—indeed, the Dodo bird in *Alice in Wonderland* is said to have been Carroll himself, who, as Martin Gardner has recounted, would stammer his name "Do-Do-Dodgson [Gardner, 1960, p. 44]." But the notion that Dodgson was a converted left-hander perhaps deserves little credence; stammering was a family characteristic, afflicting 8 of the 11 Dodgson children (Wood, 1966).

and thus produces a dislocation of speech center and center for use of hand. Or if may force also the use of a less well-developed speech center of the opposite hemisphere. In any case it disturbs the synergy between speech center and hand center, and possibly produces also a conflict between two opposite speech centers when both attempt to function. The result of this disturbance shows itself in speech defects. The fact of a synergistic or yoked relationship between the center for motor speech and that for hand movement is illustrated by the increased fluency of speech accompanying manual gesticulation or the handling of some object while speaking, such as a button, a watch chain or a pencil [Jordan, 1922, p. 382].[33]

Another manifestation of left-handers' cognitive deficiency was said to be their tendency to write in mirror, or reverse images—what the German neurologists Buchwald (1878) and Erlenmeyer (1879) called "Spiegelschrift" (Ireland, 1881, p. 361; Strack, 1893, p. 238). Probably the best-known example of "Spiegelschrift" is the manuscript of the *Codex Atlanticus* of Leonardo da Vinci—thousands of pages nearly all written in reverse script, and from right to left. Erlenmeyer, in fact, named this manuscript in his 1879 paper on mirror writing, perhaps the first neurologist to do so (see Bianchi, 1883, p. 573; Ireland, 1881, p. 365). The usual idea was that Leonardo had wished to preserve his work from the eyes of importunate readers. Ireland disagreed, noting that Cardinal Luis of Aragon had visited Leonardo during the artist's last years and later wrote "nothing more of value in painting could be expected of him, as he had paralysis of the right hand [Ireland, 1881, p. 367]." Ireland therefore suggested that Leonardo, "being unable to use his right hand, wrote with his left, and fell into the practice of writing from right to left, in obedience to a tendency which we have sought to illustrate [Ireland, 1881, p. 367; see also Bianchi, 1883].[34] Among contemporary mirror-writers, a favorite example is Lewis Carroll, whose mirror writing figured prominently in the Alice books (e.g., the first part of the "Jabberwacky" ballad) as well as in his private correspondence.

Mirror writers they were, but there is no evidence that Leonardo or Lewis Carroll were ever *confused* about spatial direction, or that their practice of mirror writing was anything but strictly controlled. However, the same phenomenon, when found to be commoner in left-handed, ambidextrous, or retarded children and adults, was widely held to be evidence of just such a disability, and by the 1920s, a huge literature had developed (see Blom, 1928). Buchanan (1908) called mirror writing a congenital anomaly

---

[33] Compare with Kinsbourne and Cook's (1971) explanation of the effects of concurrent verbalization on a repetitive motor task, according to whether the left or right hand is used.

[34] Cyril Burt also mentioned this report but added that, contrary to the implication in Cardinal Luis of Aragon's remark, practically all the well-authenticated instances of Leonardo's handwriting are written in reverse script, some dating from 20-years-old, and that according to Fra Sabba da Castiglione, Leonardo had always been left-handed (Burt, 1937, p. 343).

in left-handed children. The suggested reasons varied widely. For example, Buchanan (1908) thought it stemmed from a tendency in left-handers to write from right-to-left (the easier "abduction" movement). The reason that has lasted, in some form or other, was offered by William W. Ireland, Medical Superintendent of the Scottish National Institute for Imbecile Children. Ireland, incidentally, mentioned that his attention had been directed to the subject of left-handedness by the articles of Charles Reade (Ireland, 1880, p. 207).

Ireland (1881) described a report by Buchwald (1878) of an aphasic man with right-sided hemiplegia who, when induced to write with his left hand, wrote skillfully from right to left in mirror-script. Although the aphasia disappeared over the next few months, the tendency to mirror-write persisted. Of this case, Ireland asked,

> Is the image or impression, or change in the brain-tissue from which the image is formed in the mind of the mirror-writer, reversed like the negative of a photograph; or if a double image be formed in the visual centre, one in the right hemisphere of the brain and the other in the left, do the images lie to each other in opposite directions, e.g. C on the right side and Ɔ on the left side? We can thus conceive that the image on the left side of the brain being effaced through disease, the inverse image would remain in the right hemisphere, which would render the patient apt to trace the letters from right to left, the execution of which would be rendered all the more natural from the greater facility of the left hand to work in a centrifugal direction. Moreover, when one used the left hand to write, there would probably be a tendency to copy the inverse impression or image on the right side of the brain [Ireland, 1881, p. 367].

Some years later, Lombroso (1903) expressed a similar idea, though it was the brain of the madman that first interested him:

> There is contradiction between the two lobes of the brain, as in the case of a pair of horses, one wishing to go in one direction and the other in another, so that the great effort to act is frustrated by a complete inertia, when an extraneous influence does not intervene to re-establish order. In the same way I try to explain another and more curious fact, which occurs in certain old lunatics, that of writing backwards as is done in lithographs. We, from children, imagine and probably acquire the forms of letters correctly in the left lobe, and backwards in the right, and so we reproduce them according as the left or right lobe predominates [Lombroso, 1903, p. 443].

Still later, these same ideas were developed into a complete theory of mirror writing and reading by Samuel Orton (1925), who called mirror reading "strephysymbolia," or "twisted symbols."

Perhaps predictably, the supposed spatial confusion of the left-hander was incorporated into the analysis of homosexuality. One psychoanalyst, noting Lewis Carroll's pleasure in mirror writing and reversals, wrote that "left and right disorientation and reversals are very often symbolizations for the inability to find a definite direction in one's sexuality and for a wavering between the heterosexual and homosexual component impulses [Schilder, 1971, p. 337]."[35] In the same letter to Fliess, quoted earlier, Freud himself speculated along these lines in trying to account for his antipathy for Fliess' theory:

> It also occurred to me that you may have considered me to be partially left-handed . . . I am not aware of any [such] preference . . . I should say rather that in my early years I had two left hands. . . . I had to think which was my right; no organic feeling told me. To make sure . . . I used quickly to make a few writing movements. To the present day I still have to work out by their position, etc., which is other people's right or left hand . . . in general I have a very poor feeling for space, which made the study of geometry and all kindred subjects impossible for me.
>
> That is how it seems to me. But I know very well that it may be otherwise, and that the disinclination I have so far felt to accepting your ideas about left-handedness may be the result of unconscious motives. If they are hysterical, they have certainly nothing to do with the subject itself, but with the word. Perhaps it suggests to me something "left-handed" or guilty. If that is the case, the explanation will come sometime; heaven knows when [Freud, 4 Jan., 1898; quoted in Bonaparte *et al.*, 1954, p. 243].

Not all psychoanalysts saw a link between left–right confusion and confused sexuality. Blau (1946), for instance, asserted only that mirror reading and writing represent "essentially arrested development or faulty fixations of a phase in learning spatial orientation [Blau, 1946, p. 78]."

Speaking Out for Left-Handers

In early investigations, left-handedness was not inevitably associated with mental deficit. More left-handers continued to appear among children diagnosed as mentally retarded (e.g., H. Gordon, 1920), but comparisons of left- and right-handed children not previously diagnosed as retarded or not evincing any clinical problems such as stuttering, usually disclosed no differences between handedness groups (e.g., K. Gordon, 1924). Nevertheless, the "negative" characterization had taken hold and was hard to dislodge. There consequently developed a rising concern on the part of educators about the "problem" of the left-handed child (we saw that this same concern led to W. F. Jones advancing the "ulna plus" theory of handedness in 1915), and it is interesting to see, in the many educational publications, the expression of the full range of theories about left-

[35] Carroll will not serve the point. His sexual interests, though never consummated, nevertheless were exclusively heterosexual.

handedness. For example, *The Teacher* (McMullin, 1914) reported a questionnaire submitted to American school officials asking whether the left-handed pupil should be required to write with his right hand, and, if so, what was the expected benefit. Most of the respondents expressed strong views, and there was little consensus, with about half favoring training the right hand (particularly if the child was young and left-handed writing was not well-established) and the rest favoring letting the child use his left hand, though several commented that practice in doing other things with the right hand would be to the child's advantage because this is a "right-handed world." Most of those allowing, or even favoring, left-hand use found justification in physiology and cited the reports of lateral differences in blood supply to the hemispheres, and like evidence. By contrast, none of those favoring right-hand training referred to physiological evidence but mentioned, instead, the many practical advantages of the right-hand style (e.g., the right-handed design of desks, and the presumed right-hand design (that is, the left-to-right direction), of the English alphabet.

In the wake of the adverse publicity about left-handedness, many began to speak out on behalf of left-handers, and in the early part of the twentieth century, articles with titles like *Let Left-Handedness Alone!* (Terrell, 1917), or *The Crime Against Left-Handedness* (Jordan, 1922) appeared in popular, mass magazines like *Illustrated World, McClure's,* and *Good Health.* One especially passionate defender, George M. Gould (the author of an ocular dominance theory discussed earlier), warned "Let the left-handed child alone! Nature is quite as wise as the ignorant meddlers."[36]

One specific result of reports that converting the left-handed child to right-hand usage caused stammering and emotional upset was the rallying of the opponents of "ambidextral culture." Psychologists began to warn of the dangers of such practices as the introduction of ambidextral drawing and writing into the elementary schools. Ballard, for instance, wrote: "No kind of interference with the natural sinistrality of a child is educationally justifiable. . . . Writing should always be done by the superior hand, and *by the superior hand exclusively* [Ballard, 1911–1912, p. 309]." John B. Watson also addressed the question of changing the left-hander. Because he believed handedness to be a socially instilled habit, Watson asked,

> Should we or should we not change over the left handers—those hardy souls who have resisted social pressure? I am firmly convinced that if the job is done early enough and wisely enough not the slightest harm results [Watson, 1924a, p. 102].

[36] At least one parent took this advice to heart: Heywood Broun wrote in *Collier's* in 1920 about his left-handed son Woodie, then 3-years-old (and now the famous and still left-handed journalist). Dr. Gould's wise words, Broun Sr. confessed, saved him from a "great folly." "I had been thinking of amputation [p. 22]."

"Early enough" meant "before language develops very much [Watson, 1924a, p. 102]"—Watson was familiar with reports of language disruption when shifts were made in older children. The question whether efforts should be made to convert left-handed children to right-hand usage continued to be vigorously debated at least through the 1950s, but eventually, as Bakwin has written (1950), more and more psychologists and pediatricians came to agree that coersion was ineffective at best, and dangerous at worst (see also Arlitt, 1946, p. 120).

STUDIES OF ANIMALS

Thus far, with one exception, I have not mentioned the role of research on other species in the development of theories of handedness. A full historical analysis of this evidence would take us too far beyond the scope of the current chapter, but some examples can be given.

The exception mentioned was D. J. Cunningham (1902), who, we recall, dismissed the significance of his own evidence on lateral differences in the length of the Sylvian fissures because he had found the same condition in the ape brain; and apes, he believed, did not possess handedness. In historical perspective, Cunningham's evaluation of his findings becomes ironic. Later investigators, who have found similar asymmetries in ape as well as in fetal, infant, and adult human brains (e.g., Geschwind & Levitsky, 1968; Hochberg & LeMay, 1975; Witelson & Pallie, 1973; Yeni-Komshian & Benson, 1976) have been readier to speculate that these anatomical asymmetries are related to functional hemispheric asymmetries. Recent demonstrations of rudimentary language learning in the great apes (e.g., Gardner & Gardner, 1969) appear to have changed the intellectual climate, and the question is now being raised "whether a neuroanatomical substrate is a prerequisite for language acquisition [Yeni-Komshian & Benson, 1976: p. 389]."

As Cunningham's use of animal data suggests, the presence or absence of functional laterality in other species was seen to be of great significance in the evaluation of theories of laterality. This was especially true insofar as asymmetry began to be viewed theoretically as a phenomenon that had emerged gradually in evolution and therefore would be increasingly evident in higher, more intelligent animals. Thus, both those who proposed that handedness in man is natural, and those who opposed this view, frequently cited those reports for other species (there being sufficient number of either positive or negative reports to choose from) bolstering their theoretical positions.

Thomas Browne (1646) perhaps was the first to refer to animals to support his views.

For first, if there were a determinate prepotency in the right, and such as
ariseth from a constant roote in nature, wee might expect the same in other
animals, whose parts are also differenced by dextrality, wherein notwithstanding we cannot discover a distinct and complying account, for we find not that
Horses, Buls, or Mules, are generally stronger on this side; and as for animals
whose forelegs more sensibly supply the use of armes, they hold if not an
equality in both, a prevalency oftimes in the other [i.e., the left], as Squirrels,
Apes, and Monkeys [Browne, 1646, p. 186].

Followers of ambidextral culture likewise looked to the evidence of other
species on the grounds that if they showed no lateral preference, ambidexterity must be the more natural and thus more desirable state in man as
well. For Charles Reade, it was "all man's own doing that he is any more
semiplegiac or lop-limbed than a lion, a raccoon, a fox, a tiger, or an ape
[Reade, 19 Jan., 1878, p. 51]."

John Jackson (1905) was of like mind, but Jackson particularly wanted to
repudiate John Struthers, who from his careful measurements of the
weights of the internal organs, had adduced what looked like convincing
evidence for a mechanical theory of right-sidedness. To these findings,
Struthers had added indirect evidence from other species.

My shoemaker informs me that the right side of the hide is generally thicker
than the left; and on further inquiry at a leather merchant, who deals largely in
the hides of the calf and ox, I am informed that the above is a well-known fact
in the trade, the right being known as the "lying" side of the skin. The
quadruped would appear at any rate to lie more on the right than on the left
side [Struthers, 1863, p. 1103].

Jackson (1905), a still more fastidious observer, not only consulted his
own tanners, who disagreed with Struthers' experts, but also recorded the
sleeping positions of a total of 833 cattle and found proportions in the
reverse direction from Struthers: 60% of the cattle lay on their left sides,
40% on their right. Though the difference was statistically significant,
Jackson grandly dismissed it, concluding that if "any such peculiarity as a
preferential use of one side is ever exhibited by an individual member of a
species, it is merely a freak of nature [Jackson, 1905, p. 39]."

Blau (1946), who espoused a cultural theory, consigned the animal
literature to irrelevancy, the phenomenon of preferred laterality being "so
uniquely human . . . that we could hardly find any worthwhile information about it among the lower animals [p. 55]." He reviewed the animal
literature briefly, dismissed the few positive reports, and emphasized the
negative ones, of which they were many.

Among those who adopted an organic theory of handedness, reports of
either structural or functional asymmetries in animals found a more sym-
pathetic audience. The asymmetrical fish and crustacea, for example, were

frequently looked to for clues to the origins of handedness. Pye-Smith (1907) was impressed with the flat fishes which "make a perfectly straight start in life . . ." until the skull becomes twisted and one eye of one side migrates to the other side and becomes the upper eye.

> This transformation . . . cannot be attributed to prejudiced mothers or silly nurses, or hide-bound schoolmasters or acquired habits; and the fact that it occurs at a particular stage of growth disposes, I think, of the argument that dextral pre-eminence in the human being must be induced by education, because the baby for the first eight or nine months of its life uses both of its fore-limbs equally [Pye-Smith, 1907, p. 649].

Often mentioned, too, was "footedness" in birds. At a meeting of the British Association for the Advancement of Science, Broca is reported to have commented that birds perch on the right leg, which a Dr. Crisp explained was peculiar to one species and was a question of equilibrium—the bird was compelled to take this position from the greater weight of the liver (Bateman, 1869, p. 383). Parrots, however, were widely believed to grasp and hold food with the left claw, and similarly, there were reports of *left*-sidedness in several other animals, including such divers creatures as crabs (stronger, larger left claws and lions (on the authority, according to Lombroso, 1903, p. 441, of [Dr. David] "Livingstone").

The possibility that animals are left-sided was noted also by James Mark Baldwin (1890, 1894). Recall that he had attached no significance to the apparent "left-handed" phase preceding right-hand preference shown by his infant son. Later, he did and proposed an explanation in terms of a then popular theory about human psychological growth based on embryological development.

> If it should prove true that the lower animals are left-sided, then the current view that right-handed children have a preliminary period of left-handedness might have its explanation in the hypothesis of the repetition of phylogenetic development in the individual child [Baldwin, 1915, p. 71].

Animals also figured in the evidence brought forward to prove the inherently greater weakness of the left side. Together with data on the greater incidence of disease on the left side in humans, several writers, taking white or gray hair as an index of weakness, reported that graying was commoner on the left side, not only in man but in several other species (e.g., Allen, 1888; Girdwood, 1908; Hall & Hartwell, 1884). Girdwood explained the graying as the result of poorer blood supply to the left side.

Animal evidence also was deemed relevant to an evaluation of Von Baer's (1828) embryological theory of visceral asymmetry. Pye-Smith described examinations of "six specimens of double foetus with a single umbilical cord, and therefore presumably a single yelk-sac . . . (Pye-Smith, 1871, p. 146)." Transposition existed only in some instances.

> Moreover, one does not see how [Von Baer's theory] can explain transposition of the thoracic or abdominal viscera alone—a condition which, although rare, has been observed. Nor yet can any explanation which rests on a peculiar position of the yelk-sac apply to transposition of viscera among invertebrata [Pye-Smith, 1871, p. 146]."

Animal studies also were said to be relevant to the evaluation of genetic theories. It would be some years before attempts were made to test genetic models by breeding sidedness in laboratory animals, but certain implications were early recognized. For instance, with respect to the Mendelian recessive theory of left-handedness, Ramaley made this aside:

> It is well known that in certain species of animals, races showing particular recessive traits have less vitality and perhaps less reproductive ability than the ordinary members of the species. From the studies herein recorded, . . . it is seen that the left-handed families are quite as fertile as the normal ones [Ramaley, 1913, p. 737].

Finally, as a true experimental era began to unfold, animals began to be seen as useful subjects in neuropsychological research. For example, experiments in the style of Bouillaud's classic studies of the functions of the cortex (1830) were believed to provide a potentially critical test of cortical speech functions. Here is Bateman (1869) describing these experiments:

> The dog survived the mutilation [piercing of anterior part of the brain in the area corresponding, Bateman said, to Broca's region] but was much less intelligent than before the operation, and although he could utter cries of pain, he had entirely lost the power of barking [p. 386].

Bateman, however, discounted the relevance of this demonstration for contemporary analysis of the functions of the cortex in man, there being "little or no analogy between . . . the bark of a dog, and the articulate speech of man . . . [Bateman, 1869, p. 386]." Still, he called for more research: "It would be extremely interesting to know what would be the effect of traumatic injury to certain regions of the anterior lobes upon the quasi-articulatory powers of the parrot [p. 386]."

CONCLUSION

Here, then, are some of the early theories, facts, and fancies about left-handedness. Which of the old ideas and topics of research continue into the present day? Nearly all do, in one form or other, as we shall see in the new reports to follow. And to what extent can we now decide which ideas are fancy, which fact? To a larger extent than before, but I think the other contributors will agree that we still have a long way to go. Sinistrality is an elusive phenomenon; that is a source of its fascination and our frustration. Perhaps at times, all of us have felt the wry truth in Subirana's jocular explanation—that left-handers were "created on purpose to upset all the different conceptions which have prevailed during the last century in connection with the pathology and physiology of the two hemispheres [Subirana, 1969, p. 248]." And if created "on purpose," then by whom? The people of the Pennefather River, in Australia, are said to have known the answer long ago: "Anje-a," the nature-spirit who fashions babies "out of swamp-mud, and inserts them in the bellies of the women," makes them all right-handed. But "Thunder," who existed before Anje-a and who made him, "can also make children out of swamp-mud," and "manufactures his all left-handed [Roth, 1903, p. 23]."

Between the whims of spirits and the reasons of the natural world, sometimes one wonders which are the more inscrutable!

REFERENCES

Allen, H. The distribution of the color-marks of the mammalia. *Proceedings of the Academy of Natural Sciences of Philadelphia*, 1888, *40*, 84–105.

Anonymous. Left-handedness among the ancient Hebrews. Letter to Editor of *British Medical Journal*, 1883, 1161.

Anonymous. On left-handedness. Letter to the *British Medical Journal*, 1885, *2*, 774.

Anonymous. Left-handedness. *The Journal of Heredity*, 1914, *5*, 312.

Arlitt, A. H. *Psychology of infancy and early childhood.* New York: McGraw-Hill, 1946.

Assézat, J. Recording of discussion of Broca, P., Sur le poids relatif des deux hemispheres cerebraux et de leurs lobes frontaux. *Bulletins de la Société d'Anthropologie de Paris*, 1875, *10*, 535–536.

Audenino, E. L'homme droit, l'homme gauche et l'homme ambidextre. *Archivio di psichiatria, neuropatologia, antropologia criminale e medicina legale*, Torino, 1907, *28*, 23–31.

Baer, K. E. von. *Schädel-und Kopfmagel an embryonen von schweinen.* 1828.

Bakwin, H. Lateral dominance. *Journal of Pediatrics*, 1950, *36*, 385–391.

Baldwin, J. M. Origin of right or left handedness. *Science*, 1890, *16*, 247–48.

Baldwin, J. J. The origin of right-handedness. *Popular Science Monthly*, 1894, *44*, 606–615.

Baldwin, J. M. *Mental development in the child and the race* (3rd ed., rev.). New York: Macmillan Company, 1915.

Ballard, P. B. Sinistrality and speech. *Journal of Experimental Pedagogy and Training College Record*, London, 1911–1912, *1*, 298–310.

Ballie, M. A remarkable transposition of the viscera. *The Philosophical Transactions of the Royal Society*, 1809, *16*, 483–489; (reprint of original 1788 paper).

Bardeleben, K. von. Ueber bilaterale Asymmetrie beim Menschen und bei höheren Tieren. *Anatomischer Anzeiger. Zentralblatt für die Gasamte Wissenschaftlich Anatomie.* Ergän zungsheft zum 34 Band., 1909 (*Verhandlungen der Anatomischen Gesellschaft*, 23 Versammlung, Giessen, April 1909, 2–72).

Barr, M. L. *The human nervous system: an anatomical viewpoint.* New York: Harper & Row, 1972.

Barsley, M. *The other hand; an investigation into the sinister history of left-handedness.* New York: Hawthorn, 1966.

Barsley, M. *Left-handed man in a right-handed world.* London: Pitman, 1970.

Bastian, H. C. On the specific gravity of different parts of the human brain. *Journal of Mental Science,* 1866, *11,* 465–511.

Bastian, H. C. Note on the localisation of function in the cerebral hemispheres. *The Journal of Mental Science,* 1869, *14,* 454–460.

Bateman, F. On aphasia, or loss of speech in cerebral disease. *The Journal of Mental Science,* 1868, *13,* 521–532.

Bateman, F. On aphasia, or loss of speech in cerebral disease. *The Journal of Mental Science,* 1869, *15,* 367–392; 489–504.

Beeley, A. L. An experimental study of left-handedness. *Supplement to Education Monograph* (Vol. 2, No. 2). Chicago: The University of Chicago Press, 1918.

Beeley, A. L. Left-handedness. *American Journal of Physical Anthropology,* 1919, *2,* 389–400.

Bell, C. *The hand: Its mechanism and vital endowments as evincing design.* London: William Pickering, 1833.

Bennecke, F. W. *Die Anatomische Grundlagen der Konstitutions-Anomalien.* Marburg, 1878.

Bianchi, A. Changes in handwriting in relation to pathology. In review of the works of the following authors, viz: Marcé, Poincaré, Charcot, Buchwald, Erlenmeyer, Vogt, Swortzoff, Grasset, Ireland, and Durand. 1863–1882. *The Alienist and Neurologist: A Quarterly Journal of Scientific, Clinical and Forensic Psychiatry and Neurology,* 1883, *4,* 566–590. (Trans. by Joseph Workman, from *Il Pasani Gazetta Sicula.* Palermo, 1882).

Biervliet, J. J. van. L'asymétrie sensorielle. *Bulletins de l'Académie royale de Belgique,* 1897, *34,* 326–366.

Bischoff, E. Einige Gewichts- und Trocken-bestimmungen der Organe des Menschlichen Körpers. In Henle u. Pfeiffer's *Zeitschrift für rationelle Medicin.* 1863.

Blau, A. *The master hand: A study of the origin and meaning of right and left sidedness and its relation to personality and language.* Research Monograph No. 5, New York: American Orthopsychiatric Association, Inc., 1946.

Blom, E. C. Mirror-writing. *Psychological Bulletin,* 1928, *25,* 582–594.

Bonaparte, M., Freud, A., & Kris, E. (Eds.). *The origins of psychoanalysis: Letters to Wilhelm Fliess, Drafts, and Notes, 1887–1902 by Sigmund Freud.* New York: Basic Books, 1954.

Bonin, G. von. Anatomical asymmetries of the cerebral hemispheres. In V. Mountcastle, (Ed.) *Interhemispheric relations and cerebral dominance.* Baltimore, Johns Hopkins Press, 1962, 1–6.

Bouillaud, J. Recherches experimentales sur les fonctions du cerveau. *Journal de Physiologie, experimentale et pathologique* (Magendie), 1830, *10,* 36–98.

Boyd, R. Tables of the weights of the human body and internal organs of the sane and insane of both sexes of various ages arranged from 2,114 postmortum examinations. *Philosophical Transactions of the Royal Society,* London, 1861, *151,* 241–262.

Bramwell, B. On "crossed" aphasia and the factors which go to determining whether the "leading" or "driving" speech-centres shall be located in the left or in the right hemisphere of the brain, with notes of a case of "crossed" aphasia (aphasia with right-sided hemiplegia) in a left-handed man. *The Lancet,* 1899, *1,* 1473–1479.

Braune, W. Das Gewichtsverthältniss der rechten zur linken Hirnhälfte beim Menschen. *Archiv für Anatomie und Physiologie. Physiologische Abteilung,* 1891, *15,* 253–270.

Brewster, E. T. The ways of the left hand. *McClure's Magazine,* 1913, 168–183.

Brinton, D. G. Left-handedness in North American aboriginal art. *American Anthropologist,* 1896, *9,* 175–181.

Broca, P. Remarques sur le siége de la faculté du langage articulé, suivies d'une observation d'aphémie (perte de la parole). *Bulletins de la Société Anatomique*, 1861, *6*, 330–357.

Broca, P. Localisation des fonctions cérébrales. Siége du langage articulé. *Bulletins de la Société d'Anthropologie de Paris*, 1863, *4*, 200–203.

Broca, P. Sur le siége de la faculté de language articulé. *Bulletins de la Société d'Anthropologie de Paris*, 1865, *6*, 377–393.

Broca, P. Sur le poids relatifs du deux hémisphéres cérébraux et de leur lobes frontaux. *Bulletins de la Société d'Anthropologie de Paris*, 1875, *10*, 534–535.

Broca, P. Recherches sur la circulation cerebrale. *Bulletin de l'Academie de Medicine*. 1877, *6*, 508–539 (2e serie)

Broun, H. Let the southpaw alone. *Collier's Magazine*, 1920, *65*, 22, 62.

Brown-Séquard, C. E. Dual character of the brain. *The Toner Lectures, Lecture II. Smithsonian Miscellaneous Collections*. Washington, D.C.: Smithsonian Institution, Jan., 1877, 1–21.

Browne, T. *Pseudodoxia epidemica, or, Enquiries into very many received tenents, and commonly presumed truths*. London, printed by T. H. for Edward Dod, 1646.

Buchanan, A. Mechanical theory of the predominance of the right hand over the left, or, more generally, of the limbs of the right side over those of the left side of the body. *Address to the Philosophical Society of Glasgow*. March 12, 1862. Glasgow: Bell & Bain, 1862, 5–29. (a)

Buchanan, A. Mechanical theory of the predominance of the right hand over the left; or, more generally, of the limbs of the right side over those of the left side of the body. *Proceedings of the Philosophical Society of Glasgow*, 1862, *5*, 142–167. (b)

Buchanan, A. Theory of the right hand, —Dr. Buchanan's reply to Dr. Struthers. *Edinburgh Medican Journal*, 1863, *9*, Part 1, 184–188.

Buchanan, A. On the position of the centre of gravity in man, as determining the mechanical relations of the two sides of the body towards each other. *Proceedings of the Royal Philosophical Society of Glasgow*, 1877, *10*, 390–413.

Buchanan, L. Mirror-writing with notes on a case. *Opthalmoscope*, 1908, *6*, 156–159.

Buchwald. Spiegelschrift bei Hirnkranken. *Berliner klinische Wochenschrift, Organ fur Praktische Aerzte*, 1878, *15*, 6–8.

Burt, C. *The backward child*. New York: Appleton-Century, 1937.

Buzzard, T. *Clinical lectures on diseases of the nervous system*. London: Churchill, 1882.

Carmon, A., Harishanu, Y., Lowinger, E., & Lavy, S. Asymmetries in hemispheric blood volume and cerebral dominance. *Behavioral Biology*. 1972, *7*, 853–859.

Chamberlain, A. F. Right-handedness. *Science*, 1903, *18*, 788–789.

Chesher, E. G. Some observations concerning the relation of handedness to the language mechanism. *Bulletin of the Neurological Institute of New York*, 1936, *4*, 556–562.

Claiborne, J. H. Stuttering in a boy relieved by reversal of manual dexterity; with remarks on the subject of Symbol Amblyopia. *New York Medical Journal (International Record of Medicine and General Practice Clinics)*, 1917, *105*, 619–621.

Compton, R. H. On right- and left-handedness in barley. *Cambridge Philosophical Society Proceedings*, 1910, *15*, 495–506.

Compton, R. H. "A further contribution to the study of right- and left-handedness. *Journal of Genetics*, 1912–1913, *2*, 53–70.

Comte, A. J. Recherches anatomico-physiologiques, relatives à la prédominance du bras droit sur le bras gauche. Paris, chez l'auteur, 1828. (No. 7 in a volume of pamphlets with binders' title: *Mémoires. Physiologie. Systeme nerveux*. "Mémoire lu à l'Academie des Sciences le 25 février 1828," pp. 11–48 plus preface and figures. (Also in *Journal de Physiologie Expérimentale et Pathologie*, 1828, *8*, 41–80)

Comte, A. J. *Organisation et physiologie de l'homme.* 4th Ed. Paris: Chez Les Principaux Libraires Scientifiques, et Chez L'auteur, Rue Belle Chasse, 34, 1842.

Coren, S. & Porac, C. Fifty centuries of right-handedness: The historical record. *Science,* 1977, *198,* 631–632.

Coryell, J. F. & Michel, G. F. How supine postural preferences of infants can contribute towards the development of handedness. *Infant Behavior and Development,* 1978, *1,* 245–257.

Creamer, R. W. *Babe: a look at the life and times of George Herman Ruth.* New York: Simon & Shuster, 1974.

Crichton-Browne, J. Dexterity and the bend sinister. *Proceedings of the Royal Institution of Great Britain,* 1907, *18,* 623–652.

Cuff, N. B. The interpretation of handedness. *Journal of Experimental Psychology,* 1928, *11,* 27–39.

Cunningham, D. J. *Contribution to the surface anatomy of the cerebral hemispheres, with a chapter upon cranio-cerebral topography by Victor Horsley.* Royal Irish Academy: Dublin (Cunningham Memoirs), 1892.

Cunningham, D. J. Right-handedness and left-brainedness. The Huxley lecture for 1902. *Journal of the Royal Anthropological Institute of Great Britain and Ireland,* 1902, *32,* 273–296.

Dahlberg, G. *Twin births and twins from an hereditary point of view.* Stockholm: Bokfurlags-A.B. Tidens Tryckeri, 1926.

Darwin, C. A biographical sketch of an infant. *Mind,* 1877, *2,* 285–294.

Dax, G. Sur le même sujet. *Gazette hebdomadaire de médecine et de chirurgie (Paris), 1865, 2,* 260–262.

Dax, M. Lesions de la moitié gauche de l'encéphale coïncident avec l'oubli des signes de la pensée. *Gazette hebdomadaire de médecine et de chirurgie* (Paris), 1865, 2, 259–260.

Dearborn, G. V. N. *Motor-sensory development.* Baltimore: Warwick and York, 1910.

Desruelles, H.-M.-J. Note sur l'incurvation à gauche de la région dorsale de la colonne épinière. *Gazette des Hospitaux Civils et Militaires,* 1841, 21 Dec., *3,* No. 152, 624 (2nd series).

Dwight, T. Right and left-handedness. *Journal of Psychological Medicine,* 1870, *4,* 535–542.

Eberstaller, O. Zur Oberflächen-anatomie der Grosshirn-hemisphären. *Weiener Medizinische Blaetter,* 1884, *7,* 479–482; 542–582; 644–646.

Ecker, A. Zur Entwicklungsgeschichte der Furchen und Windungen der Grosshirn-Hemisphären im Foetus des Menschen. *Archiv für Anthropologie,* 1868, *3,* 212–223.

Erlenmeyer, A. Die Schrift. *Grundzüge ihrer Physiologie und Pathologie.* Stuttgart: Adolf Bonz & Company, 1879.

Eylmann, E. *Die Eingeborenen der Kolonie Süd-Australiens.* Berlin, 1909.

Fleury, A. de. Sur la pathogénie du langage articulé. Letter to *l'Academie des sciences, belles lettres, et arts de Bordeaux,* 9 Feb. 1865.

Fliess, W. *Der Ablauf des Lebens* (2nd Ed.) Vienna: Deuticke, 1923. (first published in 1906)

Foerster, A. *Die Missbildung des Menschen systematisch dargestellt.* Jena, 1865.

Forster, E. S. *The Works of Aristotle, Vol. VII. Problemata.* Oxford, Eng.: Clarendon Press, 1927.

Freud, S. *The interpretation of dreams.* In A. A. Brill (Ed. and Trans.), *The basic writings of Sigmund Freud.* New York: Modern Library Random House, 1938.

Freud, S. *Leonardo da Vinci: a psychological study of an infantile reminiscence.* (A. A. Brill, trans.) London: Routledge & Kegan Paul, 1948.

Freud, S. *The problem of anxiety.* New York: W. W. Norton, 1936.

Froude, J. A. *Thomas Carlyle: a history of his life in London.* New York: Scribner, 1898.

Fritsch, V. *Left and right in science and life.* London: Barrie and Rockliff, 1968.

Gardner, M. *The annotated Alice*. New York: Clarkson N. Potter, 1960.

Gaupp, E. Ueber die Maass und Gewichts-Differenzen Zwischen den Knochen der rechten und der linken Extremitäten des Menschen. *Inaug. Dissert.*, Breslau, 1889.

Gaupp, E. *Über die Rechtshändigkeit des Menschen*. Jena: A. Fischer, 1909. (a)

Gaupp, E. *Die normalen Asymmetrien des menschlichen Körpers*. Jena: A. Fischer, 1909. (b)

Geschwind, N. & Levitsky, W. Left/right asymmetries in temporal speech region. *Science*, 1968, *161*, 186–187.

Girdwood, G. P. Thoughts and facts on right and left handedness and an attempt to explain why the majority of men are righthanded. *Transactions of the Royal Society of Canada*, 1908, *2*, 179–191.

Goodfield, J. Humanity in science: a perspective and a plea. *Science*, 1977, *98*, 580–585.

Gordon, H. Left-handedness and mirror writing, especially among defective children. *Brain*, 1920, *43*, 313–368.

Gordon, K. Some notes on the mental status of the left-handed. *Journal of Juvenile Research*, 1924, *8*, 154–157.

Gould, G. M. *Righthandedness and lefthandedness with chapters treating of the writing posture, the rule of the road, etc.* Philadelphia and London: J. P. Lippincott, 1908.

Gould, G. M. & Pyle, W. L. *Anomalies and curiosities of medicine*. New York: The Julian Press, 1956; originally published by W. B. Saunders, 1896.

Granet, M. Right and left in China. ("La droite et la gauche en Chine." Communication to the Institut Francais de Sociologie, 9 June 1933). In R. Needham, (Ed.) *Right and left: Essays on dual symbolic classification*. Chicago and London: The University of Chicago Press, 1973, 43–58.

Grant, J. C. B. *Grant's atlas of anatomy, 6th Ed.* Baltimore: The Williams & Wilkins Co., 1972.

Gratiolet, P. & Leurat, F. *Anatomie comparée du système nerveux, considéré dans ses rapports avec l'intelligence*. Paris, J. B. Baillière et fils, 1839.

Hall, G. S. & Hartwell, E. M. Research and discussion, bilateral asymmetry of function. *Mind*, 1884, *9*, 93–109.

Harris, L. J. Teaching both sides of your head: An educational fad seen in historical perspective. Invited paper for Annual Meetings of Midwestern Psychological Association, Chicago, May, 1978.

Harris, L. J. Two-brain education: Historical perspective on a contemporary fad. Paper presented at Annual Meetings of the International Neuropsychology Society, New York, Feb., 1979.

Harting, P. Sur une asymétrie du squelette humain se transmettant héreditairment. *Archives Néerlandaises des sciences exactes et Naturelles*, 1869, *4*, 44–54.

Harvey, *Sheep in wolves' clothing*. Cited in Burt, 1937, p. 314.

Hécaen, H. & Dubois, J., Eds. *La naissance de la neuropsychologie du langage, 1825–1865*. Paris: Flammarion, 1969.

Hécaen, H. & Sauguet, J. Cerebral dominance in left-hand subjects. *Cortex*, 1971, *7*, 19–48.

Hertz, R. The pre-eminence of the right hand: a study in religious polarity. ("La prééminence de la main droite: etude sur la polarité religieuse," *Revue Philosophique*, 1909, *68*, 553–580). (Trans. by R. Needham.) In R. Needham, (Ed.), *Right and left: Essays on dual symbolic classification*. Chicago and London: The University of Chicago Press, 1973, 3–31.

Hewes, G. W. Lateral dominance, culture, and writing systems. *Human Biology*, 1949, *21*, 233–245.

Holland, H. On the brain as a double organ. *In Medical notes and reflections*, London: Longman, 1840.

Holland, H. On the brain as a double organ. Chap. VII in *Chapters on mental physiology.* London: Longman, Brown, Green, and Longmans, 1852, 170–191.

Hollis, W. A. Lopsided generations. *Journal of Anatomy and Physiology,* 1875, *9,* 263–271.

Holmes, J. M. *Concise medical textbooks, obstetrics.* London: Bailliere & Cassell, 1969.

Huber, J. B. Why are we right-handed? *Scientific American,* 1910, *102,* 260–261; 268–269.

Hughes, C. H. Note on the conundrum why we are right-handed. *Western Medical Reporter,* Chicago, 1890, *12,* 147.

Hyrtl, J. *Handbuch der topographischen Anatomie.* (4th Ed.), Vienna: Braumüller, 1860.

Ingalls, N. W. On righthandedness. *The Scientific Monthly,* 1928, *27,* 307–321.

Ireland, W. W. Notes on lefthandedness. *Brain,* 1880, *3,* 207–214.

Ireland, W. W. On mirror-writing and its relation to left-handedness and cerebral disease. *Brain,* 1881, *4,* 361–367.

Jackson, J. H. Hemiplegia of the left side, with defect of speech. *Medical Times and Gazette,* 1866, *2,* 210.

Jackson, J. H. Defect of intellectual expression (aphasia) with left hemiplegia. Letter to Editor of *The Lancet,* 1868, *1,* 457.

Jackson, J. *Ambidexterity or two-handedness and two-brainedness.* London: Kegan Paul, Trench, Trübner & Co., Ltd., 1905.

Jewish Encyclopedia, The. "Right and left." New York and London: Funk and Wagnalls Company, *1925, 10,* 419–420.

Johnson, W. & Wright, W. *Neolithic man in North-east Surrey.* London: E. Stock, 1906.

Jones, W. Cited in *Report on the human remains. First Annual Report of the Archaeological Survey of Nubia for 1907–1908,* 1910, 252, Cairo.

Jones, W. F. The problem of handedness in education. *Journal of Proceedings and Addresses of the National Educational Association,* 1915, *53,* 959–963.

Jones, W. F. How to detect right and left-handedness. *Literary Digest,* 1917, 741.

Jordan, H. E. The inheritance of left-handedness. *American Breeder's Magazine,* 1911, *2,* 19–28; 113–124.

Jordan, H. E. Hereditary lefthandedness with a note on twinning. *Journal of Genetics,* 1914, *1,* 67–81.

Jordan, H. E. The crime against left-handedness. *Good Health,* 1922, *57,* 378–383.

Jowett, B. (translator). *The dialogues of Plato.* Vol. IV. Oxford, England: Oxford University Press, 4th Ed., 1953.

Joynt, R. J. and Benton, A. L. The memoir of Marc Dax on aphasia. *Neurology, Minneapolis,* 1964, *14,* 851–854.

Kellogg, G. M. The physiology of right- and left-handedness. *Journal of the American Medical Association,* 1898, *30,* 356–358.

Kidd, D. *Savage childhood: A study of Kafir children.* London: A. and C. Black, 1906.

Kinsbourne, M. and Cook, J. Generalized and lateralized effects of concurrent verbalization on a unimanual skill. *Quarterly Journal of Experimental Psychology,* 1971, *23,* 341–345.

Kipiani, M. V. Ambidextrie: Etude expérimentale et critique. *Archives Internationales de Neurologie (Revue Mensuelle des Maladies Nerveuses et Mentales),* 1913, 11 Serie, *1,* 158–165.

Kolb, Eric de. *Collection: The Madonna and Child.* Art Gallery, University of Notre Dame, 1969.

Kolliker, T. Ueber das os intermaxillare des Menschen. *Nova Acta der Kaiserliche Leopoldino Carolinae. Deutsche Akademie der Neturforscher,* 1882, No. 5. (Current *Chemical Abstract* title: Nova Acta Leopoldina).

Lattes, L. Destrismo e mancinismo in relazione colle asimmetrie funzionali del cervello. *Archivio di Psichiatria, Neuropatalogia, Antropologia criminale e medicina legale,* Torino, 1907, *28,* 281–303. (Currently *Minerva Medicolegale*)

LeConte, J. Right-sidedness. *Nature*, 1884, *29*, 452(a).
LeConte, J. Right-sidedness. *Nature*, 1884, *30*, 76–77(b).
Lindsay, B. On the training of the left hand. *Northumberland and Durham Medical Journal*, 1904, *12*, 129–136.
Lithgow, R. A. Left-handedness. *The Lancet*, 1870, *2*, 660.
Lloyd, G. Right and left in Greek philosophy. In R. Needham, (Ed.), *Right and left: Essays on dual symbolic classification*. Chicago and London: The University of Chicago Press, 1973, 167–186.
Lombroso, C. Left-handedness and left-sidedness. *North American Review*, 1903, *177*, 440–444.
Lueddeckens, F. *Rechts und Linkshandigkeit*. Leipzig, 1900.
Macnaughton-Jones, H. *Ambidexterity and mental culture*. New York: Rebman, 1914.
Major, D. R. *First steps in mental growth*. New York: Macmillan, 1906.
Marienbild in Rheinland und Westfalen. 1968.
May, M. T. (trans. and commentary). Galen (Claudius Galenus) *On the usefulness of the parts of the body*. (2 Vols.) (De usu partium), Ithaca, N.Y.: Cornell University Press, 1968.
McMullin, W. G. What shall we do with our left-handed pupils? (A Symposium) *The Teacher*, 1914, *18*, 331–338.
Merkel, Fr. *Die Rechts-und Linkshandigkeit*. Wiesbaden, 1904.
Meyer, M. *Fundamental laws of human behavior: lectures on the foundations of any mental or social science*. Boston: R. G. Badger, 1911.
Meyer, M. Left-handedness and right-handedness in infancy. *Psychological Bulletin*, 1913, *10*, 52–53.
Michel, G. F. & Goodwin, R. Intrauterine birth position predicts newborn supine head position preferences. Infant Behavior and Development, 1979, *2*, 29–38.
Moorhead, T. G. The relative weights of the right and left sides of the body in the foetus. *Journal of Anatomy and Physiology*, 1902, *36*, 400–404.
Mortillet, G. de. Formations des variétés. Albinisme et gauchissement. *Bulletins de la Société d'Anthropologie de Paris*, 1890, *1*, 4 serié, 570–580.
Moss, F. A. *Applications of psychology*. New York: Houghton Mifflin, 1929.
Needham, R., (Ed.) *Right and left: Essays on dual symbolic classification*. Chicago: University of Chicago Press, 1973.
Newman, H. H. *The Physiology of twinning*. Chicago: University of Chicago Press, 1923.
Newman, H. H. Studies of human twins. II. Asymmetry or mirror imaging in identical twins. *Biological Bulletin*, 1928, *55*, 298–315.
Nice, M. M. The speech of a left-handed child, *Psychological Clinic*, 1915, *9*, 115–117.
Nice, M. M. Ambidexterity and delayed speech development. *Pedagogical Seminary*, 1918, *25*, 141–162.
Ogle, J. W. Illustrations of impairment of the power of intelligent language, in connexion with disease of the nervous system. *The Lancet*, 1868, *1*, 370–372.
Ogle, S. W. On dextral pre-eminence. *Transactions of the Royal Medical and Chirurgical Society*, 1871, *35*, 279–301.
Oppenheimer, J. M. John Hunter, Sir Thomas Browne and the experimental method. *Bulletin of the History of Medicine*, 1947, *21*, 17–32.
Orton, S. T. "Word-blindness" in school children. *Archives of Neurology & Psychiatry*, 1925, *14*, 581–615.
Overstreet, R. An investigation of prenatal position and handedness. *Psychological Bulletin*, 1938, *35*, 520–521.
Parsons, B. S. *Left-Handedness*. New York: MacMillan, 1924.
Péré, A. *Les courbures latérales normales du rachis humain*. Inaugural Dissertation Toulouse, France, 1900.

Pye-Smith, P. H. Left-handedness. *Guy's Hospital Reports,* (3rd Series), 1871, *16,* 141–146.

Ramaley, F. Inheritance of left-handedness. *American Naturalist,* 1913, *47,* 730–738.

Reade, C. "The coming man." Letters to the Editor of *Harper's Weekly.* 1878, 19 Jan., 50–51, 26 Jan., 74; 2 Feb., 94–95; 2 March, 174–175, 23 March, 234–235; 18 May, 394–395.

Rhodoginus, Lodovicus Caelius. *Sicuti antiquarum lectionum commentarios concinnarat olim vindex Ceselius, . . .* [Venetiis, In aedibus Aldi et Andreae soceri, 1516]. *National Union Catalog, 492,* p. 334 (cited under Ricchieri, L.).

Roth, W. E. Superstition, magic, and medicine. *North Queensland Ethnography: Bulletin No. 5.* Home Secretary's Department, Brisbane, Australia, Jan., 1903.

Rousseau, J. J. *Émile.* London: J. M. Dent & Sons Ltd., first publication, 1780. No. 518 of Everyman's Library, 1911; trans. by Barbara Foxley.

Sarasin, P. Über Recht- und Links-Händigkeit in der Praehistorie und die Rechts-händigkeit in der historischen Zeit. *Naturforschende Gessellschaft in Basel, Verhandlungen,* Basel, Buchdr. E. Birkhäuser, 1918, *29,* 122–196.

Satz, P. Pathological left-handedness: An explanatory model. *Cortex,* 1972, *8,* 121–135.

Sawyer, J. Ambidexterity. *British Medical Journal,* 1900, *2,* 1302–1303.

Schilder, P. Psychoanalytic remarks on Alice in Wonderland and Lewis Carroll. Reprinted in Phillips, R., (Ed.), *Aspects of Alice: Lewis Carroll's dreamchild as seen through the critics' looking-glasses 1865–1971.* Harmondsworth, England: Penguin Books Ltd., 1971, 333–343. (Orig. publ., *Journal of Nervous and Mental Diseases,* 1938).

Schiller, A. Theories of handedness. *Journal of Applied Psychology,* 1936, *19,* 694–703; *20,* 77–92.

Schonberg, H. C. *The great conductors.* New York: Simon and Schuster, 1967.

Scientific American, The Problem of Left-Handedness. 1918, *118,* 82.

Shaw, J. On right-handedness. *Journal of the Anthropological Institute,* 1877–1878, *7,* 94–97.

Shinn, M. W. *Notes on the development of a child.* Berkeley: University of California Press, 1914.

Siegel, R. E. *Galen's system of physiology and medicine: An analysis of his doctrines and observations on bloodflow, respiration, humors and internal diseases.* Basel, Switzerland: S. Karger, 1968.

Siegel, R. E. *Galen on psychology, psychopathology, and functions and diseases of the nervous system: An analysis of his doctrines, observations and experiments.* Basel, Switzerland: S. Karger, 1973.

Smith, G. E. Right-handedness. *The British Medical Journal,* 1908, *2,* 596–597.

Smith, G. E. The London skull. *The British Medical Journal,* 1925, *2,* 853–854(a).

Smith, G. E. Right- and left-handedness in primitive man. *British Medical Journal,* 1925, *2,* 1107–1108(b).

Smith, L. G. A brief survey or right- and left-handedness. *Pedagogical Seminary,* 1917, *24,* 19–35.

Stekel, W. *Die sprache des traumes. Eine darstellung der symbolik und deutung des traumes in ihren beziehengen zur kranken und gesunden seele für äzarte und psychologen.* J. F. Bergmann: Wiesbaden, 1911.

Stevens, H. C. Right-handedness and peripheral vision. *Science,* 1908, *27,* 272–273.

Stevens, H. G. & Ducasse, C. J. The retina and righthandedness. *The Psychological Review,* 1912, *19,* 1–31.

Strack, M. Mirror writing and left-handedness. *Journal of Genetic Psychology,* 1893, *2,* 236–244.

Struthers, J. On the relative weight of the viscera on the two sides of the body; and on the consequent position of the centre of gravity to the right side. *Edinburgh Medical Journal,* 1863, *8,* 1086–1104(a).

Struthers, J. The relative weight of the viscera on the two sides of the body—note by Dr. Struthers. *Edinburgh Medical Journal*, 1893, *9*, Part 1, 381–82.(b)

Subinara, A. Handedness and cerebral dominance. In P. J. Vinken, & G. W. Bruyn (Eds.), *Handbook of clinical neurology* (Vol. 4): *Disorders of speech, perception, and symbolic behavior*. New York: North-Holland Publishing Co., 1969, 248–272.

Taylor, A. E. (Trans.). Plato. *Collected Dialogues*. E. Hamilton, & H. Cairns, (Eds.), New York: Pantheon Books, Bollingen Series No. 71, 1971.

Terrell, J. J. Let left-handedness alone! *Illustrated World*, 1917, *27*, 190–192.

Thass-Thienemann, T. Left-handed writing. *The Psychoanalytic Review*, 1955, *42*, 239–261.

Theile, F. W. Gewichtsbestimmungen zur Entwicklung des Muskel-systems und des Skelets beim Menschen. *Nova Acta der kaiserlichen Leopoldino-Carolinae deutsche academie der naturforscher*, Band xlvi. No. 3, Halle, 1884. (Current *Chemical Abstract* title: *Nova Acta Leopoldina*)

Thurnam, J. On the weight of the brain and the circumstances affecting it. *Journal of Mental Science.* 1866, *12*, 1–43.

Trousseau, A. *Clinique Médicale de l'Hotel-Dieu de Paris*, 2nd Ed., 3 vols. Paris: J.-B. Baillière et fils, 1868.

Uhrbrock, R. S. Laterality in art. *Journal of Aesthetics and Art Criticism*, 1973, *32*, 27–35.

Wagner, H. *Vorstudien des Menschlichen Gehirns*, 1862, *2*, 89–92.

Wagner, H. *Massbestimmungen der Oberfläche des grossen Gehirns*. Wigand, Cassel und Göttingen, 1864.

Watson, J. B. *Behaviorism*. New York: The People's Institute Publishing Co., Inc. 1924.(a)

Watson, J. B. *Psychology from the standpoint of a behaviorist, 2nd Ed.* Philadelphia & London: J. B. Lippincott Co., 1924.(b)

Watson, J. B. What the nursery has to say about handedness. *Pedagogical Seminary*, 1925, *32*, 293–327.

Weber, E. Eine Erklärung für die Art der Vererbung der Rechtshändigkeit. *Zentralblatt für Physiologie*, 1904, *18*, 425–432.

Weitz, W. Studien an eineiigen Zwillingen. *Zeitschrift fuer Klinische Medizin*, 1925, *101*, 115–154.

Werner, A. Note on the terms used for "right hand" and "left hand" in the Bantu languages. *Journal of the Royal African Society*, 1904, *4*, 112–116.

Whitteridge, G. (Ed. and trans.) *The anatomical lectures of William Harvey*. Prelectiones anatomie universalis [16, 17, and 18 April, 1616]. De musculis [probably 1618]. Edinburgh and London: E. & S. Livingstone Ltd., 1964.

Wieschhoff, H. A. Concepts of right and left in African cultures. In R. Needham, (Ed.) *Right and left: Essays on symbolic classification.* Chicago and London: University of Chicago Press, 1973, 59–73. (Orig. publication, *Journal of the American Oriental Society*, 1938, *58*, 202–217).

Wigan, A. L. *A new view of insanity. The duality of the mind proved by the structure, functions, and diseases of the brain, and by the phenomena of mental derangement, and shewn to be essential to moral responsibility.* London: Longman, Brown, Green, and Longmans, 1844.

Williams, J. W. *Obstetrics.* New York: D. Appleton and Co., 1930.

Willius, F. A. & Dry, T. J. *A history of the heart and the circulation.* Philadelphia & London: W. B. Saunders Co., 1948.

Wilson, D. Paleolithic dexterity. *Royal Society of Canada, Proceedings and Transactions*, 1885, *3*, 119–133.

Wilson, D. Primaeval dexterity. *Proceedings of The Canadian Institute.* 1885–1886, *3*, (3rd series) 125–143.

Wilson, D. *The right hand: Left-handedness.* New York: Macmillan, 1891.

Wilson, P. T. & H. E. Jones. Left-handedness in twins. *Genetics,* 1932, *17,* 560–571.

Witelson, S. F. & Pallie, W. Left hemisphere specialization for language in the newborn: neuroanatomical evidence of asymmetry. *Brain,* 1973, *96,* 641–646.

Woo, T. L. & Pearson, K. Dextrality and sinistrality of hand and eye. *Biometrika,* 1927, *19,* 165–199.

Wood, J. P. *The snark was a boojum: A life of Lewis Carroll.* New York: Pantheon Books, 1966.

Woolley, H. T. The development of right-handedness in a normal infant. *Psychological Review,* 1910, *17,* 37–41.

Yeni-Komshian, G. H. & Benson, D. A. Anatomical study of cerebral asymmetry in the temporal lobe of humans, chimpanzees, and rhesus monkeys. *Science,* 1976, *192,* 387–389.

2

Neuroanatomical Asymmetry in Left-Handers: A Review and Implications for Functional Asymmetry[1]

SANDRA F. WITELSON

meanwhile I am annoyed that my writing should be so shaky; this is due to tiredness, even in my right hand in spite of the fact that I draw and engrave with my left. However, it seems that my right hand shares so much in the tension that it gets tired in sympathy.

M. C. Escher, 1956
(Ernst, 1976)

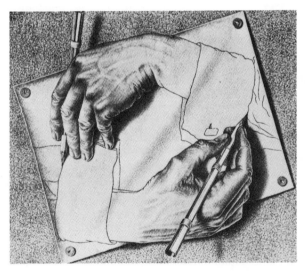

Escher, 1948. *Drawing Hands*, lithograph.

[Courtesy of the Vorpal Galleries, New York, San Francisco, Chicago, and Laguna Beach.]

[1] The writing of this chapter was supported in part by the Ontario Mental Health Foundation Research Grants Nos. 322 and 741 and by the U.S. NINCDS Contract NO 1–NS–6–2344.

NEUROPSYCHOLOGY
OF LEFT-HANDEDNESS

INTRODUCTION

Within the last decade, the study of anatomical asymmetry between the two cerebral hemispheres of man has been revived after a long interim since its first documentation around the turn of the century. Such study was not pursued at that time as it was thought that the right–left differences that were observed were insufficient to have any functional significance. However, a recent surge of studies has led to further documentation of neuroanatomical asymmetry and, consequently, its functional significance has been reconsidered.

It is frequently assumed that the anatomical asymmetry between the hemispheres is a correlate, possibly a neural substrate, of the functional specialization of the hemispheres. Such thinking is probably attributable to the dramatically simple and clear observation (Geschwind & Levitsky, 1968) of larger posterior temporal lobe regions, known to be crucial for language functions, in the left hemisphere than in the homologous regions of the right hemisphere in the majority of individuals (for review, see Galaburda, LeMay, Kemper, & Geschwind, 1978; Geschwind, 1974; Witelson, 1977b). The location, direction, magnitude, and consistency of this morphological asymmetry in the planum temporale have understandably seduced thinking to the possible premature conclusion that this asymmetry is a neural substrate of language lateralization.

Other right–left anatomical differences also have been reported: (a) a larger antero-parietal region on the left side; (b) a larger prefrontal region on the right side; (c) a larger postero-occipital region on the left side; (d) a longer occipital horn in the left lateral ventrical, suggested as an indicator of more occipital tissue on the right side; (e) larger motor pyramidal tracts on the right side; and (f) various right–left differences in cerebral vascularization. In general, the possible association of these morphological asymmetries with functional asymmetry is less obvious and more equivocal than is the temporal lobe asymmetry.

The notion that neuroanatomical asymmetry is meaningfully associated with functional asymmetry must be considered speculative to date. There is, however, considerable individual variation in the pattern of right–left differences in anatomical asymmetry, as well as in the patterns of cerebral lateralization of cognitive functions. Such variation allows for the investigation of possible correlations of different patterns of neuroanatomical asymmetry with (a) different patterns of hemispheric functional specialization and with (b) variation in other factors known to be related to functional asymmetry, such as hand preference and possibly gender. I will present a review of the available literature concerning anatomical asymmetry that particularly considers handedness. The results consistently indicate that the direction of the anatomical asymmetry is correlated with hand preference. In most cases, right-handedness is associated with anatomical asymmetry in one direction, and left-handedness with less anatomical asymmetry or asymmetry in the opposite direction. Such evidence of a double dissociation (see Teuber, 1955, p. 285) between anatomical asymmetry and hand preference provides strong support for the hypothesis that a meaningful association exists between neuroanatomical asymmetry and hand preference. With one further inferential step, the data support the hypothesis that anatomical asymmetry is associated with, or is a neural substrate of, hemispheric functional specialization.

HEMISPHERE FUNCTIONAL ASYMMETRY

The functional differences between the left and right hemispheres for cognition are well established. The two hemispheres have different roles, not only at the level of somesthetic sensation and motor control, in which case each side of the body is mainly dependent on regions in the contralateral hemisphere of the brain, but also at the level of higher mental or cognitive functions. A large body of literature indicates that numerous perceptual and mnemonic functions are differentially dependent on the two hemispheres. A synthesis of views suggests that the functional difference between the hemispheres is such that each hemisphere is specialized for a different type of information processing (see, e.g., Dimond & Beaumont, 1974). For the majority of individuals, the left hemisphere is considered to process information mainly in a phonetic, sequential, analytic, propositional mode. It may have the specific function of analyzing and executing series of discrete items in temporal arrangements. Language, because it depends heavily on such processing, would thus be subserved mainly by the left hemisphere. The right hemisphere is considered to process information predominantly in a nonlinguistic, holistic, synthetic manner and to have the specific function of synthesizing and sustaining a gestalt representation of the environment without regard to the time dimension. Consequently such skills as the perception of form, of spatial relationships, and of some aspects of music may be particularly dependent on the right hemisphere. It is still not known whether the functional differences between the hemispheres is absolute, or whether each hemisphere is capable to some degree of the other's specialized type of information processing.

Individual Differences in Functional Specialization

Left-Handedness

Although the pattern of hemisphere functional specialization previously described occurs in the large majority of individuals, this is not the case for everyone. Numerous studies of the cognitive deficits in patients with brain damage and of right–left perceptual asymmetries on dichotic stimulation and tachistoscopic tests in normal individuals indicate that specialization of the left hemisphere for linguistic functions is less frequent in left-handers than in right-handers. Additionally, when such specialization is present, it may be less complete, that is, more bihemispheric than in right-handers (e.g., Hécaen & Sauguet, 1971; Hines and Satz, 1974; Zurif & Bryden, 1969). The studies of speech lateralization as determined by the intracarotid sodium amytal test (Wada & Rasmussen, 1960) provide further verification of the association between side of preferred hand and the hemisphere dominant for language functions (Milner, 1974). The results of these latter studies clearly show that an association exists between handedness and speech lateralization, but it is not a perfect association. Although the majority of left-handers are like right-handers in that they have left-hemispheric dominance for language functions, most individuals having right-hemispheric or bihemispheric language representation are left-handers. There is much less evidence concerning right-hemispheric specialization for nonlinguistic auditory and spatial perception in left-handers compared to right-handers, and only a couple of reports indicated any difference in lateralization between groups (e.g., Levy & Reid, 1976; Varney & Benton, 1975). To sum, left-handers form a much more heterogeneous group than do right-handers regarding patterns of cerebral dominance.

An unresolved issue has been how to distinguish between sinistrals with different patterns of hemispheric specialization. Some studies indicate that the variable of a positive family history of left-handedness may be a relevant factor, and that it is the group of familial left-handers who have reversed cerebral dominance rather than the nonfamilial left-handers (e.g., Zurif & Bryden, 1969; Varney & Benton, 1975). Left-handers also show considerably more variation in the consistency and degree of their hand preference than right-handers. Some studies have suggested that it is the strongly left-handed individuals who have right-hemispheric language representation (Dee, 1971). In addition, hand posture in writing has been indicated as a dimension of handedness which may be related to the pattern of hemispheric specialization (Levy, 1974; Levy & Reid, 1976). It is well known that although almost all right-handers have a similar hand posture (i.e., the hand is held below the line of writing and the pencil is slanted upward pointing to the top of the page): left-handers show various postures. Although some left-handers write in the "normal" or "under" posture as observed for right-handers, a considerable number write with an "inverted" or "hooked" posture (i.e., the hand is curled above the line of writing, and the pencil is slanted downwards, pointing to the bottom of the page). This same posture has also been described as "crabbed" by Bonier and Hanley (1961) or, as in the words of an English handwriting teacher "there are 'pushers', 'smudgers', and 'OTT's' (over-the-top's) [Phillips, 1976]." Levy and Reid studied perceptual asymmetry on lateral verbal and spatial tachistoscopic tests in these two types of left-handers. They concluded that left-handers who write with the "normal" posture have right-hemispheric speech representation whereas those who write with the "hooked" posture have left-hemispheric speech representation. However, it is suggested that it is this latter group of left-handers who show less marked functional laterality or hemispheric specialization.

The definition of hand preference varies greatly between studies: from the hand *reported* to be used in writing, to the hand *observed* to be used consistently in a series of unimanual tasks. As left-hand (LH) preference itself varies so much, the difference between studies in the definition of LH preference is of greater magnitude and importance than in the case of right-hand (RH) preference. Left-handedness has been defined as loosely as some use of the LH for some tasks, and as stringently as strong and consistent LH preference for writing and several other unimanual tasks. It is likely for this reason that different studies report the frequency of left-handedness to be anywhere from 1 to 30% of the population (e.g. Annett, 1972; Hécaen & Ajuriaguerra, 1964). In the studies to be discussed below, the definition of handedness will be specified whenever it was given in the original study.

Gender

The sex of the individual is another factor that may be related to in-dividual differences in the pattern of functional asymmetry. Not all studies of cerebral dominance have found a sex-related difference. However, among those that did, it is almost always the male group who showed greater lateralization of function, and not the females. This is so for the lateralization of verbal functions to the left hemisphere (e.g., McGlone, 1977) and for the lateralization of spatial perception to the right hemisphere (e.g., Witelson, 1976; 1978). Some of the anatomical studies to be reviewed considered sex as a variable and these results will be summarized.

NEUROANATOMICAL ASYMMETRY

The region of the brain that has received the most consideration with regard to right–left morphological differences has been the temporo-parietal region. To date, several studies (e.g., Geschwind & Levitsky, 1968; Teszner *et al.*, 1972; Wada *et al.*, 1975; Witelson & Pallie, 1973) have

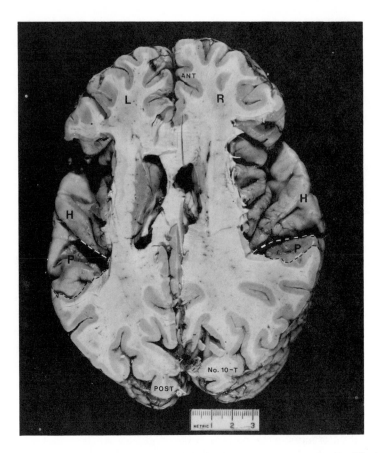

Figure 2.1. Horizontal section of an adult brain, from the series studied by Witelson and Pallie (1973), cut at the levels of the Sylvian fissures to expose the planum temporale on each side, showing the frequently observed right—left asymmetrical pattern. H, Heschl gyrus (primary auditory cortex); P, planum temporale, the area within the dashed lines (part of Wernicke's language region).

documented a larger expanse of cortex on the superior surface of the temporal lobe, posterior to the primary auditory cortex (Heschl's gyrus) in the left hemisphere than in the right. This region, called the planum temporale (see Figure 2.1), is part of Wernicke's region (see Figure 2.2), and is known to be crucial for language comprehension. In these studies, direct measurements of the length and the area of the planum were made from brain specimens, or from photographs of the specimens. The results indicated a significantly larger left than right planum in the large majority (about 70%) of individuals (for review, see Witelson, 1977b). The right–left difference is of considerable magnitude, with the right planum being about

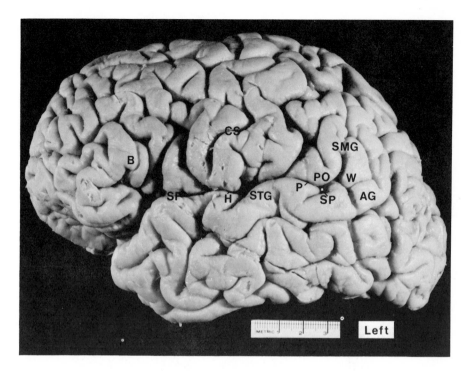

Figure 2.2. Lateral view of the left hemisphere of the brain of a human adult. AG, angular gyrus; B, core of Broca's region; CS, central sulcus; H, lateral extent of Heschl gyrus; P, lateral extent of planum temporale; PO, parietal operculum; SF, Sylvian fissure; SMG, supramarginal gyrus; SP, Sylvian point (end of fissure); STG, superior temporal gyrus; W, core of Wernicke's region.

40% smaller than the left planum (results were averaged over all studies to date).

In addition to direct measurement of the planum, other more indirect measures have been developed that may reflect indirectly the asymmetry in this neural region (for review, see Witelson, 1977b). Such measurements are the length of the lateral (Sylvian) fissure (e.g., Rubens *et al.*, 1976) and the height of the Sylvian point (e.g., LeMay & Culebras, 1972) which is the posterior tip of the Sylvian fissure (see Figure 2.2). Several studies using these measures have corroborated that the planum is usually larger in the left than in the right temporal lobe.

Of particular importance for the study of neuroanatomical asymmetry in relation to hand preference is one other indirect method concerning this region, which has the advantage that it is applicable *in vivo* (see LeMay & Culebras, 1972). In this method carotid arteriograms are obtained and the width of the angle formed by the posterior arch of the middle cerebral artery within the Sylvian fossa may be determined (see Figure 2.3). A *narrower* arch is more frequently found on the left side. This finding is considered to reflect *greater* expansion of the parietal operculum from above into the Sylvian fossa in the left hemisphere. The parietal operculum is also part of Wernicke's language region (see Bogen & Bogen, 1976).

Neuroradiological procedures such as x-rays, brain scans, and ventriculograms have also been used *in vivo* to study right–left anatomical asymmetry of various brain regions.

In spite of the consistency of the results of the anatomical studies, it is noted that there are important methodological concerns in this area of research. A more detailed account of the results of the research mentioned above and of earlier studies, as well as a discussion of the methodological issues involved, is given elsewhere (Witelson, 1977b).

Anatomical asymmetry has been most strongly documented for regions known to be crucial for the comprehension of language. Because the left hemisphere is typically the dominant one for linguistic functions and because the language regions, the planum temporale and parietal operculum, have been observed to be more frequently larger in the left hemisphere, this anatomical asymmetry has been considered to be a basis

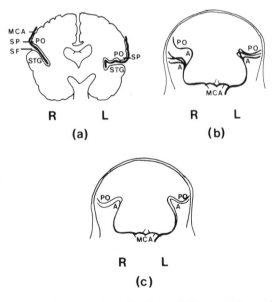

Figure 2.3. (a) Drawing of a coronal section through the posterior end of the Sylvian fissure. (b) Drawing of a carotid arteriogram from a coronal view, typical in right-handers. (c) Carotid arteriogram typical for left-handers. A, arch of artery; MCA, middle cerebral artery; PO, parietal operculum; SF, Sylvian fossa; SP, Sylvian point; STG, superior temporal gyrus. (based on LeMay & Culebras, 1972)

of the functional asymmetry. A larger neural region may indicate greater development in terms of the number of cells or in the extent of dendritic growth, or it may merely reflect more of the same tissue. Neurohistological investigation of the gross right–left differences remains as an important issue. Size, however, may not necessarily dictate greater functional relevance. Yet there are some precedents indicating that more complex functions may be represented by larger cortical areas—witness the larger cortical area subserving the control of movements of the hand or of the mouth than of the much greater body surface of the trunk. Furthermore, as cognitive capacity increased in phylogenetic development, the proportion of association cortex to primary sensory and motor cortex greatly increased.

Although in the majority of individuals the left temporo-parietal region is greater on the left than on the right side, there are considerable individual differences. An obvious next step is to determine who are the individuals who do not have a larger left planum temporale, but who have either a larger right planum or who have left and right plana of equal size (see Figure 2.4). If some factor were found to be correlated with both the direction of neuroanatomical asymmetry and with the pattern of functional asymmetry, such data would provide some support for the hypothesis that the anatomical asymmetry is a neural substrate for the well-established functional asymmetry. Such data may also reveal information about those individuals who show the less frequent pattern of a larger temporo-parietal region on the right side. There are several possibilities:

1. Such individuals may be those with speech and language functions represented in the right hemisphere.
2. They may be left-handers, perhaps familial left-handers or left-handers with "normal" writing posture (the mirror image of the typical posture of right-handers as opposed to the "hooked" posture).
3. They may be predominantly females.
4. They may be individuals with particular patterns of cognitive abilities such as low verbal skills relative to their nonverbal skills, or individuals talented in art or music.
5. They may represent none or some complex interaction of any of these factors.

Hand Preference and Neuroanatomical Asymmetry

Temporo-Parietal Region

To date, none of the studies that have directly measured the planum temporale by means of postmortem examination have reported data on the hand preference of the individuals. Wada, Clarke and Hamm (1975, p. 242)

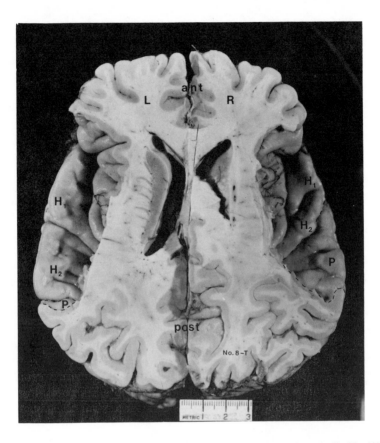

Figure 2.4. Horizontal section of an adult brain, from the series studied by Witelson and Pallie (1973), cut at the levels of the Sylvian fissures with the plana temporale exposed, showing a relatively infrequent pattern of anatomical asymmetry. H_1, first Heschl gyrus; H_2, second Heschl gyrus; P, planum temporale.

obtained handedness information about the deceased from interviews with the family, but they considered the data to be too unreliable and ambiguous and, therefore, did not use them. It is obvious that precise information concerning handedness is difficult to obtain retrospectively in such studies. However, as indicated above, some studies have employed indirect measures of the expanse of the temporo-parietal region that involve methods obtainable *in vivo*. Hand preference was documented in some of these studies.

In the first such study LeMay and Culebras (1972) examined the carotid arteriograms in a group of 44 unselected individuals and also in a group of 18 left-handers, defined as so indicated in their hospital records. With the use of arteriograms it is possible to determine the course of the middle

cerebral arteries that curve around surrounding gyri as they pass poster-
iorly within the Sylvian fossae. The anatomy of this part of the brain is
such that the size of the angle of the arch of the posterior branch of the
artery may be used as an indirect measure of the size of the parietal operculum. A smaller arterial arch is considered to reflect greater development
of the parietal operculum and, conversely, a larger arterial arch suggests a
smaller expanse of the parietal operculum on that side. Of the group of 44
individuals (most of whom were presumably right-handed), 86% showed a
narrower arterial arch on the left side and, by inference, a larger left
parietal operculum, 5% showed a narrower right arch, and 9% showed no
difference. In contrast, only 17% of the 18 left-handers showed a smaller
left arterial arch (larger left parietal operculum), 11% showed a smaller
right arch, and the majority (72%) showed no difference.

Six of the 18 left-handers had also been given the intracarotid sodium
amytal test and were considered to have speech represented in the left
hemisphere. Whether they also had some language functions represented in
the right hemisphere or whether they had long standing brain damage was
not reported. However, of those having speech represented in the left
hemisphere, not one showed a larger left parietal operculum; all six showed
no difference between right and left arterial arches. These data appear to
suggest a greater correlation of handedness than speech lateralization with
neuroanatomical asymmetry.

Subsequently, in a similar study, Hochberg and LeMay (1975) replicated
these results in larger samples of more rigorously defined right-handers and
left-handers. Hand preference was defined as the hand reported to be used
for writing and for cutting food. Of 106 right-handers examined, 67%
showed a smaller left arterial arch (greater left parietal operculum), 8%
showed a smaller right arch, and 25% showed no difference. In a group of
28 left-handers, only 22% showed a narrower arterial arch on the left side,
7% showed a narrower right arterial arch, and 71% showed no difference.
These results are very similar to those of the earlier study.

In the latter study, the size of the arch was measured and an angular difference between right and left arterial arches that was within 10 degrees
was defined as not different. In the right-handed group, the mean right–left
angular difference was 23.5 degrees. For the left-handers it was 6.6 degrees.
It is noted that the mean difference for the group of left-handers is less than
10 degrees, a difference in magnitude defined by Hochberg and LeMay as
of questionable significance.

Sylvian arterial arch asymmetry measured via carotid angiograms has
been found to be correlated with speech lateralization determined by
sodium amytal studies in a group of 59 patients studied by Ratcliff, Pila,
Taylor, and Milner (1978). Patients with evidence of early brain damage or
obvious angiographic abnormalities in the temporo-parietal areas were

omitted, thus excluding cases with possible shifted patterns of functional asymmetry. For the 39 patients with left-hemisphere speech, the mean arch asymmetry was about 27°. For the group of 11 patients with bilateral speech representation and the 9 cases with right-hemisphere speech, distribution and variance of arch asymmetries were similar to those of the former group, but the mean asymmetry of about 5° was significantly nearer zero. These results are very similar to those of Hochberg and LeMay. Such results support even more clearly the association between neuroanatomical asymmetry in this region and functional lateralization patterns.

Direct measurement of the height of the Sylvian point was also measured by LeMay and Culebras (1972) for 18 normal brains of individuals of unknown handedness and for 3 brains of known left-handers. A *lower* Sylvian point is considered to reflect *greater* development of the parietal operculum on that side, and may also indicate a greater expanse of the posterior temporal region and therefore a larger planum temporale on that side. In 78% of the group of 18 unselected specimens, the Sylvian point was lower on the left than on the right side, exhibiting greater development of the left parietal operculum. Of the 3 brains of left-handers, none showed a larger left parietal operculum, one showed a larger right parietal operculum, and two showed no right-left difference.

In addition, in one further case of a right-handed individual considered to have right-sided speech lateralization on the basis of the aphasia that followed a right temporal lesion, arteriogram measurements indicated arterial arches of similar size on the right and left sides and postmortem examination indicated a lower right than left Sylvian point. In other words, no measure indicated greater left-sided regions. Although this is only one case, the direct correlation of anatomical asymmetry with speech lateralization per se is the strongest type of evidence to support an association between anatomical and functional asymmetry.

In summary, a higher proportion of left-handers when compared to right-handers showed no asymmetry, or a reversal in the direction of anatomical asymmetry, in the temporo-parietal region. As handedness is known to be associated to some degree with functional asymmetry, these results support the hypothesis of an association between neuroanatomical and functional asymmetry.

Frontal Lobe Region

In the most recent study which considered hand preference in relation to neuroanatomical asymmetry, LeMay (1977) observed a correlation between hand preference and right–left differences in the size of frontal and occipital lobe regions. Measurements of the breadth of cortical tissue 5mm from the ends of the hemispheres were obtained from cerebral computerized transaxial tomography (CTT scans). The extent of protrusion of the frontal and occipital bones in each hemisphere was also determined from the CTT scans and in addition from basal view, skull x-rays. Greater protrusion was considered to reflect more neural tissue. These measurements may be taken *in vivo*, which allows handedness to be readily considered. The majority of the patients had normal CTT scans and minor neurological problems. Right-hand preference was defined as self-reported predominant use of the RH for graphics, tools, and sports since early childhood. Other combinations were considered as left-handed or as ambidextrous. The latter two groups were classified together as left-handers.

Complete sets of measurements from the scans and x-rays were not possible in all cases. For this reason, the size of the groups differed slightly in the comparisons with different measures. For purposes of the present paper, percent values were calculated from the given distributions of number of individuals and are based on the actual number of cases involved in each particular comparison as obtained from Table 1 in LeMay, 1977 (p. 246).

In 120 cases of right-handers, 61% showed a wider frontal expanse on the right side, whereas 19% showed a wider left frontal region. In a group of 121 left-handers, more individuals also showed a wider right frontal lobe, but the proportion of cases that did so was less: only 40% showed a wider right frontal region and 27% showed a wider left frontal region.

These results are corroborated by the measures of frontal bone protrusion. For the right-handers, 66% showed a greater right-side protrusion, whereas only 14% showed a greater left-side protrusion on scan measurements. For the x-ray measures, the values for right-handers were 39 versus 25%, respectively. In contrast, only 37% of the left-handed group showed a greater right-side protrusion, and 36% showed a greater left-side protrusion on the scan measures. For the x-ray measures, the distribution for left-handers was 26% versus 42%, respectively. LeMay noted that the x-ray measures are probably less valid than the scan measurements.

Thus, left-handers have at least a tendency to show greater right frontal expanse *less* frequently and greater left frontal regions *more* frequently than right-handers.

LeMay (1977) made a further analysis of the relationship of anatomical asymmetry to handedness, only using the scan measures. The left-handers were divided into two groups: those with and those without a positive family history of sinistrality. The nonfamilial left-handers (maximum $N = 39$) showed a pattern of asymmetry quite comparable to that of right-handers. The majority showed greater width of the right frontal region and greater protrusion of the right frontal bone (53% and 51%, respectively) via the scan measurements; only 18% showed greater left frontal width and 28% showed greater left-sided frontal protrusion. In contrast, the familial left-handers (maximum $N = 41$) showed a more equal distribution of the number of individuals with greater right and greater left measurements: Greater width of the right frontal lobe appeared in 35%, and 25% showed a greater left region. The right frontal bone showed a greater protrusion in 34% of the cases and the left in 41%. These results, which indicate that it is the familial sinistral who differs most from the dextral, are consistent with those from studies of left-handed brain-damaged individuals (e.g., Hécaen & Sauguet, 1971) and from studies of speech lateralization in normal individuals via perceptual techniques (e.g., Zurif & Bryden, 1969). In summary, the side of the brain with greater expansion in the prefrontal region was found to be correlated with hand preference, particularly when familial history of sinistrality in left-handers was considered.

Other CT brain scan measurements may eventually prove useful in studying anatomical asymmetry in neurologically intact individuals. For example, a recent report (Reese, O'Brien, Beeler, Gerding, & Romme, 1977) compared mean density measures for left and right hemispheres in 98 apparently neurologically normal individuals, although no clear asymmetry measured were noted.

The frontal region measured by LeMay is not specifically that part of the frontal region considered to be the speech zone or Broca's area. However, LeMay's finding that the prefrontal region is smaller more frequently in the left (usually speech-dominant) hemisphere is still not readily compatible with current knowledge of functional asymmetry. It is difficult to suggest what aspect of functional asymmetry may be associated with the observed anatomical asymmetry.

In this context, it is noteworthy to review the Wada, Clarke, and Hamm (1975) report, which included frontal lobe measurements in addition to measures of the planum temporale in a group of 100 adult specimens (handedness unknown) and a group of 100 infant specimens. In this study too, a frontal region was found to be slightly larger in the right hemisphere. Broca's region is difficult to measure as it does not have clearly known boundaries. Wada et al. measured a frontal region likely to be at least part of Broca's area. They made an area measurement of the lateral surface of a posterior part of the inferior (third) frontal gyrus, which included the pars opercularis and the posterior portion of the pars triangularis, and referred to it as the frontal operculum region. In a series of 100 adult brains, the mean right frontal operculum area was 26.7 planimetric units, significantly greater than the measure of 21.5 units for the left area. Only 9% of the cases showed a larger left than right area. However, because of the difficulty in unequivocally defining this area, these results must be considered with caution, as Wada and colleagues themselves indicated. The ambiguity is further compounded by their additional observation that although this area was larger on the right side, the gyri within the designated area appeared to be more tightly packed on the left side, and therefore total cortical surface may in fact have been larger on the left side in most brains.

Occipital Lobe Region

LeMay (1977) also made measures of this area from the brain scans and x-rays. In the group of 120 right-handers, 66% showed a wider expanse of tissue in the posterior part of the occipital lobe (5mm from the end) on the left side, and only 9% showed a wider right occipital lobe. In the group of 118 left-handers, there was a much smaller difference between the number of individuals showing left- and right-biased asymmetry (i.e., 38 versus 27%, respectively).

The results of measures of occipital bone protrusion from both the scans and x-rays were consistent with the tissue width measurements. As before, greater bone protrusion is considered to indicate more tissue on that side. In the right-handers, 77 and 68% of individuals showed a greater left occipital protrusion for the scan and x-ray measures, respectively; whereas only 13 and 10% showed greater right occipital protrusion, respectively. In the left-handed group, less asymmetry was observed. The frequencies of greater left versus greater right protrusion were 36 versus 35% for scan measures; and 47 versus 33% for x-rays.

LeMay's finding that a larger occipital region more frequently occurs on the left side is consistent with the results of several earlier studies (Gundara & Zivanovic, 1968; Inglessis, 1925; Kavue, 1931; Smith, 1907) that used various measures of the expanse of occipital tissue and the extent of protrusion of occipital tissue onto the cranial vault.

LeMay (1977) again analyzed the data for left-handers according to familial and nonfamilial classification. For the nonfamilial sinistrals, 59% showed greater left occipital regions on each of the scan measures (i.e., tissue width and bone protrusion). Only 19 and 26% showed greater right-sided measures, respectively. In contrast, for the familial left-handers, 37% showed greater left measurements versus 24% who showed greater right measurements for tissue width, and 29% (left) versus 39% (right) for bone protrusion. As in the case with the frontal lobe measurements, only the familial left-handers tended to show the opposite pattern of anatomical asymmetry compared to right-handers.

Thus, right–left asymmetry in the postero-occipital region also is correlated with hand preference. But in this case, a larger area is usually found in the left hemisphere in right-handers. The question again arises as to what aspect of functional asymmetry may be associated with this anatomical asymmetry in the occipital region.

On the basis of these morphological asymmetries in both the frontal and occipital regions, LeMay (1977) described the right-hander as having a brain with a counterclockwise torque and the left-hander as having a brain with a tendency to a clockwise torque.

Anatomical asymmetry in the postero-occipital region has also been investigated by means of another method, the length of the occipital (posterior) horns of the lateral ventricles (McRae, Branch, & Milner, 1968) as shown in Figure 2.5. But the results of this work appear inconsistent with those of LeMay (1977) in that a longer occipital horn was usually observed in the left hemisphere, and was interpreted as reflecting less occipital tissue on the left side.

McRae et al. measured the length of the posterior horns from the pneumoencephalograms of 100 consecutive neurological patients, many of whom had a long standing history of epileptic seizures. Handedness was defined as that hand "used for most" of a series of unimanual tasks. Of the 87 right-handers, 60% showed a longer left occipital horn, 10% a longer right occipital horn, and 30% showed horns of equal length. Of the 13 non-right-handers (i.e., ambidextrous and left-handers), 38% showed longer left horns; 31% showed longer right horns; and 31% showed no difference. Although this sample is much smaller than the right-handed group, the pattern of right–left difference observed for right-handers was not at all evident for left-handers.

However, in the same report pneumoencephalograms were studied for a second group: 140 patients, all of whom had seizures of sufficient severity to require testing for speech lateralization determined by the intracarotid sodium amytal method. Handedness was also known. In this group no cor-

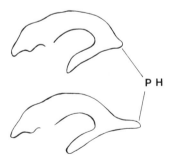

Figure 2.5. Schematic drawing of types of occipital (posterior) horns of the lateral ventricles. PH, posterior horn. (based on McRae, Branch & Milner, 1968)

relation was observed between hand preference and side of the longer horn. Both the right ($N = 68$) and non-right-handed ($N = 72$) groups showed very similar distributions: 37, 3, and 60% for the right-handers; and 31, 11, and 58% for the non-right-handers, for longer left, longer right, and equal size occipital horns, respectively.

This group was also subdivided according to the side of speech lateralization, but again no correlation was obtained with anatomical asymmetry. Of the 97 patients with speech represented in the left hemisphere, 31, 6, and 63% showed longer left, longer right, and equal size horns, respectively. For those with speech represented in the right hemisphere ($N = 34$), the distribution was 35, 9, and 56%; and for the group ($N = 9$) with bilateral speech representation, 56, 11, and 33% showed longer left, longer right and equal size horns, respectively.

For each handedness and speech-lateralization subgroup, the majority of cases showed no difference between sides: although among those with asymmetry, a greater proportion showed longer left than longer right horns. McRae *et al.* noted that of the 140 individuals in this group, there were 35 patients known to have sustained early left-sided brain damage, which may have resulted in a change of side of speech representation and may even have altered the postnatal morphological development of the occipital horns. The authors suggested that such early brain damage may have contributed to the lack of correlation between handedness and speech lateralization with occipital horn asymmetry in this group. I think that it is also possible that the factor of early brain damage may have produced a high proportion of pathological left handers in the McRae *et al.* sample (the proportion of left handers in the sample, 51%, was very high), thus further obscuring a possible correlation between hand preference and occipital horn asymmetry. However, the factor of brain damage may also have been operative in the first sample as it also included many cases of long standing epilepsy.

McRae, Branch, and Milner concluded that because the left occipital horn is more frequently the longer one, the posterior part of the language-dominant hemisphere "may be slightly smaller" than the same area on the other side. This conclusion is opposite to that of LeMay (1977). An alternate interpretation of the McRae *et al.* results may be possible, however. Perhaps a longer horn may indicate greater development in that part of the brain and thus may be considered to reflect more neural tissue on that side. In summary, the lack of correlation of this particular morphological asymmetry with speech lateralization, coupled with the possible equivocal interpretation of a longer horn in terms of size of cortical expanse, suggests that caution be exercised in interpreting the relationship of occipital horn asymmetry to functional asymmetry, particularly when measured in neurological patients. In fact, the difficulties in the interpretation of any asymmetry measures, morphological or functional, in individuals with early brain damage should be noted.

Pyramidal Tracts

Morphological asymmetry in the nervous system has also been found to exist below the level of the forebrain: in the level of and the pattern of the decussation, and in the size (cross-section) of the pyramidal (motor) tracts at the levels of the medulla and spinal chord. Yakovlev and Rakic (1966) and Yakovlev (1972) examined 179 fetal specimens and 130 adult neuraxes. Numerous serial histological sections were made from each specimen in order to examine pyramidal tract anatomy. It was observed that there were numerous patterns involving different proportions of left and right, crossed or decussating fibers (the lateral tracts) and of direct or ipsilateral fibers (the ventral tracts) in different individuals. However, there is a predominant pattern that has a systematic bias of a torque towards the right side of the body. In about 80% of the cases (adult and fetal) more fibers go from the left motor cortex via the contralateral pathway to the right side and from the right motor cortex via the ipsilateral pathway to the RH, than do fibers via the contralateral and ipsilateral tracts to the LH. In addition, in the large majority of cases, the contralateral tract from the left hemisphere crosses at a higher level in the medulla than does the contralateral tract from the right hemisphere. This pattern is presented schematically in Figure 2.6.

This morphological asymmetry has not received widespread discussion per se, nor much consideration in relation to hand preference and cerebral dominance. Yakovlev (1972) noted that it is the RH that usually receives

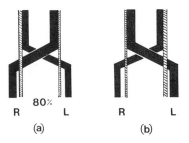

Figure 2.6. Schematic drawing of pyramidal tracts showing various patterns of decussation and distribution of tracts. Pattern (a), which occurs in approximately 80% of the population, shows the higher level of the crossing of the left contralateral tract and the more numerous fibers leading to the right side. (based on Yakovlev, 1972)

the greater amount of motor fiber innervation, the same hand that the large majority of individuals prefer to use and which is usually more skilled.

Yakovlev (1972) reported some data concerning hand preference in relation to this motor tract asymmetry. Handedness was obtained when possible from the medical charts of the adult cases. Four individuals were allegedly left handed. Analysis of these cases indicated that all four showed the typical right-sided motor tract bias. On the basis of these results, Yakovlev suggested that the right-sided torque in the motor system, as is RH preference, is a "statistical constant." He suggested further that reversed patterns in anatomy and in hand preference are not correlated with each other, but most likely are random deviations from the predominant patterns. In other words, hand preference is not a result of, nor associated with, the pyramidal anatomical bias.

Kertesz and Geschwind (1971) also studied pyramidal decussation in 158 adult cases (many of which were also included in Yakovlev's (1972) adult series), and obtained handedness data for a series of unimanual tasks from the relatives of the deceased in 132 cases. Of 125 right handers, 73% showed a higher left to right pyramidal crossing; 17% a higher right to left crossing; and 10% showed no clear difference. The similarity of this distribution to that reported for asymmetry in the planum temporale based on several independent studies is striking (see Witelson, 1977b). Of the 4 left handers and 3 ambidextrous individuals, 6 showed the common pattern and only one the reverse pattern. Kertesz and Geschwind suggested that although no relationship between handedness and decussation pattern was observed, further study of a larger group of left handers would be needed before any conclusions could be drawn.

It is well documented that the majority of left-handers have predominantly left-hemisphere representation of speech as is the case for almost all dextrals. Therefore, even if anatomical asymmetry and cerebral dominance were associated, there is no reason to expect groups of left handers to necessarily show reversed anatomical patterns compared to right-handers. This would be especially so for very small groups, as in the present case. In fact, one might expect more than only four or seven non-right-handers to be present in the total groups of 130 and 132 cases studied. Perhaps, it is only the subgroup of left handers with at least some speech representation in the right hemisphere (about 30% of all left handers) that have reversed patterns in anatomical asymmetry. What is needed to help clarify the possibility of an association of hand preference and therefore possibly of cerebral dominance with pyramidal tract asymmetry is information from a larger group of left-handers which could indicate whether a larger proportion of cases with left-sided bias in the motor system exists among left-handers than among right-handers. Or a somewhat different analysis could determine whether the proportion of left-handers is greater in a group of cases with left-sided motor bias than in a group with right pyramidal bias. A further intriguing possibility is whether any correlation exists between anatomical bias in the motor system and the dimension of "normal" versus "hooked" hand posture in writing.

The data on the left-handers presented by Kertesz and Geschwind and by Yakovlev are sufficient, however, to indicate another issue clearly. The question may be raised why it is that at least some individuals, as in the case of these left-handers, prefer to use their left hand even though morphological asymmetry in the motor tracts favors the right hand apparently from the time of birth; even though speech and language functions are most likely represented in the hemisphere contralateral to their nonpreferred (right) hand; and even though the factor of early brain damage may not be involved. The existence of such cases points to the possible operation of other factors in determining left-hand preference, such as genetic factors specific to handedness (e.g., Rife, 1950), random selection of behavioral preference (Annett, 1972), and the long considered factor of environmental influences (e.g., Collins, 1970; Corballis, 1978).

Cerebral Vascularization

Right-left differences in various aspects of cerebral vascularization have been studied and in some cases have been considered in relation to hand preference. The vascular measures, however, are even more ambiguous than the preceding ones in regard to their possible association with hemisphere functional specialization. Most explanations are *post hoc* to the observed direction of the asymmetry.

Asymmetry has been noted in venous drainage of the brain. Di Chiro (1962) examined the predominance or relative magnitude of the three main superficial veins of the brain: vein of Trolard (which is situated over the supero-parietal area), the Sylvian or middle cerebral vein (which winds around the anterior region of the temporal lobe), and the vein of Labbé (which is situated over the postero-temporal and centro-parietal regions). In a series of 180 carotid angiograms with satisfactory venous phases (all were considered to be normal angiograms but this does not rule out neurological disorders such as epilepsy, early brain damage, etc.), 72% were found to have a predominance (larger caliber) of either the vein of Trolard or of Labbé, regardless of hemisphere. Only a small minority of cases (3%) had all veins of similar caliber. The remaining cases showed the various other possible combinations of predominance of venous drainage patterns.

In a second analysis, right-left hemisphere differences were examined in a group of 65 patients for whom superficial venograms in both hemispheres were available. A significant difference between hemispheres was observed: The predominant vein in the left hemisphere was most frequently the vein of Labbé (55%) versus the vein of Trolard (18%). (Mnemonic: "L" for Left and Labbé.) In the right hemisphere, the vein of Trolard was usually the predominant one (46%) versus the vein of Labbé (24%).

As mentioned previously, the validity of an association between any neuroanatomical asymmetry and cerebral dominance is most strongly supported by correlations of anatomical measures with known functional lateralization and, to a somewhat less degree, with measures of inferred lateralization of cognitive functions. Any correlation of anatomical asymmetry with handedness requires one more inferential step, as handedness is associated, but only imperfectly, with patterns of hemisphere functional specialization.

Di Chiro presented evidence which supports an association between asymmetry in the venous channels and cerebral dominance. Venous right–left asymmetry was related to speech lateralization as determined by the intracarotid sodium amytal test in a group of 43 patients. Nine of the 43 cases demonstrated right-hemisphere speech lateralization. Labbé's vein was predominant on the left side in only 1 of the 9 cases and on the right side in 4 cases (44%). Trolard's vein was predominant on the right side in only 1 case, and on the left side in 5 cases (56%). These results were reversed in pattern and significantly different from those observed for the group with left-speech dominance whose venous pattern was similar to that of the group of 65 unselected cases described above. In summary, the vein of Labbé was found to be the predominant one in the speech-dominant hemisphere, regardless of side; and the vein of Trolard, the predominant one in the nonspeech hemisphere.

Handedness was also documented for these 43 patients. Of the total group, 16 were classified as either left-handed or ambidextrous (definition unspecified). It is noted that 8 of the 9 cases with right-speech dominance were non-right-handers (7 left, 2 ambidextrous), thus providing some cross validity for the handedness and speech lateralization classifications. Di Chiro did not analyze or discuss the handedness data in relation to venous drainage asymmetry but he did present the raw data. It should be noted, as in the McRae et al. (1968) study of occipital lobes, that any group of right-handers whose neurological status requires sodium amytal testing cannot be considered representative of right-handers in general. Recently Hardyck and Petrinovich (1977, p. 388) reported (but did not specify the analysis) that they analyzed Di Chiro's data omitting the ambidextrous individuals whom they considered ambiguous and found "that the relationship between handedness and predominant venous drainage is within the limits expected by chance." I made the following calculations from Di Chiro's raw data. Of the 27 right-handers, 16 cases showed the typical pattern of a predominance of the vein of Labbé and not of Trolard in the left hemisphere, 7 did not (4 cases had no venograms for the left hemisphere). For the 16 non-right-handers, 5 showed the typical pattern as indicated above, whereas 11 did not. This difference is significant ($\chi^2 = 4.14$, $p < 0.05$). A group difference was not observed for the pattern of predominance of the vein of Trolard. For the non-right-handers, only 5 showed the typical pattern of predominance of the vein of Trolard and not of Labbé in the right hemisphere, and 9 did not; but a similar pattern was obtained for the right handers: 7 and 12, respectively.

Hochberg and LeMay (1975) also studied the drainage pattern of the superficial veins in their series of patients and obtained similar results. Bilateral venous measures were obtained for 101 right-handed individuals. Labbé was the predominant draining vein in the left hemisphere in 33% of cases and in the right hemisphere in 15%. Trolard was the major draining vein in the right hemisphere in 31% and in the left in 20%. In contrast, for the 13 left-handers, the frequencies for both veins were almost identical between hemispheres.

An association may exist between right–left asymmetry in the venous system and cerebral dominance. How functional asymmetry may be related to this morphological asymmetry is not clear. No speculations have been offered. It may be noteworthy that the predominant vein in the left hemisphere is closely situated to language-related regions (e.g., the superior temporal, supramarginal, and angular gyri) and the predominant vein in the right hemisphere covers the supero-parietal area, which is specialized for spatial-perceptual tasks.

Another measure of vascularization, in this case one of arterial blood pressure, was used by Carmon and Gombos (1970). A difference in cerebral vascularization was expected because of the anatomical asymmetry of the vascular system peculiar to man and to anthropoid apes. In these species the blood supply of the left hemisphere is via the carotid artery which stems directly from the aortic arch, whereas the right hemisphere is supplied by the right carotid artery which shares a common trunk (the brachiocephalic artery) with the right subclavian artery supplying the upper right extremity. Carmon and Gombos measured the pressure of the ophthalmic arteries in normal young adults by the technique of ophthalmodynamometry. The ophthalmic arterial pressure is considered to be an indicator of pressure in the ipsilateral internal carotid artery that supplies the brain. Greater pressure in the carotid artery on one side may indirectly reflect greater blood flow to that hemisphere.

In this study handedness was determined by the subject's reported hand preference for a list of 10 unimanual tasks, giving a score of 20 for maximal right-handedness. In a group of 68 extremely right-handed (scores of 18–20) normal young adults, systolic ophthalmic pressure was greater on the right side in 81%, greater on the left side in 1%, and equal in 18%. Of 20 moderately right-handed individuals (scores of 14–17), pressure was greater on the right side in 60%, on the left in 15%, and was equal in 25%. In contrast, in 9 ambidextrous subjects (scores of 7–13), pressure was greater on the right side in only 22%, on the left in 11%, and was equal in 67%. Of 13 left-handed subjects (scores of 0–6), only 15% showed greater pressure on the right side, 62% showed greater pressure on the left side, and 23% showed no difference. No right–left differences were found for brachial arterial pressure in any handedness subgroups. The results indicated a significant correlation between right–left differences in systolic ophthalmic pressure and the side and degree of handedness. Carmon and Gombos suggested that this right–left pressure difference may reflect blood volume differences that in turn may be related to functional differences between the hemispheres.

In a subsequent study by Carmon, Harishanu, Lowinger, and Lavy (1972), a direct measure of hemispheric blood volume was used to study possible asymmetries in the cerebral vascular system. An intravenous injection of radioactive material was given to 85 normal young adult volunteers. Detectors were then placed on the subjects' heads to obtain gamma irradiation curves for each hemisphere separately. A greater irradiation curve was considered to reflect greater blood volume in that hemisphere. The handedness of each subject was determined by a questionnaire and hemispheric dominance for speech was inferred from perceptual asymmetry on a verbal dichotic stimulation task. Of the 85 subjects, 60 were right-handed and 61 displayed right-ear superiority.

The irradiation curve was larger in one hemisphere than the other in 75 subjects and there were significant correlations of side of the greater curve with handedness and ear superiority. Of the 60 right-handers, 62% showed a greater (higher peak) curve over the right hemisphere, 25% over the left, and 13% showed no difference. In contrast, of the 25 non-right-handers, only 28% showed a greater right-hemisphere curve, but 64% showed a greater left-hemisphere curve, and 8% showed no difference. When the total group was subdivided on the basis of ear superiority, the right–left differences observed were almost identical to those obtained for the two handedness groups. Thus, higher irradiation and, by inference, greater blood volume, was observed more frequently in the hemisphere ipsilateral to hand and ear preference, that is, the hemisphere likely to be the non-speech-dominant hemisphere. These results are consistent with those of the earlier study using ophthalmic arterial pressure (i.e., Carmon & Gombos, 1970). The correlation of hemispheric asymmetry in blood volume with handedness and ear preference suggests an association between blood volume and cerebral dominance.

The possible role that the asymmetry in cerebral blood supply may have for cerebral dominance is open to speculation. Carmon and Gombos (1970) initially suggested that the "metabolic conditions might be more favorable on the side where the pressure is less, and the hemisphere on this side (left) might acquire some function, such as speech, more easily than the other hemisphere [p. 127]." A somewhat alternate and more complex explanation was suggested by Carmon et al. (1972) in their subsequent study. They noted that the right hemisphere (usually non-speech-dominant) may develop earlier electrophysiologically. In addition, they suggested that the behavioral functions associated with the functional specialization of the right hemisphere may develop before left-hemispheric functions. The authors continued that the earlier maturation of the right hemisphere and its specialization for the earliest behavior may be related to the greater blood supply it receives.

These suggestions, of course, are highly speculative. The evidence remains scanty concerning the extent and chronological sequence of the cognitive capacities of infants for functions such as the perception of speech sounds and spatial perception. Also few data are yet available concerning the extent of and any temporal priority in the early biological maturation of the hemispheres and their functional specialization. Cerebral dominance in both hemispheres may, in fact, be preprogrammed and functional from birth (Witelson, 1977a).

It is unlikely that the neuroanatomical asymmetries observed to be associated with hand preference are a result of the effect of a bias in hand usage. In groups of left-handers, anatomical asymmetry is either attenuated or reversed in direction as compared to that of right-handers. However, a large proportion of left-handers still show the same morphological pattern observed in most right-handers. Thus, any influence resulting from the experience of using one hand preferentially must be a minor factor at most in many cases.

Furthermore, several studies have examined these anatomical features in infants, in whom hand preference may not yet be manifest and in whom little or no opportunity for biased experience has occurred. The results consistently indicate that the same anatomical asymmetries are present in infancy. Several studies have now investigated the planum temporale in neonates and the asymmetry appears to be comparable to that of adults in both the magnitude and the distribution of the asymmetry. These studies are reviewed in detail by Witelson (1977b). Since that review, another study (Chi, Dooling, & Gilles, 1977) has added to the data documenting greater left temporal regions in infants. Similar temporal lobe asymmetry has also been observed in several higher nonhuman primates such as chimpanzees and orangutans (see Witelson, 1977b for review). Yet there is no evidence indicating a distribution favoring right-paw preference within groups of these species as a group. However, there is evidence to suggest that some degree of hemispheric functional asymmetry may exist in higher primates (e.g., Harnad et al., 1977).

Several of the other anatomical measures have also been investigated in infants. A greater expanse of the left parietal operculum was observed in 100% of 10 neonate specimens (LeMay & Culebras, 1972). Greater protrusion of the right-frontal and left-occipital regions was found for a group of 22 infants, comparable to the pattern observed for dextral adults (LeMay, 1977). A greater frontal operculum was observed in the right hemisphere in a group of 100 infant specimens as in adults (Wada et al., 1975). Additionally, like adults, greater pyramidal tracts to the right side of the body were observed in fetal specimens (Yakovlev & Rakic, 1966).

In summary, there is no evidence that the experience of handedness per se (right or left) determines the direction of neuroanatomical asymmetry or that any experiential factor is necessary for the manifestation of anatomical asymmetry.

PATTERNS OF COGNITIVE SKILLS AND NEUROANATOMICAL ASYMMETRY

Several reports have indicated that in groups of musicians (Byrne, 1974), artists (Mebert & Michel, 1977) and architects (Peterson & Lansky, 1974; 1977), there is a higher proportion of non-right-handers when compared to control groups or to expected values for the general population. However, Oldfield (1969) reported no difference in hand preference between a group of 127 musicians in whom 21% showed some indication of sinistrality and a large control group, although 21% may be somewhat higher than expected. A related finding may be Deutsch's (1978) report that left-handers (particularly those with mixed handedness) showed superior auditory pitch memory compared to right-handers and strongly left-handed persons. It may be that such groups have in common more highly developed cognitive skills which are predominantly dependent on the functioning of the right (non-speech-dominant) hemisphere. It is possible, of course, that other specific cognitive profiles may prove to be associated with particular hand preference patterns.

Left-handers with such specific talents certainly do not represent left-handers as a total group. In fact, there is some inconsistency between the finding of a higher incidence of left-handers in such groups, and the observation that sinistrals are relatively worse on spatial than verbal skills when compared to dextrals (Levy, 1969; Miller, 1971). In fact it was Levy's (1969) hypothesis that bilateral language representation in left-handers resulted in the observed relatively lower spatial than verbal skills in a group of left-handers that led to several of the recent studies of hand preference and cognitive skills in these specific groups. Other studies of left-handers, however, have not observed such a verbal-spatial discrepancy in sinistrals when they are compared to dextrals (Briggs, Nebes, & Kinsbourne, 1976; Heim & Watts, 1976). Such inconsistent results may again reflect the heterogeneous nature of left-handers. It may be that left-handers who show the pattern of relatively poorer spatial than verbal skills (as do the advanced science students in Levy's, 1969, study) are one subgroup, and those left handers who do not and those who have specific talents in music or art may constitute another subgroup.

If an association does exist between hand preference and specific cognitive profiles, and if hand preference is also associated with neuroanatomical asymmetry, as the present review suggests, then perhaps there is an association between various patterns of cognitive ability and neuroanatomical asymmetry. Stated otherwise, individuals with different cognitive profiles or talents may have different brains, not only in their cognitive capabilities and likely associated physiological and neurochemical concomitants, but possibly in morphological structure.

Investigation of morphological asymmetry in the brains of individuals with various exceptional talents may yield some information about the biologic substrate of individual differences. Meyer (1977) has recently reviewed numerous different individual reports of macroscopic study of the brains of eminent persons, including musicians, orators, scientists, etc. However, as he indicates, general conclusions are currently impossible.

This line of speculation may be continued in a slightly different direction. Since handedness appears to be associated with patterns of cerebral dominance, and if there is an association between hand preference and specific talents, then individuals with particular talents may differ from the norm in their patterns of hemispheric functional specialization. This speculation is one that may be empirically examined. In fact, a few studies already exist that have looked at hemispheric specialization in musicians (Bever & Chiarello, 1974; Gordon, 1970, 1975, 1978), although these studies were not designed to compare patterns of hemispheric functional specialization. Interestingly, the various groups of musicians studied did show different patterns of ear asymmetry on monaural and dichotic stimulation tasks when compared to control groups of nonmusicians.

On tasks involving the perception of melodies, a left-ear superiority has usually been observed for nonmusicians (e.g., Bever & Chiarello, 1974; Dee, 1971; Kimura, 1964; Spellacy, 1970; Spreen, Spellacy, & Reid, 1970). In the case of the groups of musicians, who were chosen to be right-handed (on the basis of various definitions) as were the non-musicians, either no ear difference (Gordon, 1970) or a right-ear superiority (e.g., Bever & Chiarello, 1974; Gordon, 1978) was observed for the perception of melodies or rhythms. Bever and Chiarello and also Gordon suggested that, in musicians, the right-ear superiority and, by inference, the left-hemisphere predominance in the processing of the melodies indicated that the musicians used an analytic strategy in the perception of musical passages. In contrast, the left-ear superiority of the nonmusicians was suggested to reflect a holistic (right hemisphere) cognitive strategy. The perception of melodies, unlike some other cognitive tasks, may be processed via different strategies; and different individuals, either through training or due to inherently different cognitive abilities or biases, may use different strategies. It is not clear whether the musicians' apparent use of an analytic strategy is due to some inherent or experiential factor.

The implicit assumption in the experimenters' interpretation is that the pattern of cerebral dominance in musicians as a group is the typical one in which the left hemisphere is dominant for linguistic and analytic processing, and thus the right-ear superiority indicates the predominance of such cognitive processing. However, it is also possible that it is not a different cognitive strategy which differentiates musicians from nonmusicians, but rather a different pattern of cerebral dominance, such as greater bihemispheric representation of functions.

What would help to assess such varying interpretations is to establish whether musicians do, for example, show a right-ear superiority on a task that can only be processed via the strategy specific to the speech-dominant hemisphere, as in the perception of dichotic nonsense syllables. As there seemed to be no reason to ask this question, little relevant data are available. Bever and Chiarello did not give any linguistic auditory task, although Gordon (1970; 1978) administered, among other tests, verbal (digits) dichotic tasks to his groups. The surprising result is that in both studies, neither group of musicians showed the typical significant right-ear superiority, although the one control group did. This was so even though the musicians were right-handed according to various definitions. No significance was attributed to this lack of right-ear superiority. Perhaps musicians have greater bihemispheric representation of phonetic, sequential type of information processing, that is, a different brain organization.

It may be that more musicians, despite apparent right-hand preference, may have a less usual pattern of lateralization of cognitive functions as compared to the general population, and this may be related to a different morphological pattern. Such a hypothesis would need further exploration, but various experimental psychological procedures and clinical neurological methods (e.g., Luria, Tsvetkova & Futer, 1965) are available. Of interest here is a recent report (Tuge, 1975; Tuge & Ochiai, 1978) which indicated that in a talented, professional pianist and composer, who also was naturally left-handed and female, morphological study of the brain indicated a significantly larger planum temporale in the right hemisphere.

Such research is further complicated by the ambiguity of the definition of musician. It may refer to having musical activities, specific formal instruction or natural ability and to skill or activities in performance, composition or theory.

GENDER AND NEUROANATOMICAL ASYMMETRY

As indicated previously, gender has recently been reported to be associated with individual differences in the pattern of hemispheric specialization. Males appear to have a greater lateralization of verbal functions to the left hemisphere and a greater lateralization of spatial functions to the right hemisphere when compared to females. It is noted, however, that usually it is only a difference in the *degree* of functional asymmetry that is observed between the sexes rather than a difference in the *direction* of functional asymmetry as often observed between handedness groups. Experimental research with nonhuman species has indicated more directly that the functions of specific neural structures, as well as the morphology of some structures, are dependent on the sex of the animal (both genotypic sex, and phenotypic sex in atypical hormonal situations: see Dennis, 1976; Goldman, Crawford, Stokes, Galkin & Rosvold, 1974; Greenough, Carter, Steerman, & DeVoogd, 1977). For these reasons, it was considered worthwhile to review the available data pertaining to possible sex-related differences in neuroanatomical asymmetry. Because the factor of gender has only recently been considered relevant to cerebral dominance, many of the studies of anatomical asymmetry did not document gender nor analyze the results according to sex, even when data were available.

One report that did analyze sex-related differences was the Wada *et al.* (1975) study of 100 adult brains in which the authors reported that a sex-related difference existed in right–left asymmetry in the planum temporale. The sex was known for 78 of the 100 adult specimens. Only 10 of the 100 specimens showed a larger right planum (see Wada *et al.*, 1975, Table 1, p. 241). Thus the number of cases with reversed asymmetry of known sex is very small. Wada *et al.* reported that, of these reversed cases, significantly more were female than male. This sex-related difference is in somewhat the same direction as sex-related differences in functional specialization; that is, less marked left hemisphere speech representation in women. However, although a higher incidence of females was observed among the cases of reversed asymmetry, the number of such cases was very small and the large majority of women, as well as men, did show a larger left planum.

Wada *et al.* also analyzed the data of planum asymmetry for sex-related differences in their series of 100 neonates. In this case, no sex-related difference was observed. In a smaller series of 14 neonates studied by Witelson and Pallie (1973), a slight suggestion of a sex-related difference was observed in that a larger difference between left and right plana was observed for female than for male neonates of comparable postnatal age. *Post hoc,* these results were considered consistent with the earlier acquisition of speech sounds by females (McCarthy, 1954). In summary, the results concerning sex-related differences in the region of the planum temporale are of small magnitude and somewhat inconsistent, and should probably be interpreted with caution.

LeMay and Culebras (1972) found no sex-related difference in right–left measurements of the middle cerebral artery and, by inference, no sex-related difference in asymmetry in the region of the parietal operculum. In the subsequent study by Hochberg and LeMay (1975), which also measured asymmetry in arterial morphology, the distributions for right-handers were reported according to sex. Seventy-one percent of the males and only 62% of the females showed a greater right arch whereas 6% of the males and 10% of the females showed a greater left arch. However, analysis of these data indicated no statistical difference ($\chi^2 = .236$, $p > .50$). Right-left asymmetry in the expanse of occipital and of frontal regions as measured by LeMay (1977) was also analyzed for each sex, however, no sex-related difference was observed for either neural region. Additionally, Wada *et al.* (1975) found no sex-related difference for adults and neonates in asymmetry in the frontal operculum region.

Finally, in a report concerning asymmetry in venous drainage similar to that described by Di Chiro (1962), Matsubara (1960) examined the same three superficial veins in 117 normal cerebral phlebograms (from individuals with non-space-occupying lesions, nonvascular malformations, etc.). He found, as did Di Chiro, that there were variations in the patterns of predominant veins, but he only found the vein of Trolard to be the significantly more predominant one in the right hemisphere. The vein of Labbé was rarely found to be the predominant one in either hemisphere. The sex of the individuals was reported and, although no analysis of laterality in relation to sex was reported, visual inspection of Matsubara's Figure 8 (p. 89) indicated that proportionately the same number of females and males showed predominance of the vein of Trolard in the right and left hemispheres.

In relation to possible sex-related differences in motor tract asymmetry and in motor skills (e.g., fine motor-coordination), Lansdell (1964) noted a possible sex difference in neurohistological data reported by Conel. In the majority of female brains studied (four out of five), there was greater myelination in the left somesthetic cortex in the hand area than in the corresponding right hemisphere, while in the three male brains this difference was reversed.

One further study may be relevant here. The massa intermedia, a band of tissue connecting parts of the two halves of the thalamus, is absent in about one third of humans. Lansdell and Davie (1972) noted a sex-related difference in the pattern of verbal–nonverbal cognitive skills that was related to the presence or absence of this neural tissue as determined by x-ray films. Males having a massa intermedia showed lower nonverbal scores than those without the structure, but no differences were observed for verbal scores. Females showed no cognitive differences associated with different anatomical configurations.

In summary, the available evidence to date indicate little support for a sex difference in right–left neuroanatomical asymmetry. Any difference may be at a histological, neurochemical or neuroendocrinological level. The recent report that concentrations of norepinephrine are asymmetrically distributed in the human thalamus indicates the possibility of right–left neurochemical differences (Oke, Keller, Mefford & Adams, 1978).

SUMMARY

Consistent anatomical asymmetry between the hemispheres is well documented. Its possible relevance to functional asymmetry is less certain. Because handedness is associated to some degree with patterns of functional specialization, any correlation of neuroanatomical asymmetry with handedness is important to ascertain. A review was made of the studies found that considered neuroanatomical asymmetry in relation to handedness as well as to other more direct indices of speech lateralization. In almost every case a correlation of morphological asymmetry with functional asymmetry was observed.

Eight different large sets of data indicated that hand preference was correlated (sinistrals showed less or reversed asymmetry compared to dextrals) with right–left asymmetry in the parietal operculum, prefrontal region, occipital regions, venous drainage pattern, and blood volume supply. The neuroanatomical patterns associated with right- and left-hand preference are not diametrically opposed, which is consistent with the notion that dextrality and sinistrality form a dimension, as portrayed in Escher's lithograph and comment (Ernst, 1976) in the chapter lead. In only a couple of instances involving groups of patients who had intracarotid sodium amytal testing, was handedness not found to be correlated with anatomical asymmetry (i.e., for occipital horn length and for vein of Trolard predominance in the right hemisphere). In addition, there is no evidence to suggest that the experience of hand preference is essential for the manifestation of neuroanatomical asymmetry. Neonates show comparable morphological asymmetry. In four reports, speech lateralization as determined by the sodium amytal test or inferred by ear asymmetry on dichotic stimulation tasks was observed to be correlated with measures of neuroanatomical asymmetry.

In total, these data provide substantial support for the hypothesis that neuroanatomical asymmetry is associated with, and may be a substrate of, functional asymmetry. It is noted, however, that there may be a bias in the available data reviewed, as it is always possible that observed negative findings were not reported.

As in investigations of left-handers in general, the challenge remains one of discerning whether it is a particular type of sinistral who accounts for the different pattern of neuroanatomical laterality when compared to dextrals.

What may help to further document the association between anatomical and functional asymmetry are studies indicating a correlation of morphological asymmetry, including the planum temporale which is so well documented anatomically, with more direct measures of speech lateralization (e.g., the sodium amytal test, the occurrence of aphasia, asymmetry in experimental perceptual tests and in electrophysiological measures, and even possibly with specific patterns of cognitive abilities).

Although sex-related differences have been observed in functional asymmetry, to date there is almost no evidence to support a sex-related difference in neuroanatomical asymmetry. It may be that the substrate of the sex-related difference in cerebral lateralization is of a different nature than that related to hand preference.

REFERENCES

Annett, M. The distribution of manual asymmetry. *British Journal of Psychology, 1972, 63*, 343–358.

Bever, T. G. & Chiarello, R. J. Cerebral dominance in musicians and nonmusicians. *Science, 1974, 185*, 537–539.

Bogen, J. E. & Bogen, G. M. Wernicke's region—Where is it? *Annals of the New York Academy of Sciences, 1976, 280*, 834–843.

Bonier, R. J. & Hanley, C. Handedness and digit symbol performance. *Journal of Clinical Psychology*, 1961, *17*, 286–289.

Briggs, G. G., Nebes, R. D., & Kinsbourne, M. Intellectual differences in relation to personal and family handedness. *Quarterly Journal of Experimental Psychology*, 1976, *28*, 591–601.

Byrne, B. Handedness and musical ability. *British Journal of Psychology*, 1974, *65*, 279–281.

Carmon, A. & Gombos, G. M. A physiological vascular correlate of hand preference: Possible implications with respect to hemispheric cerebral dominance. *Neuropsychologia*, 1970, *8*, 119–128.

Carmon, A., Harishanu, Y., Lowinger, E., & Lavy, S. Asymmetries in hemispheric blood volume and cerebral dominance. *Behavioral Biology*, 1972, *7*, 853–859.

Chi, J. G., Dooling, E. C., & Gilles, F. H. Left-right asymmetries of the temporal speech areas of the human fetus. *Archives of Neurology*, 1977, *34*, 346–348.

Collins, R. L. The sound of one paw clapping: An inquiry into the origin of left handedness. In *Contributions to behavior-genetic analysis—The mouse as a prototype*. G. Lindzey & D. Thiessen, (Ed.) 115–136. New York: Appleton-Century-Crofts, 1970.

Corballis, M. C. Is left-handedness genetically determined? 1978. Chapter in this volume.

Dee, H. L. Auditory asymmetry and strength of manual preference. *Cortex*, 1971, *7*, 236–245.

Dennis, M. VMH lesions and reactivity to electric footshock in the rat: The effect of early testosterone level. *Physiology and Behavior*, 1976, *17*, 645–649.

Deutsch, D. Pitch memory: An advantage for the left-handed. *Science*, 1978, *199*, 559–560.

Di Chiro, G. Angiographic patterns of cerebral convexity veins and superficial dural sinuses. *American Journal of Roentgenology Radium Therapy & Nuclear Medicine*, 1962, *87*, 308–321.

Dimond, S. J. & Beaumont, J. G. (Eds.) *Hemisphere function in the human brain*. London: Paul Elek, 1974.

Ernst, B. *The magic mirror of M. C. Escher*. New York: Random House, 1976.

Galaburda, A. M., LeMay, M., Kemper, T. L., & Geschwind, N. *Science*, 1978, *199*, 852–856.

Geschwind, N. & Levitsky, W. Human brain: Left-right asymmetries in temporal speech region. *Science*, 1968, *161*, 186–187.

Geschwind, N. The anatomical basis of hemispheric differentiation. In S. J. Dimond & J. G. Beaumont, (Eds.), *Hemisphere function in the human brain*. London: Paul Elek, 1974.

Goldman, P. S., Crawford, H. T., Stokes, L. P., Galkin, T. W., & Rosvold, H. E. Sex-dependent behavioral effects of cerebral cortical lesions in the developing rhesus monkey. *Science*, 1974, *186*, 540–543.

Gordon, H. W. Hemispheric asymmetries in the perception of musical chords. *Cortex*, 1970, *4*, 387–398.

Gordon, H. W. Hemispheric asymmetry and musical performance. *Science*, 1975, *189*, 68–69.

Gordon, H. W. Left hemisphere dominance for rhythmic elements in dichotically-presented melodies. Manuscript submitted for publication, 1977.

Greenough, W. T., Carter, C. S., Steerman, C., & DeVoogd, T. J. Sex differences in dendritic patterns in hamster preoptic area. *Brain Research*, 1977, *126*, 63–72.

Gundara, N. & Zivanovic, S. Asymmetry in East African skulls. *American Journal of Physical Anthropology*, 1968, *28*, 331–338.

Hardyck, C. & Petrinovich, L. F. Left-handedness. *Psychological Bulletin*, 1977, *84*, 385–404.

Harnad, S., Doty, R. W., Goldstein, L., Jaynes, J., & Krauthamer, G. (Eds.) *Lateralization in the nervous system*. New York: Academic Press, 1977.

Hécaen, H. & de Ajuriaguerra, J. *Left handedness*. New York: Grune & Stratton, 1964.

Hécaen, H. & Sauguet, J. Cerebral dominance in left-handed subjects. *Cortex*, 1971, 7, 19–48.

Heim, A. W. & Watts, K. P. Handedness and cognitive bias. *Quarterly Journal of Experimental Psychology*, 1976, 28, 355–360.

Hines, D. & Satz, P. Cross-modal asymmetries in perception related to asymmetry in cerebral function. *Neuropsychologia*, 1974, 12, 239–247.

Hochberg, F. H. & LeMay, M. Arteriographic correlates of handedness. *Neurology*, 1975, 25, 218–222.

Inglessis, M. Uber Katazitasul-evscheide der linken und rechten Halfte am Schadel bein Menschen uber Hirn asymmetrian. *Zeitschriftfuer die Gesamte Neurologie und Psychiatrie*, 1925, 97, 354–373.

Kavue, I. Normale assymetrie des measchildchen Schadels. Philosophical dissertation, Berlin-Leipzig, 1931. (Quoted in Hochberg & LeMay, 1975.)

Kertesz, A. & Geschwind, N. Patterns of pyramidal decussation and their relationship to handedness. *Archives of Neurology*, 1971, 24, 326–332.

Kimura, D. Left-right differences in perception of melodies. *Quarterly Journal of Experimental Psychology*, 1964, 16, 355–358.

Lansdell, H. Sex differences in hemispheric asymmetries of the human brain. *Nature*, 1964, 203, 550–551.

Lansdell, H. & Davie, J. C. Massa intermedia: Possible relation to intelligence. *Neuropsychologia*, 1972, 10, 207–210.

LeMay, M. Asymmetries of the skull and handedness. *Journal of the Neurological Sciences*, 1977, 32, 243–253.

LeMay, M. & Culebras, A. Human brain morphologic differences in the hemispheres demonstrable by carotid arteriography. *New England Journal of Medicine*, 1972, 287, 168–170.

Levy, J. Possible basis for the evolution of lateral specialization of the human brain. *Nature*, 1969, 224, 614–615.

Levy, J. Psychobiological implications of bilateral asymmetry. In *Hemisphere function in the human brain*. S. J. Dimond & J. G. Beaumont, (Eds.), 121–183. London: Paul Elek, 1974.

Levy, J. & Reid, M. Variations in writing posture and cerebral organization. *Science*, 1976, 194, 337–339.

Luria, A. R., Tsvetkova, L. S., & Futer, D. S. Aphasia in a composer. *Journal of the Neurological Sciences*, 1965, 2, 288–292.

Matsubara, T. An observation on cerebral phlebograms with special reference to the changes in the superficial veins. *Nagoya Journal of Medical Science*, 1960, 23, 86–95.

McCarthy, D. Language development in children. In *Manual of child psychology*. J. Carmichael, (Ed.), 492–630. New York: John Wiley, 1954.

McGlone, J. Sex differences in the cerebral organization of verbal functions in patients with unilateral brain lesions. *Brain*, 1977, in press.

McRae, D. L., Branch, C. L., & Milner, B. The occipital horns and cerebral dominance. *Neurology*, 1968, 18, 95–98.

Mebert, C. J. & Michel, G. F. Handedness in artists. Paper presented at the 5th Annual Meeting of the International Neuropsychological Society, Santa Fe, New Mexico, 1977.

Meyer, A. The search for morphological substrate in the brains of eminent persons including musicians: a historical review. In M. Critchley & R. A. Henson, (Eds.), *Music and the brain. Studies in the neurology of music*. 255–281. London: Heinemann, 1977.

Miller, E. Handedness and the pattern of human ability. *British Journal of Psychology*, 1971, 62, 111–112.

Milner, B. Hemispheric specialization: scope and limits. In F. O. Schmitt & F. G. Worden, (Eds.), *The neurosciences. Third study program*. Cambridge, Mass.: MIT Press, 1974.

Oke, A., Keller, R., Mefford, I., & Adams, R. N. Lateralization of norepinephrine in human thalamus. *Science*, 1978, *200*, 1411–1413.

Oldfield, R. C. Handedness in musicians. *British Journal of Psychology*, 1969, *60*, 91–99.

Peterson, J. M. & Lansky, L. M. Left-handedness among architects: some facts and speculation. *Perceptual and Motor Skills*, 1974, *38*, 547–550.

Peterson, J. M. & Lansky, L. M. Left-handedness among architects: Partial replication and some new data *Perceptual and Motor Skills*, 1977, *45*, 1216–1218.

Phillips, R. C. *The skills of handwriting*. Oxford: Express LithoService, 1976.

Ratcliff, G., Dila, C., Taylor, L. B., & Milner, B. Arteriographic correlates of cerebral dominance for speech. Paper presented at the International Neuropsychology Symposium, Oxford, G. B., June 1978.

Reese, D. F., O'Brien, P. C., Beeler, G. W., Jr., Gerding, P. R., & Romme, C. R. A statistical description of the normal computerized brain scan. *American Journal Roentgenology*, 1977, *129*, 457–462.

Rife, D. C. Application of gene frequency analysis to the interpretation of data from twins. *Human Biology*, 1950, *22*, 136–145.

Rubens, A. B., Mahowal, M. W., & Hutton, J. T. Asymmetry of the lateral (sylvian) fissures in man. *Neurology*, 1976, *26*, 620–624.

Smith, G. E. On the asymmetry of the caudal poles of the cerebral hemispheres and its influence on the occipital bone. *Anatonischen Anzeiger*, 1907, *30*, 574–578.

Spellacy, F. Lateral preferences in the identification of patterned stimuli. *Journal of the Acoustical Society of America*, 1970, *47*, 575–578.

Spreen, O., Spellacy, F. J., & Reid, J. R. The effect of interstimulus interval and intensity on ear asymmetry for nonverbal stimuli in dichotic listening. *Neuropsychologia*, 1970, *8*, 245–250.

Teszner, D., Tzavaras, A., Gruner, J., & Hécaen, H. L'asymetrie droite-gauche du planum temporale: A propos de l'étude anatomique de 100 cerveaux. *Revue Neurologique*, 1972, 126, 444–449.

Teuber, H.-L. Physiological psychology. *Annual Review of Psychology*, 1955, *6*, 267–296.

Tuge, H. *An atlas of the brain of a pianist, Chiyo Tuge (1908–1969)*. Tokyo: Koseisha Koseikaku Co., 1975.

Tuge, H. & Ochiai, H. Further investigation on the brain of a pianist based upon microscopic observations with reference to cerebral laterality. Contribution from The Brain Institute, Japan Psychiatric and Therapeutic Center, Machida, Tokyo, 1978.

Varney, N. R. & Benton, A. L., Tactile perception of direction in relation to handedness and familial handedness. *Neuropsychologia*, 1975, *13*, 449–454.

Wada, J. A., Clarke, R., & Hamm, A. Cerebral hemispheric asymmetry in humans. *Archives of Neurology*, 1975, *32*, 239–246.

Wada, J. A. & Rasmussen, T. Intracarotid injection of sodium amytal for the lateralization of cerebral speech dominance: Experimental and clinical observations. *Journal of Neurosurgery*, 1960, *17*, 266–282.

Witelson, S. F. Sex and the single hemisphere: Specialization of the right hemisphere for spatial processing. *Science*, 1976, *193*, 425–427.

Witelson, S. F. Early hemisphere specialization and interhemisphere plasticity: an empirical and theoretical review. In S. Segalowitz & F. Gruber, (Eds.), *Language development and neurological theory*. New York: Academic Press, 1977a.

Witelson, S. F. Anatomical asymmetry in the temporal lobes: its documentation, phylogenesis, and relationship to functional asymmetry. *Annals of the New York Academy of Sciences*, 1977b, *299*, 328–356.

Witelson, S. F. Les différences sexuelles dans la neurologie de la cognition: implications psychologiques, sociales, éducatives et cliniques. In E. Sullerot, (Ed.), *Le Fait Féminin.* France: Fayard, 1978.

Witelson, S. F. & Pallie, W. Left hemisphere specialization for language in the newborn: Neuroanatomical evidence of asymmetry. *Brain,* 1973, *96,* 641–646.

Yakovlev, P. I. A proposed definition of the limbic system. In C.H. Hockman, (Ed.), *Limbic system mechanisms and autonomic function.* Springfield, Ill.: C. C. Thomas, 1972.

Yakovlev, P. I. & Rakic, P. Patterns of decussation of bulbar pyramids and distribution of pyramidal tracts on two sides of the spinal cord. *Transactions of the American Neurological Association,* 1966, *91,* 366–367.

Zurif, E. B. & Bryden, M. P. Familial handedness and left-right differences in auditory and visual perception. *Neuropsychologia,* 1969, *7,* 79–187.

3

The Sinistral Blastocyst: An Embryologic Perspective on the Development of Brain-Function Asymmetries[1]

CHARLES E. BOKLAGE

INTRODUCTION

This volume exists in large part because of belief in the proposition that the anatomical halves of the human brain are different in many aspects of function, and that such differences are fundamentally important in the development and use of faculties we associate with human mentation. In this chapter, I will attempt to place the subject in a cellular developmental perspective, looking from this apparently fundamental asymmetry of the functioning organ back to cellular, mechanochemical events that may serve as origins for the usual mode of development and as points of departure for the unusual.

It is argued elsewhere in this volume that non-right-handedness, and all the changes in brain lateralization it may represent, may be explained by reasonably simple genetic differences (Levy in Chapter 8). My prejudice is that this eventually shall prove to be not far wrong, but can not yet be considered proven. At best, genetic analysis will tell us how the causes get from one generation to the next, but it will not, by itself, tell us how those causes produce their consequences.

It is also argued that non-right-handedness might be traumatic or otherwise pathological in origin (Bakan 1978). I believe that this could be true in some cases. But, even if the correlations were stronger and more concrete than they are, they would, at the current level of analysis, do little more than suggest where to look for causes more specific than "birth stress." Correlated traits can be consequences of a common cause as readily as

[1] This work was supported primarily by NIH Grant GM-00006.

115

cause and effect of one another. The traces of ischemic or mechanical trauma and of hypoxic pathology, to which the effects of "birth stress" are imagined to refer, are to a large extent directly detectable, but their detection has not yet been pursued. Consequently, all such relationships so far suggested are of such an inappropriately high level of abstraction as to be useless for conclusions about cellular structural processes. Even were we to embrace wholeheartedly a pathological origin for most departures from the usual condition of right-handedness, we would still wish to explain the cellular controls responsible for producing the "normal" right-handed configuration of function, and any not-demonstrably-pathological variations. There is a good deal of difficult baseline work to be done, but we really are not asking easy questions.

In order to answer the questions I want most to address, we begin by accepting that:

1. The human brain hemispheres do indeed function with a distinctly nonrandom pattern of differences.

2. This pattern of hemispheric functional differences is subject to a certain range of minority variations over the population.

3. These minority variations in developmental outcome may originate from genomic differences and/or from variations in "environmental" determinants, for which independence from underlying genomic differences would still remain to be demonstrated.

4. At least some genomic factors must be involved in fundamental ways, given that the reasons for our interest in this subject arise most pressingly from a desire to explain differences between humans and other species, compared to which variation among humans is relatively minor. Species differences are by their nature inextricably bound up with genomic evolution. "Genomic" includes "genetic," but goes beyond it, in that most of the genome is not polymorphic (Harris, 1975), not subject to the Mendelian segregation of viable variants, and thus not capable of showing effects that can ever be defined as genetic. Evolutionary change leading to speciation is necessarily genetic at its inception and throughout the operation of selective forces, but the achievement of speciation implies the fixation of basic species-specific traits into a nonsegregating, hence "nongenetic" condition (Boklage, 1978).

The departures we observe are themselves patterned, and subject to apparent restrictions in their range and character. There is both a reduction of the predictability of relationships among the lateralities of the various functions over non-right-handers as a group and an apparent increase in flexibility of lateralization in programming. And there are limits to both. The left-handed analog of the usual "complete" right-handedness is quite rare, as is fully right-brained speech (Satz, Achenbach, & Fennell, 1967; Satz, Chapter 7 of this volume). We also observe a saving effect of unusual laterality (even when it occurs only among relatives of the victims) on recovery from aphasia (Satz, Chapter 7 of this volume; Zangwill, 1960) and on the severity of schizophrenic psychosis (Boklage, 1977a). Include the concept of relative focalization (Semmes, 1968) as a variable in a developmental process (see Brown & Jaffe, 1975, and especially Taylor, 1977), and a useful step toward a unifying hypothesis seems to emerge. It is difficult to isolate the qualitative lateral component of brain tissue specialization (which may represent a misleading dichotomization to begin with) from its quantitative and developmental, temporal aspects. In particular, sex-related differences in rate and extent of lateralization will probably require some such approach for successful explanation (Ounsted & Taylor, 1971; Taylor, 1969, 1974, 1975, 1977).

The non-right-handed minority differs in the direction of lateralization of a variety of traits, in the predictability of the directional relationships among traits, and in the degree of concentration of functions. Our list of usable clues to the number and nature of factors that may be involved seems too short. We seem not to have enough estimable parameters to solve for the apparent number of unknowns, either in the usual pattern of hemispheric differences, or in the ways it can be changed. The parameters of handedness, speech, and writing posture, all (probably falsely) dichotomized or at best awkwardly quantified, simply have not been enough.

Even at the level of the simple right-handed–left-handed dichotomy, there exists in the literature no definition or classification criterion with which a critical thinker can be comfortable. Attempts to generate quantitative measures (e.g., Oldfield, 1971) have all been based on lists of dichotomies, quantitative only in summing over the list and fitting the sum to a quasicontinuous distribution. This approach is inherently less informative than would be the use of continuous variables, but its real worst fault seems to lie in the arbitrarily equal weights assigned to the various dichotomies. Writing (together with speech, perhaps dance, and some musical performance, certainly among the most complex motor outputs of which the human is capable) takes its place alongside hammer and spoon as equally considered indicators. Although it is conceivable that this might not be wrong, I can not be comfortable with its arbitrariness. There is an opportunity for someone to do this field of endeavor a substantial service by discovering how the members of the "unusually lateralized" minority might most accurately be identified, so that their differences might most productively be analyzed.

Meanwhile, from the perspective of cellular biology, the fundamental relevance of at least one factor is clear. No matter what the character of the usual left–right differences in brain function, and even regardless of the nature and relative importance of various qualitative and quantitative aspects of minority changes, the existence of left–right differences in function demands the existence of left–right differences in structure. There could not be a nonrandom left–right pattern of differences in function without there being a means for function-assigning processes to discriminate, left from right, which tissue is to be programmed for which function. At least one determinant must be more or less purely structural, and must be traceable to the cellular processes responsible for the general differentiation of the left and right sides of the body.

The rudimentary organization of body (a)symmetry is visibly complete in the human embryo at about 14 days after conception (Moore, 1973), and must, therefore, be determined at the level of cellular commitments to differentiated developments at a still earlier point. That cellular events occurring in the first week or two of human development may have important effects on the organization of the adult human mind may be illustrated by the results of a new approach to the twin-study analysis of schizophrenia.

Twin studies have been important to both sides of the nature–nurture question in schizophrenia for a long time. The much higher concordance for schizophrenia in monozygotic (MZ) than in dizygotic (DZ) pairs has been important evidence, consistent with every other pairs-of-relatives comparison, for important genetic contributions to the causes of schizophrenia (Gottesman & Shields, 1972, for review).

On the other hand, the fact that concordance in MZ pairs is a good deal less than 100%—actually about 50–60%—has become by default the sole surviving evidence for the invocation of important "environmental" contributions. Be that as it may, several well-executed adoption studies have shown that the risk of developing illness is not reduced by being raised out of contact with biologic relatives one or more of whom are schizophrenic. Nor is the risk of illness raised for the nonbiologic relatives of the foundlings who become psychotic in their adoptive homes (Heston, 1966). Do these findings reflect an "environmental" factor not related to the presence of a schizophrenic in the family social environment, prenatal environment, or a perinatal effect? Perhaps, but Kety, Rosenthal, Wender, Schulsinger, and Jacobsen (1975) indicates that adopted-away paternal halfsiblings, who share only a sperm donor, seem to run at least as high a risk as maternal halfsiblings who shared maternal "cytoplasmic" contributions and uterine environment as well as some of the mother's genes. However, in the Kety *et al.* study, the sample is as yet too small to justify certitude in this, its most critical observation.

A mixture of unspecified "genetic" and "environmental" causative factors has been put forward to give the uneasy blessing of half-hearted concensus to this standoff (Gottesman & Shields, 1972, for review). Please, beware of that word "environmental." When "environmental" is placed in opposition to "genetic" *it is the error term* in equations modelling the effects of hypothesized Mendelian factors, and includes, exactly, everything except the effects of those factors and interactions specifically entered in that particular mathematical model. Some genetic modellers are careful to point this out, some are not; rarely is it made as clear as it should be for audiences not limited to statistically trained geneticists. In the case of schizophrenic twin concordance studies, one observable remainder—non-right-handedness—turns out to carry with it almost all of the previously unexplained variation (Boklage, 1977a). The results of studies on that point, briefly reviewed, are as follows:

1. Twins of both zygosities are roughly twice as often non-right-handed as are singletons.
2. Parents of twins, of both zygosities, are about twice as often non-right-handed as are their own same-sexed siblings.
3. Monozygotic twin pairs selected for schizophrenia-in-either-member include another approximately twofold excess over normal twins in frequency of non-right-handedness.
4. That highly significant excess is concentrated in pairs discordant for schizophrenia. The schizophrenia–concordant pairs have the same fraction of non-right-handed members as do normal MZ twins, whereas virtually every schizophrenia–discordant pair has at least one non-right-handed member (Table 3.1).

To isolate the major genetic implication of this finding: If twin pairs with non-right-handed members are removed from the dataset, on the premise that non-right-handedness represents unusual brain organization which might nosologically contaminate the sample (the same way a careful researcher might remove cases involving a suspicion of "organicity"), then the MZ pairs that remain are 92% concordant pairwise for schizophrenia, versus 10% in DZ twins or singleton siblings of schizophrenics. The conclusions one may draw from this result differ greatly from those offered by a result of 50–60% (Gottesman & Shields, 1972; Boklage, 1977a).

Certain aspects of this work, along with important work by Taylor (1975, 1977), Gruzelier and Venables (1974), Gruzelier and Hammond (1976, 1977), Flor-Henry (1969, 1974, 1976) and Gruzelier and Flor-Henry (1979) produce a very strong suspicion that schizophrenia is a disorder primarily of left-hemisphere functions, and that affective psychosis may be the "mirror image" disorder. In this particular twin sample, for instance, four of the five diagnoses of depression were given to right-handed twins of non-right-handed schizophrenics.

The differences related to handedness in these schizophrenic twins go yet deeper. The schizophrenic members of MZ pairs in which either member was non-right-handed spent less time in the hospital, were given lower

Table 3.1
Handedness in Normal Twins, their Relatives, Schizophrenic Twins,
and its Relationship to Concordance for Schizophrenia

A. *Handedness of twins relative to singletons*

White male Veteran twins, 45–55 years of age, questionnaire self-
assessment (NAS-NRC Medical Follow-up Agency; a correction of data
in Boklage, 1977a)

Monozygotic	69 LH / 500 twins	= .134
Dizygotic	65 LH / 528 twins	= .123

1975–1977 questionnaire survey of member families of the National
Organization of Mothers of Twins clubs

all twins in 773 families:

Monozygotic	176 LH / 794 twins	= .222
Dizygotic	163 LH / 752 twins	= .217

all twins 6 yrs. or older:

Monozygotic	32 LH / 210 twins	= .153
Dizygotic	50 LH / 228 twins	= .220

Other twin surveys, plus singleton surveys, reviewed by Springer
(Chapter 4, this volume)

B. *Handedness in parents of twins and same-sex siblings of parents-of-twins
from 1975-1977 survey of National Organization of Mothers of Twins
Clubs (NOMOTC) families (all reported by parents)*

Mothers of twins	101 LH / 773	= .131
Maternal aunts of twins	73 LH / 949	= .077
Fathers of twins	135 LH / 773	= .175
Paternal uncles of twins	95 LH / 1003	= .095

C. *Handedness in twins selected for [schizophrenia in either pair member]*

Monozygotic	19 LH / 56 twins	= .339
Dizygotic	8 LH / 66 twins	= .121

D. *Handedness relative to pairwise concordance for schizophrenia*

	Concordant pairs	Discordant pairs
Both right-handed	11	1
Either or both Non-right-handed	4	12

(C and D after Boklage, 1977a)

Global Psychopathology Ratings, could much less often be characterized as
having a schizophrenic illness of a nuclear subtype, and had one half the
frequency of schizoid premorbid personalities (Table 3.2).

An exponential analysis of lengths of hospital stays using this same sample reveals that there are two kinds of sick spells occurring in the group,
one type having a much lower remission rate than the other, and tending to
occur after a series of shorter hospitalizations (Boklage, Elston and Potter,
1979). The members of right-handed monozygotic pairs have the majority
of the "long" spells (Table 3.3).

It is not simply that the schizophrenics from the MZ pairs with non-

Table 3.2
Handedness Relative to Severity of Schizophrenic Illness in Monozygotic Twin Pairs

	Both members right-handed (N = 16)	Either-or-both non-right-handed (N = 26)	Fisher's exact significance levels of differences
Not working at close of study	11	7	0.0094
Total hospitalized 1 year or more	12	9	0.0123
Total hospitalized 2 year or more	9	4	0.0075
Global psychopathology rating ≥ 5.5/7.0	10	5	0.0061
Global psychopathology rating ≥ 6.0/7.0	8	1	0.0017

Note: For comparisons of Nuclearity and Premorbid Personality distributions, refer to Boklage, 1977a.

Table 3.3
Number of Hospitalizations of 75 weeks or more, or less than 75 weeks, by Zygosity and Handedness within Monozygotic Pairs

Recurrences in cases from pairs	"Long," ≥ 75 weeks	"Short," ≤ 75 weeks	
Monozygotic, both right-handed	14	57	(19.7% "long")
Monozygotic, either or both non-right-handed	5	50	(9.1% "long")
Dizygotic	7	117	(5.6% "long")

$\chi^2_2 = 12.76, p < 5 \times 10^{-4}$

right-handed pair members "aren't really schizophrenic"; they received the same average number of "votes" from the panel of six (three English, two American, and one Japanese) diagnosticians. However, most of this subgroup did not rate the stricter Scandinavian diagnosis, and most of them received subtype diagnoses which hedge away from the "core" of the syndrome (e.g., schizoaffective, atypical, reactive, pseudoneurotic, and the like). The diagnosis of schizophrenia for research purposes remains a delicate proposition, and differences in the diagnostic range from one investigation to the next continue to exert important influence on results. The effects I am discussing here would all have vanished had the diagnosis been done entirely by Scandinavian criteria (Table 3.4).

In writing about this effect to date I have treated it as an interaction effect exerted by some developmental correlate of unusual laterality on the penetrance of a (presumed unitary) genotypic predisposition to schizophrenia. It could conceivably represent the existence of two, developmen-

Table 3.4
Scandinavian Diagnosis (by Erik Essen-Möller) versus Concensus Diagnosis (Gottesman & Shields, 1972), by Zygosity and Handedness within Monozygotic Pairs

Cases from pairs	Scandinavian diagnosis:		Concensus schizophrenics
	"True schizophrenia" or "schizophreniform psychosis"	Other	
Monozygotic, both right-handed	12	3	15
Monozygotic, either or both non-right-handed	6	10	16
Dizygotic	27	9	36

$\chi_i^2 = 8.54$, $p < 0.025$

tally distinct, paths leading to a schizophrenic outcome. That would require a rather more complex explanation of the results, which only family segregation studies could verify. For a variety of preliminary reasons the possible existence of two paths seems to deserve further consideration.

There is only one pair in this sample of 28 MZ pairs that is discordant for schizophrenia without having a non-right-handed pair member. Furthermore, all of the above-mentioned distributions hold with high significance when either member of the pair is non-right-handed, yet none of these effects is significant when the comparisons are done by way of *individual* handedness. This last observation provides a serious obstacle to any effort to relate these effects to trauma or pathology affecting the individual. The real but often too casually invoked "birth stress" of twinning has been shown to be almost exclusive to the second twin born (Derom & Thiery, 1976). In this open-ascertainment sample of schizophrenic twin pairs, there is a nonsignificant excess of *first*born twins among either the schizophrenic or the non-right-handed subsample. In another MZ sample, selected as rigorously as possible for discordance in (presumably, therefore, "nongenetic") schizophrenia, a majority of the schizophrenics are the secondborn of the pair (Pollin, Stabenau, Mosher, & Tupin, 1966; Pollin & Stabenau, 1968). The "birth stress" effects of twinning are in general significantly more frequent and severe among males than females (Hay & Wekrung, 1970; Myrianthopoulos, 1976); but the results from this sample are quite independent of sex. Further, while the "birth stress" of twinning is by no means confined to MZ twins, these effects of handedness among MZ pairs selected for schizophrenia are not found to operate significantly among the DZ pairs. In fact, there is a weak, but intriguing, suggestion of a reciprocal relationship.

Where non-right-handers are greatly over-represented among MZ schizophrenics, they are nonsignificantly under-represented among DZ schizophrenics. Although non-right-handedness in MZ pairs strongly predicts concordance and relatively mild illness, it nonsignificantly associates with concordance and relative severity in DZ pairs. Carter-Salzman and her colleagues (1976) led me to heed this weak, but consistent, relationship in these data, and only on the interest of their findings do I bother to mention my weaker ones. In three of five cognitive tests they administered to a sample of twins (Raven Progressive Matrices, Columbia Test of Mental Maturity, and Peabody Picture Vocabulary) they found that the observed correlations between handedness and test scores were significantly opposite in direction for the two zygosity groups of handedness-discordant pairs.

Whether you want to believe that deviations from "normal" right-handedness represent obviously useful genetic variation in an evolving biologic program, or rather some manner of pathological development, the use of unusual laterality as an index has helped to remove the last remaining evidence for any major involvement of nonbiologic factors in the origin of schizophrenia. It has contributed major support to a theory of schizophrenia as a cellular brain-development disorder involving lateralized functions. It has produced profound uncertainties in behavioral applications of the century-old twin-study technology (Galton, 1875; Elston & Boklage, 1977), and it has raised serious doubts in at least my mind as to the prevailing theories of the cellular origins of twins of both zygosities.

Some very intriguing questions are raised by a surprising complex of observations; (a) that there can be special relationships between the development of brain-function asymmetry and each of two mechanisms of twinning thought to be quite unrelated cellularly; (b) that some of these special relationships are the same and some quite different between zygosities; and especially (c) that some of these effects act significantly on the pair as a unit and not on the individual. What is held in common by the predominantly single-born parents of twins which correlates with their handedness as compared with the handedness of their non-twin-producing siblings? What can happen to distinguish the development of twins of both zygosities from that of singletons including their own siblings? Among those differences, what further can happen to MZ twin pairs that either does not happen to DZ pairs or must happen differently, and that might exert strong influences upon multiple aspects of brain asymmetry development, and especially upon different aspects of brain development for each twin? These questions lead to an examination of the first few days after conception of human life, where the development of MZ, DZ, and singleton embryos may differ in a symmetry-related way.

Monozygotic twinning must itself be considered as an anomaly of embryonic symmetry development. Two separate body symmetries must be

constructed from a group of cells that are somehow programmed to produce a single bilateral body symmetry in 99.7% of viable human embryos.
Many of us still think of identical twins as embarking upon separate
destinies after the first cleavage of the fertilized egg, in crude analogy to the
results of separating the first two blastomeres of the starfish. In fact, about
70% of MZ twins are born in the same outer membrane (Bulmer, 1970), indicating that they were together at least until after the cells which form the
chorionic membrane differentiated around them. Chorion differentiation
usually happens on about the fourth day, at a definitely multicellular stage
(see Moore, 1973). It should be stated early in this discussion, and em-
phatically, that we have in fact *no* clear idea of the cellular mechanisms by
which twinning of either zygosity occurs.

The literature on MZ twinning is based on imagining some sort of division of the embryo into two subsets of cells that must go on to form
separate embryos. That such a physical separation must occur at some
point, albeit rarely incomplete in the case of conjoined pairs, *does not*
mean that it must be the initial event in an MZ twinning process, even
given that in some much simpler creatures an artificial division of that sort
may lead to a roughly analogous result.

The mouse is the most complex animal from which we have experimental
evidence bearing on this point. Monozygotic twinning has been estimated
to occur in the mouse with a frequency higher than that in humans (1% according to Wallace & Williams, 1965 versus 0.38% according to Bulmer,
1970). Yet in thousands of experiments in which inner-cell-mass cells from
different strains of mice, or even from rats, have been placed into whole
mouse blastocysts, twinning has never resulted, but rather in all cases fusion occurred to form a single embryonic mass of mixed cell type (Gardner,
personal communication, 1974). If we can extrapolate that observation to
the human at even the grossest level, it would seem reasonable to suppose
that there is something special about embryos that produce and unfold two
or more separate development-organizing schemata within an otherwise
undisrupted inner cell mass.

With no further concern about the quite unknown nature of the twinning
"split," but vaguely aware of a dependence on its timing and direction, we
go on to imagine that each twin embryo receives a variable proportion of
cells that would normally form part of a right side for the body but that
now must form a whole left side, and vice versa. In some "splits" this effect
might be imagined to produce unusual development in only one twin, in
other splits it might affect both. Additionally, this "split" could presumably
affect some aspects of body symmetry and not others, again depending on
the stage of development already reached by the cells involved.

We will presumably not see live normal twins born of "divisions" that are not reasonably equal. There is, further, no way to estimate how many people are born as singletons following grossly unequal "twinning" events. Monozygotic twins are unique not only in being genetic clones of $N = 2$, but also in that they are the only live humans known to have undergone at least temporary disruptions of early embryonic development in a time span coinciding with cellular definition of bilateral symmetry. Knowing as little as we do about what that may mean in terms of subsequent cellular development, there is very little to keep us from imagining that every left hander in the world is the survivor of just such an embryonic disturbance. By such a process, non-right-handedness, and twinning, could arise from genomic factors only weakly correlated with the corresponding phenotypes of relatives, and perhaps better explained by the transmission of a subtle pleiotropic developmental instability (Layton, 1976).

I am sometimes asked to comment on the phenomenon known as mirror imaging in MZ twins. At face value, it is a simple concept to appreciate. For example, the outer ears of each twin may have different shapes, and the shape of the left ear of one twin may match that of the other twin's right ear. This sort of difference may occur in any of several facial features, hair-whorls, handprints, and conceivably any other feature, whether or not within a normal range of development, for which both twins are asymmetric. In practice, it is normally noticed only in traits derived from the embryonic ectoderm.

The term "mirror imaging," however, has been applied to discordance in twins for handedness and dichotic ear dominance, ostensibly with the same meaning (Springer, Chapter 4 of this volume). The nervous system is in fact derived from the same embryonic cell layer that is responsible for the development of the skin and all its derivatives. The cells in the bilaminar disc embryo that are responsible for brain development are surrounded immediately on three sides by cells that will form the skin of the head and face. From there they fold down and inward to form the neural tube, and the skin structures of face, head, and back close over it in a zipperlike fashion.

Thus brain symmetry development could be subject to some of the same processes which may result in "mirror imaging" for nearby skin structures. "Mirror imaging" in brain functions is, in fact, much more frequently observable than that in other features, because it essentially always fulfills the requirement of being a feature in which both twins display noticeable asymmetry. In most twin studies of handedness, about a third of the pairs are discordant for handedness. This is much more frequent than the observation of mirroring in ear wrinkles and the like. As usual, however, the observation is not so difficult as is the interpretation. The standard presumption is that "mirror imaging" results from each embryo being derived primarily from opposite lateral "halves" of the original embryo, each replacing its "missing half" from developmental potential not yet fully committed.

That much is conceptually very simple—deceptively simple; it almost sounds as if we know what that means. We do not, as I explained above, but a few conceptual limits may be put in place. To begin with, no preprogrammed asymmetry can in any such simple way be mirror imaged. A "left half" would replace a missing "right half" either with normal right-sided structure or with something more like the left side or otherwise anomalous, depending on the remaining uncommitted developmental potential, and vice-versa for the "right half." The left-half embryo would still be left-sided on its left side; the right half still right-sided on its right side. Although it is conceivable that these original halves could suffer some changes due to the compensations they might have to perform in their subsequent separate developments, what would result would not be a mirror image with respect to the original preprogrammed asymmetry. It might, however, be mirror imaged with respect to any matching anomaly in the replaced "missing halves"; one twin anomalous on the right side, the other anomalous on the left.

This latter possibility might arise whether or not the trait in question was originally programmed to be asymmetric. So it remains a reasonably imaginable possibility that aspects of brain function laterality might be subject to such embryonic "mirror imaging" as a consequence of MZ twinning. However, the form it might take is by no means obvious. We do not know what kinds of developmental anomalies are possible in these tissues, which anomalies allow survival, which may be fully functional, and which dysfunctional. Among the possible and survivable dysfunctional consequences, we do not know which consequences would be subtle, which would be prominent and pervasive, which would show effects directly, and which only through other cell groups interacting either in development or in ongoing function.

There may be much in these obvious questions or in less obvious others, that might eventually force abandonment of the notion that embryonic "mirror imaging" explains anything about handedness discordance in MZ twins. Meanwhile, there are two ideas that already caution us severely against a simplistic application of the concept of mirror imaging. The first is the realization that it merely begs a question by explaining one phenomenon with another which itself can not be explained. The second is the observation that, with barely detectable differences, the distribution of handedness in MZ twins is the same as that in DZ twins, whose origins are not thought to involve any splitting of embryos. It can not be said that cellular disturbances of embryogenesis could play no part at all in handedness discordance of MZ twin pairs. But it can be said firmly that we presently have no clear idea what part, if any, they may play, or how. Such cases as the pairs mentioned earlier wherein the left-hander is schizophrenic and the right-hander depressive, or another pair group of similar size with two left-handed members, one schizoaffective and one diagnosed as an inadequate personality, will keep the question intriguingly open.

With what frequency, for example, do there occur MZ pairs in which one twin has unusual left-brain function and the other, unusual right-brain function? Is such pairing really typical of handedness-discordant MZ pairs, as the concept of mirror imaging seems to imply? If non-right-handedness is considered to be an anomaly of left-brain function, frequently attributed in MZ twin pairs to "mirror imaging," should we not expect right-handed members of mixed-handed MZ pairs to include a high proportion of people with anomalous right-brain function? The pairs mentioned above, with left-handed schizophrenic and right-handed depressive members, support that possibility, but their numbers hardly call for its being given much generality. Does the similarity in distributions of handedness between MZ and DZ twins and their families really arise from independent mechanisms?

What about the apparently special relationships in brain symmetry also seen in DZ twins? It is common knowledge that DZ twins are the product of separate ovulations, and that there should be no cause to invoke embryonic disturbances. It happens that this knowledge is of a very common sort indeed, for there is not a shred of proof. The only critical evidence in existence bearing on the point is a report in the literature of one pair of twin fetuses, DZ with probability in excess of 90%, in the ovaries accompanying which *only one corpus luteum* could be found (Wieman and Weichert, 1936). This sample of one represents an alternative that cannot presently be excluded. Dizygotic twins must be the product of separate gametes, but in at least some cases those gametes may be the products of an unusual division of one primary, or more likely secondary, oöcyte—the normal immediate precursors of the ovum in its development.

In reducing the egg pronucleus to a half-set of chromosomes for union with the sperm's half-set, the normal process throws out one whole set and one half-set of chromosomes as polar bodies, essentially spare nuclei with little or no cytoplasm. If one of those divisions were more equal (i.e., more symmetrical) than it should be, yielding two fertilizable gametes, then DZ twinning could broadly be viewed as an anomaly of symmetry development at a subcellular level. The abstriction of the polar bodies involves the movement of the spindle, in meiotic cell divisions, far away from the center of the oöcyte, and its rotation through 90° in the cytoplasm, to place one end against the membrane (Austin, 1951; see Figure 1), normally resulting

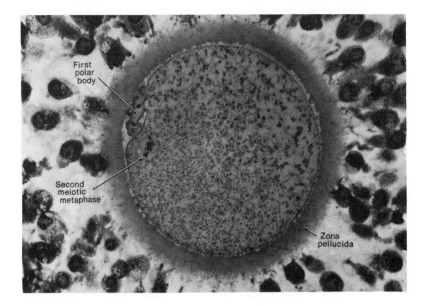

Figure 3.1: Human secondary oöcyte, showing first polar body and second meiotic spindle in position for abstriction of second polar body. Separation of two distinct patterns of cytoplasmic staining approximately along diameter through the position of the first polar body. After L. Zamboni, Figure 33–18, p. 874, in Bloom and Fawcett, A Textbook of Histology, Tenth Edition, courtesy W. B. Saunders Co., Philadelphia

in the most extreme possible asymmetry of cell division. It would be at least as simple biochemically to produce the failure of either component of that spindle movement, as to allow two instead of one follicle (out of hundreds in apparently equivalent stages of development) to ripen into an oöcyte.

The possibility of this kind of twinning has previously been considered (e.g., Mijsberg, 1957), but its prevalence has been subjected to estimation based on the erroneous assumption that the maternal genetic contribution to such "polar body" twins would be identical. Only in the total absence of sister-chromatid recombination could this be true, an unlikely circumstance by current measurements of the frequency of recombination in the human. Protocols for a new test are now being developed which we believe will not only be theoretically correct, but which should also be more powerful (Elston & Boklage, 1977). In addition to the special symmetry relationships of both kinds of twins, there are a few other observations more simply explained by this model. These have to do, for example, with anomalies of chromosome number (Mai, 1974). This is not really an odd juxtaposition, since the chromosomes are segregated in meiosis by the same programmatically displaced spindle.

From twin data there can also be derived a fairly firm assertion that the basic bilateral symmetry of the human body is irreversibly committed at least as early as the time of differentiation of the inner, amnionic membrane on about day 7, which is 6 or 7 days before the embryo's symmetry becomes visible in the microscope. About 32% of MZ twins separate before the outer membrane, the chorion, differentiates on about day 4 or 5. About 97% of viable MZ pairs achieve separation before the amnion forms on about day 7; that is, they are born in separate amnions within a common chorion (Table 3.5). Separation as late as amniogenesis is developmentally very dangerous; such twins include all conjoined twins, most of the twin births in which the body symmetry of only one twin is complete, and a good many apparently otherwise normal twin pairs in which one or both members is dead from knotting of the umbilical cords (Foglmann, 1976). Conjoinment may occur at nearly any point on the head or trunk, usually side-by-side, but always by corresponding parts of the anatomy. It represents, therefore, incomplete separation of the two body symmetries.

It seems, in short, that MZ twinning is an unusual way of doing what the embryo usually does in the process of laying out body symmetry, as most of each process occurs in the time span during which the inner cell mass is rearranging itself into the bilaminar disk stage, between day 4 and day 7 (Figures 3.2 and 3.3.) Shortly thereafter, the full three-axis symmetry is visibly fixed by the appearance of the prochordal plate and primitive streak, which mark anterior and posterior respectively, and thus left and right by reference to the dorsoventral axis already established by the polar orientation of the inner cell mass within the blastocyst (Moore, 1973). Even in MZ pairs whose basic body symmetries are well separated, other anomalies are apparently in excess, as MZ twins are grossly overrepresented among cases of anencephaly, spina bifida, and midline neurological abnormalities, all of which represent failures of the symmetrical closure of the neural tube from which the nervous system must develop (Nance, 1969; Davies, Chazen, & Nance, 1971).

Over all published twin samples, pooled data indicate that the distribution of handedness is essentially perfectly binomial among DZ pairs; among MZ pairs there is a small deficit of handedness-discordant pairs, significant only in large pooled samples (Boklage, 1977a). In an unpublished study of 40 pairs of MZ twins by Satz and his colleagues, dichotic ear advantage also fit closely to a binomial distribution among the pairs. The usual strong association between right-handedness and dichotic right-ear advantage is not significantly observed in this twin sample, probably

Table 3.5
Chorionicity and Amnionicity in Twin Pairs

Frequency of dichorionic and monochorionic placentae in monozygotic twin pairs

Dichorionic N (%)	Monochorionic N (%)	Reference
297(33.3)	595(66.7)	Totals from Bulmer's (1970) review of 10 reports, minus Corney, Robson, and Strong (1968) and Edwards and Cameron (1967), each replaced by later totals from the same group
47(28.8)	116(71.2)	Edwards, Cameron, and Wingham (1967)
48(30.1)	111(69.9)	Myrianthopoulos (1970)
45(37.5)	75(62.5)	Nylander (1970)*
42(27.8)	109(72.2)	Fujikura and Froehlich (1971)*
28(18.5)	123(81.5)	Corney, Robson, and Strong (1972)*
12(35.3)	22(64.7)	Nylander and Corney (1975)* *reviewed by MacGillivray, Nylander, and Corney (1975)
519(31.08)	1151(68.92)	31.8% dichorionic overall ± 2.73%; 2σ, 95% confidence interval of the estimated proportion

Frequency of monoamnionic twin pairs

Monoamnionic N (%)	Diamnionic N (%)	Reference
40(1.26)	3144(98.74)	Totals from Bulmer's 1970 review of 10 reports, minus Corney, Robson, and Strong, replaced by later total from the same group
13(0.452)	2865(99.55)	Totals from Simonsen (1966) review of 13 studies
9(1.44)	615(98.56)	Myrianthopoulos (1970)
10(2.15)	455(97.85)	Fujikura and Froelich (1971)
8(1.49)	528(98.51)	Corney, Robson, and Strong (1972)
80(1.04)	7607(98.96)	1.04% of all twin pairs ÷ 0.304 MZ pairs/all pairs (Bulmer's 1970 estimate over pooled European populations studies mid-1950s to mid-1960s
		3.34% of MZ twin pairs monoamnionic ± 0.74%; 2σ, 95% confidence interval of the estimated proportion

Remainder, 65.58%, ± 2.83%, monochorionic, diamnionic

due in part to a very stringent definition of left-handedness. This reduced the left-handed subsample to a marginal size for hypothesis testing, and probably placed some incompletely lateralized subjects among the right-handers, increasing the frequency of their failure to demonstrate right-ear advantage, but not significantly. Dr. Springer (Chapter 4 of this volume) has tested a larger sample of twins more critically, and will hopefully clarify this particular issue.

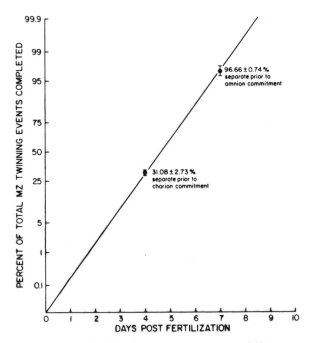

Figure 3.2: Normal Probability Plot of Time Distribution of Monozygotic Twinning Events, as Inferred from Chorionicity and Amnionicity.

I have reviewed the evidence here and elsewhere (Elston & Boklage, 1977; Boklage, 1977b) for asserting that the large departure from full concordance in handedness among MZ twins cannot straightforwardly be used as evidence against a genomic determination. I believe the relationships discussed in this chapter call for the interpretation that, almost regardless of how handedness may prove to be programmed, the twin data tell us where and when the cardinal programming effect is exerted—in the first eight days of embryogenesis. The word "cardinal" is chosen to represent the assertion that all further development of laterality hinges on the basic outline established in these early cellular steps. Any left–right functional difference derives at least part of its definition from the existence of left and right, and may begin only when there exists a left and a right to be prepared for different uses.

However, we still have not traced the basic bilateral symmetry to its source. The vast majority of animal species are bilaterally symmetrical; even apparent exceptions like starfish and sea urchins have bilaterally symmetrical larval forms, traces of which remain in the adult. In many organisms, it is clear that the basic organization of the body symmetry is laid down in the structure of the egg, as evidenced by gradients of

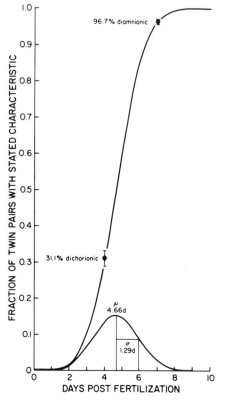

Figure 3.3: Cumulative Distribution and its first-derivative normal curve, corresponding to plot in Figure 3.2.

cytoplasmic constituents, by fixed point of sperm entry, or by variable point of sperm entry (this point then defines a pole of the body symmetry), or by an axis defined by a polar body on one side and a polar lobe diametrically opposite.

We have very little information about the determinants of symmetry in mammals, and virtually none in the primates as embryologic study is vastly more difficult in viviparous organisms. In the rat, the first few divisions are independent of the orientation of visible cytoplasmic gradients. However, cells derived from the pole with most of the dark RNA granules end up on one side, whereas cells with many vacuoles and little RNA are found on the other side, from whence they migrate to envelop the high-RNA cells that will become concentrated in the embryogenic inner cell mass (Jones-Seaton, 1950). So the dorsal-ventral axis, at least, is defined in some subcellular correlate of that vacuole-to-RNA gradient (just as it is for frogs and sea urchins). The control is not exerted on the orientation of the cleavage spindle in the first few divisions, but is apparently exerted through the cell–surface interactions responsible for the later relative migration.

The first few cleavages of the human egg may be predicted by cytoplasmic structure, but the available sample of very early human embryos is much too small for drawing a conclusion. Figure 3.1 seems to show two distinct patterns of cytoplasmic staining on opposite sides of the diameter through the first polar body, parallel to the axis of the second meiotic spindle. Figure 3.4, quite independently obtained, seems to show a similar difference between the first two blastomeres, perhaps not incidentally seen to have divided on a similar plane through the polar bodies visible in the upper notch between the blastomeres.

Whether the human embryo uses one of these mechanisms for establishing its symmetry, or some other mechanism, it is unreasonable to suppose

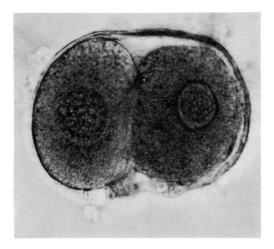

Figure 3.4: Two-cell human embryo, showing cleavage of first two blastomeres in plane through the position of polar bodies, at least one of which is visible in upper notch between blastomeres. Notice difference in patterns of cytoplasmic staining between blastomeres. After Hertig, Rock, and Adams, Figure 33-35A, p. 891 in Bloom and Fawcett, A Textbook of Histology, Tenth Edition, courtesy W. B. Saunders Co., Philadelphia

that it could be free of the need to pass information about its symmetry development from one generation to the next through this stage of its development (Boklage, 1978). Where then is this information encoded? In the organisms examined to date, there is no measurable RNA synthesis during the first few cleavages (i.e., no detectable messages being sent from the genes in the nucleus, *de novo*). The developmental program is being run on information already expressed, enzymes already synthesized or coded for in stable messages, and/or "template" structure already laid down in the egg cortex or in local variations of the concentration of components of the cytoplasm. This is information that was laid down well before conception, in cells that (according to the dominant theory of egg formation) have not divided or grown since the mother was an embryo (*cf.* Davidson, 1976, for review). Here are the first expressions of our normally symmetric-asymmetric development. Anything that comes later must build from this foundation. And here too are the first places in which causes of deviations from the plan, or choices of alternatives, might operate.

Whatever you may imagine about the nature of brain tissue specializations underlying functional asymmetries; at whatever level you may imagine them to operate (cortical, ganglionic, thalamic, or some mixture); either different kinds of cell networks must be elaborated as substrate for laterally different functions, or the same kind of cell network does different jobs because it is differently programmed or differently activated through the functioning of other cell networks that *are* laterally differentiated. Something must know left from right on the basis of cellular, mechanochemical, or structural information, usually knows it well, and is built from cells that knew where they were going before your mother suspected she was pregnant.

SUMMARY

It is possible, from direct observation and straightforward deduction, to state that the basic (a) symmetries of the human body are established at a cellular level in the first two weeks of gestation. All further elaborations of asymmetric form and function derive at least part of their specification from these early cellular events.

Monozygotic twinning events represent temporary disruptions of the normal course of these events. Two body symmetries must be formed from a group of cells that are somehow programmed to produce one bilaterally symmetrical body in 99.7% of viable human embryos. Depending on the timing and directionality of the twinning split, some of the earliest cellular commitments to lateralized differentiations must, with some probability, be diverted from the timing and/or directionality of their normal elaboration. Monozygotic twins are unique not only in being clones of two, but also in being the only humans known to have undergone early, temporary disturbances of embryonic (symmetry) development.

This line of reasoning promotes what seems a promising new approach to the study of aspects of usual and unusual human mental development in which brain functional asymmetries may be of fundamental importance. This chapter has concerned itself with the givens, assumptions, and implications of this approach, and some results from applying it to the study of the genetics and neuropsychology of schizophrenia.

REFERENCES

Austin, C. R. Observations on the penetration of the sperm into the mammalian egg. *Australian Journal of Scientific Research*, 1951, 4:581

Bakan, P. Why left-handedness? *The Behavioral and Brain Sciences*, 1978, 1(2):279-280.

Boklage, C. E. Schizophrenia, brain asymmetry development, and twinning: A cellular relationship with etiologic and possibly prognostic implications. *Biological Psychiatry*, 1977a, 12(1):19.

Boklage, C. E. Embryonic determination of brain programming asymmetry-A caution concerning the use of data on twins in genetic inference about mental development. *Annals of the New York Academy of Sciences*, 1977b, 299:306.

Boklage, C. E. (1978) On cellular means of heritably transmitting structural information. *The Behavioral and Brain Sciences*, 1978, 1(2):282-286.

Boklage, C. E., Elston, R. C., & Potter, R. H. Cellular origins of functional asymmetries: Evidence from schizophrenia, handedness, fetal membranes and teeth in twins. In J. H. Gruzelier & P. Flor-Henry (Eds.) *Hemisphere asymmetries of function and psychopathology*. London: Elsevier-North Holland, in press.

Brown, J. W. & Jaffe, J. Hypothesis on cerebral dominance. *Neuropsychologia*, 1975, 13:107.

Bulmer, M. G. *The biology of twinning in man*. Oxford: Clarendon Press, 1970.

Carter-Salzman, L., Scarr-Salapatek, S., Barker, W. B. & Katz, S. Left-handedness in twins: Incidence and patterns of performance in an adolescent sample. *Behavior Genetics*, 1976, 6(2):189.

Davidson, E. H. *Gene activity in early development*, (2nd ed.). New York: Academic Press, 1976.

Davies, J., Chazen, E., & Nance, W. E. Symmelia in one of monozygotic twins. *Teratology*, 1971, 4(3):367.

Derom, R. & Thiery, M. Intrauterine hypoxia—A phenomenon peculiar to the second twin. *Proceedings of the First International Congress on Twin Studies, Acta Geneticae Medicae et Gemellologiae*, 1976, 25:314.

Edwards, J. H., Cameron, A. H., & Wingham, J. *The Birmingham twin survey*, cited in S. J. Strong & G. Corney, *The placenta in twin pregnancy*. Oxford: Pergamon Press, 1967.

Elston, R. C. & Boklage, C. E. (1977) An examination of fundamental assumptions of the twin method. In W. E. Nance, G. Allen, & P. Parisi (Eds.), *Twin research, part A—Psychology and methodology*, Vol. 24A, *Progress in clinical and biological research*. New York: Alan R. Liss, Inc. 1978.

Flor-Henry, P. Psychosis and temporal lobe epilepsy: A controlled investigation. *Epilepsia,* 1969, *10*:363.

Flor-Henry, P. Psychosis, neurosis, and epilepsy: Developmental and gender-related effects and their ætiological contributions. British Journal of Psychiatry, 1974, *124*:144.

Flor-Henry, P. Lateralized temporal-limbic dysfunction and psychopathology. *Annals of the New York Academy of Sciences,* 1976, *280*:777.

Foglmann, R. (1976) Monoamniotic twins. *Proceedings of the First International Congress on Twin Studies, Acta Geneticae Medicae et Gemellologiae,* 1976, *25*:62.

Galton, F. The history of twins as a criterion of the relative powers of nature and nurture. *Journal of the Royal Anthropological Institute of Great Britain and Ireland,* 1875, *5*:391–406.

Gottesman, I. I. & Shields, J. *Schizophrenia and genetics: A twin-study vantage point.* New York: Academic Press, 1972.

Gruzelier, J. H. & Flor-Henry, P. (Eds.) *Hemisphere asymmetries of function and psychopathology.* London: Elsevier-North Holland, in press.

Gruzelier, J. H. & Hammond, N. V. Schizophrenia: A dominant hemisphere temporal-limbic disorder? *Research Communications in Psychology, Psychiatry, and Behavior,* 1976, *1*:33.

Gruzelier, J. H. & Hammond, N. V. The effect of chlorpromazine upon bilateral asymmetry of bioelectrical skin reactivity in schizophrenia. *Studia Psychologica,* 1977, *19*:40.

Gruzelier, J. H. & Venables, P. H. Bimodality and lateral asymmetry of skin conductance orienting activity in schizophrenics: Replication and evidence of lateral asymmetry in patients with depression and disorders of personality. *Biological Psychiatry,* 1974, *8*:55.

Harris, H. (1975) *The principles of human biochemical genetics,* (2nd ed.). Amsterdam: North-Holland Publ. Co., 1975.

Hay, S. & Wehrung, D. A. Congenital malformations in twins. *American Journal of Human Genetics,* 1970, *22*:262.

Heston, L. L. Psychiatric disorders in foster-home-reared children of schizophrenic mothers. *British Journal of Psychiatry,* 1966, *112*:819.

Jones-Seaton, A. Étude de l'organisation cytoplasmique de l'oeuf des rongeurs, principalement quant à la basophilie ribonucleique. *Archives Biologique, Paris,* 1950, *61*:291–444. (cited in B. I. Balinsky, *An introduction to embryology,* Philadelphia: Saunders, 1960)

Kety, S. S., Rosenthal, D., Wender, P. H., Schulsinger, F., & Jacobsen, B. Mental illness in the biological and adoptive families of adopted individuals who have become schizophrenic: A preliminary report based on psychiatric interviews. In *Genetic research in psychiatry,* R. R. Fieve, D. Rosenthal, & H. Brill, (eds.). Baltimore: Johns Hopkins University Press, 1975.

Layton, W. M., Jr., (1976) Random determination of a developmental process: Reversal of normal visceral asymmetry in the mouse. *The Journal of Heredity,* 1976, *67*:336.

Macgillivray, I., Nylander, P. P. S., & Corney, G. (1975) *Human multiple reproduction,* London: Saunders, 1975.

Mai, L. L. Down syndrome in twins: Lack of evidence for independence of non-disjunction and dizygotic twinning, *Anthropology UCLA,* 1974, *6*(1).

Mijsberg, W. A. Genetic-statistical data on the presence of secondary oöcytary twins among non-identical twins. *Acta Genetica,* 1957, *7*:39.

Moore, K. L. *The developing human,* Philadelphia: Saunders, 1973.

Myrianthopoulos, N. C. Congenital malformations in twins. *The Proceedings of the First International Congress on Twin Studies, Acta Geneticae Medicae et Gemellologiae,* 1976, *25*:331.

Nance, W. E. Anencephaly and spina bifida: A possible example of cytoplasmic inheritance in man. *Nature,* 1969, *224*:373.

Oldfield, R. C. The assessment and analysis of handedness: The Edinburgh inventory. *Neuropsychologia*, 1971, 9:97.

Ounsted, C. & Taylor, D. C. (eds.). *Gender differences: Their ontogeny and significance*, London: Churchill Livingstone, 1971.

Pollin, W., Stabenau, J. R., Mosher, L., & Tupin, J. Life history differences in identical twins discordant for schizophrenia. *American Journal of Orthopsychiatry*, 1966, 36:492.

Pollin, W. & Stabenau, J. R. Biological, psychological and historical differences in a series of monozygotic twins discordant for schizophrenia. In *The transmission of schizophrenia*, D. Rosenthal, S. S. Kety, (eds.). London: Pergamon Press, 1968.

Satz, P., Achenbach, K., & Fennell, E. Correlations between assessed manual laterality and predicted speech laterality in a normal population. *Neuropsychologia*, 1967, 5:295.

Semmes, J. Hemispheric specialization: A possible clue to mechanism. *Neuropsychologia*, 1968, 6:11.

Simonsen, M. Monoamniotic twins. *Acta Obstet. Gynec. Scand.*, 1966, 45:43.

Taylor, D. C. Differential rates of cerebral maturation between sexes and between hemispheres. *Lancet*, 1969, ii, 140–142.

Taylor, D. C. (1974) The influence of sexual differentiation on growth, development, and disease. In *Scientific foundations of paediatrics*, J. Davies, and J. Dobbing, (eds.). London: Heinemann, 1974.

Taylor, D. C. Factors influencing the occurrence of schizophrenia-like psychosis in patients with temporal-lobe epilepsy. *Psychological Medicine*, 1975, 5:245.

Taylor, D. C. Epileptic experience, schizophrenia, and the temporal lobe. *McLean Hospital Journal*. Special Issue. June 1977, 22–39.

Wallace, M. E. & Williams, D. A. Monozygotic twinning in mice. *Journal of Medical Genetics*, 1965, 2:26.

Wieman, H. L. & Weichert, C. K. An unusual double human pregnancy with a single corpus luteum. *Anatomical Record*, 1936, 65:201.

Zangwill, O. L. *Cerebral dominance and its relation to psychological function*. London: Oliver and Boyd, 1960.

4

Left-Handedness in Twins: Implications for the Mechanisms Underlying Cerebral Asymmetry of Function[1]

SALLY P. SPRINGER
ALAN SEARLEMAN

INTRODUCTION

The high incidence of left-handedness in twins, roughly twice that of the singleton population according to some reports (Carter-Saltzman, Scarr-Salapatek, Barker, & Katz, 1976; Stocks, 1933), poses an interesting challenge to those concerned with the factors determining handedness. The increase, present in both monozygotic (MZ) and dizygotic (DZ) twins, derives primarily from a large number of pairs discordant for handedness, with one member of a pair predominantly right-handed and the other member predominantly left-handed (Rife, 1940).

Collins (1970) has computed the proportion of right-handers and left-handers among MZ twins from data compiled by Newman, Freeman, and Holzinger (1937), Wilson and Jones (1932), and Rife (1940, 1950), and calculated expected frequencies for the three intrapair handedness relationships (R/R, R/L, L/L) assuming the pairs are binomially, that is, randomly, distributed. The resulting frequencies did not differ significantly from those actually observed. A similar calculation for DZ pairs produced equivalent results.

Dizygotic twins are a consequence of the fertilization of two separate eggs and hence are no more similar genetically than siblings born at different times (Bulmer, 1970). They do have, however, an average of 50% of their genes in common. Therefore, a genetic model of handedness would

[1] This research was supported by NIMH Grant RO3MH27101.

NEUROPSYCHOLOGY
OF LEFT-HANDEDNESS

predict a nonchance relationship between the handedness of one member of a pair and that of his cotwin. An even stronger relationship would be expected for MZ pairs as MZ twins are genetically identical, the end product of the division of a single embryo early in development to form two individuals (Bulmer, 1970). Collins (1970) concluded that the knowledge of one twin's preference provides no additional information regarding the hand usage of the cotwin, and that the twin data provide no support for the view that hand preference is determined by genetic factors.

Nagylaki and Levy (1973) have argued that it is inappropriate to test predictions of a genetic model of handedness with twin data because special mechanisms operate to produce the handedness patterns observed in twins. The logic of the twin study method as a tool for investigating heritability requires that the trait under consideration occur with the same frequency and be affected by the same factors as in singletons. Nagylaki and Levy (1973) suggested that pathogenic effects (affecting all twins), and mirror imaging (occurring only in MZ pairs), can account for the high incidence of discordance among twins.

In this chapter we will review the literature dealing with handedness in twins and the factors hypothesized to account for the elevated rates of sinistrality. Many of the ideas to be considered in this regard are modern versions of theories prevalent in the 1920s and 1930s. Although early investigators interested in handedness and twinning were aware of an association between hand preference and hemispheric asymmetry of function (Newman, 1928), it is only relatively recently that behavioral tools have become available enabling the study of cerebral organization in neurologically intact subjects (Kimura, 1961). In addition, new findings have suggested that cognitive abilities may vary as a function of handedness (Levy, 1969; Miller, 1971). We will examine what little is known about the consequences of being a left-handed twin from these two perspectives, and present the results of our own investigation of the relationship between handedness and brain organization in twins. While we agree with Nagylaki and Levy (1973) that there are difficulties associated with using twins to test genetic models of handedness, we feel that important insights concerning the mechanisms operating to produce brain laterality may be gleaned from twin studies.

THE INCIDENCE OF SINISTRALITY AMONG TWINS

Consistent estimates of the incidence of left-handedness among twins have been difficult to obtain. This problem, however, is not limited to twins alone. Indeed, contemporary estimates of left-handedness in the general population range from a low of 1% to a high of 30% (Hardyck & Petrinovich, 1977).

One factor contributing significantly to the variability from study to study in both twin and singleton groups is the lack of consensus among researchers concerning just how handedness should be measured. Many investigators determine handedness through simple self-classification or the use of questionnaires, whereas others observe which hand is used to perform various tasks such as writing or throwing a ball. The relative strength and/or dexterity of the two hands is used to categorize individuals in studies that employ such measures as grip strength or speed of finger tapping. In their review of the literature on the incidence of left-handedness in the general population, Hardyck and Petrinovich (1977) demonstrate that the incidence figures from various studies are closely related to the method of handedness determination used in those studies.

A second, related source of variability derives from the fact that handedness is best conceptualized as a graded characteristic that varies along a continuum. As such, it requires the establishment of somewhat arbitrary criteria for assigning individuals to one of the two handedness classifications. To the extent that studies differ in the way this assignment is made, variability is introduced.

Sociocultural factors are also responsible, in part, for the differences in the frequency of left-handedness that have been reported. Levy (1976) has shown that the incidence of sinistral writers increased monotonically over the 40 year period, 1932–1972, an increase she attributed to relaxation of cultural pressure to be right-handed. She supported this view with data from Pyle and Drouin (1932) showing that 7.5% of the children in the Detroit school system in 1932 were left-handed writers compared with 2.2% of the children in other school systems. The Detroit school system was notable at the time for the absence of pressure toward dextrality exerted by teachers.

Additional evidence for the importance of social influence on manifested handedness has been reported by Teng, Lee, Yang, and Chang (1976). They conducted a questionnaire survey on handedness in a large Chinese population in Taiwan, where social pressure for right-handed writing and eating is still strong. Out of 4143 subjects, 0.7% used the left hand for writing. This is strikingly lower than the value of 6.5% observed in a sample of 538 Oriental school children living in the United States (Hardyck, Goldman, & Petrinovich, 1975) where cultural pressures to write with the right hand have been relaxed.

Ideally, one would want to restrict attention to those studies that included MZ, DZ, and singleton subjects of the same age and cultural background and tested in the same manner, to achieve greater accuracy in determining the relative incidence of sinistrality in these populations. Unfortunately, few studies meet such criteria (Wilson & Jones, 1932). Table 4.1 tabulates the distribution of handedness relationships among MZ twins, DZ twins, and singletons compiled by a number of different investigators.

When the results of the different studies are combined, it is clear that the incidence of sinistrality in both MZ and DZ twins is substantially greater than that found in singletons ($p < .001$ in each case). The incidence of left-handedness ranges from 8.3% to 31.0% for the MZ samples, and from 6.0% to 19.3% for the DZ samples. The range for singletons was 4.3% to 9.6%. The frequency of left-handedness collapsed across all studies did not differ significantly for the MZ and DZ pairs.

FACTORS RESPONSIBLE FOR ELEVATING
THE INCIDENCE OF SINISTRALITY AMONG TWINS

Pathogenic Factors

The pathogenic model of left-handedness holds that as a consequence of damage to the hemisphere genetically programmed to control handedness, a certain percentage of individuals will experience a shift in manifested handedness (Gordon, 1920; Satz, 1972, 1973). Assuming that 90% of all individuals are genotypically left-hemisphere dominant, and thus would normally develop into right-handers, such damage to the right hemisphere would not be reflected in a handedness shift in most cases, although left hemisphere damage would be expected to produce a sizable number of so-called "pathological left-handers" (Satz, 1972, 1973).

The model of pathological left-handedness receives support from the observation that significantly higher percentages of left-handers may be found among such clinical populations as stutterers, epileptics, the learning disabled, and the mentally retarded (Bingley, 1958; Hécaen & Ajuiaguerra, 1964; Hildreth, 1949; Palmer, 1964). For example, Gordon (1920) reported that the incidence of left-handedness was 7.3% in regular elementary schools whereas it was 18.2% in schools for the mentally defective. He concluded that the brain damage responsible for cerebral dysfunction produced the increase in left-handedness as well.

Indices of cerebral pathology are found to be in excess among both MZ and DZ twins. Rosanoff, Handy, and Plesset (1937), Allen (1955), and Allen and Kallman (1955) report a high rate of mental abnormality among twins. Howard and Brown (1970) have indicated that the incidence of pathology observed in twins warrants the consideration of twinning as a marker for biological insults. The link between handedness and pathology

Table 4.1
Handedness Distributions

Investigator	Monozygotic Twin Pairs			
	R/R	R/L	L/L	
Gordon (1920)[a]	116	21	1	
Siemens (1924)[b]	26	10	1	
Weitz (1924)[b]	10	7	1	
Lauterbach (1925)[a]	115	22	6	
Dahlberg (1926)[b]	89	29	5	
von Verschuer (1927)[b]	58	16	5	
Newman (1928)[c]	25	19	6	$p(L) = .145$
Hirsch (1930)[c]	25	18	0	
Wilson and Jones (1932)	56	13	1	
Stocks (1933)	35	6	1	
Newman, Freeman, and Holzinger (1937)	30	17	3	
Rife (1950)	231	76	6	
Carter-Saltzman, Scarr-Salapatek, Barker, and Katz (1976)	132	46	9	

Investigator	Dizygotic Twin Pairs			
	R/R	R/L	L/L	
Gordon (1920)[a]	53	25	3	
Lauterbach (1925)[a]	48	14	1	
Dahlberg (1926)[b]	111	16	1	
von Verschuer (1927)[c]	28	10	0	
Newman (1928)[c]	35	13	2	
Hirsch (1930)[c]	51	7	0	$p(L) = .140$
Wilson and Jones (1932)	55	13	1	
Stocks (1933)	44	8	1	
Newman et al. (1937)	39	11	3	
Rife (1950)	164	45	2	
Carter-Saltzman et al. (1976)	115	54	7	

Investigator	Singletons		
	R	L	
Gordon (1920)	3057	241	
Wilson and Jones (1932)	482	39	
Stocks (1933)	156	7	$p(L) = .085$
Rife (1940)	3273	269	
Hardyck, Goldman, and Petrinovich (1975)	6947	741	

[a] Frequencies based on same sex versus opposite sex classification
[b] Cited in Newman (1928)
[c] Cited in Wilson and Jones (1932)

in twins is provided by an observation made by Gordon (1920), the first investigator to propose that the incidence of left-handedness in twins is attributable in part to pathogenic factors associated with twinning. Out of 219 twin pairs, he found 8 handedness discordant pairs in which the left-handed cotwin was in a school for the mentally retarded whereas the right-hander was not. He noted that his sample did not contain any discordant pairs in which only the right-handed twin attended a school for the mentally defective.

Taken together, these findings are consistent with the hypothesis that some of the increase in sinistrality observed in twins is attributable to pathogenic factors related to the twinning process. It is important to note, however, that an elevated incidence of sinistrality occurs even in twin samples drawn from a normal population for which there are no additional signs of cerebral insult. Although this poses a problem for the pathological model of left-handedness, it is possible that sophisticated measures of brain function would reveal the subtle effects of the minimal brain damage thought to underlie the increased incidence of left-handedness in presumably normal twins.

Position *in Utero*

Several investigators have suggested that the position of the fetus in *utero* may affect subsequent hand preference (Wilson & Jones, 1932; Rife, 1940). They note that fetal position *in utero* for twins differs considerably from that of singletons and that, in some way, this may be responsible for the high incidence of discordance.

This model of left-handedness in twins has not been elaborated upon, however, and Carter-Saltzman *et al.* (1976) note that an adequate evaluation of it would require, among other things, information regarding the amount of rotation and shifting of position occurring prenatally in twins as well as the prenatal stage at which handedness is presumably determined. They conclude that there is little evidence to support the position *in utero* theory. It is also unclear whether this hypothesis should be considered separately from the pathogenic model of left-handedness discussed in the previous section.

Of historical interest is the suggestion made by Danforth (1919) that the position taken by the twins *after* birth may be important in determining handedness. He noted that twin babies generally face each other in their cribs, and if they are not frequently moved their heads may become asymmetrical on opposite sides. Danforth (1919) concluded that "this may possibly affect the hemisphere of the brain differently and certainly influences the amount of use that is made of the left hand in one infant and the right in the other [p. 400]."

Mirror Imaging

The term "mirror imaging" refers to the phenomenon, reported by Newman (1928, 1937), among others (Dahlberg, 1926; Rife, 1940), that MZ pairs are frequently discordant for handedness and other bodily asymmetries (e.g., eye dominance and direction of head-hair whorl). Newman (1928) proposed that the presence of reversals of this nature within a twin pair were a consequence of the stage in development at which the twinning event occurs.

Monozygotic twins, it will be recalled, result from the division of a single embryo to form two individuals. The best embryological evidence to date indicates that such a division may produce two viable offspring at any time during the early development of the embryo up to 2 weeks following ovulation. Visible signs of differentiation are present by Day 4, and by Day 14 the previously radially symmetrical germ disk starts to show bilateral symmetry with the formation of the axis of the primitive streak (Nance, 1959). Approximately two-thirds of all MZ twinning events are believed to occur between Day 4–14 (Macgillivray, Nylander, & Corney, 1975). See Boklage (Chapter 3 of this volume) for a more complete discussion of the embryology of twinning.

Newman (1928) proposed that there is considerable variation from pair to pair in the developmental stage at which twinning takes place, and that those twins separating before the establishment of bilateral symmetry and asymmetry would be concordant for various asymmetries, whereas those dividing subsequent to it would exhibit intrapair differences. Newman's own research with the nine-banded armadillo, an animal that characteristically produces MZ quadruplets, supported these views. The second stage in the process that produces armadillo quadruplets takes place during the establishment of the axis of symmetry, and Newman (1928) observed numerous instances in which markings appeared on the left side of one armadillo twin and on the right side of another. He states that "by analogy, we may infer that twinning in man takes place in close association with, and possibly as an aberration of, the process of establishing and fixing the relations of symmetry and asymmetry in the embryo [Newman, 1928, p. 312]."

Newman (1928) believed that there were two distinct kinds of handedness. One form of handedness was genetically determined whereas the other was a consequence of twinning. He referred to the latter as "epigenetically determined." In the absence of twinning, genetic factors will determine the handedness of the individual. Similarly, such factors will determine the handedness of both members of a twin pair if twinning occurs before any asymmetry is fixed in the developing embryo. Thus, given that the original embryo was genetically right-handed, both twins would develop as right-handers. If twinning takes place after the initial bodily asymmetry has been established, however, the left half of the embryo will develop into a right-handed individual, reflecting the contralateral relationship between dominant hand and dominant hemisphere, while the right half would form an epigenetically left-handed individual.

Fifty years after Newman proposed it, the possible role played by such a mirror imaging mechanism in the development of human twins is still controversial (Bulmer, 1970; Macgillivray *et al.*, 1975; Rife, 1940; Torgerson, 1950). Although mirror imaging is briefly mentioned in many of the sources discussing the embryology of twinning, very little in the way of new evidence either supporting or refuting the mirror-imaging hypothesis has been advanced in the ensuing years.

THE RELATIONSHIP OF HANDEDNESS, CEREBRAL ORGANIZATION, AND COGNITIVE ABILITIES IN TWINS

Our own investigations of laterality in twins involved 122 same-sex twin pairs, 75 MZ and 47 DZ. Using writing hand as a criterion, 88 of the pairs were both right-handed (R/R), whereas 19 MZ and 8 DZ pairs were discordant; one right-handed and one left-handed (R/L). Of the remaining 7 pairs, 2 were MZ and left-handed (L/L), 3 were DZ L/L, and 1 MZ and 1 DZ pair had at least one ambidextrous member. The twins ranged in age from 13–38, with a mean age of 17.6. Zygosity was determined by serological analysis of the ABO, Rh, MNSs, Kell, and p systems (Race & Sanger, 1975) or by a zygosity questionnaire previously shown to determine zygosity with 95% accuracy (Cohen, Dibble, Grawe, & Pollin, 1973).[2]

The primary purpose of our work was to determine if the variation in direction and extent of hemispheric asymmetry for the perception of speech in right-handers had a heritable component. This involved a comparison of the intrapair differences for MZ R/R twins on measures of hemispheric asymmetry with that of DZ R/R twins. The results of these analyses may be found in Springer and Searleman (1978). The study also yielded valuable data, to be considered here, concerning the general relationship between handedness and brain laterality in twins, and the relationship of handedness and performance on various tests of verbal and spatial abilities in twins.

Dichotic listening was used to provide a measure of degree and direction

---

[2] There were four additional pairs for which zygosity could not be determined with certainty. These pairs were not included in any of the data analyses.

of hemispheric asymmetry in speech perception. Kimura (1961) had demonstrated that when two different spoken messages are simultaneously presented to subjects through headphones, one message to each ear, most right-handed subjects are better able to report the material delivered to the right ear. She interpreted her findings as reflecting the specialization of the left hemisphere for speech in most people as well as the suppression, at some level, of ipsilateral ear–cortex connections during dichotic presentation. Subsequent dichotic listening work with patients previously tested with sodium amytal to determine the hemisphere controlling language confirmed that subjects showed superior performance in the ear opposite the hemisphere housing the speech center.

The dichotic listening test employed in the present study involved single pairs of consonant–vowel syllables selected from among the sequence pa, ta, ka, ba, da, ga. Similar stimuli have been shown to produce a right-ear advantage in right-handers, and possibly to reflect an underlying continuum of hemispheric asymmetry for the processing of speech in the general population (Shankweiler & Studdert-Kennedy, 1967; 1975). Subjects received two exposures to a 120 pair dichotic tape and were asked to write down the first letter of each of the two sounds heard on a trial. Results were analyzed in terms of the ϕ coefficient (Kuhn, 1973),[3] a positive value of which indicates a right-ear advantage whereas a negative value indicates a left-ear advantage, and the total number of correct identifications regardless of ear (TC). The TC scores were not correlated with the ϕ values. Split-half reliability corrected for attenuation exceeded .90 for both measures.

To provide a more complete picture of the hand preferences of the twins, each was asked to complete a Crovitz and Zener (1962) questionnaire which asks which hand is used to perform various tasks. Scores on the questionnaire can range from 14, for a strongly right-handed individual, to 70, for a strongly left-handed individual. In addition, each twin pair was asked if any members of their immediate family was left-handed or ambidextrous. Twins answering affirmatively were considered to have a family history of sinistrality (FS+) whereas twins not reporting left-handers in their immediate family were classified as having a negative history of familial sinistrality (FS−). Rife (1940) and others have reported that both MZ and DZ twin pairs that are discordant for handedness have a higher incidence of FS+ than concordant R/R pairs. We sought to determine if a similar relationship would be observed in our sample. In addition, several

---

[3] Considerable controversy exists concerning the most appropriate measure of ear asymmetry in the dichotic task. We employed several different measures, discussed in more detail in Springer and Searleman (1977). Results did not vary greatly as a function of the measures used and we report ϕ scores here as a representative measure.

recent studies (Hines & Satz, 1971: Zurif & Bryden, 1969) have reported that FS+ singletons differ from their FS− counterparts in terms of cerebral organization so we examined this possibility as well with our data.

The pairs discordant for handedness were also observed to determine the manner in which they positioned their hand when writing. Levy and Reid (1976) reported a relationship between normal and inverted (i.e., hooked position with hand primarily above the line of writing) hand posture and contralateral and ipsilateral hemispheric control of speech, respectively. Left-handers who wrote in a hooked fashion are those who showed left-hemispheric specialization for language, whereas straight writers appeared to have right-hemispheric specialization. Similar relationships were reported to hold for right-handers as well. We sought to determine if the hand postures of discordant pairs would vary as a function of zygosity, and if hand posture would be related to performance on dichotic listening tests.

Table 4.2 displays the mean ϕ, handedness, and TC scores for the 53 MZ and 35 DZ R/R twin pairs and a right handed singleton group. Table 4.2 also presents the incidence of FS+ and the number of individuals showing a right-ear advantage for the three groups. There were no significant differences on any of these measures for the MZ–DZ comparisons, nor for either zygosity group tested against the singleton sample.

Table 4.3 presents a similar display of data obtained from the 27 R/L pairs, the right-handed singletons, and a group of left-handed singletons. The "I" column indicates how many individuals in each group showed the inverted hand posture. Left-handers had lower ϕ scores than right-handers in all three groups, but the difference was significant only in the MZ group ($p < .05$). As expected, the Crovitz and Zener scores were significantly higher for the left-handed members of each group ($p < .01$). Total correct performance did not differ significantly as a function of handedness,

Table 4.2
Test Scores as a Function of Zygosity for Right-Handed Twin Pairs

Pair type	ϕ	Handedness	Total correct	Frequency of positive family history	Right ear advantage
Monozygotic (N = 53)	.142	21.3	338.9	23 (43%)	92 (87%)
Dizygotic (N = 35)	.139	21.3	336.5	14 (40%)	56 (80%)
Singletons (N = 30)	.117	20.6	335.8	12 (40%)	24 (80%)

Table 4.3
Test Scores as a Function of Zygosity for Discordant Twin Pairs

Pair type	ϕ	Hand	TC	FS+	REA	I
Monozygotic						
Left Hand						
(N = 19)	.018	54.7	355.4	8 (42%)	13 (68%)	5 (26%)
Right Hand						
(N = 19)	.120	20.4	346.5	8 (42%)	17 (89%)	0
Dizygotic						
Left Hand						
(N = 8)	.032	50.2	337.5	6 (75%)	5 (63%)	3 (38%)
Right Hand						
(N = 8)	.145	20.2	316.1	6 (75%)	6 (75%)	0
Singletons						
Left Hand						
(N = 20)	.040	58.8	361.7	12 (60%)	13 (65%)	10 (50%)
Right Hand						
(N = 30)	.117	20.6	335.8	12 (40%)	24 (80%)	1 (3%)

although there was a tendency for the left-handers to outperform right-handers in each of the three groups. Neither left- nor right-handed MZ twins differed significantly on hand posture, ϕ scores, or TC performance from their DZ counterparts or the appropriate singleton groups.

The incidence of FS+ did not vary significantly when both MZ and DZ groups were compared with each other and separately with each of the singleton groups, nor was FS+ significantly different for either MZ or DZ pairs when compared to their R/R counterparts. This latter observation is at variance with the observation of Rife (1940) that discordant MZ and DZ pairs had a greater incidence of FS+ than concordant pairs. For singletons, the incidence of FS+ for left-handers was not significantly greater than that found among right-handers.

The findings relating the ϕ scores to FS+ are complex and will be only briefly mentioned here. We expected to find that FS+ individuals, regardless of handedness, would show smaller ϕ scores than those individuals without left-handers in their immediate family. Contrary to expectation, FS+ left-handed twins had significantly higher ϕ scores than FS− twins ($t_{25} = 3.18$, $p < .01$). Similar results, although not significant, were obtained for left-handed singletons. Right-handed cotwins showed a difference in the same direction that did not approach significance. At this point we have no explanation for these findings.

The incidence of handedness inversion among left-handers was not significantly different for MZ and DZ pairs, nor for either group when compared to singletons. However, although the differences were not significant, the left-handed cotwins of MZ pairs discordant for handedness appear to have a lower incidence of hand posture inversion than either their DZ counterparts or left-handed singletons. Although this difference may well be due to sampling error associated with the small sample size, this observation is consistent with the hypothesis that discordance for handedness in MZ pairs is often reflected in discordance for hemispheric asymmetry of function as well. The data of Levy and Reid (1976) suggest that left-handed noninverted writers have right-hemispheric specialization for speech and language.

The hypothesis that hand posture is related to cerebral organization as measured by dichotic listening was tested by comparing the mean ϕ score for the left-handed inverted twins to the mean ϕ scores for the left-handed noninverted twins, collapsing across zygosity. The scores of the inverted twins were significantly greater ($t_{2s} = 2.48$, $p < .02$). A similar comparison for the right-handed cotwins of these individuals did not approach significance. Although these findings are consistent with Levy and Reid's (1976) model, an analysis of the ϕ scores for inverted and noninverted left-handed singletons was not significant, with the means falling in the opposite direction.

To complete our presentation of these data, Table 4.4 displays the various measures for the remaining seven pairs of twins. Five of these pairs are L/L, while one contains two ambidextrous (A/A) individuals and one contains a right-hander and an ambidextrous cotwin. Although sample size precludes meaningful statistical analysis, scores on all variables for the left-handed or ambidextrous individuals are consistent with those found for the left-handed members of L/R discordant pairs, whereas the lone right-handed twin in this display obtained a ϕ score typical of that of right-handers.

Hand–Brain Organization Relationships in Twins

Boklage (Chapter 3 of this volume) has suggested that, as a consequence of the disruption of the gradients that are responsible for the development of bilateral asymmetry in many MZ pairs, the relationship between handedness and brain organization in such twins is random. Our data argue strongly against this view.

The data indicate that whatever processes are responsible for handedness discordance in MZ twins, they extend to cerebral organization as well. That mirror imaging may be the important factor is suggested by the comparison of MZ with DZ discordant pairs. Dizygotic discordant pairs in some percentage of the cases are discordant presumably because of genetic

Table 4.4
Test Scores as a Function of Zygosity for Left-handed and Ambidextrous Twin Pairs

Pair type		ϕ	Hand	TC	FS+	REA	I
Monozygotic							
L/L (N = 2)		.077	54.8	320.2	1	3	0
A/A (N = 1)	Twin 1	−.042	37.0	345.0	1	0	0
	Twin 2	−.048	36.0	307.0	1	0	0
Dizygotic							
L/L (N = 3)		.067	58.7	339.8	2	3	3
R/A (N = 1)	Twin 1	.190	26.0	281.0	1	1	0
	Twin 2	−.038	39.0	295.0	1	0	0

differences, whereas the remainder may involve pathological left-handers. Monozygotic pairs, however, cannot involve genetic differences, and hence discordance may be attributable to mirror imaging and pathogenic factors. The extent to which MZ pairs are more discordant than DZ pairs may be due to the mirror imaging mechanism.

To test this possibility, intraclass correlations were calculated for MZ and DZ pairs for ϕ and TC scores. The MZ correlation for ϕ was $-.34$ whereas it was $+.09$ for DZ. Although the size of the sample precluded these values attaining conventional levels of significance, the data suggest the MZ discordant pairs have a greater percentage of their total variance occurring within a twin pair than DZ twins. The TC measure, however, produced a correlation of $+.81$ for MZ and $+.16$ for DZ twins, consistent with the hypothesis that TC performance has a heritable component that is not affected by handedness discordance.

In summary, the data from MZ and DZ R/R and R/L pairs suggest that handedness–brain organization relationships are similar to those found among singletons, and that whatever factors are responsible for discordance also result in discordance for brain organization to a greater extent in MZ than DZ twins. Mirror imaging is suggested as a possible mechanism, operating only among MZ pairs, that might be responsible for this difference.

Handedness and Cognitive Abilities in Twins

In addition to dichotic testing, 26 of the 27 discordant pairs were given a battery of verbal and spatial abilities tests. These tests were administered in collaboration with Richard Harshman and Sheri Berenbaum. Performance on the tests may be examined to determine if discordance for handedness has implications for the cognitive function of twins. The three tests of spatial ability employed were the Spatial subtest of the Thurstone Primary Mental Abilities Test (1962), Surface Development (French, Ekstrom, & Price, 1963), which involves mentally folding boxes into three-dimensional structures, and the Harshman Figures Test which is a gestalt completion task. Tests of verbal ability included Nonsense Syllogisms (French et al., 1963) which required the subject to decide if a given conclusion followed necessarily from a set of premises, and Word Beginnings and Endings (French et al., 1963) which asked the subject to list as many words beginning and ending with particular letters as possible in a three-minute period. A sixth test, Number Comparisons (French et al., 1963), is a test of perceptual speed that required the subject to scan pairs of multidigit numbers for a possible mismatch. The mean scores, corrected for guessing, for each test by zygosity and hand are given in Table 4.5.

The differences between the scores of the left- and right-handed members

Table 4.5
Mean Scores on Cognitive Tests as a Function of Zygosity and Hand

Pair type	PMA space	Surface development	Harshman figures	Nonsenses syllogisms	Word beginnings and endings	Number comparisons
Monozygotic (N = 19)						
Left Hand	69.6	13.3	5.3	2.1	10.4	20.6
Right Hand	73.2	14.4	4.4	.6	10.2	21.6
Dizygotic (N = 7)						
Left Hand	84.3	15.7	5.9	2.7	9.7	16.9
Right hand	71.4	10.1	5.1	2.3	7.9	13.1

of the MZ twin pairs were not significantly different for any of the tests. For DZ pairs, the only test where the difference between the scores of left- and right-handed cotwins attained significance was Surface Development $(t_6 = 2.81, p < .05)$, in which the left-handed twins attained a higher mean score. This superior performance by the left-handed DZ cotwins was reflected, although not significantly, in the remaining five tasks. Monozygotic–dizygotic comparisons were statistically insignificant on all tests except Number Comparisons, where right-handed MZ twins were superior to their DZ counterparts $(t_{24} = 3.73, p < .01)$.

The left–right comparisons in the present study are at variance with the findings obtained by Carter-Saltzman et al. (1976) in which different patterns of performance were found for MZ and DZ discordant pairs on a battery of cognitive tests. In their study, MZ left-handers did better than their right-handed cotwins on the Ravens Progressive Matrices, the Columbia Test of Mental Maturity, and the Peabody Picture Vocabulary Test, whereas among DZ twins the right-handers were superior to their left-handed cotwins. The difference reached statistical significance, however, only in the Columbia Test of Mental Maturity.

The Peabody and Columbia tests are primarily verbal in nature, while the Ravens test measures nonverbal reasoning. Two additional tests, the Benton Revised Visual Retention Test and a paired associate learning test, both measuring spatial or nonverbal abilities were administered as well in the Carter-Saltzman et al. (1976) study, but these did not show any differences between handedness groups for either zygosity.

Our own findings indicate that left-handed DZ twins perform better than right-handed cotwins on both verbal and spatial abilities tests. Even though this pattern of results is not consistent with the findings of Carter-Saltzman et al. (1976), it does argue, as they do, that left-handedness is not necessarily associated with a cognitive deficit in spatial abilities as proposed by Levy (1969). We had hoped that the pattern of results in the cognitive tests would reflect the presumed differences in the etiology of left-handness in the two twin groups. The fact that our sample is small and that the findings conflict with those of Carter-Saltzman et al. (1976) suggest that further research will be required before this goal will be realized.

CONCLUSIONS

We have reviewed evidence showing that the incidence of left-handedness in twins, resulting primarily from the existence of a large number of pairs discordant for handedness in both MZ and DZ groups, is considerably above that found in the singleton population. Although the proportion of left-handers is similar for both MZ and DZ groups, it is likely that different mechanisms are responsible for handedness discordance in the two twin groups. There is reason to believe that discordance in MZ twins may be due to either pathological or mirror imaging factors. Among DZ pairs, genetic differences between cotwins probably play a significant role, though pathological factors may also contribute to the incidence of discordance in the group.

Our own research sought to determine if such differences in the mechanisms presumed to underlie sinistrality in MZ and DZ twins would be reflected in other measures. In particular, if mirror imaging effects are responsible for handedness discordance in some MZ twins, these effects may extend to cerebral organization as well. Three aspects of our data support this hypothesis. First, intraclass correlations calculated for MZ and DZ pairs using the ϕ coefficient scores suggest that a greater proportion of the total variance in these scores is attributable to variation within twin pairs in the MZ group than in the DZ group. This is contrasted with the non-laterality-related TC scores that show less variation within pairs for MZ twins than DZ twins. Second, when left- and right-handers are compared on the basis of their ϕ scores, the MZ twins are the only group to produce a statistically significant difference. Third, the incidence of hand inversion among MZ discordant pairs is lower, though not significantly, than that found in DZ pairs and left-handed singletons. If, as Levy and Reid (1976) suggest, normal writing posture in left-handers reflects right hemispheric specialization for language, these data are consistent with the hypothesis that left-handed MZ twins are more likely to be right-hemisphere dominant.

Admittedly, each of these pieces of evidence taken alone is not strong and is at best suggestive. A better test could be made if MZ pairs showing other signs of asymmetry reversal in addition to handedness could be identified. The handedness–brain organization for these pairs could then be compared with those obtained from discordant pairs not showing other signs of mirror imaging. In the present work we endeavored to determine the direction of head-hair whorl in discordant pairs. Such a determination proved exceedingly difficult in many cases and reliability was so low that the resulting data were useless. More sophisticated indices of asymmetry may be obtained from dental casts and x-rays, as well as dermatoglyphics, and future studies employing such procedures should provide important information regarding mirror imaging and its consequences.

The wide variety of research reported in this volume leads unavoidably to the conclusion that many different factors are potentially responsible for the hand preference shown by a given individual. There is considerable evidence to indicate that hand preference is heritable, although pathological and sociocultural pressures exert their effects as well. Levy and Nagylaki (1972) have argued that handedness is transmitted from generation to generation in Mendelian fashion, whereas others have suggested that information coded in the cytoplasm of the egg, rather than nuclear DNA, is the determining factor (Morgan, 1977).

Although these two forms of inheritance make different predictions, as yet not adequatedly tested, with regard to the patterns of handedness among relatives, they would both ultimately influence handedness through their effects on the developing embryo. Boklage (Chapter 3 of this volume) states that "regardless of how handedness may prove to be programmed, the twin data tell us where and when the cardinal programming effect is exerted—in the first eight days of embryogenesis." [p. 131]. Our preliminary data suggest that a similar statement may be true for hemispheric asymmetry of function as well.

REFERENCES

Allen, G. Cases of cerebral palsy in a series of mentally defective twins. *American Journal of Mental Deficiency*, 1955, *59*, 629–639.

Allen, G., & Kallman, F. J. Frequency of mental retardation in twins. *American Journal of Human Genetics*, 1955, *7*, 15–20.

Bingley, T. Mental symptoms in temporal lobe epilepsy and temporal lobe gliomas with reference to laterality of lesion and the relationship between handedness and brainedness. *Acta Psychiatrica et Neurologica*, 1958, *33*, Supplement 120.

Bulmer, M. G. *The biology of twinning in man.* Oxford: Clarendon Press, 1970.

Carter-Saltzman, L., Scarr-Salapatek, S., Barker, W. B., & Katz, S. Left-Handedness in twins: Incidence and patterns of performance in an adolescent sample. *Behavior Genetics*, 1976, *6*, (2), 189–203.

Cohen, D. J., Dibble, E., Grawe, J., & Pollin, W. Separating identical from fraternal twins. *Archives of General Psychiatry*, 1973, *29*, 465–469.

Collins, R. L. The sound of one paw clapping: An inquiry into the origin of left-handedness. In G. Lindzey & D. D. Thiessen (Eds.), *Contributions to behaviour-genetic analysis: The mouse as prototype.* New York: Appleton-Century-Crofts, 1970.

Crovitz, H. F., & Zener, K. A group test for assessing hand and eye dominance. *American Journal of Psychology*, 1962, *73*, 271–276.

Dahlberg, G. *Twin births and twins from a hereditary point of view.* Stockholm: Tidens, 1926. (Cited by Newman, 1928.)

Danforth, C. H. Resemblance and difference in twins. *Journal of Heredity*, 1919, *10*, 399–409.

French, J. W., Ekstrom, R. B., & Price, L. A. *Manual for kit of reference tests for cognitive factors* (revised 1963). Princeton, N.J.: Educational Testing Service, 1963.

Gordon, H. Left-handedness and mirror writing especially among defective children. *Brain*, 1920, *43*, 313–368.

Hardyck, C., Goldman, R., & Petrinovich, L. Handedness and sex, race, and age. *Human Biology*, 1975, *47*, 369–375.

Hardyck, C., & Petrinovich, L. Left-Handedness. *Psychological Bulletin*, 1977, *84* (3), 385–404.

Hécaen, H., & de Ajuriaguerra, J. *Left-handedness.* New York: Grune & Stratton, 1964.

Hildreth, G. The development and training of hand dominance: Part I. *Journal of Genetic Psychology*, 1949, *75*, 197–220.

Hines, D., & Satz, P. Superiority of right visual half-fields in right-handers for recall of digits at varying rates. *Neuropsychologia*, 1971, *9*, 21–25.

Hirsch, N. D. M. *Twins, heredity, and environment.* Cambridge: Harvard University Press, 1930. (Cited by Wilson & Jones, 1932.)

Howard, R. G., & Brown, A. M. Twinning: A marker for biological insults. *Child Development*, 1970, *41*, 519–530.

Kimura, D. Cerebral dominance and the perception of verbal stimuli. *Canadian Journal of Psychology*, 1961, *15*, 166–171.

Kuhn, G. M. The phi coefficient as an index of ear differences in dichotic listening. *Cortex*, 1973, *9*, 450–457.

Lauterbach, C. E. Studies in twin resemblance. *Genetics*, 1925, *10*, 525–568.

Levy, J. Possible basis for the evolution of lateral specialization of the human brain. *Nature*, 1969, *224*, 614–615.

Levy, J. A review of evidence for a genetic component in handedness. *Behavior Genetics*, 1976, *6*, 429–453.

Levy, J., & Nagylaki, T. A model for the genetics of handedness. *Genetics*, 1972, *72*, 117–128.

Levy, J., & Reid, M. Variations in writing posture and cerebral organization. *Science*, 1976, *194*, 337–339.

Macgillivray, I., Nylander, P., & Corney, G. *Human multiple reproduction.* London: W. B. Saunders Co., Ltd., 1975.

Miller, E. Handedness and the pattern of human ability. *British Journal of Psychology*, 1971, *62*, 111–112.

Morgan, M. Embryology and inheritance of asymmetry. In S. Harnad, R. W. Doty, L. Goldstein, J. Jaynes, & G. Krauthamer (Eds.), *Lateralization in the nervous system.* New York: Academic Press, 1977.

Nagylaki, T., & Levy, J. "The sound of one paw clapping" isn't sound. *Behavior Genetics*, 1973, *3*, 279–292.

Nance, W. E. Twins: An introduction to gemellology. *Medicine*, 1959, *38*, 403–414.

Newman, H. H. Asymmetry reversal or mirror imaging in identical twins. *Biological Bulletin*, 1928, *55*, 298–315.

Newman, H. H., Freeman, F. N., & Holzinger, K. J. *Twins: A study of heredity and environment.* Chicago: University of Chicago Press, 1937.

Palmer, R. D. Development of a differentiated handedness. *Psychological Bulletin*, 1964, *62*, 257–273.

Pyle, W. H., Drouin, A. Left-handedness: An experimental and statistical study. *School and society*, 1932, *36*, 253–256.

Race, R. R., & Sanger, R. *Blood groups in man,* (6th ed.). Oxford: Blackwell Scientific Publications, 1975.

Rife, D. C. Handedness, with special reference to twins. *Genetics*, 1940, *25*, 178–186.

Rife, D. C. An application of gene frequency analysis to the interpretation of data from twins. *Human Biology*, 1950, *22*, 136–145.

Rosanoff, A. J., Handy, L. M., & Plesset, I. R. The etiology of mental deficiency with special reference to its occurrence in twins: A chapter in the genetic history of human intelligence. *Psychological Monographs*, 1937, No 216.

Satz, P. Pathological left-handedness: An explanatory model. *Cortex*, 1972, *8*, 121–135.

Satz, P. Left-handedness and early brain insult: An explanation. *Neuropsychologia*, 1973, *11*, 115–117.

Shankweiler, D., & Studdert-Kennedy, M. Identification of consonants and vowels presented to left and right ears. *Quarterly Journal of Experimental Psychology*, 1967, *19*, 59–63.

Shankweiler, D., & Studdert-Kennedy, M. A continuum of lateralization for speech perception? *Brain and Language,* 1975, *2,* 212–225.

Siemens, H. W. Die Bedeutung der Zwillingspathologie für die aetiologische Forschung erläutert an Beispiel der Linkshändigkeit. 1924. (Cited by Newman, 1928.)

Springer, S. P., & Searleman, A. The ontogeny of hemispheric specialization: Evidence from dichotic listening in twins. *Neuropsychologia,* 1978, *16,* 269–281.

Stocks, P. A biometrical investigation of twins and their brothers and sisters. *Annals of Eugenics,* 1933, *5,* 1–55.

Teng, E. L., Lee, P., Yang, K., & Chang, P. Handedness in a Chinese population: Biological, social, and pathological factors. *Science,* 1976, *193,* 1148–1150.

Thurstone, T. G. *Adult primary mental abilities.* Science Research Associates, Inc., 1962.

Torgersen, J. Situs inversus, asymmetry, and twinning. *American Journal of Human Genetics,* 1950, *2,* 361–370.

von Verschuer, O. Der Vererbungsbiologische Zwillingsforschung. *Ergebnisse der inneren Medizin und Kinderheilkunde,* 1927, *31.* (Cited by Newman, 1928.)

Weitz, W. Studien an eineiigen Zwillingen. *Zeitschrift für Klinische Medizin,* 1924, *101.* (Cited by Newman, 1928.)

Wilson, P. T., & Jones, H. E. Left handedness in twins. *Genetics,* 1932, *17,* 560–571.

Zurif, E., & Bryden, M. P. Familial handedness and left-right differences in auditory and visual perception. *Neuro-psychologia,* 1969, *7,* 179–187.

5

Is Left-Handedness
Genetically Determined?[1]

MICHAEL C. CORBALLIS

INTRODUCTION

There can be few topics more disputed than the inheritance of handedness. Even in the 1970s speculation ranges from one extreme to another. For instance Levy and Nagylaki (1972) have proposed a model in which variations in both handedness and cerebral lateralization are attributed entirely to genetic variation, according to Mendelian principles. This model is in a tradition of genetic models dating back to early in the century (Chamberlain, 1928; Rameley, 1913; Rife, 1950; Trankell, 1955). Collins (1970, 1975), on the other hand, has argued for an extreme environmental position, suggesting that handedness is transmitted from one generation to the next by means of cultural and environmental biases. In this, he echoes the earlier conclusion of Blau (1946) who, after a careful review of the evidence, wrote as follows:

> Preferred laterality is not an inherited trait. There is absolutely no evidence to support the contention that dominance, either in handedness or any other form, is a congenital, predetermined human capacity. Despite the popularity it has enjoyed with many investigators and the attempts to prove it by various techniques and in relation to different organs of the body, the theory of heredity must be put down as erroneous [p. 180].

He went on to argue that dextrality is a learned response to a right-handed

[1] This work was supported by a grant from the National Research Council of Canada.

NEUROPSYCHOLOGY
OF LEFT-HANDEDNESS

bias in our environment, and that left-handedness is essentially a failure to learn this, due to physical defect, faulty education, or "emotional negativism."

Annett (1972) has proposed a model that is, in some respects, a compromise between these extreme positions. She supposed that there is a large random component to the distribution of intermanual differences due to unsystematic environmental influences. Most people, however, inherit a "right shift" factor, so that the mean of the distribution favors the right hand (RH). According to Annett the right shift is genetically determined, perhaps by a single gene. Some individuals may lack this gene, and on an unbiased test of handedness these individuals should be equally divided between left- and right-handers. In a later article, Annett (1974) presented evidence that the lack of a right shift has the property of a Mendelian recessive: Children of left-handed couples were shown to be equally divided into left- and right-handers. These children, like their parents, evidently lacked the right shift. Annett screened out those couples in which one or the other parent, or both, had some record of birth trauma or early perinatal difficulty which might have explained their left-handedness and found that the children of these couples were predominantly right-handed. She thus recognized two sources of left-handedness, one pathological (Baken, 1971; Bakan, Dibb, & Reed, 1973) and the other the inherited lack of the right shift.

My own view, which I owe largely to M. J. Morgan and which is discussed in more detail elsewhere (Corballis & Beale, 1976; Morgan, 1976), is that the right shift is not directly coded in a gene (or genes), but is rather a genetically controlled expression of a more fundamental underlying gradient which normally favors more advanced development on the *left*. This gradient may be expressed in phenomena as diverse as the leftward displacement of the heart in vertebrates, the doubling of the habenular nuclei on the left side of the brain in amphibia (Braitenberg & Kemali, 1970), the left-hypoglossal control of song in passerine birds (Nottebohm, 1971, 1972), and the enlargement of the left temporal planum of the brain in chimpanzee (Yeni-Komshian & Benson, 1976), orangutan (LeMay & Geschwind, 1975), and man (Geschwind & Levitsky, 1968; Wada, Clarke, & Hamm, 1975; Witelson & Pallie, 1973). According to this view, both right-handedness and the left-cerebral control of speech in humans are species-specific manifestations of the same gradient. Estimates based on the sodium amytal test (Wada & Rasmussen, 1960) administered to patients about to undergo brain surgery for focal epilepsy suggest that some 96% (Milner, 1975) to 99% (Rossi & Rosadini, 1967) of right-handers have speech control localized in the left cerebral hemisphere. As these estimates may be contaminated by some degree of pathology, it may not be an exaggeration to claim that *all* normal right-handers have speech localized in the left hemisphere. This would of course be consistent with the view that the same fundamental gradient underlies both right-handedness and the left cerebral control of speech.

The critical question now is, why do some people depart from this general pattern? That is, why are some people left-handed, and why do some have speech represented bilaterally or in the right cerebral hemisphere (Milner, 1975)? I wish to examine two possible explanations, one based on Annett's idea that there is genetic control over the presence or absence of a lateralization factor (the "right shift"), the other based on the more parsimonious notion, due to Collins, that variations in lateralization are due largely, if not entirely, to environmental causes. I have chosen to examine Annett's theory because it seems to me to represent the most plausible genetic model that has been proposed to date. It admits a significant random component which, as we shall see, is a point in its favor over more deterministic models. It is also consistent with a general biologic perspective on genetic influences over asymmetries that implies that the genes are on the whole "left–right agnosic [Morgan, 1976]." The evidence on asymmetries, other than handedness or cerebral lateralization, suggests that the genes may control the presence or absence of asymmetries, perhaps through interaction with nongenetic sources of asymmetry, but there is very little indication that the genes may control the *direction* of an asymmetry (Corballis & Beale, 1976; Morgan, 1976; Stern, 1955). However, although Annett's model is in line with this perspective, I shall suggest that it may still overestimate the extent of genetic control over the variations in handedness and cerebral lateralization. I shall focus on the fit of the model to data supplied by Rife (1940, 1950) on the handedness of children as a function of parental handedness (Table 5.1) and on the distribution of handedness among twins and among paired siblings (Table 5.2).

First, some comments on these data. The breeding ratios shown in Table 5.1 make it clear that handedness is a function of parental handedness; a person is more likely to be left-handed if one parent is left-handed than if both are right-handed, and more likely still if both are left-handed. This might be taken as evidence that handedness is genetically determined,

Table 5.1

Handedness of Offspring as a Function of Parental Handedness in Rife's (1940) Survey

| | Parental categories | | |
	R–R	R–L	L–L
Number of families	620	62	5
Number of offspring	1993	174	11
Proportion offspring right-handed	.9242	.8046	.4545

Table 5.2

Observed and Predicted Distributions of Handedness among Monozygotic
Twins, Dizygotic Twins, and Nontwin Sibling Pairs

Source	Pairings			
	R–R	R–L	L–L	ϕ
Monozygotic twins				
Observed frequencies (Rife, 1950)	261	76	6	
Observed proportions	.761	.222	.017	.009
Binomial prediction	.760	.224	.016	0
Prediction from Annett's model	.853	.088	.059	.525
Corrected prediction from				
Annett's model	.804	.136	.060	.393
Dizygotic twins				
Observed frequencies (Rife, 1950)	164	45	2	
Observed proportions	.777	.213	.009	– .039
Binomial prediction	.781	.205	.013	0
Prediction from Annett's model	.824	.147	.029	.203
Paired nontwin siblings				
Observed frequencies (Rife, 1940)	3067	475	41	
Observed proportions	.856	.133	.011	.075
Binomial prediction	.851	.143	.006	0
Prediction from Annett's model	.824	.147	.029	.203
Weighted solution from				
Annett's model	.857	.125	.018	.156
Binomial solution weighted				
by families	.834	.156	.010	.027

although it is also consistent with the view that children learn their hand
preferences from their parents (Collins, 1970). Hicks and Kinsbourne
(1976) have argued in favor of the genetic hypothesis on the basis of a
survey showing that the handedness of young adults was positively correlated with that of their biologic parents but uncorrelated with that of
their stepparents. I find this evidence inconclusive, however, because the
respondents, whose average age was just over 20 years, had only been living with their stepparents an average of 7.24 years ($SD = 3.12$ years). If we
suppose that the first few years of life are critical to the establishment of
handedness (e.g., Gesell & Ames, 1947), then it would not be surprising,
even according to an environmental hypothesis, that the stepparents
exerted little directional influence, at least among the great majority of
subjects.

The data on the distribution of handedness among twins and among siblings, shown in Table 5.2, argue more strongly against a genetic
hypothesis. In fact, the proportions of pairs who are both right-handed, of
opposite-handedness, and both left-handed conform remarkably well to the

binomial distribution, implying that handedness within families is distributed on a chance basis, although with an overall bias toward right-handedness. Knowing a person's handedness tells us virtually nothing about the handedness of his or her sibling. It is important to note that this is as true (if not more so) of monozygotic (MZ) twins as of dizygotic (DZ) twins or of nontwin siblings. As Collins (1970) points out, these and other comparable data rule out any simple genetic model, such as those of Rife (1950) and Trankell (1955). I have argued elsewhere that the data are also inconsistent with Levy and Nagylaki's (1972) genetic model (Corballis & Beale, 1976). The concordance between pairs of siblings or twins is most succinctly expressed by the ϕ coefficient:

$$ \phi = \frac{p_{RR} - p_R^2}{p_R(1 - p_R)} $$

where p_{RR} is the proportion of pairs who are both right-handed and p_R is the overall proportion of right-handers. Levy and Nagylaki's model predicts a ϕ score of about .319 for paired siblings or for DZ twins, and a ϕ score of unity for MZ twins, but the data yield ϕ scores close to zero in both cases. Nagylaki and Levy (1973) claim that twins are subject to special pathological and "mirror imaging" effects that render them unsuitable for testing genetic hypotheses, but the discrepancies between data and theory are still too wide for any such special pleading (Hudson, 1975). Annett's (1972) model, outlined previously, does make allowance for a large random component as well as a genetic component, and the question of whether this model can provide an acceptable fit to the data is taken up in the following discussion.

ANNETT'S MODEL

Estimating Parameters

Following Annett (1972), let us suppose that the presence or absence of the "right shift" in the distribution of handedness is governed by a diallelic gene locus. For purposes of fitting the model, it is irrelevant whether the gene codes handedness directly, or whether it controls expression of some more fundamental gradient. The dominant allele (D) represents the right shift, or dextrality, whereas the recessive allele (s) represents the absence of the right shift, or symmetry. We may suppose that D occurs with some probability (α) in the population. Some small proportion (β), of those carrying a dominant allele (i.e., DD and Ds individuals) would be classed as left-handed because of extreme environmental (including pathological) influences. These individuals represent an extreme leftward tail of the distribution of handedness among those manifesting the right shift. Some larger propotion (γ) of those symmetrically disposed (ss) individuals would also be classed as left-handed. According to an unbiased test of handedness one would expect γ to equal .5 (Annett, 1974), but the criterion adopted by Rife (1940) was almost certainly biased quite strongly in favor of left-handedness. Rife classified subjects as right-handed only if they reported using their RHs exclusively on all of 12 familiar operations, otherwise they were classed as left-handed. In fitting Annett's model to Rife's data, therefore, we might expect γ to be greater than .5.

There are therefore three different genotypes, DD, Ds and ss, each of whom may be phenotypically right-or left-handed. The expected proportions of the six different kinds of individuals are readily expressed in terms of α, β, and γ. Thus the proportion of right handed DD individuals is $\alpha^2(1 - \beta)$, whereas that of left-handed DD individuals is $\alpha^2\beta$. The corresponding expressions for Ds individuals are $2\alpha(1 - \alpha)(1 - \beta)$ for right-handers and $2\alpha(1 - \alpha)\beta$ for left-handers, and those for ss individuals are $(1 - \alpha)^2(1 - \gamma)$ for right-handers and $(1 - \alpha)^2\gamma$ for left-handers.

The six different kinds of individuals give rise to 21 different mating combinations, whose expected proportions are simply determined from the expressions just given. Mendelian laws then predict the proportions of each genotype among the offspring of each parental pairing, and each genotype gives rise to the two possible phenotypes. For instance, matings of DD with DD, DD with Ds, or DD with ss yield offspring who are either DD or Ds, and are therefore left-handed with a probability of β. Mating Ds with Ds yields DD or Ds with a probability of .75, and these individuals in turn have a probability of β of being left-handed, whereas ss individuals are produced with a probability of .25 and have a probability of γ of being left-handed. Ultimately, then, we can write complex expressions in α, β and γ which yield the expected proportions of left- and right-handers born to each of the parental combinations. These in turn can be gathered and summed to yield the expected proportions of left- and right-handers born to the different combinations of left- and right-handed parents. The expressions are too complex to present here, but are essentially straightforward and can be obtained from the author upon request.

The expressions for the proportions of right-handers born to each of the three categories of parents were equated to the actual proportions obtained by Rife (1940), shown in Table 5.1. This yielded three independent equations in the three unknowns, α, β and γ. (The equations for left-handed offspring are of course not independent of these). These equations were solved exactly by means of a computer algorithm to give the following values:

$$\alpha = .6244, \qquad \beta = .0136, \qquad \gamma = .6457$$

The next and critical question is whether we can use these estimates to obtain reasonable fits to other data. First, let us consider the concordance of handedness between MZ twins, shown in Table 5.2.

Prediction of Distribution among Monozygotic Twins

Annett's model clearly does not predict perfect concordance between MZ twins, as does Levy and Nagylaki's (1972) model for example. Monozygotic twins must share the same genotype (DD, Ds, or ss), but may exhibit different phenotypes, depending on environmental influences. I assume that these influences are random and apply independently to each of a pair of twins, so that within each genotype the expected proportions of right-handed, mixed, and left-handed twin pairs are given by the binomial distribution. That is, within the DD and Ds genotypes, the proportions are β^2, $2\beta(1-\beta)$ and $(1-\beta)^2$, respectively, and within the ss genotype they are γ^2, $2\gamma(1-\gamma)$ and $(1-\gamma)^2$, respectively. Using the estimated values of β and γ given on p. 164, and weighting the genotypes according to their expected relative frequencies, yielded the expected proportions shown in Table 5.2 as the "prediction from Annett's model." The computed value of ϕ is .525, which is well above the value of .009 obtained from the observed proportions.

It should be noted however that the *overall* proportion of left-handers is higher than that predicted by the model. In Rife's survey, .1283 of the MZ twins were classified as left-handed, whereas the model predicts proportions of .1028. One possible reason for this discrepancy is that there is an increased incidence of left-handedness due to pathological influences among twins, resulting perhaps from intrauterine crowding (Nagylaki & Levy, 1973). In an attempt to model this, I let the parameter β increase until the predicted proportion of left-handers matched the observed proportion. This occurred when β equaled .0433 (representing a "pathology" factor some three times that estimated from the sample as a whole), and yielded the estimated proportions shown in Table 5.2 as "corrected prediction from Annett's model." The computed value of ϕ from these estimates is .393, which is still considerably higher than the value of .009 derived from the observed proportions. Converting the expected proportions to expected frequencies and comparing them to the observed frequencies yielded a score ($\chi^2 = 27.90$) that with two degrees of freedom is significantly ($p < .001$) greater than zero. This indicates that the model still provides an extremely poor fit to the data.

One might perhaps question my initial assumption that handedness is determined independently in each of a pair of twins. To the extent that pathological influences due to intrauterine crowding are shared by both

twins, one might expect the environmental influence to be positively correlated, and the predicted value of ϕ might therefore be considered an
underestimate. However, it has also been claimed that there are special
"mirror-imaging" effects operating in twins that would actually serve to
create a *negative* correlation between them (Nagylaki & Levy, 1973;
Newman, 1940). The extent of mirror imaging is actually a moot point
(Corballis & Beale, 1976), but it is conceivable that it serves effectively to
cancel the positive correlation predicted by Annett's model.

It is at least debatable, however, whether it is plausible or even legitimate
to continue to seek *post hoc* influences that might somehow explain why
the predicted value of ϕ remains stubbornly above the empirical value.
Adding further assumptions only serves to complicate the model. The difficulty is that the distribution of handedness among twins, both MZ and DZ,
is predicted to a remarkable degree of accuracy by the binomial distribution, both in Rife's (1950) data shown in Table 5.2 and in several other
tabulations summarized by Collins (1970). On the grounds of parsimony,
then, adding further assumptions to the genetic model can only strengthen
the case against it, and in favor of the much simpler hypothesis that the
distribution of handedness among twins is simply a matter of chance.

Prediction of Distribution among
Dizygotic Twins and Nontwin Siblings

Let us now turn to the prediction of the distribution of handedness between fraternal siblings (i.e., between DZ twins and between nontwin siblings). If we again assume environmental influences to be random and to
apply independently to each of a pair of siblings, we can use the solutions
on p. 164 to generate the expectations shown in Table 5.2 as the "prediction
from Annett's model." The computed value of ϕ is .203, which is again
above the value of $-$ .039 for DZ twins and .075 for nontwin siblings obtained from the observed proportions.

It is again apparent, however, that the predicted proportions fail to
match the actual proportions in terms of the overall incidence of right-
handedness. The actual proportion of right-handers among DZ twins is
lower than that predicted by the parameters of the model, perhaps again
because of a higher incidence of "pathological" left-handedness among
twins. Among nontwin sibling pairs, however, the actual incidence of
right-handers is *higher* than that predicted. Because the value of ϕ tends to
decrease the more extreme the proportion, this could explain at least some
of the discrepancy between the observed and predicted values of ϕ. The
overrepresentation of right-handers among the observed pairs can be attributed to the fact that right-handed parents, on the average had more
children (and therefore more *pairs* of children), than parents of mixed

handedness, who were in turn more prolific than left-handed parents. The average family sizes were 3.21, 2.81, and 2.20 children, respectively. Unfortunately it is not possible to tell from Rife's (1940) report how many sibling pairs there were in each parental category, and thus how the distributions should have been weighted to compensate for the variations in family size. (In generating the proportions given in the previous paragraph, I assumed equal family size across parental groups.) However, I attempted to gain some understanding of how different weights might have influenced the fit of the model in the following way.

Suppose that the relative proportions of sibling pairs born to right-handed, mixed-handed, and left-handed couples are w_{RR}, w_{RL} and w_{LL}, respectively. These weights are constrained, firstly, in that they must add to unity, and secondly, in that they should yield a distribution of sibling pairs with the same overall proportion of right-handers as in the actual distribution. This leaves one parameter, say w_{RR}, free to vary. I therefore built in the two constraints and generated solutions with varying values of w_{RR}. A limiting case occurred with w_{RR} equal to .963, in which case w_{RL} would equal .027 and w_{LL} would equal 0. It was a limiting case in that smaller w_{RR} yielded a larger ϕ and poorer fit to Rife's data, whereas a larger w_{RR} yielded negative w_{LL} which is impossible. But even in this case, the solution was a poor fit to the data. The predicted proportions are shown in Table 5.2 as the "weighted solution from Annett's model" and yielded a ϕ of .156. Although this value of ϕ is itself an underestimate, it is still clearly above the empirical value of .075. If the predicted proportions are converted to expected frequencies and compared with the actual frequencies, we obtain a score $x^2 = 8.908$), that, with two degrees of freedom, can be considered significantly greater than zero ($p < .02$). This is not strictly legitimate as a test of significance, however, because the sibling pairs are not independent of one another (e.g., in families of three siblings, each sibling is counted in two pairings), but it does reinforce the point that the predictions fail to match the data even when one "leans over backwards" to compensate for the distortion due to unequal family sizes.

The Relationship between Handedness and Cerebral Lateralization

Annett's model can be extended to make predictions about the relationship between handedness and cerebral lateralization for the control of speech. As suggested earlier, one can suppose that Annett's postulated "right shift" is more fundamentally a *left* shift, and that DD and Ds individuals are genetically predisposed to be right-handed and to have speech localized primarily in the left cerebral hemisphere. Let us also assume that environmental (or pathological) influences are less likely to cause a switch in cerebral lateralization for speech than a switch in handedness (Satz, 1972); that is, let the proportions of DD and Ds individuals with right-hemispheric control of speech be for all practical purposes zero, whereas the proportion of those who are left-handed remains at β ($\beta = .0136$), as before. Let us further suppose that among ss individuals, who are without any genetic predisposition to cerebral or manual asymmetry, the directions of handedness and cerebral lateralization for speech are determined at random and independently of each other.

According to the parameters estimated on p. 164, the proportion of the population who are genetically ss and who thus lack the lateralization factor should be .1411. Using Rife's (biased) criterion for determining handedness, we can divide this proportion into .0911 ($.0911 = .1411 \times .6457$) who are left-handed and .0500 who are right-handed. Assuming handedness and cerebral lateralization for speech to be independent, we can further divide these proportions into equal parts to yield the proportions of those assumed to have speech localized primarily in the left cerebral hemisphere and those with speech localized in the right. Among the .8589 who do inherit the lateralization factor, we calculate .0117 ($.0117 = .8589 \times .0136$) to be left-handed and .8472 to be right-handed by Rife's criterion, and assume all to have speech control localized in the left cerebral hemisphere. The total proportion of *right-handers* is thus .8972, and of these .8722 should be left cerebrally dominant for speech. Expressing this as a proportion, we predict that .972 of right-handers are left cerebrally dominant for speech, which is within the empirical estimates of .96 (Milner, 1975) and .99 (Rossi & Rosadini, 1967). The total proportion of *left-handers*, according to the model, is .1028, and of these we calculate that .05725 should have speech localized primarily in the left cerebral hemisphere. Expressing this as a proportion yields .557, which is close to the empirical estimate of .53 reported by Goodglass and Quadfasel (1954). However, other more recent estimates suggest that the proportion of left-handers who are left cerebrally dominant for speech is considerably higher than this, perhaps in the vicinity of .70 (Milner, 1975; Warrington & Pratt, 1973).

The above estimates from Annett's model are presumably somewhat distorted in that they depend upon Rife's biased criterion of handedness. I attempted to compensate for this in the following way. I assumed the distribution of intermanual differences to be normal within each category, those who inherit and those who do not inherit the lateralization factor (Annett, 1972). Among the latter, an unbiased criterion for handedness should yield equal proportions of left- and right-handers (Annett, 1974), whereas Rife's data yield estimates of .6457 and .3543, respectively. Rife's criterion thus corresponds to a standard normal deviate of .374 (the area to the right is .3543, the area to the left .6457). Subtracting .374 would thus remove the bias. If we move the criterion for those who *do* inherit the lateralization factor by the same amount, the estimate of .0136 of left-handedness is reduced to .0049. If we now recompute the estimates using these "unbiased" estimates of left-handedness, we discover that the proportion of right-handers with left cerebral control of speech is estimated to be .962, which is still within the range of empirical estimates, whereas the proportion of left-handers with left cerebral control of speech is .528, which is even closer to the empirical estimate reported by Goodglass and Quadfasel (1954) but remains deviant from the estimates reported by Milner (1975) and Warrington and Pratt (1973).

According to Annett's model and the additional assumptions I have made, the extent to which the proportions of left-handers with left-cerebral speech dominance deviates upwards from .5 depends on β. This, in turn, might be considered at least partially a measure of the degree of pathologically determined left-handedness among those who are genetically predisposed to be right-handed. Rife's (1940) sample consisted of university students, who, in the late 1930s, might be considered to have been something of an intellectual elite. Perhaps this explains why the estimate of left-handers with left-cerebral speech representation is lower than that based on neurological patients (Milner, 1975) or on subjects more representative of the population as a whole (Warrington & Pratt, 1973).

This extended version of Annett's theory also helps explain why left-handers are generally more diffusely lateralized than right-handers, in terms both of handedness itself and of cerebral lateralization (e.g., Zangwill, 1960). Because those recessive individuals assumed to lack the lateralization factor comprise the majority of those classified as left-handed or ambidextrous, but only a small minority of those classified as right-handed, it follows that left-handed or ambidextrous individuals should be the more diffusely lateralized. Milner (1975) reports that about 15% of left- and mixed-handed patients without signs of early brain damage exhibited bilateral representation of speech according to the sodium amytal test. She also notes that there was no essential difference between left-handers and mixed-handers in the distribution of speech representation, which lends support to my earlier assumption that cerebral and manual asymmetry may be determined independently among these individuals. Indeed, there is even evidence that different measures of cerebral lateralization are uncorrelated with each other among left-handers, but positively correlated among right-handers (Hines & Satz, 1974). By contrast, in a comparable sample of 140 right-handers, Milner reports that there was *none* with bilateral speech representation. If there is any surprise here, it is that there were not at least a few with bilateral representation of speech, as one would expect some of the recessive individuals to have been classified as right-handed.

Annett's theory also implies that those left-handers with some family history of left-handedness should display less pronounced cerebral lateralization than those without such a history. Those with positive family histories should include the larger proportion of those recessives who inherit the absence of the lateralization factor, whereas those without a family history should include the larger proportion of those who are left-handed for pathological reasons. There is indeed some evidence showing that familial left-handers do not show consistent cerebral dominance whereas nonfamilial left-handers show the usual left-cerebral dominance for speech and verbal processing (Hécaen & Sauguet, 1971; Zurif & Bryden, 1969). But the evidence is inconsistent: Bryden (1975) failed to confirm the effect, Warrington and Pratt (1973) found familial left-handers to be *less* likely than nonfamilial left-handers to display right-cerebral representation of speech, and Lake and Bryden (1976) report that familial sinistrality reduced lateralization according to a dichotic-listening test among their female subjects but increased it among their male subjects!

Conclusions

To summarize, we have seen that Annett's model can be fitted to the data on breeding ratios of handedness to yield parameters that are at least plausible. In this context, we should also remember Annett's (1974) demonstration that the children of left-handed couples display, on average, no consistent handedness according to an unbiased test, which supports the idea that the absence of a lateralization factor is indeed a genetically recessive condition. With additional assumptions, the model also provides a reasonable account of the relationship between handedness and cerebral lateralization for speech. But the real difficulty with the model is its failure to predict the distribution of handedness among twins and among paired nontwin siblings. Even if one can allow that "special factors" may operate in the case of twins (Nagylaki & Levy, 1973), which is debatable (Corballis & Beale, 1976; Hudson, 1975), the model still fails to account for the distribution among paired nontwin siblings.

Of course the issue is by no means closed. There are doubtless many influences I have overlooked in attempting to fit the model to the data. Rife's data are themselves far from ideal. The criterion for determining handedness was clearly biased in favor of left-handedness, and the use of a questionnaire rather than some more objective test certainly introduces a measure of unreliability. The data on the distribution of handedness among paired nontwin siblings are particularly inadequate in that they do not reveal the relative contributions from the different parental categories, yet these data are perhaps the most critical for a test of the theory. To many, the notion that lateralization is controlled by a single gene locus will seem unreasonable, yet it would be premature to develop a multiple-gene model. I have ignored sex-related differences. For instance, it is commonly observed that a child is more likely to be left-handed if the mother is left-handed than if the father is left-handed; in Rife's (1940) own data the proportions were .256 versus .218, respectively. Annett's model does not make provision for this, unless perhaps it is supposed that pathological left-handedness may be subject to a weak maternal influence.

As I have already suggested, the question is whether it is really worth the effort at this stage to add still further elements to Annett's model to achieve a closer fit to the data. On the one hand, the model does suggest certain insights about the nature of lateralization and about the relationship between handedness and cerebral lateralization. But on the other hand, although the model does predict the distribution of handedness among twins and among nontwin siblings better than any other genetic model known to me, it still fails to do so as accurately as the simple proposition that handedness is distributed according to the binomial distribution (i.e., without any genetic component at all).

A NONGENETIC APPROACH

We have seen that the data on the distribution of handedness among twins and among nontwin siblings, summarized in Table 5.2, suggest that handedness is distributed on an apparently random basis. Collins (1970) was the first to clearly point out that this poses extreme difficulties for any genetic theory. However there is still something of an inconsistency between the data of Table 5.2 and those of Table 5.1, which show that there are systematic differences between families. Why are these differences not reflected in the distributions among siblings?

Let us suppose that there are indeed systematic differences *between* families, but that the distribution *within* families is binomial, and then enquire as to what distribution one would expect to observe between paired siblings when one averages across families. We can obtain from Table 5.1 direct estimates of the probability that a child will be right-handed in each of the three parental categories, and thus compute the binomial expectancies for pairs of siblings. Among the offspring of right-handed couples the probability of a child being right-handed is estimated to be .9242, so that the expected binomial probabilities of right-handed, mixed-, and left-handed pairs are $.9242^2$ which is .8541, $2 \times .9242 \times .0758$ which is .1401, and $.0758^2$ which is .0057, respectively. Similarly, the binomial probabilities among the offspring of mixed couples are .6474, .3144, and .0382, respectively, whereas those among the offspring of left-handed couples are .2066, .4959, and .2976 for right-handed, mixed-, and left-handed, respectively. Again we face the difficulty that we do not know how these sets of estimates should be weighted to compensate for different family sizes, but if we ignore family size and weight simply according to the number of families within each category, we obtain the averaged proportions shown in Table 5.2 as "binomial solution weighted by families." The computed value of ϕ is only .027. This value of ϕ would presumably be even smaller if more weight were given to the families of right-handed couples. Consequently, systematic differences between families contribute only minimally to raising the expected overall intersibling correlation above zero.

As a first (and close) approximation, then, the data of Tables 5.1 and 5.2 are consistent with the interpretation that there are consistent differences between families in the distribution of handedness, but that the distribution within families is binomial. This applies equally to MZ twins, DZ twins, and nontwins. Clearly, this conclusion is difficult to reconcile with any simple genetic hypothesis, and suggests in fact that variations in handedness are due to environmental influences. These influences must be partly postnatal, as it is difficult otherwise to explain how parental handedness, especially that of the father, could play a role before a child is born. However, the probability of a child being left-handed is not zero even if both parents are right-handed, suggesting that there may be some influence that is prenatal or that is associated with birth trauma (Bakan, 1971; Bakan, Dibb, & Reed, 1973). The slight maternal influence might also be attributed in part to prenatal factors.

This account is not at odds with the everyday observation that left-handedness often appears to be congenital—an infant may display a persistent, not to say stubborn tendency to use the left hand despite parental encouragement to use the right, even if both parents are right-handed. We do not need to suppose that this is simply a matter of "emotional negativism [Blau, 1946]," although this may conceivably be a factor. The influence may well be prenatal or associated in some way with birth stress. However, it is also worth noting that most children destined to become right-handed display and initial preference for the left hand, and show cyclic changes until the right hand finally predominates (Gesell & Ames, 1947). (The same phenomenon has also been observed in a baby chimpanzee—see Chorazyna, 1976). It is not inconceivable that some parents are so struck by the early left-hand preference that they switch their training strategies accordingly, and encourage their fundamentally right-handed children to become left-handed.

What of cerebral lateralization in the control of speech? According to the present view, departures from left-cerebral speech dominance would also be attributed simply to environmental, including traumatic causes. It is now fairly clear that reversals of speech dominance occur less frequently than do reversals of handedness (Milner, 1975). Obviously, it is more difficult (perhaps impossible) to train a child to be right-brained for speech than to be left-handed; the one is covert, the other overt. There may be some degree to which the one depends on the other, so that if one trains a child to be left-handed one increases the probability that the control of speech will be bilateral or represented in the right cerebral hemisphere. However, Milner (1975) notes that there appears to be little if any correlation between the degree of left-handedness and the degree of right-cerebral dominance for speech. It is likely that there is considerable plasticity both in the direction of handedness and in the direction of cerebral lateralization, partly because bilateral symmetry itself confers certain advantages, and partly because a mechanism for reversal seems to be involved in equipotentiality (Basser, 1962; Corballis, & Beale, 1976),.

I recognize that it is somewhat facile and *post hoc* to attribute variations in cerebral lateralization to environmental factors. Clearly, there is a strong need for empirical data on this point. However, in a preliminary study using dichotic listening to measure laterality, Bryden (1975) found low positive correlations between parents and children, but *negative* correlations between siblings. These data are certainly difficult to reconcile with a genetic model, but are no doubt contaminated by the unreliability of the dichotic listening test and by the difficulties associated with measuring laterality (Richardson, 1976). In any case, until more conclusive data are available, the present account should be considered more as a null hypothesis than as a fully articulated theory, at least with respect to cerebral lateralization.

CONCLUSIONS

I have examined in detail a somewhat extended version of Annett's theory of handedness. I chose this theory because it seemed to me to be the most plausible genetic theory that is currently available. Although the theory suggests an elegant formulation of the relationship between handedness and cerebral lateralization, it still seems to fail to explain the distribution of handedness within families. However, it is possible that the data, not the theory, are at fault, and we should continue to seek further empirical tests. In particular, we need more data on the inheritance of cerebral lateralization. For the present, it appears to be unnecessary to postulate any genetic contribution to the distribution of handedness and cerebral lateralization.

It should not be concluded that I fully endorse Collins' views on handedness. Collins (1975) has recently suggested that even *right-*handedness can be attributed to environmental influences, largely on the grounds that mice, initially without overall preference for either paw, became predominantly right-pawed if exposed to an environment that was biased to favor right-pawedness. Some 10% remained persistently sinistral, as in the human population. It is of course true that we humans also live in a biased world favoring right-handers, but this does not easily explain why all known cultures, past and present, have been predominantly right-handed (Annett, 1972: Needham, 1973). Moreover, Collins' argument fails to consider cerebral lateralization.

If cerebral lateralization were influenced by handedness but were otherwise randomly determined, one might expect a higher incidence, if anything, of right-handedness than of left-cerebral speech dominance—but the reverse appears to be the case. Moreover, there is growing evidence that left-cerebral lateralization for speech can be detected early in the first year of life (Entus, 1977; Molfese, Freeman, & Palermo, 1975), or even at or before birth (Wada, Clarke, & Hamm, 1975; Witelson & Pallie, 1973). These data are more consistent with the view that right-handedness and the left-cerebral control of speech are preprogrammed at birth than with the view that they are environmentally determined. They are also consistent with the notion, expressed earlier, that these manifestations of human laterality are genetically controlled, species-specific expressions of a fundamental underlying gradient.

But if Collins is wrong in claiming that right-handedness depends on environmental influences, he may be correct in asserting that left-handedness does. A genetic factor may well explain the overall bias among humans toward right-handedness and the left-cerebral control of speech, but I know of no convincing evidence to suggest that variations from this pattern are due to anything other than environmental causes.

REFERENCES

Annett, M. The distribution of manual asymmetry. *British Journal of Psychology*, 1972, 63, 343–358.

Annett, M. Handedness in the children of two left-handed parents. *British Journal of Psychology*, 1974, 65, 129–131.

Bakan, P. Birth order and handedness. *Nature*, 1971, 229, 195.

Bakan, P., Dibb, G., & Reed, P. Handedness and birth stress. *Neuropsychologia*, 1973, 11, 363–366.

Basser, L. S. Hemiplegia of early onset and the faculty of speech, with special reference to the effects of hemispherectomy. *Brain*, 1962, 85, 427–460.

Blau, A. *The master hand.* Research Monograph No. 5. New York: American Orthopsychiatric Association, 1946.

Braitenberg, V., & Kemali, N. Exceptions to bilateral symmetry in the epithalamus of lower vertebrates. *Journal of Comparative Neurology,* 1970, *138,* 137–146.

Bryden, M. P. Speech lateralization in families: A preliminary study using dichotic listening. *Brain & Language,* 1975, *2,* 201–211.

Chamberlain, H. D. The inheritance of left handedness. *Journal of Heredity,* 1928, *19,* 557–559.

Chorazyna, H. Shifts in laterality in a baby chimpanzee. *Neuropsychologia,* 1976, *14,* 381–384.

Collins, R. L. The sound of one paw clapping: An inquiry into the origin of left handedness. In G. Lindzey & D. D. Thiessen (Eds.), *Contributions to behavior-genetic analysis—The mouse as a prototype.* New York: Meredith Corporation, 1970.

Collins, R. L. When left-handed mice live in right-handed worlds. *Science,* 1975, *187,* 181–184.

Corballis, M. C., & Beale, I. L. *The psychology of left and right.* Hillsdale, N. J.: Lawrence Erlbaum Associates, 1976.

Entus, A. K. Hemispheric asymmetry in processing of dichotically presented speech and non-speech by infants. In S. J. Segalowitz & F. Gruber (Eds.), *Language development and neurological theory.* New York: Academic Press, 1977.

Geschwind, N., & Levitsky, W. Human brain: Left-right asymmetries in temporal speech region. *Science,* 1968, *161,* 186–187.

Gesell, A., & Ames, L. B. The development of handedness. *Journal of Genetic Psychology,* 1947, *70,* 155–175.

Goodglass, H., & Quadfasel, F. A. Language laterality in left-handed aphasics. *Brain,* 1954, *77,* 521–548.

Hécaen, H., & Sauguet, J. Cerebral dominance in left-handed subjects. *Cortex,* 1971, *7,* 19–48.

Hicks, R. E., & Kinsbourne, M. Human handedness: A partial cross-fostering study. *Science,* 1976, *192,* 908–910.

Hines, D., & Satz, P. Cross-modal asymmetries in perception related to asymmetry in cerebral function. *Neuropsychologia,* 1974, *12,* 239–247.

Hudson, P. J. W. The genetics of handedness—a reply to Levy and Nagylaki. *Neuropsychologia,* 1975, *13,* 331–339.

Lake, D. A., & Bryden, M. P. Handedness and sex differences in hemispheric asymmetry. *Brain & Language,* 1976, *3,* 266–282.

LeMay, M., & Geschwind, N. Hemispheric differences in the brains of great apes. *Brain, Behavior, & Evolution,* 1975, *11,* 48–52.

Levy, J., & Nagylaki, T. A model for the genetics of handedness. *Genetics,* 1972, *72,* 117–128.

Milner, B. Psychological aspects of focal epilepsy and its neurosurgical management. In D. P. Purpura, J. K. Penny, & R. D. Walters (Eds.), *Advances in neurology, Vol. 8.* New York: Raven Press, 1975.

Molfese, D. L., Freeman, R. B., Jr., & Palermo, D. S. The ontogeny of brain lateralization for speech and nonspeech sounds. *Brain & Language,* 1975, *2,* 356–368.

Morgan, M. J. Embryology and inheritance of asymmetry. In S. R. Harnad, R. W. Doty, L. Goldstein, J. Jaynes, & G. Krauthamer (Eds.), *Lateralization in the nervous system.* New York: Academic Press, 1976.

Nagylaki, T., & Levy, J. "The sound of one paw clapping" isn't sound. *Behavior Genetics,* 1973, *3,* 279–292.

Needham, R. (Ed.). *Right and left: Essays on dual symbolic classification.* Chicago: University of Chicago Press, 1973.

Newman, H. H. *Multiple human births.* New York: Doubleday, Doran & Co., 1940.

Nottebohm, F., Neural lateralization of vocal control in a passerine bird. I. Song. *Journal of Experimental Zoology,* 1971, *177,* 229–262.

Nottebohm, F. Neural lateralization of vocal control in a passerine bird. II. Subsong, calls, and a theory of vocal learning. *Journal of Experimental Zoology*, 1972, *179*, 25–50.

Ramaley, F. Inheritance of left-handedness. *American Naturalist*, 1913, *47*, 730–738.

Richardson, J. T. E. How to measure laterality. *Neuropsychologia*, 1976, *14*, 135–136.

Rife, D. C. Handedness, with special reference to twins. *Genetics*, 1940, *25*, 178–186.

Rife, D. C. Application of gene frequency analysis to the interpretation of data from twins. *Human Biology*, 1950, *22*, 136–145.

Rossi, G. F., & Rosadini, G. Experimental analysis of cerebral dominance in man. In C. H. Millikan & F. L. Darley (Eds.), *Brain mechanisms underlying speech and language*. New York: Grune & Stratton, 1967.

Satz, P. Pathological left-handedness: An explanatory model. *Cortex*, 1972, *8*, 121–135.

Stern, C. Gene action. In B. H. Williere, P. A. Weiss, & V. Hamburger (Eds.), *Analysis of development*. New York: Hafner Publishing Co., 1971. (Facsimile of 1955 edition).

Trankell, A. Aspects of genetics in psychology. *American Journal of Human Genetics*, 1955, *7*, 264–276.

Wada, J. A., Clarke, R., & Hamm, A. Cerebral hemispheric asymmetry in humans. *Archives of Neurology*, 1975, *32*, 239–246.

Wada, J. A., & Rasmussen, T. Intracarotid injection of sodium amytal for the lateralization of speech dominance: Experimental and clinical observations. *Journal of Neurosurgery*, 1960, *17*, 266–282.

Warrington, E. K., & Pratt, R. T. C. Language laterality in left handers assessed by unilateral ECT. *Neuropsychologia*, 1973, *11*, 423–428.

Witelson, S. F. & Pallie, W. Left hemisphere specialization for language in the newborn: Neuroanatomical evidence of asymmetry. *Brain*, 1973, *96*, 641–646.

Yeni-Komshian, G. H., & Benson, D. A. Anatomical study of cerebral asymmetry in the temporal lobe of humans, chimpanzees, and rhesus monkeys. *Science*, 1976, *192*, 387–389.

Zangwill, O. L. *Cerebral dominance and its relation to psychological function*. Edinburgh: Oliver & Boyd, 1960.

Zurif, E. B., & Bryden, M. P. Familial handedness and left-right differentiation in auditory and visual perception. *Neuropsychologia*, 1969, *7*, 179–187.

6

A Model for the Ontogeny of Cerebral Organization in Non-Right-Handers

MARCEL KINSBOURNE

INTRODUCTION

Almost all right-handers are left lateralized for language, but many non-right-handers are right lateralized or have bilateral language representation (Rasmussen & Milner, 1976). Their anomalous cerebral dominance could be due either to brain damage effects or to variations in the genetic control of cerebral dominance itself. Both mechanisms appear to operate. In populations with a presumptively high incidence of brain damage, non-right-handedness is represented in a proportion well in excess of the 10–11% customarily found in the general population. Thus, among the mentally retarded, left-handers are more prevalent the more severe the retardation (Hicks & Barton, 1975). This excess could be due to damage to the left motor cortex that sufficiently impairs right-hand (RH) dexterity to make it expedient to switch hand preference (Satz, 1972). But in samples of the general population, no such impairment of RH dexterity among non-right-handers is to be found (Briggs, Kinsbourne, & Chow, 1977) and there is good evidence that most non-right-handedness in the general population is genetically determined (Hicks & Kinsbourne, 1976). What is the mechanism that establishes laterality of cerebral function, and what are the genetically determined variations in that mechanism which account for the anomalies in cerebral organization that are prevalent among non-right-handers?

NEUROPSYCHOLOGY
OF LEFT-HANDEDNESS

HYPOTHESES ABOUT THE BRAIN BASIS OF
CEREBRAL SPECIALIZATION

The brain basis of cerebral specialization is not known, but there are two alternatives to choose from. One is that neuronal interconnections are differently structured in different cerebral locations, so that each location is structured in a manner conducive to the optimal performance of a particular mental operation. The other is that no such differentiation initially exists, but that there is provision for the differential activation of different areas of cerebrum when different mental operations are called for.

Although it has been suggested on theoretical grounds that neuronal networks are more focally interconnected in the left than the right hemisphere, thus adapting the left hemisphere for analytic and the right for more global types of processing (Semmes, 1968), there is no evidence to support this contention. The minor asymmetries in the gross configuration of the cerebral hemispheres that have been reported are equivocal in interpretation. The significance for left lateralized language of a longer planum temporale on the left (Geschwind & Levitsky, 1968; Witelson & Pallie, 1973) is offset by the greater extent of Broca's area (Wada, Clark, & Hamm, 1975) and Wernicke's area (Akesson, Dahlgren, & Hyde, 1975) on the right side. In any case, the prevalence of systematic, measureable, anatomical asymmetries between the hemispheres does not approach the figure of some 95–96% that is required to match the actual incidence of left-sided language dominance in the population. Furthermore, if the neuronal hardware in each hemisphere is specified from the start, it would be hard to account for the ability of each hemisphere to assume the cognitive role of the other when the latter is damaged, particularly early in life (Kohn & Dennis, 1974: Smith, 1974). Finally, it is highly doubtful whether the mere bulk of cerebal tissue can be equated with the degree of functional sophistication (Lenneberg, 1967). It therefore becomes worthwhile to search for alternative determinants of lateralization of cerebral function.

The fact that a particular part of the cerebrum usually assumes a particular role in cognitive processing does not necessarily imply that it is uniquely fitted for this role. The area in question could have obtained ascendency over another area of comparable potential as a control center by virtue of being more activated at the relevant times. In other words, the area in question might be selectively more activated, or competing areas selectivley inhibited, whenever circumstances call for the relevant processing mode. Adaptive behavior results from two consecutive brain based events: The adoption of the appropriate response set ("switching in" of the relevant processor) and the execution of the response (activity of the switched-in professor). For instance, adopting a verbal response set must precede verbal activity. There must be a mechanism in the brain for switching-in the cerebral language processor when its assistance is called for.

Evidence is accumulating for a brain stem role in cognition. Left-brain-stem (especially thalamic) injury and stimulation affect verbal processes and right-sided injury and stimulation affect spatial processes (Brown, 1975; Ojemann, 1975; Ojemann & Ward, 1971; Riklan & Levita, 1970). The exact nature of the brain stem contribution to these cognitive modes is not known, but it is clear that asymmetrical brain stem stimulation can elicit a selective orienting response from the ipsilateral cortex (Heilman & Watson, 1977). Ojemann and Ward (1971) and Ojemann (1975) have credited the ventrolateral thalamus with a role in the selective activation of one cerebral hemisphere. Our model will assume that asymmetrical cerebral activation results from asymmetrical brain stem activity. In other words, each cerebral hemisphere is "switched-in" by the corresponding side of the brain stem.

BRAIN STEM ACTIVITY AND CEREBRAL ASYMMETRY

Given this presumption, it becomes illuminating to consider asymmetries in brain stem activity in individuals who lack cognitive capabilities (i.e., newborn infants). Can we detect in them the brain stem antecedent of cerebral dominance? That is, can we identify a brain stem selector system that develops ahead of the cerebral processors that it will ultimately select?

The idea that selection can develop ahead of processing is consistent with known facts of behavioral development. Thus, infants show interactional synchrony (i.e., move in the rhythm of an adult's speech) well before they can decode the message (Condon, 1971). Much of infant play, and certainly babbling, can be understood as form preceding content; the selectors activate response systems before these come under the control of higher level processors. Does symmetrical stimulation in newborn infants generate asymmetrical response? So it has been shown (Davis & Wada, 1977; Molfese, Freeman, & Palermo, 1975; Gardiner, Schulman, & Walter, 1973). But, although the recordings are made over cortex, this does not necessarily imply a cortical processing activity. It could instead indicate a lateralized alerting of the cortex by the brain stem in a material-specific fashion.

Perhaps the most generally prevalent consequence of lateralized alerting is orienting (turning) contralateral to the side of the activated brain (Kinsbourne, 1974), and asymmetrical turning tendencies are conspicuous in infant behavior. Preponderantly right-sided orienting, either in a free field or in response to symmetrical stimulation, was noted by Gesell (1938), Siqueland and Lipsitt (1966) and Turkewitz, Gordon, and Birch (1965).

Liederman and Kinsbourne (in press) have shown that this asymmetry is not accounted for by positional biases, applies to withdrawal from negatively valenced stimuli as well as approach to positively valenced stimuli, and must be considered to be an asymmetrical response set that is species-specific in nature. This asymmetry of motor control could be an antecedent of the asymmetry of grasp which was demonstrated as early as 3-months-of-age by Caplan and Kinsbourne (1976), and this in turn may be a precursor of the subsequent asymmetry of manual preference and dexterity. It is therefore important to note that this asymmetry in turning was found only for the offspring of parents both of whom were right-handed. It was not found for offspring of one or two non-right-handed parents (Liederman & Kinsbourne, submitted).

THE SELECTIVE ACTIVATION MODEL OF CEREBRAL LATERALIZATION

We are now in a position to suggest a precursor for left-sided cerebral control of verbal response. It is a special case of the more general bias toward left-sided control of responding. By the same token, we expect, and find, left hemisphere control of nonspeech skilled motor behavior (Kimura & Archibald, 1974). The postulated mechanism is a greater readiness of the left brain to adopt a response set. In newborns this involves the primitive approach and withdrawal synergisms (Schneirla, 1939). Subsequent to cerebral maturation, the bias carries over to various specialized and even internalized response sets. The left cerebral hemisphere assumes control over verbal responding not because it contains specialized neuronal hardware suited to the purpose, but because it is selectively activated under circumstances that call for such responding.

The following, then, is the model as it applies to genotypic right-handers:

1. Cerebral dominance is based on left-lateralized cerebral activation during the adoption of a verbal mental set.
2. This lateralized activation results from lateralized brain stem (thalamic) activity exclusively projected to the left cerebral hemisphere.
3. It follows that a loss (i.e., pathology) of the left hemisphere leaves the individual with an intact residual hemisphere that has language potential, but *cannot* be accessed by the brain stem selector system.
4. The gradual evolution of recovery from severe aphasia would then represent the gradual establishment of connections between the brain stem selector for adoption of a verbal response set and the right hemisphere as this has become responsible for the aphasic speech (Kinsbourne, 1971; Czopf, 1972).

5. Such compensation occurs more readily in the immature and, therefore, more plastic nervous system (though it may not compensate totally even at a very early age—see Kohn & Dennis, 1974) and still does occur when the brain is mature (Kinsbourne, 1971; Czopf, 1972).

Let us now consider how this mechanism might differ in non-right-handers. When the wealth of comparative data about asymmetries other than manual in non-right-handed versus right-handed groups is considered in overview, the following generalization is justified (Hicks & Kinsbourne, 1978): Non-right-handers are, as a group, less asymmetrical in virtually every respect—physically, neuropsychologically, and behaviorally. We propose that they are also less asymmetrical with regard to the distribution of their cortical activation during the adoption of various cognitive sets. That is, their selector system is less exclusive in its cerebral connections, and activates the cerebrum more diffusely.

We have already seen that the right-sided response bias in newborns is missing from the group of non-right-handed parentage (Liederman & Kinsbourne, submitted). There are also good grounds for supposing that a more diffuse (bilateral) activation occurs in many non-right-handers during cognitive function when the nervous system is fully mature.

An extensive literature attests to the superiority of right-handers' response to verbal information (visual or acoustic) deriving from the right as compared to the left side of space. These hemifield and dichotic asymmetries can be regarded as due to orientational biases contralateral to the hemisphere specialized for verbal processing. A paradigm introduced by Kinsbourne (1972) makes this explicit. Given verbal problems to solve, subjects turn their head and eyes to the right while preparing their response (whereas they turn up and to the left for spatial and numerical problems). This finding has been supported by several studies (Gur, Gur, & Harris, 1975; Kocel, Galin, Ornstein, & Merrin, 1972; Schwartz, Davidson, & Maer, 1975). It makes overt the fact that a selective lateral orienting response can be a marker for asymmetrical cerebral activation (see also Bowers & Heilman, 1976). With respect to all these behavioral asymmetries, non-right-handers, where investigated, yield less asymmetrical and more variable findings—that is, they show a more bilaterally diffuse pattern of cerebral activation. Such relative diffuseness of cerebral activation could result in exactly the range of anomalies in cerebral dominance relationships that prevails among non-right-handers (i.e., some left, some right, and some bilaterally specified for language processes).

Here, then, is the model adapted for the non-right-handed genotype:

1. Cerebral dominance is based on diffuse cerebral activation during the adoption of a verbal mental set.

2. This diffuse activation results from less laterally polarized brain stem (thalamic) influence that is projected to both cerebral hemispheres.
3. It follows that a loss (i.e., pathology) of the language-dominant hemisphere leaves the individual with an intact residual hemisphere that has language potential, and *can* be accessed by the brain stem selector system.
4. The more rapid recovery of non-right-handers from aphasia (Subirana, 1958) would be due to the ready availability of connections between the brain stem selector system for the adoption of a verbal response set and the residual hemisphere.
5. This would give non-right-handers an advantage in recovery from aphasia at any level of maturation of the nervous system.

Incidentally, the model draws a distinction that is often overlooked between area of brain that is activated and area of brain that is specifically involved in a particular process. Once we understand dichotic, visual hemifield, and kindred effects as representing the distribution of activation across the brain (i.e., cerebral selective orienting response), then we realize that this could be a misleading indicator of the actual location of the active processor. For instance, both right-handers and many left-handers are left lateralized for language. If during verbal activity, the left-hander yields less marked dichotic or visual hemifield asymmetries, this does not necessarily indicate a different location of the language processor. It could merely imply that in the left-handed group, activity is not *confined* to the left hemisphere (even if the left hemisphere happens to do all the cognitive work). Finally, to illustrate the heuristic value of the selective activation model of cerebral lateralization, we refer to the unresolved question of whether anomalous cerebral organization per se, as distinct from any antecedent brain damage, is in any way detrimental to cognitive functioning.

Although it has repeatedly been suggested that non-right-handers are at a cognitive disadvantage, large-scale studies have not confirmed these claims (Hardyck & Petrinovich, 1977; Hicks & Kinsbourne, 1978). Yet indications of differences in the cognitive development of right- and non-right-handers persist (Kocel, Chapter 14 of this volume; Swanson, Kinsbourne & Horn, Chapter 13 of this volume). The present model suggests why that might be. As long as the individual is engaged in one task at a time, and that task calls solely for one mode of thinking, then there is no obvious reason why it would matter which part of the brain is doing the processing, and how diffusely about that area the activation spreads. It would be different, however, if psychometric test instruments included dual task performance, for the following reason: The cerebrum is highly linked neuronally.

If a person is concurrently engaged in uncorrelated tasks, then the two active loci are at risk of generating mutually interfering cross-talk. According to the functional cerebral space model (Kinsbourne & Hicks, 1978), the greater the functional distance between the two loci (i.e., the less interconnected they are), the less the risk of cross-talk interference and the greater the efficiency of concurrent performance. If subjects concurrently perform a verbal and a spatial task and these are programmed in separate hemispheres, the cross-talk will be minimal. But if representation is diffuse, as in those non-right-handers who are diffusely lateralized, then there will be little or no functional distance between the two active loci, and cross-talk interference will be severly handicapping.

The model therefore predicts that some non-right-handers will be disproportionately at a disadvantage if given tasks that call for conjoint use of the two hemispheres in different tasks. This prediction remains to be tested specifically. However, a task analysis of certain psychometric instruments from this perspective might illuminate some curious recent findings. We refer to reports in this volume by Kocel (Chapter 14) and by Swanson, Kinsbourne, and Horn (Chapter 13), that non-right-handers show a decline relative to right-handedness in late childhood on certain intelligence tests. Perhaps the more difficult tests given the older children are more difficult because they tend to call for a combination of processing modes, rather than just one at a time. According to our model, this is the kind of test on which non-right-handers would experience disproportionate difficulty. Then it could be that the relative decline in IQ is an artifact of differences in the kind of questions asked of the children at an earlier and a later age.

REFERENCES

Akesson, E. J., Dahlgren, W. J., & Hyde, J. B. Memory and growth in the superior temporal gyri. *The Canadian Journal of Neurological Sciences*, 1975, 2; 191–194.

Barnet, A., De Sotillo, M., & Campos, E. *EEG sensory evoked potentials in early infancy malnutrition.* Paper presented at Society for Neuroscience, St. Louis, 1974.

Bowers, D., & Heilman, K. M. Material specific hemispheric arousal. *Neuropsychologia*, 1976, *14*, 123–127.

Briggs, G. G., Kinsbourne, M., & Chow, S. L. Relation of finger tapping skill and handedness: A test of the prevalence of pathological left handedness in the general population. Unpublished manuscript.

Brown, J. W. On the neural organization of language: Thalamic and cortical relationships. *Brain and Language*, 1975, 2, 18–30.

Caplan, P., & Kinsbourne, M. Baby drops the rattle: Asymmetry of duration of grasp by infants. *Child Development*, 1976, 47, 532–534.

Condon, N. S. & Ogston, Speech and baby motion synchrony of the speaker–hearer. *The Perception of Language*, D. Horton & J. Jenkins, (Eds.). Columbia, Ohio: Merrill, 1971.

Czopf, J. Uber die Rolle der nicht dominanten Hemisphere in der Restitution der Sprache des Aphasischen. *Arch. Psychiatr. Nervenkr.*, 1972, *216*, 162–171.

Davis, A., & Wada, J. Hemispheric asymmetries in human infants: Spectal analysis of flash and click evoked potentials. *Brain and Language*, 1977, *4*, 23-31.

Gardiner, M. F., & Walter, D. O. Evidence of hemispheric specialization from infant EGG. In S. Harnad, R. W. Dody, L. Goldstein, J. Jaynes, & G. Krauthamer (Eds.) *Lateralization in the nervous system.* New York: Academic Press. 1976.

Gardiner, M. F., Schulman, C., & Walter, D. O. Facultative EGG asymmetries in infants and adults. *Cerebral Dominance, Brain Information Service Conference Report*, 1973, *34*, 37-40.

Gesell, A. The tonic neck reflex in the human infant. *Journal of Pediatrics*, 1938, *13*, 455-464.

Gur, R. E., Gur, R. C., & Harris, L. J. Cerebral activation, as measured by subjects' lateral eye movements, is influenced by experimenter location. *Neuropsychologia*, 1975, *13*, 35-44.

Geschwind, N ., & Levitsky, W. Human brain: Left-right asymmetries in temporal speech region. *Science*, 1968, *161*, 186-187.

Hardyck, C., & Petrinovich, L. F. Left-handedness. *Psychological Bulletin*, 1977, *84*, 385-404.

Hilman, K. M., & Watson, R. T. The neglect syndrome—A unilateral defect of the orienting response. In E. Weinstein (Ed.) *Hemi-inattention and hemisphere specialization.* New York: Raven Press, 1977.

Hicks, R. E., & Barton, A. K. A note on left-handedness and severity of mental retardation. *Journal of Genetic Psychology*, 1975, *127*, 323-324.

Hicks, R. E., & Kinsbourne, M. *Human handedness: A partial cross-fostering study. Science*, 1976, *192*, 908-910.

Hicks, R. E., & Kinsbourne, M. Handedness differences—Human handedness. In M. Kinsbourne (Ed.) *Asymmetrical function of the brain.* New York: Cambridge University Press, 1978.

Kimura, C., & Archibald, Y. Motor functions of the left hemisphere. *Brain*, 1974, *97*, 337-350.

Kinsbourne, M. The minor cerebral hemisphere as a source of aphasic speech. *Archives of Neurology*, 1971, *25*, 302-306.

Kinsbourne, M. Eye and head turning indicate cerebral lateralization. *Science*, 1972, *176*, 539-541.

Kinsbourne, M. Lateral interactions in the brain. In M. Kinsbourne & W. L. Smith (Eds.) *Hemispheric disconnection and cerebral function.* Springfield, Ill.: Thomas, 1974.

Kinsbourne, M., & Hicks, R. E. Functional cerebral space: A model for overflow, transfer and interference effects in human performance. In J. Requin (Ed.) *Attention and performance VII.* New York: Academic Press, 1978.

Kocel, K., Galin, D., Ornstein, R., & Merrin, E. Lateral eye movement and cognitive mode. *Psychonomic Science*, 1972, *27*, 223-224.

Kohn, B., & Dennis, M. Patterns of hemispheric specialization after hemidecortication for infantile hemiplegia. In M. Kinsbourne, & W. L. Smith (Eds.) *Hemispheric disconnection and cerebral function.* Springfield, Illinois: Thomas, 1974.

Lenneberg, E. H. *Biological foundations of language.* New York: Wiley, 1967.

Liederman, J., & Kinsbourne, M. The mechanism of the neonatal rightward turning bias: a sensory or motor asymmetry? Infant Behavior and Development, in press.

Molfese, D. L., Freeman, R. B., & Palermo, D. S. The ontogeny of brain lateralization for speech and non-speech stimuli. *Brain and Language*, 1975, *2*, 356-368.

Ojemann, G. A. Language and the thalamus: Object naming and recall during and after thalamic stimulation. *Brain and Language*, 1975, *1*, 101-120.

Ojemann, G., & Ward, A. Speech representation in ventrolateral thalamus. *Brain*, 1971, *94*, 669-680.

Rasmussen, T., & Milner, B. Clinical and surgical studies of the cerebral speech areas in man. In K. J. Zülch, O. Creutzfeldt & G. Galbraith (Eds.) *Otfried Foerster Symposium on Cerebral Localization.* Heidelberg: Springer, 1976.

Riklan, M., & Levita, B. Psychological and electroencephalographic relationships and cryo-thalamectomy for Parkinsonism. *Perceptual and Motor Skills,* 1970, *30,* 799–810.

Satz, P. Pathological left handedness: An explanatory model. *Cortex,* 1972, *8,* 121–135.

Schneider, G. E. Two visual systems. *Science,* 1969, *163,* 895–902.

Schneirla, T. C. A theoretical consideration of the basis for approach-withdrawal adjustments in behavior. *Psychological Bulletin,* 1939, *37,* 501–502.

Schwartz, G. E., Davidson, R., & Maer, F. Right hemisphere lateralization for emotion in the human brain: Interactions with cognition. *Science,* 1975, *190,* 286–288.

Semmes, J. Hemispheric specialization: A possible clue to mechanism. *Neuropsychologia,* 1968, *6,* 11–26.

Siqueland, E., & Lipsitt, L. Conditioned head turning in human newborns. *Journal of Experimental Child Psychology,* 1966, *4,* 356–357.

Smith, A. Dominant and nondominant hemispherectomy. In M. Kinsbourne & W. L. Smith (Eds.) *Hemispheric disconnection and cerebral function.* Springfield, Illinois: Thomas, 1974.

Subirana, H. The prognosis in aphasia in relation to the factor of cerebral dominance and handedness. *Brain,* 1958, *8,* 415–425.

Turkewitz, G., Gordon E., & Birch, H. Head turning in the human neonate: Spontaneous patterns. *Journal of Genetic Psychology,* 1965, *107,* 143–158.

Wada, J. A., Clark, R., & Hamm, A. Cerebral hemispheric asymmetry in humans: Cortical speech zones in 100 adult and 100 infant brains. *Archives of Neurology,* 1975, *32,* 239–246.

Witelson, S. F., & Pallie, W. Left hemisphere specialization for language in the newborn: Neuroanatomical evidence for asymmetry. *Brain,* 1973, *96,* 641–646.

II

CEREBRAL VARIATION: THE MOST CONSISTENT SINISTRAL ATTRIBUTE

7

Incidence of Aphasia in Left-Handers: A Test of Some Hypothetical Models of Cerebral Speech Organization[1]

PAUL SATZ

INTRODUCTION

Considerable controversy still exists concerning the cerebral organization of speech and language in left-handed adults. One of the earliest theories was advanced by Hughlings Jackson (1880). Jackson invoked the classical rule that the dominant speech hemisphere is contralateral to the preferred hand—namely, the right hemisphere in left-handers and the left hemisphere in right-handers. Exceptions to this classical rule were later reported in left-handers by a number of investigators who observed aphasic symptoms more often after left-hemispheric lesions. Bramwell (1899) introduced the term "crossed aphasia" to describe cases of aphasia due to a lesion of the hemisphere ipsilateral to the preferred hand, particularly in left-handers.

The major evidence against the classical theory of cerebral speech dominance in left-handers was based on the large series of epileptic patients followed by Penfield and Roberts in Montreal (1959). They showed that transient dysphasia followed surgery on the left hemisphere no more frequently in right-handers (73%) than in left-handers (72%). Moreover, dysphasia following surgery on the right hemisphere was not significantly more frequent in the left-handed than in the right-handed. Based on these results, they concluded that the left hemisphere is dominant for speech in the vast majority of left- and right-handers. According to the authors: "The

[1] This research was supported, in part, by funds from the National Institute of Health (NS08208).

189

reason why the right hemisphere is sometimes dominant for speech remains unclear, but it is not related solely to handedness [Penfield & Roberts, 1959, p. 102]."

This *unilateral* position of brain lateralization (left hemispheric speech) is discrepant with more recent findings that report a more variable pattern of cerebral speech dominance in left-handers (Hécaen & Sauguet, 1971). Briefly, three different positions have been advanced with respect to hemispheric speech lateralization in left-handers. The first might be referred to as a *variable unilateral* position, which assumes that speech representation is lateralized either in the left or the right hemisphere in left-handers, with the majority being left-sided (approximately 66%). This position represents a fusion of both the classical theory (Jackson, 1880) and the concept of "crossed aphasia" advanced by Bramwell (1899). Support for this position comes from studies of unilaterally brain-injured adults (Piercey, 1964) and non-brain-injured psychiatric patients who have undergone unilateral electroconvulsive therapy (ECT) for depression (Warrington & Pratt, 1973). This latter position, however, contrasts with studies that have used sodium amytal to determine hemispheric speech dominance in epileptic patients awaiting surgery (Milner, 1973). The latter findings lend support for a more *variable unilateral and bilateral* representation of speech in left-handers. This position postulates three different types of hemispheric speech dominance in left-handers, a left-sided group (70%), a right-sided group (15%) and a bilateral group (15%). Despite differences in the two latter positions, it should be noted that the majority of left-handers are nevertheless postulated to have left-sided dominance for speech and language.

This concept of different types of functional brain lateralization in left-handers is also reflected in a third position that postulates a much greater representation of bilateral speech. For convenience, one might refer to the latter as a *bilateral and variable unilateral* position. Support for this position, based on the results of unilaterally brain-injured left-handers, is as follows: (a) a higher incidence of expressive aphasia (Broca's type); (b) fewer comprehensional defects; (c) fewer symptoms of aculculia, agraphia, and alexia; (d) less symptom severity and (e) faster recovery. The most striking phenomenon concerns the differential recovery course in left-handers. In fact, Luria (1947) and Subirana (1958) have reported a dramatic remission of aphasic symptoms not only in left-handers but in those right-handers having a history of familial sinistrality (FS+). These findings led Hécaen and Ajuriaguerra (1964) to hypothesize "that the cerebral mechanisms of language in the left-handed have an organization which is comparatively less resistant to an acute disturbance (due to greater equipotentiality) but which is nevertheless more capable of being reorganized after the occurrence of the lesion than are the 'more organized' mechanisms of the right-handed [p. 113]." Despite the attractiveness of this hypothesis, some investigators have failed to demonstrate a more rapid recovery course in left-handers following unilateral brain injury (Newcombe & Ratcliff, 1973; Russell & Espir, 1961).

More consistent support for this position is based on reports of a higher frequency of aphasia (largely Broca's type), regardless of prognosis, in unilaterally brain-injured left-handers (Hécaen & Ajuriaguerra, 1964; Hécaen & Sauguet, 1971; Gloning, Gloning, Haub, & Quatember, 1969). This raised incidence of aphasia has prompted some investigators to postulate an incomplete functional lateralization of speech in the vast majority of left-handers resulting in a greater sensitivity to acute brain lesions (Gloning et al., 1969; Hécaen & Ajuriaguerra, 1964; Zangwill, 1960). By contrast, other investigators have taken more moderate views postulating different subtypes of hemispheric organization that include both bilateral and variable unilateral representation of speech. Hécaen and Sauguet (1971) have recently taken this view. They postulate at least three different types of cerebral speech organization in left-handers: a unilateral speech group (left- or right-sided) and a bilateral speech group who are primarily FS+. Unfortunately, no evidence is available at present to estimate the proportion of left-handers in the population who fall into each of these hypothetical speech–brain groups. At one extreme of this controversy, Penfield and Roberts (1959) estimate that the vast majority of left-handers are left-brained for speech whereas, at the other extreme, Gloning and associates (1969) estimate that the majority of left-handers are bilaterally represented for speech.

Although studies reporting a higher incidence and recovery from aphasia suggest a different pattern of hemispheric speech lateralization in left-handers, they provide no information on the *type* of brain lateralization that might be involved. For example, an increased frequency of aphasic symptoms, following unilateral brain-injury in left-handers, merely suggests that the pattern of speech lateralization is different than in right-handers. Beyond that, it provides no information on whether the pattern of hemispheric speech lateralization is compatible with a variable unilateral representation (left- or right-sided) or a more complex form of bilateral and variable unilateral speech. The reason is that in none of the positions previously described, including the *unilateral* position for right-handers, has one determined the specific upper limit of aphasia that would be expected, assuming that aphasia invariably occurred following random unilateral damage to the dominant speech hemisphere in adults (left, right, or bilateral). If these upper limits could be quantitatively established, then one could use the observed data in the literature, on the frequency of aphasia following unilateral brain-injury in left-handers, to determine the type or pattern of hemispheric speech lateralization involved. The present chapter is addressed to this problem.

METHOD

Hypothetical Models

Each of the preceding hemispheric speech positions (for left- and right-handers) has been incorporated into a separate hypothetical model that includes the probability estimates for speech lateralization (rows) and the probability estimates for lesion side (columns). In other words, the distribution of hemispheric speech (rows), in each model, is based largely on empirical findings, and lesion side is assumed to be random in nature (columns). Consequently, if one assumes that aphasia will always occur following injury to the dominant speech hemisphere, then one can compute the upper limit of aphasia that can be expected for each model.

Model 1 (Unilateral Model)

This model is presented in Table 7.1 for 100 hypothetical cases and represents the presumed pattern of speech lateralization for right-handers and left-handers based on the findings of Penfield and Roberts (1959; left-sided speech lateralization occurs in 96%, right-sided speech lateralization occurs in 4%). In addition, lesion side is random so that half the cases are left-brain-injured and half are right. Consequently, if aphasia always followed injury to the dominant speech hemisphere, the expected upper limit of aphasia in this model would be 48 (following left-sided damage) plus 2 (following right-sided damage) or 50% (i.e., out of 100 cases).

Table 7.1
Unilateral Model (1): Right-Handers or Left-Handers[a]

| | Lesion hemisphere | | |
Speech hemisphere	Left	Right	Percentage
Left	48 (Aphasic)	48	96
Right	2	2 (Aphasic)	4
Total	50	50	100

[a] The expected incidence (upper limit) of aphasia equals $(48 + 2)/100$ or $50/100(50\%)$.

Model 2 (Variable Unilateral Model)

This model is presented in Table 7.2 for 100 hypothetical cases and represents the presumed lateralization of speech for left-handers (Piercy, 1964; Warrington & Pratt, 1973). In this model, the percentage of left- and right-hemispheric speech is 66% and 34%, respectively; also, half of the cases are left-brain-injured and half are right-brain-injured. Inspection of Table 7.2 shows that the expected upper limit of aphasia [(33 + 17)/100 or 50%] is identical to Model I (Unilateral Model), despite the more variable unilateral pattern of speech representation in this model. This finding shows that the incidence of aphasia following unilateral brain injury could not be used to differentiate Model 1 from Model 2.

Model 3 (Variable Unilateral and Bilateral Model)

This model is presented in Table 7.3 for 100 hypothetical cases and represents the presumed lateralization of speech for left-handers based on sodium amytal studies (Milner, 1973). In this table, the distribution of speech lateralization is as follows: left comprises 70%, right comprises 15%, and bilateral comprises 15%. Inspection of Table 7.3 shows that the

Table 7.2
Variable Unilateral Model (2): Left-Handers[a]

	Lesion hemisphere		
Speech hemisphere	Left	Right	Percentage
Left	33 (Aphasic)	33	66
Right	17	17 (Aphasic)	34
Total	50	50	100

[a] The expected incidence (upper limit) of aphasia equals (33 + 17)/100 or 50/100 (50%).

Table 7.3
Variable Unilateral and Bilateral Model (3): Left-Handers[a]

	Lesion hemisphere		
Speech hemisphere	Left	Right	Percentage
Left	35 (Aphasic)	35	70
Right	7.5	7.5 (Aphasic)	15
Bilateral	7.5 (Aphasic)	7.5 (Aphasic)	15
Total	50	50	100

[a] The expected incidence (upper limit) of aphasia equals (35 + 7.5 + 7.5 + 7.5)/100 or 57.5/100 (57.5%).

expected upper limit of aphasia following unilateral brain injury would be higher here than for either of the preceding two models [Model 3 level would be (35 + 7.5 + 7.5 + 7.5)/100 or 57.5%].

Model 4 (Bilateral and Variable Unilateral Model)

This model (Table 7.4) is presented for 100 hypothetical cases and represents the presumed distribution of speech based on studies that reveal three different patterns of hemispheric speech representation in left-handers (Hécaen & Sauguet, 1971)—a bilateral speech group and a variable unilateral speech group (left- and right-sided). Lacking empirical data, these frequency estimates are postulated to be as follows: left-hemispheric speech comprises 40%, right-hemispheric speech comprises 20%, and bilateral speech comprises 40%. These prior probability values, in contrast to the preceding models, represent more subjective estimates of speech lateralization. This procedure is permissable because the model merely postulates a hypothetical distribution of speech–brain lateralization that generates the upper limit of aphasia to be expected in the model based on these assumptions. Evaluation of the model must rest ultimately on the basis of observed data (i.e., the incidence of aphasia following unilateral left- and right-sided brain injury in left-handers). Inspection of Table 7.4 shows that the upper limit of aphasia to be expected in this model is much higher than in the preceding models, largely because of the increased percentage of bilateral speech [(20 + 10 + 20 + 20)/100 or 70%].

RESULTS

Test of Models

The test for each of the models is based on a review of those studies that reported the observed frequency of aphasia following unilateral brain in-

Table 7.4
Bilateral and Variable Unilateral Model (4): Left-Handers[a]

| Speech hemisphere | Lesion hemisphere | | Percentage |
	Left	Right	
Left	20 (Aphasic)	20	40
Right	10	10 (Aphasic)	20
Bilateral	20 (Aphasic)	20 (Aphasic)	40
Total	50	50	100

[a] The expected Incidence (upper limit) of aphasia equals (20 + 10 + 20 + 20)/100 or 70/100 (70%).

jury (left- and right-sided) in left-handed adults. Twelve studies (1935–1973) were found that met these requirements and they are presented in Table 7.5. Five of the studies also reported data for right-handed patients and results are presented at the bottom of Table 7.5. The data have been recalculated to show the frequency of aphasia following left- and right-sided brain injury in each study (rows) and a computed frequency (percentage) for combined lesions in each study (final column). The overall mean frequency of aphasia across studies is presented at the bottom of the table.

Inspection of this table shows that the incidence of aphasia, following unilateral left- and right-sided brain injury in *left-handers*, ranged from a low of 30% (Newcombe & Ratcliff, 1973) to a high of 92% (Chesher, 1936). Nine of the twelve studies (75%) revealed a mean frequency of aphasia (unilateral combined) that equalled or exceeded the maximal limit predicted by Models 1 and 2. Seven of the twelve studies (58%) revealed a

Table 7.5

Observed Incidence of Aphasia in Left-Handers in Relation to Side of Lesion and Study[a]

		Test of Models				
		Left Side		Right Side		
Studies[b]	Cases	Aphasia	No Aphasic	Aphasia	No Aphasic	Aphasia Frequency Total[c]
1	8	4(67%)	2(33%)	2(100%)	0(0%)	75%
2	12	5(83%)	1(17%)	6(100%)	0(%)	91%
3	20	5(50%)	5(50%)	5(50%)	5(50%)	50%
4	10	5(100%)	0(%)	4(80%)	1(20%)	90%
5	9	6(86%)	1(14%)	2(100%)	0(0%)	90%
6	14	7(59%)	5(41%)	0(0%)	2(100%)	50%
7	13	5(83%)	1(17%)	5(70%)	2(30%)	77%
8	33	13(72%)	5(28%)	1(7%)	14(93%)	42%*
9	63	11(37%)	19(63%)	8(27%)	25(73%)	30%*
10	58	28	?	20	?	83%*
11	59	27(73%)	10(27%)	13(59%)	9(41%)	68%*
12	14	2(50%)	2(50%)	3(30%)	7(70%)	36%*

[a] Frequency of aphasia in right-handers (combined unilateral lesions) as follows: 8(116/353 = 33%); 9(237/704 = 34%); 10(231/650 = 36%); 11(62/163 = 38%); 12(68/200 = 34%). Overall Mean Frequency = 35%(714/2070).

[b] *Studies:* 1(Weisenburg & McBride, 1935); 2(Chesher, 1936); 3(Conrad, 1949); 4(Humphrey & Zangwill, 1952); 5(Zangwill, 1954); 6(Critchley, 1954); 7(Goodglass & Quadfasel, 1954); 8(Penfield & Roberts, 1959); 9(Newcombe & Ratcliff, 1973); 10(Gloning & Quatember, 1966); 11(Hecaen & Ajuriaguerra, 1964); 12(Bingley, 1958).

[c] Overall mean frequency of aphasia in left-handers (combined unilateral lesions) = 60% (187/313).

combined frequency of aphasia that exceeded the maximal limit predicted by Model 3. This means that, even if aphasia occurred each time a lesion encroached on the dominant speech side, the observed frequencies in the majority of the studies would still be higher than the frequencies predicted by Models 1–3. In fact, when the overall mean frequency of aphasia was computed across studies, a value of 60% was obtained which again exceeded the limit predicted by Models 1–3. This overall mean frequency (60%) is felt to be most compatible with Model 4 (Bilateral and Variable Unilateral Model) whose upper limit of aphasia is predicted to be 70%.

These observed frequencies are further strengthened by the findings for *right-handers*. The percentages of aphasia, following unilateral left- and right-sided brain injury, were consistently lower, ranging from 33 (Penfield & Roberts, 1959) to 38% (Hécaen & Ajuriaguerra, 1964). In fact, the overall mean frequency of aphasia in right-handers (35%) remained consistently below the 40% level which would be compatible with Model 1 (Unilateral Model) or Model 2 (Variable Unilateral Model). The upper limit of aphasia predicted from either model is 50% which would only occur if aphasia consistently followed damage to the dominant speech hemisphere.

DISCUSSION

The present findings, based on the observed incidence of aphasia following unilateral brain injury in adults, demonstrate that a different model of hemispheric speech lateralization exists for left-handers and right-handers. A unilateral model represents the best estimate of brain lateralization in right-handers and a more complex model of bilateral and variable unilateral speech represents the best estimate of brain lateralization in left-handers. This latter finding, if true, should encourage more vigorous efforts to identify subgroups of left-handers in the normal population as it relates to brain lateralization and behavioral competence. It certainly buttresses the claim that in terms of hemispheric brain lateralization left-handers represent a more heterogeneous group than right-handers (Zangwill, 1960).

Future studies might well profit from attempts to identify these subgroups on an *a priori* basis and then proceed to test more theoretical problems relating to genetics and behavior (e.g., cognition). For example, Model 4 demonstrates that a large number of left-handers may have bilateral speech (40%). This is the subgroup that Hécaen and Sauguet (1971) suggest may have FS+ for left-handedness. Is this also the subgroup that accounts for the greater recovery from aphasia following unilateral brain injury? It would also be important to know whether the greater hemispheric equipotentiality of speech in this subgroup confers a special disadvantage in Gestalt-spatial functions as compared with left-handers having unilateral speech representation. Unfortunately, this hypothesis has recently been tested on left-handers, most of whom have been presumed to have bilateral hemispheric speech (Levy, 1969). No reliable differences between handedness groups have been found when left-handers are treated alike with respect to hemispheric organization (Fennell, Satz, Van den Abel, Bowers, & Thomas, 1977; Newcombe & Ratcliff, 1973).

One might note that the distribution of speech–brain groups in this model (4) is such that 80% of the left-handers are predicted to have *at least* partial representation of speech in the left hemisphere. This finding would partially explain why some of the more indirect measures of cerebral speech dominance fail to detect robust or reliable differences between handedness groups (Altman, Sutker, & Satz, 1974). The model would also predict that, on dichotic, verbal, listening tasks, a right-ear superiority should occur for both left- and right-handers, with a more pronounced asymmetry for right-handers (group by ear interaction). Although this interaction has long been reported (Satz, Achenbach, Pattichall, & Fennell, 1965), it provided no information as to whether the effect was due to a variable unilateral or more complex model of hemispheric speech organization in left-handers.

Finally, the existence of different speech–brain groups in Model 4 should caution future investigators against the use of small unselected samples of left-handers in their studies on the relationship between brain function and handedness.

REFERENCES

Altman, A., Sutker, L. & Satz, P. Hemispheric processing of verbal information in right and left handers. Paper presentation, International Neuropsychology Society, Boston, 1974.

Bingley, T. Mental symptoms in temporal lobe epilepsy and temporal lobe gliomas. *Acta Psychiatrica et Neurologica Scandinavica*, 1958, *33*, Supplementum 120.

Bramwell, B. On "crossed" aphasia and the factors which go to determine whether the "leading" or "driving" speech-centers shall be located in the left or in the right hemisphere of the brain. *Lancet*, 1899, *1*, 1473–1479.

Chesher, E. C. Some observations concerning the relation of handedness to the language mechanism. *Bulletin Neurological Institute New York*, 1936, *4*, 556–562.

Conrad, K. Über aphasische Sprachstorungen bei hiruverletzten Linkshanderm. *Nervenarzt*, 1949, *20*, 148–154.

Critchley, M. Parietal syndromes in ambidextrous and left-handed subjects. *Zbl. Neurochir.*, 1954, *14*, 4–16.

Fennell, E., Satz, P., Van den Abell, T., Bowers, D. & Thomas, R. Visuo-spatial competency, handedness and cerebral dominance. *Brain and Language*, 1978, *5*, 206–214.

Gloning, I., Gloning, K., Haub, G. & Quatember, R. Comparison of verbal behavior in right-handed and non-right-handed patients with anatomically verified lesion of one hemisphere. *Cortex*, 1969, *5*, 43–52.

Gloning, I. & Quatember, R. Statistical evidence of neuropsychological syndrome in left-handed and ambidextrous patients. *Cortex*, 1966, *2*, 484–488.

Goodglass, H. & Quadfasel, F. A. Language laterality in left-handed patients. *Brain*, 1954, *77*, 521–548.

Hécaen, H. & Ajuriaguerra, J. *Left-handedness*. New York: Grune and Stratton, 1964.

Hécaen, H. & Sauguet, J. Cerebral dominance in left-handed subjects. *Cortex*, 1971, *7*, 19–48.

Humphrey, M. E. & Zangwill, O. L. Dysphasia in left-handed patients with unilateral brain lesions. *Journal of Neurology and Psychiatry*, 1952, *15*, 184–193.

Jackson, J. H. On aphasia, with left hemiplegia. *Lancet*, 1880, *1*, 637–638.

Levy, J. Possible basis for the evolution of lateral specialization of the human brain. *Nature*, 1969, *224*, 614–615.

Luria, A. R. *Traumatic aphasia: Its syndromes, psychopathology and treatment*. Moscow: Academy of Medical Sciences, 1947.

Milner, B. Effects of early left hemisphere lesions on cerebral organization of function in man. Paper presentation, American Psychological Association, New Orleans, 1973.

Newcombe, F. & Ratcliff, G. Handedness, speech lateralization and ability. *Neuropsychologia*, 1973, *11*, 399–407.

Penfield, W. & Roberts, L. *Speech and Brain Mechanisms*. Princeton: Princeton University Press, 1959.

Piercy, M. The effects of cerebral lesions on intellectual function; a review of current research trends. *British Journal of Psychiatry*, 1964, *110*, 310–352.

Russell, W. R. & Espir, M. L. E. *Traumatic aphasia*. London: Oxford University Press, 1961.

Satz, P., Achenbach, K., Pattishall, E. & Fennell, E. Order of report, ear asymmetry and handedness in dichotic listening. *Cortex*, 1965, *1*, 377–396.

Subirana, A. The prognosis in aphasia in relation to cerebral dominance and handedness. *Brain*, 1958, *81*, 415–425.

Warrington, E. K. & Pratt, R. T. C. Language laterality in left-handers assessed by unilateral E. C. T. *Neuropsychologia*, 1973, *11*, 423–238.

Weisenburg, T. & McBride, K. E. *Aphasia: A clinical and psychological study*. New York: Hildred, 1935.

Zangwill, O. L. Agraphia due to a left parietal glioma in left-handed man. *Brain*, 1954, *77*, 510–520.

Zangwill, O. L. *Cerebral dominance and its relation to psychological function*. Edinburgh: Oliver and Boyd, 1960.

Note Added in Proof

This chapter represents the First Formal demonstration of the method for testing hypothetical speech models from aphasia data. Since then, two mathematical revisions have been completed.

(a) Satz, P. A test of some models of hemispheric speech organization in the left- and right-handed. *Science*, 1979, *203*, 1131–1133.

(b) Hohenegger, M., Carter, R. L. & Satz, P. Handedness and aphasia: An inferential method for determining the mode of cerebral speech specialization. *Neuropsychologia*, in press.

8

Individual Differences in Psychoneurological Organization[1]

JERRE LEVY
RUBEN C. GUR

INTRODUCTION

During the past 10 years there has been a growing interest in problems relating to the functional asymmetry of the brain. Much of this research has been directed toward gaining a deeper understanding of the differing specialties of the two cerebral hemispheres as inferred from patients with unilateral brain damage, split-brain patients, and by the use of dichotic and tachistoscopic tests of normal individuals. Although a great deal remains to be learned about the details of left- and right-hemispheric functioning, most investigators would be in fair agreement regarding general differences in the two sides of the brain.

The left hemisphere in the majority of right-handers may be described as verbal, propositional, categorical, analytic, symbolic, logical, and abstract. The right hemisphere, in contrast, may be described as perceptual, appositional, wholistic, synthetic, literal, analogical, and concrete (Dimond & Beaumont, 1974). These descriptions are not meant to suggest that either hemisphere is totally incompetent in the other's specialty, but rather that the body of currently available research strongly supports the view that the hemispheres are differentially competent in the various processes.

One of the major questions still confronting researchers concerns the cognitive characteristics, not of a single hemisphere, but rather of the integrated brain in action. We are still almost totally ignorant about the rela-

[1] This work was supported by NSF Grant BNS75-23061 to Jerre Levy, Ruben Gur, and Raquel Gur, and by PHS 5507RR07029-14 to Jerre Levy

199

tionship between measurable features of neurological organization in normal people and psychological function in ordinary behavior. The fact that people display ear asymmetries in dichotic tests, visual hemifield asymmetries in tachistoscopic tests, or manual asymmetries in dichhaptic tests tells us very little regarding the consequences for ordinary human activity. In essence, the problem comes down to finding systematic covariances between neurological and psychological organization.

The basic stumbling block in this endeavor has been that while we all recognize the multitude of characteristics on which people differ psychologically, we tend to think of all human beings as having similarly organized brains with respect to anything we can directly measure. In fact, people who are known to differ from the majority are typically excluded from investigations. The vast proportion of studies on laterality are restricted to right-handers, and often, to right-handed males with no left-handed first-degree relatives. If our experimental designs are such that we have no variance in the neurological variable, then of necessity, we can find no covariance between this and our psychological variables.

In order to make progress in understanding the neuropsychological relationship, it is necessary to determine just how much neurological variation exists and to determine its association with psychological functioning. Fortunately, more and more researchers are coming to appreciate this approach and at least certain answers are beginning to emerge.

It has been recognized, since biblical times, that left- and right-handers differ, not only in the preferred hand, but also in other behavioral traits (Judges 3:15 and Judges 20:16). Some have variously suggested that left-handedness is a pathological sign (Bakan, Dibb, & Reed, 1973; Bolin, 1953; Gordon, 1920; Mintz, 1947; Wilson & Dolan, 1931), that it is a sign of negativity in personality traits (Blau, 1946), that it is learned from parents (Collins, 1970), and that it is a normal genetic variant (Baldwin, 1890; Chamberlain, 1928; Levy & Nagylaki, 1972; Ramaley, 1913; Rife, 1940). Although there is evidence that pre- and perinatal pathogenic factors affect manifest handedness, and, in particular, increase the frequency of sinistrality (Bakan, Dibb, & Reed, 1973; Gordon, 1920; Hécaen & De-Ajuriaguerra, 1964; Mintz, 1947; Wilson & Dolan, 1931) and that cultural pressure can inhibit manifest sinistrality (see Nagylaki & Levy, 1973), these factors are insufficient to account for the major portion of variance in manual asymmetry and for the associations between handedness and other traits.

Right-handedness, though clearly reinforced by the culture, is not a consequence of cultural determinants, and left-handedness, though increased in frequency in the presence of pre- and perinatal trauma, is not merely a result of pathology. In support of these assertions, handedness has been found to be significantly correlated with asymmetries in palm prints and fingerprints (Beltman, 1932; Cromwell & Rife, 1942; Cummins, 1940; Cummins, Leche, & McClure, 1931; Newman, 1934; Rife, 1943) which are known to be under strong genetic control and are formed by the eighteenth gestational week (Rife, 1955). Furthermore, handedness is correlated with structural asymmetries of the brain (Hochberg & LeMay, 1975; LeMay & Culebras, 1972; McRae, Branch, & Milner, 1968)—asymmetries that are present at birth and in fetal specimens and that cannot be the result of birth trauma. There is even a highly significant association between nasal and manual asymmetry (Sutton, 1967), and it would be difficult to suggest either pathological or cultural factors that could produce a covariation of the magnitude reported between handedness and nose asymmetry. Based on these and other data to be discussed, it appears that a major portion of the variance in handedness is genetic.

ORIGINS OF LATERAL ASYMMETRY

The evidence that the human brain is laterally differentiated at birth comes from anatomical (LeMay & Calebras, 1972; Wada, Clarke, & Hamm, 1975; Witelson & Pallie, 1973), psysiological (Gardiner & Walter, 1977; Molfese, Freeman, & Palermo, 1975), and behavioral studies (Entus, 1975; Turkewitz, 1977). In the majority of infants the left planum temporale (Wada, Clarke, & Hamm, 1975; Witelson & Pallie, 1973) and the left parietal operculum (LeMay and Culebras, 1972) are larger than their counterparts in the right hemisphere. Lesions of these regions in adults typically produce severe aphasic symptoms (Hécaen, 1962). Electrophysiological data show that the infant right and left hemispheres become selectively activated in the presence of musical and verbal stimuli, respectively (Gardiner & Walter, 1977; Molfese, Freeman & Palermo, 1975), leaving little doubt that the anatomical asymmetries have cognitive consequences from the outset. Behaviorally, also, Entus (1975) has shown that babies manifest a right-ear superiority for verbal stimuli and a left-ear superiority for musical stimuli. Selective activating effects of linguistic and tonal stimuli on the left and right hemispheres were demonstrated by Turkewitz (1977) who found that neonates shift their eyes to the right when they hear words and to the left when they hear tones.

These findings rule out the possibility that cerebral lateralization is produced by sociocultural factors. A vast body of neurological literature shows that variations in cerebral laterality are associated with variations in handedness. Only a small fraction of right-handers have right-hemispheric language. Among left-handers a much larger proportion have language specialized to the right hemisphere (Levy, 1974). Even among those right- and left-handers in whom the language hemisphere is ipsilateral to the writing hand, the control of fine manual movements derives from the language hemisphere, mediated via the callosum or ipsilateral pyramidal pathways. Hécaen, Angelergues, and Douzens (1936) found that in left-handed patients with left-hemispheric lesions, the presence of aphasia was associated with the presence of agraphia, whereas the absence of aphasia was associated with the absence of agraphia and the presence of constructural apraxia. Evidently, even when the language hemisphere is ipsilateral to the dominant hand, it controls writing movements. This finding is to be expected as writing requires access to the language centers. Thus, the dominant writing hand always appears to be under the control of the language hemisphere. Variations in the laterality of hemispheric specialization within handedness groups is almost certainly due to the fact that in some left- and right-handers the control pathways from the language hemisphere lead, directly or indirectly, to the ipsilateral hand and in others, to the contralateral hand.

When a child is forced by sociocultural pressures to shift handedness, there is no evidence that the direction of cerebral laterality changes. Instead, it is the control pathway that is likely to have changed from ipsilateral to contralateral or vice-versa. Indeed, when individuals are asked to write with their nondominant hands, it is obvious that the language hemisphere does not shift and, in fact, the only change that occurs is in the control pathways. Therefore, were there some index of control pathways, this index, in conjunction with handedness, could perfectly predict hemispheric laterality if the latter could be perfectly measured.

BEHAVIORAL INDICES OF CEREBRAL LATERALITY

It appears that an index of control pathways has been discovered. Levy and Reid (1976) found that individuals who use the normal writing posture (i.e., hand held below the line of writing, pencil pointed toward the top of the page), regardless of handedness, have their language hemispheres contralateral to the writing hand. This association was manifested in 100% of 48 subjects (half were left-handed) by two tachistoscopic tests of cerebral laterality. Individuals using the inverted posture (hand held above the line of writing, pencil pointed toward the bottom of the page) have their language hemispheres ipsilateral to the writing hand. Of 25 such subjects (one right-handed) all but three left-handers showed this relationship. Thus, hemispheric laterality was correctly predicted in 45 out of 48 left-handers and in all right-handers.

In spite of the strength of this association, people have criticized the hand posture variable as reflecting no more than a peripheral adaptation to situational demands. It has been suggested, for example, that the inverted posture is a compensation for the left-to-right writing system of English, the need of left-handers to see what they write, their need to avoid smearing ink, their adjustment to the orientation of paper imposed by elementary school teachers, etc. Were any of these suggestions correct, it would imply, in light of Levy and Reid's finding, that cerebral laterality itself was determined by environmental events. Additionally, such explanations cannot account for the inverted writing posture found among some American right-handers and a substantial proportion of Israeli left-handers.

Gur and Gur (1974) inferred from data relating the direction of conjugate, lateral eye movements to hemispheric activation (Bakan, 1971; Day, 1964; Kinsbourne, 1972; Kocel, Galin, Ornstein, & Marin, 1972) that left- and right-eye dominance in sinistrals was associated respectively with right- and left-hemispheric language specialization. Eye dominance refers to the fact that, typically, individuals consistently use either the left or the right eye for sighting when conditions compel the use of a single eye. Most people are unaware of eye dominance, either in themselves or in others and consequently, eyedness, unlike handedness or hand posture, is relatively insusceptible to cultural influences. Furthermore, eyedness has been found to run in families, inherited equally in the maternal and paternal lines (Merrell, 1957).

About 70% of right-handers are also right-eyed, but among left-handers, right-eyedness occurs only in about half (Gur & Gur, 1977a). Although it has been suggested that currently available data do not allow the conclusion that eyedness and handedness are associated (Porac & Coren, 1976), this conclusion has been shown to be invalid (Gur & Gur, 1977b). The association between the two traits is, in fact, highly significant and it is quite probable that the correlation is mediated through the causal effects that hemispheric laterality has on both.

Some of the variation in eyedness appears to be a consequence of birth stress. Gur, Levy, and Van Auken (1979) examined the birth history records, as reported by their mothers, of 174 right-handers and rated the degree of birth stress on a scale from 0–3, based on a variety of stress indices. There was a high, positive, and linear relationship between the probability of left-eyedness and the degree of birth stress. Further, Gur (1977) has recently found that among right-handed males, those who are right eyed manifest a strong right-visual-field superiority for verbal material and a strong left-field superiority for spatial material, whereas those who are left eyed, though having a left-field superiority for spatial stimuli, showed no significant asymmetry for verbal stimuli. It may well be that perinatal birth trauma tends to bilateralize language functions into both hemispheres while shifting eye dominance from a contralateral to an ipsilateral position with respect to the congenital language hemisphere.

SEX-RELATED DIFFERENCES IN CEREBRAL ORGANIZATION

During the past few years a number of studies have been consistent in reporting that the degrees of cerebral lateralization is less in females than in males. Data from both dichotic (Harshman, 1976) and tachistoscopic tests (Kimura, 1969; Levy & Reid, 1976), whether stimuli are verbal or nonverbal, indicate that females display a relatively small sensory field asymmetry. Levy and Reid (1976) found that this sex-related difference was also obtained in left-handers, even in those having the inverted writing posture (a group in which all subjects, regardless of sex, were very weakly lateralized in comparison to other groups).

Until recently, there had been no evidence either that the direction of lateralization or the cognitive consequences of a given pattern of lateralization differed in males and females. However, we found that 66% of left-handed males, but only 31% of left-handed females have the inverted writing posture. Levy and Reid found just as strong an association between hand posture and the direction of cerebral lateralization in males and females. This result implies that right-hemispheric language is much more frequent in left-handed females than in left-handed males. Only about 15–20% of the neurological population from which cerebral dominance estimates have been obtained are female, so that if our data correctly reflect the proportion with left-hemispheric language in male and female left-handers, the expected estimate from neurological data would be about 60%, not significantly different from the estimates reported. This difference has implications for psychological differences in the sexes because left-handed people with left- and right-hemispheric language differ in a number of psychological dimensions, as will be discussed subsequently.

Reid (1979) has confirmed the hand-posture–hemispheric-lateralization association in 5- and 8-year-old children. Her most remarkable finding, however, was that at age 5 the left hemisphere of females and the right hemisphere of males, regardless of their cognitive functions, were sufficiently developed to manifest an asymmetric superiority on either a verbal or a spatial task. In contrast, no hemispheric asymmetry was seen on tasks that would subsequently be specialized to the right hemisphere in females and the left hemisphere in males. Thus, in children with left-hemispheric language, males showed an asymmetry on a spatial task, but none on a verbal task, whereas females showed the reverse. In children with right-hemispheric language, males displayed an asymmetry on the verbal task, but none on the spatial task, and vice-versa for females. In addition, girls with left-hemispheric language performed better on a standardized test of verbal function than on one for spatial function, boys having the opposite profile. Precisely the reverse pattern of sex-related differences were seen in children with right-hemispheric language. High levels of fetal sex hormones may promote lateralization and enhance the development of the right hemisphere, whereas low levels may result in enhanced development of the left hemisphere.

Reid's results strongly suggest that the well-known differences in the cognitive structure of males and females is a secondary consequence of the fact that most people have left hemispheric language, and that the left hemisphere of females and the right hemisphere of males are relatively enhanced in development, and probably ultimate functional capacity.

THE POPULATION VARIANCE
IN HEMISPHERIC LATERALIZATION

It should be obvious from the foregoing sections that human species is quite variable in hemispheric organization and its behavioral concomitants, much more so than has been realized from clinical reports. Since Broca (1861) first reported the association between left-hemispheric damage and aphasia, it has been assumed that, except for a very small fraction of the population, the direction and degree of cerebral lateralization were invariant. Variations in symptomatology following brain lesions were typically attributed to variations in the extent and location of the lesions. It appears from our work with normal subjects that the description of hemispheric organization given in clinical neurology textbooks is valid only for right-handed males who have no sinistral first-degree relatives, who use the normal writing posture, and even, perhaps, who are right-eyed. Such individuals may constitute no more than 25% of the population.

First, right-handers having sinistral relatives have been shown to have a much higher probability of recovery from aphasia following left-hemispheric lesions than those with only dextral relatives (Luria, 1970). The implication that such people are only weakly laterally differentiated is confirmed by studies of normal individuals who show variations in the magnitude of sensory field asymmetries as a function of the handedness of their relatives (Hines and Satz, 1971; Zurif & Bryden, 1969). As previously noted, recent data also suggest that left-eyedness in right-handed males is associated with weak cerebral lateralization (i.e., as measured by tachistoscopic tests—see Gur, 1977). Second, as mentioned, females in all handedness–hand posture groups display smaller field asymmetries than males, and are found to have a smaller degree of neuroanatomical asymmetry (Wada, Clarke,, & Hamm, 1975). Lansdell (1970) also reported that following lesions to the brain, both verbal and spatial functions were affected in females, whereas only one was affected in males.

In possibly half of all left-handers, the direction of cerebral lateralization is reversed. Such individuals, as found in Levy and Reid's study (1976), are very well lateralized. However, they found that sinistrals with left-hemispheric language displayed extremely weak lateral differentiation. Thus, essentially all left-handers, 12–15% of the population, deviate significantly in cerebral organization from the plurality of right-handers, either having a mirror-image laterality pattern or being less strongly lateralized.

Among right-handers, the neurological literature indicates that a small fraction, ranging from less than 1% to slightly over 4%, have right-hemispheric language (see Levy, 1974). These estimates are based on a predominantly male patient population. In a survey of about 900 people, we found that only 1–2% of right-handed males used the inverted hand posture (presumed right-hemispheric language), where the corresponding proportion among dextral females was 10–12%. If hand posture is as accurate an index of the direction of hemispheric lateralization as the Levy and Reid study would seem to suggest, the estimates of the proportion of dextrals with right-hemispheric language derived from the neurological literature are valid for males, but greatly underrepresent the true proportion in females.

To summarize, there is sufficient evidence to conclude that there is considerable variation, both in the direction and in the degree of hemispheric lateralization, and such variations are a function of sex, handedness, hand posture in writing, eye dominance, familial handedness, and possibly other, currently unidentified variables. Theoretically, it should be possible to deduce the cognitive organizations associated with these cerebral variants.

PREDICTIONS REGARDING THE COGNITIVE COVARIATES OF CEREBRAL ORGANIZATION

Variations in neurological patterns ought to have predictable cognitive consequences. We shall now discuss what these consequences might be. First, the well-known sex-related differences in cognitive structure (Harris, 1975; Maccoby & Jacklin, 1974) (i.e., males being relatively superior in visuo-spatial functions, females in verbal fluency) may pertain only to people having language in the left hemisphere. If Reid's conclusions are correct, and the left hemispheres of females and the right hemispheres of males are functionally enhanced regardless of their specialties, the reverse cognitive pattern may obtain in individuals with right-hemispheric language. Furthermore, sex-related differences in cognition might be increased in populations having weak hemispheric differentiation. Verbal functions may tend to be bilateralized in females and spatial functions bilateralized in males when the main language hemisphere is on the left, with the reverse occurring when the main language hemisphere is on the right. We are suggesting that bilateralization of one function should produce incomplete specialization of the hemisphere mainly responsible for the other function, leading to good ability in the bilateralized function and depressed ability in the other.

If this hypothesis is correct, the following predictions may be advanced regarding relative verbal and spatial abilities in various groups of people. First, among right-handers having the normal hand posture, verbal ability should exceed spatial ability in females, the reverse being the case in males. Among left-handers with the normal hand posture, females should display unusually good spatial abilities, compared to right-handed females, and males should have unusually good verbal abilities, when compared to right-handed males. In people using the inverted hand posture, females who are left-handed should be greatly superior on verbal as compared to spatial ability, whereas those who are right-handed should be greatly superior on spatial as compared to verbal ability. Precisely the reverse should be seen in males.

Eye dominance should act as a moderating variable in all varieties of brain organization patterns. When eye dominance is contralateral to the language hemisphere, the predicted associations ought to be most strongly manifested. When an ipsilateral relationship is seen, overall performance should be reduced, and the predicted effects attenuated.

Whether any or all of these predictions are correct can only be determined in careful empirical investigations in which the measures of the various dimensions outlined are highly valid indexes of the underlying properties they are designed to assess. Variations in cognitive function, currently viewed by most psychologists as "error variance," may someday be found to reflect measureable fundamental variations in the neurological organization of the human species.

SUMMARY

In this chapter we have reviewed the evidence for biologically based variations in the patterns of cerebral asymmetry of function. These variations, present at birth, seem to have a genetic origin and seem to be moderated by fetal sex hormones and the degree of perinatal stress to the brain. We have outlined a series of rather simple and straightforward behavioral indices of the direction and magnitude of hemispheric asymmetry.

We postulate that high levels of fetal sex hormones, as occur in males, promote the expression of cerebral lateralization and selectively enhance the maturational rate and cognitive capacity of the right hemisphere. This postulate can account for the stronger degree of hemispheric differentiation in males as compared to females, and for the fact that males with left hemispheric and females with right hemispheric language are relatively better on spatial than on verbal tasks, with the reverse obtaining in the other two groups.

Within both males and females, verbal and/or spatial functions tend to be bilateralized when the dominant writing hand is ipsilateral to the controlling language hemisphere. Such individuals are generally cognitive specialists, being superior in the bilateralized function, and showing a relative deficiency in that function for which no fully specialized hemisphere exists. The various relationships we have proposed would be expected to be weakened if birth stress had produced some degree of brain reorganization. One sign of such stress is an ipsilateral relationship between eye dominance and the main language hemisphere.

On the basis of these considerations, we have outlined a set of predictions regarding the relationship between neurological patterns and cognitive performance. Preliminary observations are consistent with these predictions.

REFERENCES

Asher, H. *Experiments in Seeing.* New York, Basic Books, Inc., 1969.
Bakan, P. The eyes have it. *Psychology Today,* 1971, *4,* 64–69.
Bakan, P., Dibb, G., & Reed, P. Handedness and birth stress. *Neuropsychologia,* 1973, *M,* 363–366.
Baldwin, J. M. Origin of left or right handedness. *Science,* 1890, *16,* 247–248.
Beltman, S. Die Papillarleistenzeichnung der Hankflache in ihrer Beziehung zur Handigkeit. *Zeitschrift für und Entwicklungslgeschichte,* 1932, *98,* 149–174.
Blau, A. *The Master Hand.* New York: Research Monograph No. 5, American Orthopsychiatry Association, 1946.
Bolin, B. J. Left handedness and stuttering as signs diagnostic of epileptics. *Journal of Mental Science,* 1953, *99,* 483–488.
Broca, P. Remerques sur le siège de la faculté du langage articulé surves d'une observation d'aphemie. *Bulletin Societie Anatomique (Paris),* 1861, *6,* 330–357.
Chamberlain, H. B. Inheritance of left handedness. *Journal of Heredity,* 1928, *19,* 557–559.
Collins, R. L. The sound of one paw clapping: An inquiry into the origin of left-handedness. In G. Lindzey, and D. D. Thiessen, (Eds.), *Contributions to Behavior-Genetic Analysis: The Mouse as Prototype,* New York: Appleton-Century-Crofts, 1970.
Cromwell, H., & Rife, D. C. Dermatoglyphics in relation to functional handedness. *Human Biology,* 1942, *14(4),* 517–526.
Cummins, H. Finger prints correlated with handedness. *American Journal of Physical Anthropology,* 1940, *26,* 151–166.

Cummins, H., Leche, S. & McClure, K. Bimanual variations in palmer dermatoglyphics. *American Journal of Anatomy*, 1931, *48*, 199–230.

Day, M. E. An eye-movement phenomenon relating to attention, thought and anxiety. *Perceptual and Motor Skills*, 1964, *19*, 443–446.

Dimond, S., & Beaumont, J. G. (Eds.) *Hemisphere function in the human brain.* New York: Wiley, 1974.

Entus, A. Hemispheric asymmetry in processing of dichotically presented speech and non-speech stimuli by infants. Paper presented at the meetings of the Society for Research in Child Development, Denver, Colorado, April, 1975.

Gardiner, M. F., & Walter, D. O. Evidence of hemispheric specialization from infant EEG. In S. Harnad, R. W. Doty, L. Goldstein, J. Jaynes, & G. Krauthamer (Eds.), *Lateralization in the Nervous System.* New York: Academic Press, 1977.

Gordon, H. Left handedness and mirror writing especially among defective children. *Brain*, 1920, *43*, 313–368.

Gur, R. E. Left hemisphere dysfunction in schizophrenia: Evidence from a tachistoscopic study. Manuscript submitted for publication, 1977.

Gur, R. C., & Gur, R. E. Eye dominance is associated with cerebral organization. Manuscript submitted for publication, 1977b.

Gur, R. C., & Gur, R. E. Handedness, sex, and eyedness as moderating variables in the relation between hypnotic susceptibility and functional brain asymmetry. *Journal of Abnormal Psychology*, 1974, *83*, 635–643.

Gur, R. E., & Gur, R. C. Sex differences in the relations among handedness, sighting-dominance and eye-acuity. *Neuropsychologia*, 1977a, *15*, 481–498.

Gur, R. E., Levy, J., & Van Auken, C. The effects of birth stress on eye dominance for sighting in right handers. In preparation, 1979.

Harris, L. J. Sex differences in spatial ability: possible environmental, genetic, and neurological factors. In M. Kinsbourne (Ed.) *Hemispheric asymmetries of function.* Springfield, Ill.: C. C. Thomas, 1975.

Harshman, R. A. Sex, language, and the brain: adult sex differences in lateralization. In D. O. Walter, L. Rogers, & J. M. Finzi-Fried (Eds.), *Conference on human brain function: Brain information service.* Los Angeles: BRI Publications Office, U.C.L.A., 1976.

Hécaen, H. Clinical symptomatology in right and left hemisphere lesions. In V. B. Mountcastle (Ed.), *Interhemispheric Relations and Cerebral Dominance*, Baltimore: Johns Hopkins Press, 1962.

Hécaen, H., & DeAjuriaguerra, J. Left Handedness. New York: Grune & Stratton, 1964.

Hécaen, H., Angelergues, R., & Douzens, J. A. Les agraphies. *Neuropsychologia*, 1963, *1*, 179–208.

Hines, D., & Satz, P. Superiority of right visual half-fields in right-handers for recall of digits presented at varying rates. *Neuropsychologia*, 1971, *9*, 21–25.

Hochberg, F. H., & LeMay, M. Arteriographic correlates of handedness. *Neurology*, 1975, *25*, 218–222.

Kimura, D. Spatial localization in left and right visual fields. *Canadian Journal of Psychology*, 1969, *23*, 445–458.

Kinsbourne, M. Eye and head turning indicates cerebral lateralization. *Science*, 1972, *176*, 539–541.

Kocel, K., Galin, D., Ornstein, R., & Marin, E. Lateral eye movement and cognitive mode. *Psychonomic Science*, 1972, *27*, 223–224.

Lansdell, H. Relation of extent of temporal removals to closure and visuo-motor factors. *Perceptual and Motor Skills*, 1970, *31*, 491–498.

LeMay, M., & Culebras, A. Human Brain-Morphologic differences in the hemispheres demonstrable by carotid arteriography. *New England Journal of Medicine*, 1972, *287*, 168–170.

Levy, J. Psychobiological implications of bilateral asymmetry. In S. Dimond & J. G. Beaumont (Eds.), *Hemisphere Function in the Human Brain*, London: Paul Elek, Ltd., 1974.

Levy, J., & Nagylaki, T. A model for the genetics of handedness. *Genetics*, 1972, *72*, 117–128.

Levy, J., & Reid, M. Variations in writing posture and cerebral organization. *Science*, 1976, *194*, 337–339.

Luria, A. R. *Traumatic Aphasia*. Paris: Mouton, 1970.

Maccoby, E. E., & Jacklin, C. N. *The psychology of sex differences*. Stanford, Ca.: Stanford University Press, 1974.

McRae, D. L., Branch, C. L., & Milner, B. The occipital horns and cerebral dominance. *Neurology*, 1968, *18*, 95–100.

Merrell, D. J. Dominance of hand and eye. *Human Biology*, 1957, *29*, 314–328.

Mintz, A. Lateral preferences of a group of mentally subnormal boys. *Journal of Genetic Psychology*, 1947, *1*, 75–84.

Molfese, D., Freeman, R., & Palermo, D. The ontogeny of brain lateralization for speech and nonspeech stimuli. *Brain and Language*, 1975, *2*, 356–368.

Nagylaki, T., & Levy, J. The sound of one paw clapping is not sound. *Behavior Genetics*, 1973, *3*, 279–292.

Newman, H. H. Dermatoglyphics and the problem of handedness. *American Journal of Physical Anthropology*, 1934, *33*, 421–428.

Porac, C., & Coren, S. The dominant eye. *Psychological Bulletin*, 1976, *83*, 880–897.

Ramaley, F. Inheritance of left handedness. *American Naturalist*, 1913, *47*, 730–738.

Reid, M. Cerebral lateralization in children: An ontogenetic and organismic analysis. Doctoral Dissertation, Univ. of Colorado, 1979.

Rife, D. C. Handedness, with special reference to twins. *Genetics*, 1940, *25*, 178–186.

Rife, D. C. Genetic interrelationships of dermatoglyphics and functional handedness. *Genetics*, 1943, *28*, 41–48.

Rife, D. C. Hand prints and handedness. *American Journal of Human Genetics*, 1955, *7*, 170–179.

Sutton, P. R. Handedness and facial asymmetry: Lateral position of the nose in two racial groups. *Nature*, 1967, *198*, 909.

Turkewitz, G. The development of lateral differentiation in the human infant. *Annals of the New York Academy of Sciences*, New York: N.Y. Academy of Sciences, 1977.

Wada, J. A., Clarke, R., & Hamm, A. Cerebral hemispheric asymmetry in humans. Cortical speech zones in 100 adult and 100 infant brains. Archives of Neurology, 1975, *32*, 239–246.

Wilson, M. O., & Dolan, L. B. Handedness and ability. *American Journal of Psychology*, 1931, *43*, 261–268.

Witelson, S. F., & Pallie, W. Left hemisphere specialization for language in the newborn: Neuroanatomical evidence of asymmetry. *Brain*, 1973, *96*, 641–647.

Zurif, E. B., & Bryden, M. P. Familial handedness and left-right difference in auditory and visual perception. *Neuropsychologia*, 1969, *7*, 179–187.

9

Handedness and Individual Differences in Hemispheric Activation

RUBEN C. GUR
RAQUEL E. GUR

INTRODUCTION

Much of the research on the cognitive concomitants of left-handedness has centered on identifying differences between left-handers and right-handers with regard to the direction and the degree of hemispheric specialization. It is quite clear, by now, that left-handers are different from right-handers in the extent to which the two hemispheres are specialized for different functions. It has also been demonstrated that, at least for some left-handers, the hemispheres are organized differently in that verbal-analytic processing is localized in the right hemisphere whereas spatial-holistic processing is lateralized to the left hemisphere (see Levy & Gur, Chapter 8 of this volume, for a summary). It is reasonable to expect that this research would eventually explain the differences in cognitive organization found between left-handers and right-handers as the degree of hemispheric specialization, and perhaps even the direction of specialization, appear to have profound effects on cognitive capacity and style (cf. Levy & Reid, 1976, 1978; McGlone & Davidson, 1973).

More recently, experimental attention has been paid to yet another aspect of hemispheric specialization that pertains to the circumstances under which a given hemisphere becomes more activated relative to the other. Logically, this dimension may be independent of competence differences between the hemispheres. Regardless of which hemisphere is better

211

NEUROPSYCHOLOGY
OF LEFT-HANDEDNESS

suited for solving a particular problem type, either hemisphere could be activated when a problem is actually presented to an individual. In reality, however, one would expect to find that the dimension of hemispheric activation would be highly, if not perfectly correlated with the dimension of hemispheric competence since pressures for competent performance would eventuate in the development of a match between problem type and the activation of the hemisphere most suited for its solution. Nevertheless, to the extent to which the correlation is imperfect and, in particular, if deviations from the ideal problem–hemisphere match can be related systematically to either situational or to intraindividual variables, then investigating the dimension of hemispheric activation may help elucidate mechanisms involved in the ongoing process of problem solving. Furthermore, identification of variables affecting hemispheric activation in a way that optimizes the problem–hemisphere match may help devise control systems that improve problem-solving capabilities without the much more elaborate efforts involved in improving hemispheric capacity. Additionally, the identification of variables that account for a reduction of this match may help in the understanding of dysfunctional problem-solving behavior.

That such mismatches between hemispheric activation and the nature of the task can occur is suggested by Levy & Trevarthen (1976), who identified a metacontrol mechanism that activates the two hemispheres selectively and is under the influence of priming manipulations. Other studies have shown that such mismatches may be due, at least in part, to individual differences in the tendency to activate one or the other hemispheres. Thus, Bogen (1969) observed individual differences in what he called "hemisphericity;" Ornstein (1972) discussed individual differences in logical versus intuitive cognitive styles; and Bakan (1971) offered the typology of right-hemispheric and left-hemispheric or "right-brained" and "left-brained" individuals.

One way of finding out whether this dimension of individual differences significantly accounts for the variation in cognitive organization is to examine the extent to which the association between "brainedness" or "hemisphericity" and cognitive organization is influenced by factors that are known to affect the direction and/or degree of hemispheric specialization (e.g. handedness, sex, eye dominance). If, for example, it is found that characteristic activation of the left, relative to the right, hemisphere in right-handed males is associated with a particular pattern of performance on a given task, then one would expect the effect to be smaller, and even in the opposite direction, for left-handers. Investigating the effects of such variables on the association between hemisphericity and cognitive organization may help in validating the existence of the individual differences dimension. The investigation of individual differences in hemispheric specialization may also help uncover other mechanisms that could account for cognitive style differences between left- versus right-handers and males versus females, as these groups may differ not only in the direction and degree of hemispheric specialization, but also in characteristic tendencies to activate one or the other hemisphere.

HEMISPHERIC ACTIVATION: THE CONCEPT AND ITS OPERATIONALIZATION

Clearly, as long as an individual is alive, the central nervous system (CNS) is constantly active in maintaining a dynamic equilibrium of excitation and inhibition. The amount of activity that takes place in the brain, however, can be assumed to vary as a function of the state of arousal of a given individual. Indeed, various measures that can be expected theoretically to reflect the amount of activity in the nervous system show that, barring some specificity related to individual differences in somatic compliance (Lacey, 1967) and, perhaps (and this is far from being proven), to some specificity of type of arousal (Ax, 1953), increased stimulation generally results in increased activity in the nervous system as a whole. With regard to CNS activation, measures of electrical cortical activity (electroencephalographs and evoked potentials) were linked to variations in general states of arousal (Orne & Wilson, 1977), in attention (Mulholland, 1969), and even in mental load (Creutzfeldt, Grunewald, Sinonova, & Schmitz, 1969; Lindsley, 1952).

Similarly, studies of cerebral hemodynamics have shown that changes in the blood supply to the brain, which are to be expected as a result of changes in metabolic rate, are associated with changes in arousal level (Obrist, Thompson, Wang, & Wilkinson, 1975) and increase with mental activity (Risberg & Ingvar, 1973). By *hemispheric activation* we refer, therefore, to any changes that occur in a given hemisphere and that result in concomitant changes on measures that were previously shown to be associated with increased CNS arousal or stimulation. Thus, an electroencephalograph (EEG) pattern that is characteristic of a state of high arousal will be taken to indicate that a given hemisphere is relatively more activated than the other hemisphere if this pattern is detected to a larger extent on that hemisphere. We would likewise tend to conclude that a given hemisphere is more activated by a given task than the other if it can be shown that the blood flow to that hemisphere has increased relative to the other hemisphere when this task has been presented to a subject. It is obvious, then, that a technique intended to measure hemispheric activation should produce measures that can be shown to relate, theoretically and empirically, to the degree of hemispheric arousal. The popular tachistoscopic method of presenting stimuli to the two visual fields, which is designed to investigate hemispheric lateralization of function inferred from differences in the quality of responses as a function of visual fields, will not do for this purpose as it probably taps differences in hemispheric cognitive capacity or proficiency rather than differences in activation. On the other hand, measures such as EEG, regional cerebral blood flow, and the direction of conjugate lateral eye movements during cognitive activity seem, at least theoretically, to be indices of hemispheric activation.

When such measures are obtained from subjects during the performance of cognitive tasks, it has been shown that an association exists between the nature of the cognitive task and the hemisphere that is being activated. It has also been shown, however, that this association is far from being perfect—a fact that may not in itself be interesting unless it can be demonstrated that the variance contributing to the attenuation of the relationship is not simply due to random measurement error but is in some way lawful and explainable. The following discussion will attempt to show that such variances are both lawful and explainable.

The first findings of laterality in measures of EEG activity pertained to asymmetries in the amount of α activity over the two hemispheres. In perhaps the earliest report, Rancy (1939) generally found more α activity in the right versus left hemisphere. This finding was replicated by a number of investigators (Cornil & Gestaut, 1947; Lindsley, 1940; Subirana & Olier-Daurelia, 1960). In a later development, however, a number of studies have indicated that the relative amount of α activity in one hemisphere versus another also depends on the nature of the cognitive task the subject is engaged in when the measurements are taken. Thus, Morgan, McDonald, and MacDonald (1971) found more α activity in the left versus the right hemisphere during the performance of a spatial (right-hemispheric) task, and more α activity in the right versus the left hemisphere during the performance of verbal or analytic tasks. This finding was replicated by Morgan, MacDonald, and Hilgard (1974) and by others (e.g., Doyle, Ornstein, & Galin, 1974; Galin & Ellis, 1975; Galin & Ornstein, 1972; Mckee, Humphrey, & McAdam, 1973).

In all of these cases the association between hemispheric activation (as measured by EEG α activity) and the nature of the cognitive task, although significant, was not terribly impressive and did not approach the uniformity of effect one would expect from clinical data and split-brain studies regarding the differences in functioning between the two hemispheres. In an attempt to account for some of the error variance by investigating individual differences in hemisphericity or "brainedness", Dumas and Morgan (1975) measured α asymmetries during the performance of verbal and spatial tasks in a group of artists and a group of engineers, expecting the artists to show greater right-hemispheric activation. No group differences were obtained but, as Furst (1976) has pointed out rather convincingly, occupational choice may be determined by a large number of variables other than cognitive predispositions and further, a number of approaches resulting in adequate performance within a given occupation can be adopted. Thus, mathematicians tend to divide into "geometry types" and "algebra types," architects and engineers are known to vary with respect to their tendency to be analytic or impressionistic in their approach to problems in design, etc. Furst (1976) tested the hypothesis of the influence of systematic individual differences more directly by measuring the size of the difference between left- and right-hemispheric EEG activity during the performance of a spatial task and correlating this measure with performance on the task. He obtained a significant correlation (.55), indicating that the higher the magnitude of the right–left (R–L) ratio, the better the performance. Perhaps even more interesting for our purpose here was his finding that the R–L ratio taken during baseline measures was an equally good predictor of performance (.51) on the spatial task as the same measure taken during actual performance. This seems to indicate, as Furst has pointed out, that subjects come into the laboratory with varying degrees of activation in the right or the left hemisphere, and that these variations are predictive of performance in a cognitive task involving spatial manipulations.

Another method for analyzing brain waves is through the study of evoked potentials. When this method was applied in initial attempts to detect hemispheric asymmetries, it was found that the visual evoked response (VER) is larger in the right versus the left hemisphere (Bigum, 1969; Cohn, 1963, 1964; Groberg, 1967). Further studies showed that evoked potentials are different over the left or the right hemisphere as a function of cognitive task (Buchsbaum & Fedio, 1970; Cohn, 1971; McAdam & Whitaker, 1971; Morrell & Salamy, 1971; Shucard, Shucard, & Thomas, 1977; Wood, Goff, & Day, 1971). Although a number of studies failed to detect such differences (Friedman, Simson, Ritter, & Rapin, 1975; Galambos, Benson, Smith, Schulman-Galambos, & Osier, 1975; Shelburne, 1972), there were only eight subjects in each of these studies and individual differences in hemisphericity could have wiped out the effects. The influence of such individual differences on this measure apparently has not been investigated.

Another measure of hemispheric activation applied to the study of hemispheric asymmetry of function is that of regional cerebral blood flow. As the feedback mechanisms that may operate to enhance blood flow to the brain when it is becoming increasingly activated are yet to be fully specified and understood, the first step required to justify the use of this measure was a demonstration that blood flow to the brain does indeed increase as a function of cognitive activity. A very large portion of the total blood supply goes to the brain and the brain has virtually no reservoires of blood. Therefore, a mechanism ought to exist that would regulate blood flow to correspond to changes in brain metabolism resulting from increased activity due to engagement in cognitive effort. A recent noninvasive method for measuring regional cerebral blood flow uses xenon-133 gas which is inhaled by the subject and its clearance from the brain is measured with NaI (sodium iodide) crystal emission detectors placed on the subject's head.

Using this method, Obrist et al. (1975) and Risberg and Ingvar (1973) demonstrated that blood flow to the brain is correlated with the amount of cognitive activity. Risberg, Halsey, Blavenstein, Wilson, and Wills (1975) went on to show that blood flow increases differentially in the two hemispheres as a function of cognitive task. They used the ^{133}Xe inhalation method with 24 normal, right-handed males and 30 patients recovering from aphasias produced by cerebral infarctions. Subjects were presented with a verbal reasoning test (i.e., analogies) and with a spatial test of perceptual closure (i.e., incomplete figures). Hemispheric activation during task performance was compared to a rest period. It was found that regional cerebral blood flow (rCBF) increased in both hemispheres during problem solving but the increase in the left hemisphere was significantly greater during the solution of the verbal problems, whereas the increase in the right hemisphere was significantly greater during the performance of spatial problems.

To find out whether individual differences in hemispheric activation are reflected in the blood flow response to cognitive stimulation, we tested 36 male, right-handed subjects using tasks similar to those employed by Risberg et al. (1975), except that we also measured performance (Gur & Reivich, 1979). The results show a significant increase ($p < .01$) in blood flow to the left hemisphere during the performance of the verbal task, and a nonsignificant increase in flow to the right hemisphere during the performance of the spatial task. However, when we divided our subjects into those who showed an increase in blood flow to the right hemisphere for the spatial task and those who did not show such an increase or even had a decrease, we found that the 20 subjects who responded in the expected direction performed significantly better ($p < .025$) than the 16 subjects who did not show the expected increase. Furthermore, a significant correlation (.39) was obtained between performance on the spatial task and the increase in ratio of right–left hemispheric blood flow during the performance of the spatial task as compared to baseline levels. These results seem to suggest, again, that subjects with asymmetrically active hemispheres excell in tasks that are presented to their more active hemisphere.

The fact that no such hemisphericity effects were obtained for the verbal task can either mean that the verbal task is too "hardwired" to the left hemisphere to leave much room for cognitive style effects to take place, or it could mean that the range of variations in left-hemispheric style was too restricted in our sample to allow for an expression of its influence. Clearly, we would need to use a larger variety of tasks on larger samples of subjects before we can answer this question, but even at this point it seems that we have obtained, using a more direct measure of hemispheric activity, results congruent with Furst's EEG study.

The story is a bit more complicated with regard to a third potential measure of hemispheric activation, that is, conjugate lateral-eye-movement directionality. The course of events in studies using this measure was chronologically reversed from what took place in the investigation of the two earlier measures, in that individual differences were explored before it was demonstrated that eye movements were related to task specific effects. Teitelbaum (1954) was the first to report the observation that when a subject is faced by a questioner he usually breaks eye contact, following the presentation of each question, and moves his eyes either to the right or left. This phenomenon was later investigated more thoroughly by Day (1964), who found that the direction in which the eyes move is fairly consistent for a given individual. Duke (1968) offered more experimental support for these observations and suggested a new typology, "left-movers" and "right-movers." A series of investigations by Day (1964, 1967a, 1968) revealed various differences between "left-movers" and "right-movers" in cognitive style and a number of personality traits. Bakan and Shotland (1969) found performance differences between these two groups. Right-movers performed better than left-movers on tasks requiring focused visual attention, whereas left-movers reported clearer visual images (Bakan, 1969) and were verbally more fluent. In addition, left-movers had more waking EEG α activity, more frequently majored in the humanities and social sciences in college, and performed better on the verbal than on the quantitative section of the Scholastic Aptitude Test (SAT). Right-movers were less likely to display waking α activity on EEGs, preferred majors in science, and had higher scores on the quantitative section of the SAT (Bakan, 1969, 1971; Bakan & Svorad, 1969).

To account for these personality and cognitive style differences, Bakan (1971) advanced the hypothesis that eye movements are indicative of individual differences in what he called ease of "triggering of activity in the hemisphere contralateral to the direction of eye movement." In other words, he postulated that the consistency in the direction in which the subjects' eyes moved in response to questioning reflected what has been referred to here as "brainedness" or hemisphericity.

This hypothesis, far fetched and bizarre as it may seem at first glance, has since received considerable experimental support and, as we shall see, is not that outlandish. As Trevarthen (1972) has pointed out, it is evolutionarily advantageous for an organism to orient itself toward a source of stimulation thereby bringing the source of stimulation into the center of the visual field. In the human species in which cognitive activity is lateralized according to its nature, cognitive processing that results in higher levels of activity in one hemisphere may mimic the effect of unilateral stimulation and produce an orienting response to a direction contralateral to the activated hemisphere. Furthermore, as Mott and Shafer (1890) have demonstrated in animals and as Penfield and Roberts (1959) have demonstrated in humans, electrical stimulation in many parts of the cortex produces contralateral eye deviations. Because each cerebral hemisphere is a rather tightly linked system, it is not unreasonable to expect (Kinsbourne, 1972) that increased activity in the cognitive area will "overflow" to the motor area and produce eye movements in the contralateral direction.

If the above is correct, one should expect that a problem-specific direction for eye movements could also be demonstrated, as in the case of the EEG and the blood flow studies. Indeed, Kinsbourne (1972) recorded eye and head movements in subjects while they responded to verbal, spatial, and numerical questions asked by an experimenter sitting behind them. The recordings were made by a hidden videotape camera. Subjects moved their eyes more to the right for verbal questions and more to the left for spatial questions, showing no significant tendency to move more frequently to either direction for the numerical questions. In a subsequent study (Gur, Gur, & Harris, 1975; Gur, 1975) we replicated Kinsbourne's findings when an experimenter was seated behind the subject and did not obtain the problem-specific effect when the experimenter was seated in front of the same subject (the procedure used by Bakan, Day, and Duke). In this condition, subjects manifested characteristic tendencies to move in the same direction, some to the left and some to the right, regardless of problem type. To account for this effect of experimenter location, we hypothesized that when the experimenter is behind the subject the problem itself is the most salient stimulus and the subject, more nearly free to attend exclusively to it, can use the hemisphere that more nearly serves the cognitive strategies needed for solving the problem. Furthermore, the experimenter-facing-subject condition is more personal and, therefore, more likely to produce interpersonal anxiety that would tend to elicit stereotypic or habitual modes of responding in the subject, thereby enhancing stylistic effects. These hypotheses received some support from analysis of the quality of subjects' responses in the two experimental conditions. Subjects who moved their eyes in accordance with problem type in the experimenter-behind condition and became unidirectional movers in the experimenter-facing condition performed more poorly in the latter condition than subjects who continued to produce eye movement in problem-appropriate directions. Furthermore, overall performance was poorer in the experimenter-facing condition, a fact that may attest to subjects' anxiety or to the increased distraction produced by the experimenter who faces them. The anxiety hypothesis was not supported, however, in a study by Hiscock (1977), who replicated the experimenter location effect but failed to produce more stereotyped eye-movement directionality with a direct manipulation designed to increase anxiety (i.e., telling subjects that the questions presented to elicit eye movements were designed to measure I.Q.). Clearly, then, more research is needed before we can begin to understand the circumstances that produce eye movements in the direction predicted from problem type and those that produce eye movements that reflect enduring cognitive styles.

In the meanwhile, some studies appear to show mainly the problem-type effect on eye-movement directionality (e.g., Combs, Hoblick, Czarnecki, & Komler, 1977; Gur, 1978; Kocel, Galin, Ornstein, & Marin, 1972; Schwartz, Davidson, & Maer, 1975), others show mainly the individual differences in cognitive styles associated with consistent movements in one direction (e.g., Gerdes & Kinsbourne, 1974; Hiscock, 1977; Libby & Yaklevich, 1973; Meskin & Singer, 1974; Sackeim, Packer, & Gur, 1977), and still others report both effects (e.g., Combs et al., 1977; Gur, 1978; Tucker, Roth, & Arneson, 1977). As we have seen in the studies with EEG and with blood flow, however, it is not inconceivable that both effects may be present in most studies and appear only when specific types of data analyses are performed. It is also possible that some of the studies that did not find the individual differences effect used a restricted range of subjects who happened to belong mostly to one or the other hemisphericity groups. Only samples that are large enough to allow for the variation to express itself can be reasonably expected to show an effect for individual differences in "brainedness."

Recently, Schwartz et al. (1975) reported on another variable that seems to produce differential eye-movement directionality. They administered verbal and spatial questions but made half the questions in each problem-type emotional. They found that emotional questions, whether verbal or spatial, elicited more leftward eye movements than nonemotional questions, indicating that emotional material produces increased activation in the right versus the left hemisphere. This conclusion agrees with clinical data (Gardner, King, Flamm, & Silverman, 1975; Heilman, Scholer, & Watson, 1975) and with experimental findings that indicate that emotions are expressed more intensely on the left side of the face (Campbell, 1976; Levy & Heller, 1977; Sackeim, Gur, & Saucey, 1978). Furthermore, Tucker *et al.* (1977) found that the number of leftward eye movements in response to questions increased with stress manipulations which they described as increasing their subjects' emotional arousal.

In a study we have just completed, we tested the effect of both problem type (verbal versus spatial and emotional versus nonemotional) and experimenter location in a group of 24 subjects (12 male, 12 female). We found, again, that experimenter location had an effect, but this time the effect was somewhat more complicated than in the Gur *et al.* (1975) study, as indicated by a significant three-way interaction. The nature of this interaction is illustrated in Figure 9.1.

As can be seen in this figure, our earlier results were replicated for the nonemotional questions (of the type that were used in our earlier study) in that problem-type had a larger effect in the experimenter-behind than in the experimenter-facing condition. Regarding the emotional question, however, subjects moved their eyes more to the left if the problems were spatial and more to the right if the problems were verbal in the experimenter-facing condition, whereas the effect was attenuated in the experimenter-behind condition. This finding suggests that the results of Schwartz *et al.* may be due, in part, to experimenter location, but an understanding of what all this means with regard to the roles of the hemispheres in processing emotional input must await further study.

Complications of this nature, however, seem to reflect primarily the clumsiness with which our current knowledge permits us to approach the problem of identifying the optimal conditions for studying the different dimensions of our subject matter. They should not cloud the fact that a considerable degree of congruence of findings emerges out of a rather divergent set of measurements of the underlying theoretical concepts. Brain waves, blood flow measures, and eye movements all point to the existence both of a correlation between hemispheric specialization and hemispheric activation and of a pattern of individual differences regarding the extent to which people characteristically activate a given hemisphere across problem types. In the section to follow we will present a series of studies that have examined the effect of handedness, sex, and eye dominance on hemispheric activation as measured by conjugate lateral-eye-movement directionality.

THE EFFECT OF HANDEDNESS, SEX, AND EYE DOMINANCE ON HEMISPHERIC ACTIVATION

In the first study in which we examined eye directionality in left-handers (Gur, Gur, & Harris, 1975), our sample of left-handers ($N = 17$) was too small to warrant any firm conclusions with regard to subgroups of left-

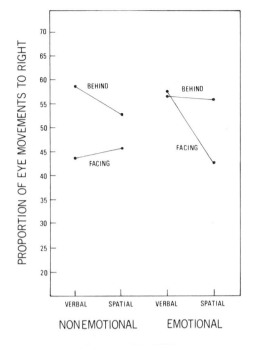

Figure 9.1. The figure shows the effect of problem type and experimenter location on eye movement directionality.

handers. As a group, however, they failed to show an effect of problem-type on the direction of eye movement either in the experimenter-facing or in the experimenter-behind condition. In this sense, the results were congruent with other findings indicating weaker hemispheric specialization among left-handers.

When the results were analyzed by individual subjects, rather than by groups, there were indications that the left-handers had far less homogenous responses than their right-handed counterparts. We divided the subjects who did not show a characteristic direction of movement in the experimenter-behind condition into *discriminators* (i.e., subjects who moved their eyes differentially according to problem type—left in response to spatial questions and right in response to verbal questions, or the reverse which was against the theoretically expected direction) and *non-discriminators* (i.e., subjects whose eye movements were inconsistently related to problem type and appeared haphazard). This classification revealed that whereas most right-handers were discriminators (18 out of

28), most left-handers (11 out of 13) were nondiscriminators ($\chi^2(1) = 6.65$, $p < .01$). Furthermore, both left-handed discriminators were "reverse" discriminators in that they moved their eyes to the left for verbal questions and to the right for spatial questions. Only one right-hander was a "reverse" discriminator.

It thus appeared that some left-handers show little evidence of activating a particular hemisphere as a function of problem type, whereas other left-handers show activation patterns suggestive of right-hemispheric language specialization and left-hemispheric specialization for spatial processing.

These results are consistent with clinical as well as experimental data which indicate that some left-handers have weakly lateralized brains whereas some have the direction of specialization reversed (see Levy & Gur, Chapter 8 of this volume, for a review). More recent research has suggested that hand posture in writing could serve as a rather simple behavioral index of the direction of hemispheric specialization among left-handers. Specifically, left-handers using the inverted writing posture appear to have language subserved in the left hemisphere and functionally are less well lateralized, whereas left-handers who use the noninverted writing posture have language in the right hemisphere and appear to be better lateralized. If eye movements reflect hemispheric activation, and given the expected correlation between hemispheric activation and hemispheric competence, one would expect these two groups of left-handers to differ in patterns of eye directionality as a function of question type. Specifically, left-handers using the noninverted writing posture should move their eyes to the right for spatial questions and to the left for verbal questions, whereas left-handers using the inverted writing posture should show a weaker problem-type effect and in a direction similar to that found among right-handers.

We tested these hypotheses in a study recently completed in our laboratory (Van Auken, 1977). The subjects were 60 undergraduates, 30 males and 30 females. Within each sex group, 10 of the subjects were right-handers using the noninverted writing posture (RN), 10 were left-handers who use the noninverted writing posture (LN), and 10 were left-handers using the inverted writing posture (LI). The subjects were presented with 50 questions, 25 verbal and 25 spatial. The questions also varied with regard to being emotional or nonemotional, but this aspect need not concern us here. The dependent measure was the proportion of rightward eye movements out of the total number of movements.

The major finding was a three-way interaction between handedness and writing posture, sex, and problem type ($F(2, 56) = 3.86$, $p < .05$). The interaction is illustrated in Figure 9.2. As can be seen in this figure, the LN group for both sexes showed patterns of eye movements opposite in direc-

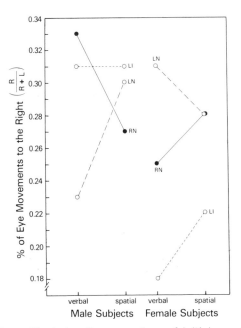

Figure 9.2. The figure illustrates the percentage of initial eye movements to the right after verbal or spatial question. Subjects are grouped by sex, handedness, and handwriting posture.

tion to the pattern showed by (RN) subjects, whereas the LI group seems to show little problem-type effects. Post hoc comparisons among the means indicated that problem-type had a significant effect in males, in opposite directions, for the RN and the LN groups. The other differences did not reach statistical significance. It appears, then, that the direction of lateral eye movements as a function of problem-type is influenced by the same variables that are known to affect the direction and degree of hemispheric specialization.

So far we have examined the effect of handedness on eye directionality as a function of problem-type. As we have discussed earlier, individual differences in hemispheric activation are also revealed by the study of eye directionality. These individual differences in characteristic activation of a particular hemisphere, regardless of problem-type, have also been observed in studies using EEG and blood flow measures of cerebral activity.

Whenever a dimension of individual differences in cognitive, conative, or affective styles is identified, a potentially profitable strategy for gaining an understanding of its effect is to investigate correlates of this dimension in areas where such correlates can be expected. If people vary with regard

to the degree to which they activate a given hemisphere, this should influence the manner in which they approach intellectual and emotional
problems. The manner of approach in turn should be reflected in personality structure insofar as personality variables measure enduring characteristics of individuals.

If we reflect for a moment on how an extreme "left-brained" individual
should differ from an extreme "right-brained" individual (leaving aside for
the moment variations in the direction of hemispheric specialization), a
description of the functions associated with each hemisphere would lead us
to the expectation that the former would be a more logical, rational,
unemotional and well-organized person, whereas the latter would be more
intuitive, imaginative, emotionally expressive, and impulsive. A number of
descriptions of individuals who vary in the extent to which they display
particular personality traits are strikingly similar to the above expected
description of extreme hemisphericity types. It is not surprising, therefore,
that such descriptions served as initial guides in directing research into the
personality correlates of hemisphericity. A case in point is hypnotic susceptibility.

Hypnotic susceptibility, when measured by standardized scales, is a
stable and enduring personality trait (Hilgard, 1965), as hard to modify
substantially by situational manipulations as IQ scores (Gur, 1975). Hypnosis has been described as a "regressive" mode of relating interpersonally
(Gill & Brenman, 1959), requiring an "imaginative involvement" on the
part of the subject (J. R. Hilgard, 1970) and an ability to concentrate on an
object without thinking discursively or analytically (Van Nuys, 1973). According to current views of right-hemispheric functions, the requirements
of the hypnotic task would seem to involve primarily the right hemisphere.
One might accordingly expect hypnotizability (in right-handed subjects)
to be related to a subject's tendency to rely predominantly on right-
hemispheric functioning.

This prediction was supported by Bakan's (1969) research on eye directionality, in which he found that right-movers tend to be less hypnotizable
than left movers. He asked subjects five questions and found a significant
correlation of $-.44$ between the number of eye movements to the right in
response to questioning and hypnotic susceptibility as measured by the
Stanford Hypnotic Susceptibility Scale, Form C (Weitzenhoffer & Hilgard,
1962). Morgan et al. (1971) have replicated this finding, again obtaining a
significant, albeit lower ($-.22$) correlation between the number of eye
movements to the right and hypnotic susceptibility. Gur and Reyher (1973)
found that left-movers performed better than right-movers on a hypnotic
induction scale with instructions phrased in a passive and emotional style
and calling for focusing attention on internal subjective feelings and ex-

periences. Right-movers performed better on a hypnotic induction scale phrased in an active and intellectual style and calling for focusing on external events.

If hypnotic susceptibility is related to right-hemispheric functioning, one would expect handedness to be a moderating variable in this relationship. Some suggestive evidence that handedness may be related to hypnotizability was provided by Bakan (1970), who found that left-handers were more likely than right-handers to score at the extremes, either high or low, on a hypnotic susceptibility scale, and less likely to score in the middle. Gender was not examined in Bakan's (1969, 1970) studies, and only right-handed males were used in Gur and Reyher's (1973) study.

As an initial step toward explicating the effect of handedness on personality correlates of individual differences in hemispheric activation, we tested the hypothesis that the association between eye directionality and hypnotic susceptibility is moderated by handedness (Gur & Gur, 1975). We also expected sex to moderate the association and we included measures of eye dominance as another potential indicator of the direction of hemispheric specialization (e.g. Humphrey, 1951; Levy & Gur, Chapter 8 of this volume). Unfortunately, Levy and Reid's (1976, 1978) data with regard to the effect of writing posture were not available at the time and the subjects' writing posture was not recorded.

Sixty right-handers (30 male, 30 female) were randomly selected from a total sample of 270 undergraduate volunteers. From this total sample, all 30 left-handers (19 males and 11 females) were also selected. Initially, handedness was defined on the basis of the response to the question "Are you right-handed, left-handed, or ambidextrous?" Subsequently, the subjects chosen were administered Part A of Humphrey's (1951) questionnaire which assesses hand usage for a variety of tasks.

Hypnotic susceptibility was measured both by a group scale (the Harvard Group Scale of Hypnotic Susceptibility; Shor & Orne, 1962) and by a more advanced scale administered individually (the Stanford Hypnotic Susceptibility Scale: Form C: Weitzenhoffer & Hilgard, 1962). The main findings were as follows:

1. For the total sample, eye movements to the left and hypnotic susceptibility were moderately related ($r = -.21$, $p < .05$).
2. When handedness was introduced as a moderating variable, the results showed that this relationship existed for right-handed subjects only.
3. When gender was introduced as a moderating variable, the results showed the relationship to be present only for males.
4. When the combined moderating effect of both gender and handedness was considered, the results showed that hypnotizability was associated

with left eye movements (right hemisphere bias) for right-handed males and with right eye movements (left hemisphere bias) for left-handed females (see Figure 9.3). As can be seen in Figure 9.3, the magnitude and direction of the correlations apparently depend on both handedness and gender. Left-hemispheric activation (right eye movements) correlated negatively with hypnotizability for males and positively for females, with left-handed females being somewhat of a "mirror image" of right-handed males.

5. When eye dominance was introduced as a moderating variable for left-handed males and right-handed females, the results showed that for left-handed, left-eyed males, hypnosis is associated with right eye movements, whereas for left-handed right-eyed males hypnotic susceptibility is associated with left eye movements. As for the right-handed females, the correlation between leftward eye movements and hypnotic susceptibility was positive for the left-eyed females and negative for the right-eyed females. The difference between these correlations, however, was not significant.

The results seem to support the idea that the ability to become hypnotized is related to a tendency to rely on the nonverbal, holistic, synthetic,

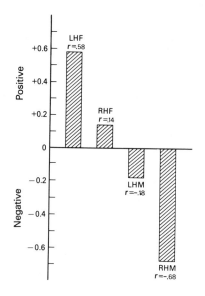

Figure 9.3. The figure demonstrates the magnitude and direction of correlations between number of eye movements to the right and hypnotic susceptibility for right-handed males (RHM), left-handed males (LHM), right-handed females (RHF), and left-handed females (LHF).

or "intuitive" hemisphere. The results simultaneously provide some additional support for eye directionality as an index of hemispheric activation and for the idea that individuals differ in the degree to which they tend to activate one or the other hemisphere. A position which rejects either view would be hard pressed to account for the pattern of correlations that were obtained in this study.

SUMMARY

In this chapter we have attempted to present the case for considering hemispheric activation as an important dimension for understanding the role of functional brain asymmetry in cognition. We have summarized evidence supporting the view that, in addition to variations in the direction and degree of lateral specialization and in competence of problem-solving capacities in the two hemispheres, individuals differ also in characteristic activation of the two hemispheres. We suggested a number of methods for measuring this dimension of "brainedness" or hemisphericity (Bogen, 1969), and showed how studies using such measures converged to support the hypothesis that such a dimension may exert significant influences on problem solving strategies. We proceeded to focus on lateral eye movements as an index of hemispheric activation and described a series of studies indicating that the direction of eye movements in response to questioning reflects hemispheric activation both as a function of cognitive task demands and as a function of individual differences in characteristic activation. Finally, we examined the effect of handedness and other variables known to affect the direction and degree of hemispheric activation on eye directionality.

The results, in the main, support the hypothesis that left-handedness is associated with a weaker degree of hemispheric specialization and, at times, with a reverse direction of specialization. They also suggest the possibility that individual differences in hemispheric activation patterns may account for some of the variation in cognitive organization that is associated with variations in manual and ocular asymmetries.

REFERENCES

Ax, A. The physiological differentiation between fear and anger in humans. *Psychosomatic Medicine*, 1953, *15*, 433–442.

Bakan, P. Hypnotizability, laterality of eye movement and functional brain asymmetry. *Perceptual and Motor Skills*, 1969, *28*, 927–932.

Bakan, P. Handedness and hypnotizability. *International Journal of Clinical and Experimental Hypnosis*, 1970, *18*(2), 99–104.

Bakan, P. The eyes have it. *Psychology Today*, 1971, *4*, 64–69.

Bakan, P., & Shotland, J. Lateral eye movement, reading speed, and visual attention. *Psychonomic Science*, 1969, *16*, 93–94.

Bakan, P., & Svorad, D. Resting EEG alpha and asymmetry of reflective lateral eye movements. *Nature*, 1969, *223*, 975–976.

Bigum, H. Visual and somatosensory evoked responses form mongoloid and normal children. Unpublished doctoral dissertation, University of Utah, 1969.

Bogen, J. E. The other side of the brain II: An appositional mind. *Bulletin of the Los Angeles Neurological Societies*, 1969, *34*, 135–162.

Buchsbaun, Monte & Fedio, Paul. Hemispheric differences in evoked potentials to verbal and nonverbal stimuli to the left and right visual fields. *Physiology & Behavior*, 1970, *5*(2), 207–210.

Campbell, R. Asymmetries in interpreting and expressing posed facial expressions, Unpublished manuscript, Birkbeck College (University of London), 1976.

Cohn, R. Average evoked cortical responses from visual stimulation. *Electroencephalography and Clinical Neurophysiology* (Amsterdam), 1963, *15*, 156–165.

Cohn, R. Differential cerebral processing of noise and verbal stimuli. *Science*, 1971, *192*, 599–601.

Combs, A. L., Hoblick, P. J., Czarnecki, M. J., & Komler, P. Relationship of lateral eye-movement to cognitive mode, hemispheric interaction and choice of college major. *Perceptual and Motor Skills*, 1977, *45*, 983–990.

Cornil, L., & Gestaut, H. Données electroencephalographiques sur la dominance hemispheric (abstract). *Revue Neurol.*, 1947, *79*, 207.

Creutzfeldt, O., Grunewald, G., Sinonova, O., Schmitz, H. Changes of the basic rhythms of the EEG during the performance of mental and visuomotor tasks. In C. R. Evans & T. B. Nulholland (Eds.) *Attention in Neurophysiology*. New York, Appleton, Century and Crofts, 1969, 148–168.

Day, M. E. An eye-movement phenomenon relating to attention, thought and anxiety. *Perceptual and Motor Skills*, 1964, *19*, 443–446.

Day, M. E. An eye-movement indicator of type and level of anxiety. Some clinical observations. *Journal of Clinical Psychology*, 1967(a), *23*, 433–441.

Day, M. E. An eye-movement indicator of individual differences in the physiological organization of attentional processes and anxiety. *The Journal of Psychology*, 1967(b), *66*, 51–62.

Day, M. E. Attention, anxiety and psychotherapy. *Psychotherapy Theory, Research and Practice*, 1968, *5*, 146–149.

Doyle, J. C., Ornstein, R., & Galin, D. Lateral specialization of cognitive mode: ii EEG frequency analysis. *Psychophysiology*, 1974, *11*(5), 567–578.

Duke, J. Lateral eye-movement behavior. *Journal of General Psychology*, 1968, *78*, 189–195.

Dumas, R., & Morgan, A. EEG asymmetry as a function of occupation, task, and task difficulty *Neuropsychologia*, 1975, *13*, 219–228.

Friedman, D., Simson, R., Ritter, W., & Rapin, I. Corticle evoked potentials elicited by real speech words and human sounds. *Electroencephalography and Clinical Neurophysiology*, 1975, *38*,13–19.

Furst, C. J. EEG asymmetry and visuospatial performance. *Nature*, 1976, *260*, 254–255.

Galamobs, R., Benson, P., Smith, T. S., Schulman-Gialamoos, C., & Osier, H. On hemispheric differences in evoked potentials to speech stimuli. *Electroencephalography & Clinical Neurophysiology*, 1975, *39*(3), 279–283.

Galin, D., & Ornstein, R. Lateral specialization of cognitive mode: An EEG study. *Psychophysiology*, 1972, *9*(4), 412–418.

Galin, D., & Ellis, R. R. Asymmetry in evoked potentials as an index of lateralized cognitive processes: Relation to EEG alpha asymmetry. *Neuropsychologia*, 1975, *13*(1), 45–50.

Gardner, H., King, R. K., Flam, L., and Silverman, J. Comprehension and appreciation of humerous material following brain damage. *Brain*, 1975, *98*, 399–412.

Gerdes, E. P., & Kinsbourne, M. Lateral eye movements and state anxiety. *Catalogue of selected documents in psychology*, 1974, *4*, 118–119.

Gill, Merton, M. & Brenman, Margaret. *Hypnosis and related states: Psychoanalytic studies in regression.* New York: International Univer Press, 1959.

Groberg, D. H. Handedness and late components of visual and somatosensory cerebral evoked responses. Unpublished doctoral dissertation, University of Utah, 1967.

Gur, R. E. Conjugate lateral eye movements as an index of hemispheric activation. *Journal of Personality and Social Psychology*, 1975, *31*, 751–757.

Gur, R. E. Left hemisphere dysfunction and left hemisphere overactivation in schizophrenia. *Journal of Abnormal Psychology*, 1978, *87*, 226–238.

Gur, R. E., & Gur, R. C. Defense mechanisms, psychosomatic symptomatology, and conjugate lateral eye movements. *Journal of Consulting and Clinical Psychology*, 1975, *43*, 416–420.

Gur, R. E., Gur, R. C., & Harris, L. J. Cerebral activation, as measured by subject's lateral eye movements, is influenced by experimenter location. *Neuropsychologia*, 1975, *13*, 35–44.

Gur, R. C., Reivich, M. Cognitive task effects on hemispheric blood flow in humans. *Brain and Language*, in press.

Gur, R. E. & Reyher, J. The relationship between style of hypnotic induction and direction of lateral eye movement. *Journal of Abnormal Psychology*, 1973, *82*, 499–505.

Heilman, K. M., Scholer, R., & Watson, R. T. Auditory affective anagnasia. *Journal of Neurology, Neurosurgery, and Psychiatry*, 1975, *38*, 69–72.

Hilgard, Ernest R. *Hypnotic susceptibility.* New York: Harcourt, Brace & World, 1965.

Hilgard, J. R. *Personality and hypnosis: A study of imaginative involvement.* Chicago, Ill.: University of Chicago Press, 1970.

Hiscock, Merrill. Effects of examiner's location and subject's anxiety on gaze laterality. *Neuropsychologia*, 1977, *15*(3), 409–417.

Humphrey, M. E. Consistency of hand usage: A preliminary inquiry. *British Journal of Educational Psychology*, 1951, *21*, 214–225.

Kinsbourne, M. Eye and head turning indicates cerebral lateralization. *Science*, 1972, *176*, 539–541.

Kocel, K., Galin, D., Ornstein, R., & Merrin, E. Lateral eye movement and cognitive mode. *Psychonomic Science*, 1972, *27*, 223–224.

Lacay, J. I. Somatic response patterning and stress: Some revisions of activation theory. In M. H. Appley & R. Trumbull (Eds.), *Psychological stress: Issues in research.* New York: Appleton, 1967.

Levy, J. & Reid, M. Variations in writing posture and cerebral organization. *Science*, 1976, *194*, 337–339.

Levy, J. & Reid, M. Variations in cerebral organization as a function of handedness, hand posture in writing, and sex. *Journal of Experimental Psychology*, 1978, *107*, 119–144.

Levy, J. & Trevarthen, C. Metacontrol of hemispheric function in human split brain patients. *Journal of Experimental Psychology: Human Perception and Performance*, 1976, *2*(3), 299–312.

Levy, J. & Heller, W. Laterality and the perception of emotion. Unpublished manuscript, University of Pennsylvania, 1977.

Libby, W. L. & Yaklevich, D. Personality determinants of eye contact and direction of gaze aversion. *Journal of Personality and Social Psychology*, 1973, *27*(2), 197–206.

Lindsley, D. B. Psychological phenomena and the electroencephalogram. *Electroenceph-alography and Clinical Neurophysiology*, 1952, *4*, 443–456.

Lindsley, D. B. Bilateral differences in brain potentials from the two cerebral hemispheres in relation to laterality and stuttering. *Journal of Experimental Psychology*, 1940, *26*, 211–255.

Mott, F. W., & Shafer, E., On associated eye movements produced by cortical faradization of the monkey's brain. *Brain*, 1890, *13*, 165–173.

Meskin, B. B., & Singer, J. L. Daydreaming, reflective thought and laterality of eye movements. *Journal of Personality and Social Psychology*, 1974, *30*, 64–71.

McAdam, Dale, W. & Whitaker, Harry A. Language production: Electroencephalographic localization in the normal human brain. *Science*, 1971, *172*, 499–502.

McGlone, J., & Davidson, W. The relation between cerebral speech laterality and spatial ability with special reference to sex and hand preference. *Neuropsychologia*, 1973, *11*, 105–113.

McKee, G., Humphrey, B., & McAdams, D. Scaled lateralization of alpha activity during linguistic and musical tasks. *Psychophysiology*, 1973, *10*, 441–443.

Morrell, L. K., & Salamy, J. G. Hemispheric asymmetry of electrocortical responses to speech stimuli. *Science*, 1971, *174*, 164–166.

Morgan, A. H., McDonald, P. J., & MacDonald, H. Differences in bilateral alpha activity as a function of experimental task with a note on lateral eye movements and hypnotizability. *Neuropsychologia*, 1971, *9*, 459–469.

Morgan, A. H., MacDonald, H., & Hilgard, E. R. EEG alpha: Lateral asymmetry related to task, and hypnotizability. *Psychophysiology*, 1974, *11*, 275–282.

Mulholland, T. B. The concept of attention and the electroencephalographic alpha rhythm. In C. R. Evans & T. B. Mulholland (Eds.), *Attention in neurophysiology*. New York: Appleton-Century-Crofts, 1969, pp. 100–127.

Obrist, W. D., Thompson, H. K., Wang, H. S., and Wilkinson, W. E. Regional cerebral blood flow estimated by 133 xenon inhalation. *Stroke*, 1975, *6*, 245–256.

Orne, M. T. & Wilson, S. K. Alpha, biofeedback and arousal/activation. In J. Beatty & H. Legewie (Eds.), *Biofeedback and behavior*. New York: Plenum Press, 1977, pp. 107–120.

Ornstein, R. E. *The psychology of consciousness*. San Francisco: W. H. Freeman and Co., 1972.

Penfield, W., & Roberts, L. *Speech and brain mechanisms*. Princeton, N.J.: Princeton University Press, 1959.

Rancy, E. T. Brain potentials and lateral dominance in identical twins. *Journal of Experimental Psychology*, 1939, *24*, 21–39.

Risberg, J., & Ingvar, D. M. Patterns of activation in the gray matter of the dominant hemisphere. *Brain*, 1973, *96*, 737–756.

Risberg, J., Halsey, J. H., Blavenstein, V. W., Wilson, E. M. & Wills, E. L. Bilateral measurements of the rcBf during mental activation in normals and in normals and in dysphasic patients. In A. M. Harper, W. B. Jennett, J. D. Miller & J. O. Brown (Eds.). *Blood flow and metabolism in the brain*. London: Churchill Livingstone, 1975.

Sackeim, H. A., Gur, R. C., & Saucy, M. Emotions are expressed more intensely on the left side of the face. *Science*, 1978, *202*, 434–436.

Sackeim, H. A., Packer, I. K., & Gur, R. C. Hemisphericity, cognitive set and susceptibility to subliminal perception. *Journal of Abnormal Psychology*, 1977, *86*, 624–630.

Schwartz, G. E., Davidson, R. J., & Maer, F. Right hemisphere lateralization for emotion in the human brain: Interactions with cognition. *Science*, 1975, *190*, 286–288.

Shelburne, S. A. Visual evoked responses to word and nonsense syllable stimuli. *Electroencephalography and clinical neurophysiology*, 1972, *32*(1), 17–25.

Shucard, D. W., Shucard, J. L., & Thomas, D. G. Auditory evoked potentials as probes of hemispheric differences in cognitive processing. *Science,* 1977, *197,* 1295-1298.

Subirana, A., & Olier-Daurella, L. Laterality, maturity and EEG. *Current Problems Phoniat. Logotp.,* 1960, *1,* 141.

Teitelbaum, H. A. Spontaneous rhythmic ocular movement. Their possible relationship to mental activity. *Neurology,* 1954, *4,* 350-354.

Trevarthen, C. Brain bisymmetry and the role of the corpus callosum in behavior and conscious experience. Paper presented at the *International Colloquium on Cerebral Hemispheric Relations,* Smolenice, Chechoslovakia, 1969 (subsequently published in J. Cernacek, & F. Podivinsky (Eds.), Cerebral hemispheric relations. Bratislava: The Publishing House of the Slovak Academy of Science, 1972).

Tucker, D. M., Roth, R. S., Arneson, B. A., & Buckingham, V. Right hemisphere activation during stress. *Neuropsychologia,* 1977, *15,* 697-700.

Van Auken, C. L. The effects of handedness, hand writing posture and sex on the direction of conjugate lateral eye movements in response to questioning. Unpublished Masters Thesis, University of Pennsylvania, 1977.

Van Nuys, D. Meditation, attention, and hypnotic susceptibility: A correlational study. *Inter. Journal of Clinical and Experimental Hypnosis,* 1973, *21,* 59-69.

Weitzenhoffer, A. M., & Hilgard, E. R. *Stanford Hypnosis Susceptibility Scale Form C.* Palo Alto, California: Consulting Psychologists, 1962.

Wood, C. C., Goff, W. R., & Day, R. S. Auditory evoked potentials during speech perception. *Science,* 1971, *173,* 1248-1251.

10

Two Hands, Two Brains, Two Sexes

JEANNINE HERRON

INTRODUCTION

Several chapters in this book are devoted to studies of patterns of hemisphere specialization in left-handers. It is not necessary to repeat the evidence that suggests that these patterns vary more among left-handers than among right-handers, and that in left-handers at least half control speech primarily with the left hemisphere, while for the remainder the right hemisphere seems to share control or dominate to a far greater extent in the speech process. How patterns vary for spatial abilities is even less well-understood.

Although Subirana (1969) bemoaned this variation in left-handers and declared that it existed for the sole purpose of confounding and dismaying neurologists, a more cheerful view suggests that this select population provides researchers with a rich source of different patterns of cortical specialization for studying the relationship of brain organization to individual traits like personality, cognitive skills, cognitive deficits, cognitive style, motor abilities, creativity, psychosis, even genius.

Researchers have only begun to develop accurate measures to identify different patterns of cortical organization and to assess the extent of the specialization. In previous work at Langley Porter, we studied hemisphere specialization in right-handers by examining EEG alpha asymmetry between the two hemispheres while the subjects performed different cognitive tasks (Galin & Ornstein, 1972; Doyle, Ornstein & Galin, 1974). We found that

233

NEUROPSYCHOLOGY
OF LEFT-HANDEDNESS

the left hemisphere generally was more engaged during language tasks and that the right was more engaged during spatial tasks, as might be predicted from clinical lesion studies.

We decided to extend our investigation to left handers, in order to explore several questions. First, we predicted that patterns of alpha asymmetry would differ between right- and left-handers because left-handed groups would include significantly more individuals whose specialization for speech would be more "bilateral" or even the "reverse" of the usual right-handed pattern. In particular, we wanted to see if there were differences in patterns of hemisphere activity between (a) "pure" left-handers and ambidexters (b) male and female left-handers, and (c) left-handers who use the inverted hand posture for writing and those who use the noninverted posture.

More commonly used measures, dichotic listening and tachistoscopic hemifield stimulation, seemed initially promising as ways to infer the laterality of speech in normal subjects. Unfortunately, correlations between the results obtained with these methods are low (Fennel, Bowers, & Satz, 1977; Bryden, 1965). Perhaps the correlations are low partly because the methods do not assess the same language behaviors. The auditory test assesses auditory–verbal specialization, whereas the visual test measures visual–verbal specialization. "Language" involves reading, writing, speaking, and listening. It has many different components including kinesthetic and motor components and, in some individuals, these components may not all be lateralized in the same hemisphere. Consequently, the lateralization of language per se in an individual subject cannot be safely inferred from a single measure. Hines and Satz (1974) found that ear superiority and visual half-field superiority were correlated in right-handers but not in left-handers, indicating some dissociation between visual and auditory processes. The *extent* of specialization in individuals cannot be easily inferred because factors other than hemispheric specialization may influence the degree of ear and visual-field superiority (e.g., attention, set, physical characteristics of the stimulus).

In the early 1970s, an EEG technique was developed which arose from the observation that alpha (α) waves (8–13 Hz) tend to appear more frequently when the brain is *not* engaged in a task. The technique involves recording activity at two homologous sites, (i.e., one over the left hemisphere, the other over the right) and comparing the amount of 8–13 Hz activity at each electrode lead. Characteristically, a task that engages the *left hemisphere* in most right-handed subjects, a language task such as mentally composing a letter will produce relatively *less* α at the left hemisphere lead. A task that engages the *right hemisphere* in most right-handed subjects, a spatial task such as reproducing a design with colored blocks, will produce relatively less α at the right hemisphere lead. It is the relative *absence* of α that marks the active hemisphere. In comparing the activity of the two hemispheres, we use a ratio between right and left (R/L) power, to express the relationship. A high R/L ratio (more α in the right than the left hemisphere) indicates greater engagement in the *left* hemisphere. The reverse, a low R/L ratio, indicates greater engagement of the *right* hemisphere. Our laboratory has used this paradigm extensively (Doyle, Ornstein, & Galin, 1974; Galin & Ornstein, 1972; Galin, Johnstone, & Herron, 1978; Galin, Ornstein, Herron, & Johnstone, 1979), and other investigators have used it with similar results (McKee, Humphrey, & McAdam, 1973; Davidson & Schwartz, 1977; Ehrlichman & Weiner, 1977).

The EEG technique has the advantage that it reflects the events that are actually occurring in the brain more directly than do behavioral measures. Although it is a fairly crude instrument, one electrode picking up the electrical activity of literally thousands and thousands of cells, it nevertheless enables an investigator to measure the relative participation of the two hemispheres during everyday tasks such as reading, speaking, singing, etc. Other methods are usually constrained to brief stimuli that do not represent natural cognitive processing. The relative *activation* of the two hemispheres is not *necessarily* a reflection of hemispheric "specialization"; the pattern of activation might be influenced by attention, strategy, cognitive style, etc., as well as by the "specialization" of the hemispheres. Nevertheless, the EEG is one of the most direct tools for evaluating how the two hemispheres participate in ongoing tasks in different subjects.

Our subjects were 30 left-handed, 30 right-handed, and 30 ambidextrous normal adults with 15 males and 15 females in each group. We classified them on the basis of a 12 item questionnaire that asked hand preference on unimanual tasks such as writing, drawing, throwing, etc. (after Annett, 1967). ("Right hand" responses scored $+1$; "left-hand" responses scored -1; "either" scored 0. The right-handed group scored $+12$ to $+8$, ambidexters scores $+7$ to -6, and left-handers scored -7 to -12.)

The EEG was recorded from leads C_3, C_4, (centrals), P_3, P_4 (parietals) 0_1 and 0_2 (occipitals), all references to C_z, with a grass model 7 polygraph (.5 A cutoff $= 1$–35 Hz). The signal was led to an on-line, hard-wired analysis system which filtered the narrow alpha band (9.0–11. Hz), summed the alpha power over 30 second epochs, and printed values for each of the six channels every 30 seconds. All six channels of the polygraph and analysis system were adjusted for equal output with a standard 120 μV, 10 Hz signal and calibrated each day before and after testing. The EEG was recorded while the subjects performed six cognitive tasks entitled Blocks, Sing, Read, Listen, Speak and Write.

In Blocks, the subjects memorized a two-dimensional geometric pattern

(Kohs) for one minute, then reconstructed the pattern from memory using both hands to arrange multicolored blocks. We presented additional designs until we obtained 3 min of recording. For Sing, the subjects sang without words, familiar melodies like "Happy Birthday." In Read, the subjects read a factual but not difficult 1000 word passage on biologic rhythms, concentrating on facts and ideas that they knew they would be asked to summarize later. For the Listen task, the subjects listened to a tape of a similar passage. For Speak, the subjects gave an oral summary of what they had just heard or read. For Write, the subjects wrote as many of the facts as they could recall from what they had just heard or read. All the tasks were 3 min long and were repeated twice in counterbalanced order.

The basic data are the integrated α power for each task at six leads and the R/L log ratios between homologous leads. (All computations involving ratios were performed on logarithmic transforms of the ratios because the log values are linearly and symmetrically distributed.) The R/L ratios from the central leads for all tasks for each group are shown in Table 10.1 and Figure 10.1

RIGHT- VERSUS LEFT-HANDED DIFFERENCES

We found that ratios for individual tasks did not differ significantly between the right- and left-handed groups, except for the Write task where the difference was highly significant. This task is discussed more fully in later sections of this chapter. We did find, however, that significant differences appeared when we analyzed the *relationship* between two individual tasks, Speak and Blocks, for the right-handed and left-handed groups. Speak and Blocks differ significantly in the right-handed group but not in the left-handed group. We express the relationship between Speak and Blocks with a Speak minus Blocks score, (actually a ratio of ratios) that gives us a single number representing a rough estimate of the extent of hemispheric asymmetry a subject can show when these tasks are compared. A high Speak— Blocks difference would imply strong left hemisphere participation in Speak, and strong right hemisphere participation in Blocks. A difference around zero would imply less differentiation between the hemispheres, while a difference of less than zero would imply a reversal of the first pattern (this is, more right hemisphere participation in Speak and more left-hemisphere participation in Blocks). When we compared Speak—Blocks scores for right- and left-handers (see Table 10.2), we found the right-handers scored higher ($F = 2.79$, $p = .067$).

If no further analysis were done, it might be concluded that left-handers as a group had a somewhat more "reversed" pattern of activation.

Table 10.1
C_4/C_3 Task Log Ratios

Subjects	Blocks	Sing	Listen	Read	Speak	Write
Male right-handers[a]						
$\overline{X}$	−.107	−.044	−.043	−.008	.048	.122
SD	(.153)	(.159)	(.130)	(.132)	(.136)	(.128)
Female right-handers[a]						
$\overline{X}$	−.080	.044	.059	.058	.072	.191
SD	(.158)	(.178)	(.161)	(.128)	(.125)	(.165)
All right-handers[b]						
$\overline{X}$	−.094	.000	.008	.025	.060	.156
SD	(.153)	(.171)	(.152)	(.132)	(.129)	(.149)
Male ambidexters						
$\overline{X}$	−.113	−.065	−.051	−.033	−.023	.027
SD	(.166)	(.168)	(.162)	(.167)	(.148)	(.236)
Female ambidexters						
$\overline{X}$	−.047	−.036	−.066	−.017	.009	−.010
SD	(.144)	(.149)	(.160)	(.085)	(.111)	(.192)
All ambidexters						
$\overline{X}$	−.080	−.050	−.058	−.025	−.007	.009
SD	(.157)	(.157)	(.158)	(.131)	(.130)	(.212)
Male left-handers						
$\overline{X}$	−.062	.055	.038	.042	.069	−.091
SD	(.129)	(.119)	(.107)	(.119)	(.107)	(.164)
Female left-handers						
$\overline{X}$	−.022	−.031	−.010	−.004	−.032	−.113
SD	(.157)	(.180)	(.151)	(.117)	(.156)	(.181)
All left-handers						
$\overline{X}$	−.042	.012	.014	.019	.019	−.102
SD	(.143)	(.156)	(.131)	(.118)	(.141)	(.170)

Analysis of Variance

Source	SS	df	MS	F	p
Sex	.0165	1	.0165	.199	.656
Hand	.3197	2	.1598	1.937	.151
Sex–Hand	.2399	2	.1200	1.454	.240
Error	6.6011	80	.0825		
Task	.5290	5	.1058	9.7931	.000
Task–Sex	.0402	5	.0080	.7433	.591
Task–Hand	.9204	10	.0920	8.5191	.000
T–S–H	.1324	10	.0132	1.2252	.273
Error	4.3216	400	.0108		

[a] $N = 13$
[b] $N = 26$

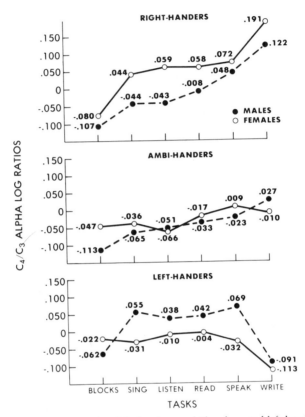

Figure 10.1 C_4/C_3 Log ratios for right-handers, ambi-handers, and left-handers during six cognitive tasks

However, when male and female left-handers are considered separately (see Table 10.2), it becomes clear that, at least in this population of 30 left-handers, the pattern among the females is much more "reversed." The female left-handers have significantly lower Speak minus Blocks scores than the male left-handers, ($t = 2.11$, $p < .05$), or the female or the male right-handers ($t = 2.70$, $p < .02$). Ambidextrous females show the same tendency, but not as strongly.

Another way to look at this phenomenon is to examine the correlation between Speak − Blocks score and handedness questionnaire scores for the 45 males and 45 females. The correlation for females is positive and significant ($r = .42$, $p < .01$): the more right-handed the women are, the higher the Speak − Blocks scores and the more left-handed the women are, the lower the Speak − Blocks scores. The correlation for males is not significant

Table 10.2
Relationship of Speak and Blocks Tasks in
Handedness Groups (log C_4/C_3 Speak — log C_4/C_3
Blocks)

Hand group		Speak-Blocks
Male right-handers	$\overline{X}$	.152
	SD	(.145)
Female right-handers	$\overline{X}$	.146
	SD	(.114)
All right-handers	$\overline{X}$	.149
	SD	(.128)
Male ambi-handers	$\overline{X}$	.090
	SD	(.144)
Female ambi-handers	$\overline{X}$	.056
	SD	(.162)
All ambi-handers	$\overline{X}$	.073
	SD	(.152)
Male left-handers	$\overline{X}$	.131
	SD	(.174)
Female left-handers	$\overline{X}$	− .010
	SD	(.192)
All left-handers	$\overline{X}$	.061
	SD	(.193)

$(r = .03)$. When the Speak task is considered by itself, the correlation between Speak log ratios and handedness is again significant among the women $(r = .35, p = < .05)$ but not among the men $(r = − .01)$. For the Blocks task alone, the correlation for women is not significant but it shows a trend in the predicted direction $(r = − .158)$. The correlation for males again is not significant $(r = − .130)$.

These results suggest that there is an orderly relationship among these females between handedness and the pattern of hemispheric activation during speaking. As the left hand is more consistently preferred, the right hemisphere is more consistently engaged during speaking.

The relationship with Blocks ratios is not so clear. Although Speak ratios show a significant correlation with handedness in women, Blocks ratios do not. It seems that in an individual, participation of the right hemisphere in speaking does not *necessarily* imply a similar "reversal" (that is, more participation of the left hemisphere) for spatial tasks.

The relationship of handedness with Speak is consistent with lesion studies (Goodglass & Quadfasel, 1954; Gloning & Quatember, 1965; Gloning et al., 1969; Hécaen & Ajuriaguerra, 1964) and with dichotic listening studies (Kimura, 1961; Curry, 1967; Zurif & Bryden, 1969; Satz et al.,

1967, Hines & Satz, 1974; Shankweiler & Kennedy, 1975). However, most of the studies have grouped men and women together, assuming that the relationship between handedness and hemispheric specialization is expressed similarly in both groups.

Our findings indicate sex related differences in hemispheric specialization among left-handers, but *not* among right-handers. A number of other reports have indicated sex related differences in hemispheric specialization although not specifically among left-handers. Wada, Clark, and Hamm (1975) showed that more women than men have a larger planum temporale (language area) on the right. Some lesion studies support the idea that women may have more right hemispheric participation in language than men (Goodglass & Quadfasel, 1954; Ettlinger *et al.*, 1956; Landsdell, 1961; 1962; 1968; McGlone & Kertesz, 1973). In addition, a stronger right-ear superiority on verbal dichotic listening tests was found for males by Lake and Bryden (1977). Regarding tachistoscopic measures, Ehrlichman (1971) found that males have a stronger right visual-field superiority for verbal material. It must be emphasized, however, that these studies were largely of right-handers and that in our experiment we found no differences in EEG asymmetry between male and female right-handers but only between male and female left-handers.

LEFT-HANDED VERSUS "AMBI-HANDED" DIFFERENCES

"Ambidexterity" implies equal dexterity with both hands. It also implies that both hands are right hands, a bit of "dextro-chauvinism" I prefer to replace with the term "ambi-handed." The implication is that an ambidexter is a right hander who can also use the left hand, whereas it is just as likely that the ambidexter is a left-hander who can also use the right. The more radical term "ambi-sinistral" might evoke an image of an individual with two awkward hands rather than two "dextrous" hands. However, it seems that left hands can be adequately "dextrous." In our experiment we tested our subjects' performance on finger tapping speed, grip strength, and manual dexterity, and left-handers performed just as well with the left hand as right-handers did with the right (Johnstone, Galin, & Herron, 1979).

Actually, most ambi-handers do not do the same task equally well with both hands. It is extremely rare to find individuals who write or draw equally well with both hands. The usual pattern is for the distal small muscles tasks to be accomplished better by one hand than the other. Our questionnaire allowed subjects to respond that they usually performed the 12 actions with their *left* hand, their *right* hand, or *either* hand. Tasks carried out by more proximal large muscles (e.g., throwing, playing a game with a racquet) were more frequently answered "either" hand than were small muscle tasks (e.g., writing or drawing). On the small parts dexterity test, which requires skilled finger coordination, the ambi-handers usually performed better with one hand than the other. They were not more bilaterally skilled than the left-handers or right-handers. The mean right − left score for the group was misleading in that respect, because some individuals performed better with the left hand and other with the right hand (Johnstone et al., 1979). On "footedness," however, ambi-handers leaned more definitely to the right, preferring the right foot for skilled kicking, while left-handers preferred the left.

Studies of hemisphere specialization comparing strongly left-handed individuals with those who use both hands are not in agreement. Hecaen and Sauget (1971) and Dee (1971) believe strong left-handers to have language more consistently in the left hemisphere, whereas others claim strong left-handers are more bilaterally organized (Knox & Boone, 1973; Satz, Achenbach, & Fennel, 1967; Shankweiler & Studdert-Kennedy, 1975).

In our experiment, the ambi-handers produced an unexpected and interesting result. In general, their R/L ratios were *lower* than either right-handers' or left-handers', implying more right hemispheric engagement overall. Specifically, at the parietal leads the mean ratio across all tasks was lowest for the ambi-handers and produced a main effect for hand group in the analysis of variance (ANOVA). We found this surprising because we had expected ambi-handed ratios to fall somewhere between right- and left-handers' ratios. We also expected to find differences in *task-dependent* asymmetry, but not differences in hemispheric asymmetry regardless of task.

When tasks were examined individually at the parietal leads, we found that during the Speak task, the ambi-hander mean ratio was the lowest of the three groups ($F = 3.39$, $df\ 2, 480$, $p < .05$), significantly lower than the right-hander Speak ratio, and lower than the left-handers' Speak, but not significantly so. During the Sing task, ambi-handers showed lower ratios than both right-handers and left-handers ($F = 4.86$, $p < .01$), who were not different from each other.

The Write task needs special consideration, because it is a unimanual task and was not performed the same way by all subjects. The 30 right-handers wrote with their right hand; the 30 left-handers wrote with their left hand; But 11 of the ambi-handers wrote with their right hand and 19 wrote with their left hand. The Write ratios seem to be strongly influenced by the laterality of the motor component. Those ambi-handers who wrote with their left hand produced Write ratios similar to left-handers. Conversely, the 11 who wrote with the right hand produced Write ratios similar to right handers. The other three tasks, Listen, Read, and Blocks, also have lower mean ratios in the ambi-handers than in both right and left-handers, although the difference for each task does not reach significance.

One possible explanation for this phenomenon is that ambi-handers may all have thinner skulls on the left side of the head (or thicker skulls on the right) than left-handers or right-handers. Alpha activity has been shown to be attenuated where the skull is thicker (Leissner, 1970). However, this explanation does not seem plausible unless one could rationalize a relationship between skull thickness and ambidexterity. We must also consider the possibility that some kind of right hemisphere engagement, mostly at parietal areas, is occurring more continuously in ambi-handers—either some cognitive component common to all the tasks is taking place in the right (i.e., sequencing, analytical or gestalt processing, sensory/motor function) or an attentional bias is causing more right parietal participation in the tasks.

INVERTED VERSUS NONINVERTED HAND POSTURE DIFFERENCES

One of the most intriguing aspects of left-handedness is the inverted hand posture used by most left-handers when writing. In the inverted posture, the hand is positioned above the line with the pencil pointing toward the bottom of the page. Usually the paper is positioned either straight in front of the writer, or with the top of the page slanted to the left. About two-thirds of all left-handers use this posture, and most are male. The other third slant the paper to the right and use a posture that is a mirror image of the usual right-handed position—that is, the hand is positioned below the line with the pencil pointing towards the top of the page (noninverted hand posture). Most of these individuals are female.

Two questions puzzle me: (a) Why do *any* left-handers adopt the inverted posture? and (b) Why do some adopt inverted and others noninverted hand postures? The inverted posture seems a relatively inefficient way to write. With the wrist in the flexed position, the fingers and thumb tend to extend, making it even harder to bend the fingers around a pencil, and probably requiring more pressure to do so. Certainly the inverted position appears clumsy; the writer does not use the fingers much, relying more on the wrist, or even the whole arm for movement. Many authors have speculated about the reason for adopting this posture. One theory is that "hooking" the hand around somehow keeps the ink from smearing, but this is true only if the writer is a partial "hooker" to begin with. In the noninverted position there is no problem of ink smear because the hand is below the line, just as in right-handed writing. In fact, some inverted writers, including myself, switched to noninverted writing for this reason.

Other authors have suggested that children adopt the inverted position because they are told by a teacher or parent to slant the top of the paper to the left. When the paper is in this position, there is virtually *no other way* a left-hander can write except in the inverted position. However, in many American schools children today are free to experiment with their hand-writing, yet they do not seem consistently to choose the noninverted position as more natural even in a situation where they are allowed to select what seems comfortable.

Of course there are always subtle influences on children. They may copy the way other children have slanted their paper, for example. It remains to be seen whether inverted position is caused by external influences, but the fact that so many left-handers adopt this position without undue pressure leads me to believe that there may be internal factors involved.

If so, what might they be? Jerre Levy and Marylou Reid (1976; 1978), and Levy and Gur (Chapter 8 of this volume) have suggested that hand posture is related to hemispheric specialization. They postulate that left-handers who use the inverted posture have linguistic abilities primarily in the left hemisphere, whereas noninverted left-handers use their right hemisphere more for language tasks. Employing verbal and spatial tachistoscopic measures, they found that in right- and left-handed noninverters, the hemisphere contralateral to the writing hand was superior on the syllable task, whereas the ipsilateral hemisphere was superior on the dot location task. The reverse was true for a group of left-handed inverters and also for a right-handed inverter. They conclude that "hand posture can reliably predict which hemisphere is predominantly linguistic and which predominantly 'spatial'."

To explain the inverted hand posture, Levy and Reid proposed an additional theory: Left-handers with language in the left hemisphere (the inverters) may control the writing hand via ipsilateral pyramidal pathways. (There are some individuals who have larger uncrossed than crossed pyramidal bundles; however, it has not been demonstrated that these people are left-handed.) The authors point out that in cases of callosal agenesis and in hemiplegics, synkinesis occurs, where the actions of one hand are accompanied by mirror movements of the other. The motor control for one hand seems to stimulate the same muscles in the other hand, "presumably via ipsilateral pathways in the absence of inhibiting signals from the other side of the brain." They continue, "quite possibly the writing motions of an inverted ipsilateral hand are, in some way, a mirror reflection of certain aspects of the writing motions of a noninverted contralateral hand [Levy & Reid, 1978]."

This explanation does not seem likely for several reasons. To begin with, the motor programs of the "contralateral hand" (the right in the case of an inverted left-hander) are relatively *clumsy.* The right hand cannot write well. If its programs were sent via ipsilateral pathways to the same muscles in the left hand, then the left would write mirror writing, and it would write as clumsily as does the nonpreferred hand. A "mirror" reflection of noninverted writing of the right hand would be what is normally called "mirror writing," that is, writing with the left hand also in the *noninverted* position, but proceeding "backwards" from right to left. If that hand were moved around to the inverted position, it would produce mirror writing *upside down* although the writing *would* run from left to right as normal writing does (see Figure 10.2–A).

The various studies that have examined the relationship of hand posture to cerebral organization do not agree that hand posture can be used as a reliable index of the linguistic hemisphere. Moscovitch and Smith (1977), using Levy's tachistoscopic measure, replicated her results, but found no difference between hand posture groups on a dichotic test. They also found that inverters have faster reaction time to visual hemifield targets with the ipsilateral hand, supporting the idea of ipsilateral motor control. However, they did not obtain the same reaction time effect with auditory or tactile stimuli. Corballis (1978) and McKeever and VanDeventer (1978) used similar but not identical tachistoscopic measures and found no differences between inverters and noninverters. However, in the latter study, the authors used their own criteria rather than Levy's for classifying inverters and noninverters. Milner (1978), using the Wada sodium amytal technique

Figure 10.2 A. Mirror writing with the left hand. The hand started the word "Left" in the non-inverted position and continued to write as the paper was turned gradually from slanting right to slanting left, until the hand was in the inverted position. Continuing exactly the same mirror writing produced upside down mirror writing. B. Mirror with the left noninverted hand. The wrist extends on up-stroke, flexes on down-stroke. Fingers, if used, make clockwise circle (flex, extend, flex). C. with the inverted left hand. Wrist extends on up-stroke, flexes on down-stroke. Fingers, if used, make counterclockwise circle (extend, flex, extend). D. with noninverted right hand. Wrist extends on up-stroke, flexes on down-stroke. Fingers, if used, make counterclockwise circle (flex, extend, flex). While the action of the fingers differs, the action of the wrist is the same in all three cases.

with clinical patients, has reported finding no relationship between hand posture and the speech hemisphere. In summary, there is some support from *visual* studies for the idea that inverters have at least some aspect of *visual language* in the left hemisphere. The other studies employing auditory and speech measures are not in accord.

Evidence from our EEG studies suggests that (*a*) inverters and noninverters may differ in the organization of visual language processes but not language per se, and (*b*) that contralateral rather than ipsilateral pathways are being used during all writing, contrary to Levy's second hypothesis. We will describe our hand posture study, then propose an alternative theory to explain inverted hand posture.

We used, in addition to the EEG measure, a dichotic listening test to assess ear superiority in verbal tasks (Herron *et al.*, 1979). There were 49 subjects who wrote with the left hand (30 left-handers and 19 ambi-handers). Thirty-three subjects were inverters and 13 were noninverters. Three subjects were deleted from the analysis because they showed equivocal hand posture. This incidence of inverters (72%) is slightly higher than that found in other hand posture studies and higher than the number of left-handers predicted by clinical studies to have speech in the left hemisphere. Of the 33 inverters, 64% were male and 36% were female; of the 13 noninverters, 23% were male and 77% female. The distribution of males in each group is significantly different from chance ($\chi^2 = 6.20$, $p = .013$). Levy and Gur (Chapter 8 of this volume) and McKeever and VanDeventer (1978) found similar distributions.

We found no difference in ear advantage with the dichotic measures between inverters and noninverters, or between right-handers and either hand posture group. However, the dichotic measure did discriminate right-handers from the 30 "pure" (excluding ambi-handed) left-handed subjects. This is consistent with other studies that have been unable to distinguish inverters from noninverters on the basis of auditory or speech tests.

When EEG R/L log ratios for central and parietal lead pairs are examined, the results show that inverters and noninverters differ from right-handers in several ways but do not differ from each other at all (see Table 10.3). For example, the Write task mean ratio is dramatically higher in right-handers than in the other two groups.

As was seen earlier, for right-handers the Speak mean ratio was significantly higher than the Blocks mean ratio at the central ($p < .01$) and parietal ($p < .05$) leads, indicating relatively more left hemisphere participation during Speak task and relatively more right hemispheric participation during Blocks. In inverted and noninverted groups there were no significant differences between Speak and Blocks tasks at central or parietal leads, suggesting that neither inverters nor noninverters have a pattern of hemisphere specialization similar to right-handers at these leads.

Table 10.3
R/L Alpha[a] in RH, IHP, and NHP Groups[b]
(Full Sample)

Groups	N	Blocks	Read	Speak	Write	Listen	Speak/Blocks
				Log C4/C3			
RH	30	−.093	.013	.056	.159	.003	.149
		(.146)	(.135)	(.126)	(.147)	(.149)	(.128)
IHP	33	−.061	.008	−.002	−.100	−.014	.059
		(.149)	(.117)	(.138)	(.179)	(.149)	(.185)
NHP	13	−.043	.021	.032	−.089	−.001	.075
		(.100)	(.125)	(.130)	(.161)	(.146)	(.169)
				Log P4/P3			
RH	30	−.001	.016	.060	.130	.013	.061
		(.101)	(.097)	(.092)	(.108)	(.073)	(.117)
IHP	33	−.031	.005	.016	−.050	.013	.047
		(.096)	(.091)	(.116)	(.107)	(.150)	(.148)
NHP	13	.009	.024	.010	−.052	−.026	.001
		(.068)	(.113)	(.102)	(.150)	(.121)	(.117)

[a] Expressed in log ratios: Entries are means and standard deviations.
[b] Right-handers (RH); inverted left-handers (IHP); noninverted left-handers (NHP)

The fact that there is a difference between Speak and Blocks mean ratios in right-handers and not in left-handers, is consistent with the common finding that when left-handers are grouped together, fewer individuals show strong lateral specialization. But the results for each hand posture group do not support the prediction from Levy's model that inverters would be similar to right-handers, and noninverters would show a more "reversed" pattern of specialization. The conclusion is the same when we examine α power for the individual leads instead of the R/L log ratio. There is no difference between inverters and noninverters at either central or parietal leads for Write, Speak, or Blocks tasks. The means are almost identical. Thus, by EEG criteria at the central and parietal leads, each hand posture group appears to contain the same mixture of individual patterns of specialization found in any group of unselected left-handers. However, at the occipital leads, the two groups *do* differ significantly on two tasks.

Because the studies that have demonstrated differences between inverters and noninverters have used a visual test (tachistoscopic hemifield stimulation) we examined the visual area recordings (O_1, O_2). Some subjects tensed their neck muscles during certain tasks and produced artifact in the occipital EEG. These subjects were dropped from the analysis of the occipital data. To be sure the remaining subjects were representative of the total sample, we again examined R/L log ratios at the central and parietal leads (see Table 10.4). These subjects show the same results as the larger population: Right-handers differ from inverters and noninverters on the Write task and in the relationship of the Speak to the Blocks task, whereas the inverters and noninverters do not differ from each other. However, on the Write task, the noninverters have lower ratios than the inverters ($p < .05$) and the right-handers ($p < .01$); inverters are not different from right handers. The differences are similar but smaller for the Read task: inverters have lower ratios than right-handers ($p < .05$). Although a full analysis of sex related differences was not possible due to the small number of males in the noninverter group, analysis of the O_2/O_1 ratios revealed differences between female inverters and female noninverters for the Read task ($t = 1.91$, $p = .077$) and the Write task ($t = 2.16$, $p = .049$). Thus the differences seen between inverters and noninverters at O_2/O_1 for these tasks are not due to the fact that there are more male inverters and more female noninverters.

Table 10.4
R/L Alpha in RH, IHP and NHP Groups

(Sub-Sample[a])

Groups	N	Blocks	Read	Speak	Write	Listen	Speak/Blocks
				Log C4/C3			
RH	13	− .043 (.135)[b]	.058 (.176)	.108 (.159)	.195 (.180)	.061 (.176)	.151 (.109)
IHP	21	− .047 (.121)	− .020 (.105)	− .009 (.151)	− .087 (.178)	− .007 (.164)	.038 (.175)
NHP	9	− .038 (.108)	− .012 (.105)	.003 (.136)	− .102 (.171)	− .027 (.166)	.041 (.158)
				Log P4/P3			
RH	13	.032 (.063)	.043 (.082)	.079 (.107)	.161 (.097)	.020 (.099)	.047 (.103)
IHP	21	− .042 (.098)	− .007 (.098)	− .017 (.119)	− .045 (.082)	− .009 (.157)	.025 (.156)
NHP	9	.023 (.063)	.017 (.117)	.028 (.110)	− .042 (.163)	− .019 (.132)	.005 (.112)
				Log 02/01			
RH	13	.056 (.096)	.042 (.087)	.043 (.077)	.058 (.082)	.008 (.078)	− .013 (.086)
IHP	21	− .010 (.081)	.018 (.080)	.027 (.095)	.001 (.083)	.028 (.084)	.037 (.100)
NHP	9	− .019 (.033)	− .044 (.061)	− .010 (.065)	− .064 (.055)	− .044 (.094)	.009 (.053)

[a] Smaller n to include only Ss with occipital as well as central and parietal data.
[b] Standard deviation

When α power at individual occipital leads O_1 and O_2 is examined (see Table 10.5), it is clear that ratio differences between groups are due entirely to changes at the right hemisphere lead. The noninverters seem to be using the right occipital area during the Read and Write tasks relatively more than do the right-handers and inverters. Thus, at the occipital leads and *only* at the occipital leads, over visual areas, during visual language tasks, there is a relationship between hand posture and hemispheric participation in "language" as predicted by Levy and Reid (1976).

On the spatial task, inverters and noninverters do not differ: The O_2/O_1 Blocks ratios are nearly identical. This is contrary to the prediction suggested by Levy's tachistoscopic data that implied that for noninverters the left hemisphere would be more engaged in spatial tasks, while for inverters and right-handers, the right hemisphere would predominate. Thus, no difference between inverters and noninverters in spatial specialization was seen at any lead pair. Neither were any differences found during the Speak, Listen, or Sing tasks.

Our assessment of hemispheric specialization with EEG and dichotic measures suggests that the differences found between the two hand posture groups may be based primarily on *visual mechanisms* rather than auditory or proprioceptive motor specialization. This would explain the absence of significant differences between inverter and noninverter groups at anterior leads, and the presence of differences during visual tasks at the occipital leads. The repeated failure to find a difference between inverters and noninverters with dichotic listening tests would also be explained if hand posture is related to visual processing only. Levy's successful tachistoscopic method reflects the visual specialization.

A correlation between hand posture and the relative engagement of the two occipital poles during these tasks could suggest that a pattern of visual specialization somehow influences the choice of hand posture, *or* that the choice of hand posture (which may relate to paper position, head position, side of body space, emphasis of one visual field, eye movements, etc.)

Table 10.5
Alpha Power at O_1 and O_2

		Read				Write			
		O_1		O_2		O_1		O_2	
		$\overline{X}$	SD	$\overline{X}$	SD	$\overline{X}$	SD	$\overline{X}$	SD
RH	$N = 13$	555	(185)	648	(345)	357	(141)	424	(197)
IHP	$N = 21$	555	(281)	572	(272)	343	(135)	339	(123)
NHP	$N = 9$	539	(283)	483	(243)	345	(172)	292	(123)

somehow influences the relative engagement of left and right occipital areas during these tasks. It seems worth noting that we read continuously as we write; in that sense, these two tasks, which revealed EEG differences between the groups, are behaviorally the most closely related to hand posture.

It does not appear that hand posture can be used to reliably index the language hemisphere. But it may be related to *some* aspect of language lateralization. Language is not a unitary function. In left-handers (or groups such as the learning-disabled and stutters) whose cerebral organization is alleged to be less lateralized than typical right-handers, it may be only particular components of language that are differently lateralized. The concept of a "language hemisphere" may be most useful when describing typical right-handers in whom the various language behaviors seem to be lateralized fairly consistently to the left hemisphere; it may be misleading when applied to non-right-handers, whose patterns of specialization might differ for specific aspects of language.

The suggestion that the inverter group controls the writing hand via ipsilateral pathways is not supported by our data during the Write task at the central leads (presumably located close to motor hand areas). If the inverter group has speech in the left hemisphere and controls writing from the left hemisphere via ipsilateral pathways, then one would expect the mean Write ratio for inverters to be similar to the mean Write ratio for right handers, and significantly higher than the Write ratio for noninverters. As can be seen in Table 10.3, at the central leads there are dramatic group differences on the Write task ($F = 22.49$, $df = 2$, $p < .001$): The mean Write ratio for right-handers is significantly higher than the mean Write ratio for *both* inverters and noninverters (both $p < .01$). Inverters do not differ from noninverters on the Write task. This evidence strongly suggests contralateral control of the writing hand. The evidence is given further emphasis by our finding that Write ratios are significantly *higher* than Speak ratios in right-handers ($p < .01$) and significantly *lower* than Speak ratios for inverters ($p < .01$) and for noninverters ($p < .05$).

To determine how activity in each hemisphere contributes to these R/L ratio differences in writing, we examined the α power for separate leads C_3 and C_4 (Table 10.2). Because no differences were seen between inverters and noninverters, the two groups were pooled as "left-handers." In right-handers, Writing engages the left hemisphere (C_3) significantly more than the right hemisphere (C_4) ($t = -4.24$, $df = 29$, $p = .0002$) and in left-handers engages the right hemisphere (C_4) significantly more than the left (C_3) ($t = 3.28$, $df = 45$, $p = .0002$). Therefore, we conclude that the

Write task primarily engages the central region of the hemisphere contralateral to the writing hand, and regardless of hand posture, the right hemisphere central region is activated for left-handed writing.

In addition, we found that even in those left-handers selected by EEG criteria for processing speech primarily in the left hemisphere, writing with the left hand involves considerable right hemisphere participation: The task ratio for Write is significantly lower than the Speak task ratio in the selected left-hand group. If writing were controlled by the same hemisphere as speech in these selected left-handers, one would expect Write task ratios to be the same as or higher than Speak task ratios, as is the case in right-handers.

Therefore, our EEG recording during writing in normal left-handed subjects leads us to conclude that the right hemisphere is strongly engaged during left-handed writing regardless of hand posture or hemispheric specialization for speech. In left-handers with speech primarily in the left hemisphere, this process is presumably mediated across the corpus callosum.

Heilman *et al.* (1973) present excellent support for the idea that control of a hand might be executed across the corpus callosum. Since 1908 it has been recognized that in patients with callosal lesions, the "minor" hand is apraxic (cannot carry out verbal commands) because it is disconnected from the control of the language hemisphere. These authors describe their own experience with an adult patient who had suffered a right hemisphere injury. The man had been originally left-handed, but had been taught as a child to write with his right hand and had done so all his life. As a result of the right hemisphere lesion, this patient lost motor control of the left hand, but he did not become aphasic. Presumably speech and other language functions were being carried out in the intact left hemisphere. But strangely, he became *agraphic* and *apraxic* with the right hand! How could this occur when the left hemisphere was not injured and language was preserved? The authors suggest that because he was originally left-handed and had been "switched," this man had a unique pattern of neural organization for writing. They speculate that he had to transmit all verbal information across the corpus callosum to the right hemisphere to access the "executive motor" function for the left hand. However, because he was taught to write with the *right* hand, this patient had to re-transfer the signal back across the corpus callosum in order to achieve writing with the right hand. Therefore, when his right hemisphere was injured, he could no longer connect with this "executive motor" function and lost the ability to write with his right hand despite an intact left hemisphere and preserved speech. The Heilman *et al.* study raises fascinating questions about how frequently the control of a hand for a complex process may be mediated across the corpus callosum.

Writing is a very complex task, and the complexity of information being transferred across the corpus callosum may affect the fidelity of the transmission. Myers (1962) studied information transfer with chiasm-sectioned cats. When he trained one hemisphere, he found that the information had been transferred to the untrained hemisphere. When the corpus callosum was sectioned and the experiment repeated, there was no longer any transfer. Furthermore, when the discrimination task was made more difficult, less transfer occurred. Myers concluded that "the intercommunication through the corpus callosum lacks the refinement and capability of the direct intrahemispheric integrating mechanisms."

In the light of our EEG evidence that writing in some left-handers may involve the integration of visual language and motor mechanisms across the corpus callosum, it is necessary to reconsider the original question, "Why do any left-handers use the inverted posture?" My speculations require a consideration of the nature of English script, the mechanical properties of the arm joints (i.e., elbow, wrist, and fingers) and the pattern of neural organization in left-handers. My reasoning is this:

1. English script requires many strokes that go diagonally from down-left to up-right (e.g. ╱).

2. The extension-flexion movement of the wrist is important in making such a stroke in normal right-handed writing.

3. The right hand cannot use the wrist to make the *mirror image* of that stroke in the *right to left* direction (╲), unless the hand posture is changed to the inverted posture.

4. Likewise, left-handers using noninverted posture to write English from left to right cannot use the wrist to make that stroke, but must learn a much more complex *pushing* movement using the fingers and thumb.

5. Left-handers, by using the *inverted* posture, can use the wrist in the same way as right-handers (an extension movement to produce ╱) without calling on elaborate finger movements.

6. Young children learning to write frequently do not have very sophisticated fine motor (pyramidal) control of fingers and thumb (especially boys). Therefore, some left-handers (especially boys) may adopt the inverted posture to write English script in order to take advantage of the easier wrist movement.

The reasoning thus far leaves several glaring questions unanswered such as, don't the children with "immature" pyramidal systems eventually "switch" postures when they get older, and why don't right-handed writers of Hebrew use the inverted posture? Speculative answers can be offered but they are not entirely satisfying. Perhaps the children fail to "switch" because writing patterns when well-learned become automatic and are hard to change. Perhaps right-handed Hebrew writers do not use the inverted posture because languages written from right to left are designed with fewer consecutive diagonal up-strokes and with more isolated down-strokes, which are easier for the fingers to accomplish.

But other questions are even more puzzling. For example, why do any left-handed Israeli writers use the inverted posture and why are there any right-handed inverters? If we assume that the inverted posture has such disadvantages that it would not be adopted by chance and maintained for convenience, then we must continue to search for a reason for its adoption. Thus far we have not considered the rather strong evidence presented by Levy and Reid (1978) and McKeever and VanDeventer (1978) that hand posture groups can be distinguished on the basis of tachistoscopic hemifield tests, and our EEG evidence that occipital participation in visual verbal tasks may vary between inverters and noninverters. If neural patterns do differ in these two groups, there are three possible ways in which these patterns could relate to hand posture: (a) there might be no causal relationship at all; (b) the hand posture might influence the neural patterns; and (c) the neural pattern might influence the choice of hand posture.

In order to continue the original line of reasoning I will postulate that the latter condition is true and propose four additional points:

7. Evidence from our experiment does not support the theory that the inverted posture is related to motor control via ipsilateral pathways.

8. The laterality of *visual* verbal processing (as distinct from speech) may differ in the two hand posture group: Visual verbal information may be processed by inverters in the left hemisphere and by noninverters in the right.

9. Visual verbal information generated in the left hemisphere is transmitted across the *corpus callosum* to be expressed via motor/kinesthetic mechanisms in the right hemisphere by the left hand.

10. If pyramidal control is immature and myelination of the corpus callosum is still being completed in the young child, then this pathway may be less efficient, or some information might be lost in transfer, creating, in effect, a functional partial disconnection or dyspraxia. Such individuals may have special difficulty controlling the thumb and digits of the left hand for a verbal task and therefore may resort to the use of the wrist in the inverted posture. Each of these points will be discussed in the following pages. The purpose of the discussion is to raise issues that will generate further research rather than to defend a position.

The act of writing takes advantage of elbow and wrist joints as well as fine motor movement of the fingers. For illustration, observe the movements of your own right arm during writing (left-handers can experiment with this as well as right-handers). The first consideration must be given to the elbow. Keeping your elbow in the same place, move your hand around the desk. The elbow joint is the center of the circle, the radius being the arm. If you start with your right elbow flexed and the hand at the leftmost point in the arc and then gradually extend the elbow moving the hand toward the right, the arm describes a quarter circle (the top left quarter of a circle). In order to move with ease from left to right (or right to left in the case, for example, of Hebrew or Arabic), the writer takes advantage of the arc of this circle, placing his paper at a slant that orients the lines of the paper tangential to the circumference of the circle. Most written work is done within this quarter circle. You probably have slanted your head to the left so that your eye movements along the line of writing are from left to right. This puts the paper in the range of view of your right eye. If your nose suddenly grew so large that it divided your face in half, you would be unable to see the writing at all with your left eye.

It is the same for the left-handed noninverted writer except in reverse. The quarter circle described by the left arm is the top right quarter instead of the top left. The paper is slanted in the opposite direction and the head is slanted to the right, leaving the writing in the left half of the visual space. The writing, of course, is from left to right, but in the case of the right hand, the elbow is extending, whereas in the case of the left, the elbow is flexing. Elbows accommodate easily to both directions for writing. The same is not true for the wrist.

The wrist seems to be the crucial joint. As the right-hander writes, the primary stroke in English script is accomplished mostly by the rhythmical extension and flexion of the wrist with the emphasis in the rhythm given to the extension stroke as the elbow also extends. For the left-hander, relying on wrist movement in the noninverted posture produces "backslanted" writing, and is not easy because the wrist is extending while the elbow is flexing. In order to slant the letter forward in the noninverted posture the left-hander must minimize wrist movement and learn to rely on finger–thumb movement instead. To accomplish this, the hand and wrist are pronated more flatly against the writing surface and fingers and thumb must learn to cooperate precisely in that uniquely human (and late developing) capacity of opposing finger and thumb. If control of fingers and thumb is difficult, the left-hander may search instead for a posture in which a forward slant can be accomplished by using the wrist. The wrist must be rotated outward to a vertical position with the lateral edge of the hand against the table. The writer must then orient the hand to the line on the paper in such a way so as to produce a forward slant when the wrist extends. The paper is turned to the left, the hand above the line. Behold! It is the inverted posture (see Figure 10.2-c).

To continue your experiment, use the normal noninverted position with the right hand (see Figure 10.2-d) and make some lower case *l*'s in script across a page from left to right. Note that the arc described by the wrist in flexion or extension is *the same as* the arc described by flexion or extension of your elbow. (That is, they are both the top left quarter or a circle, and they are both oriented in the direction of the slant of English script so that the diagonal left to right stroke is easy.) If you now try to make the *l*'s in the opposite direction from right to left across the page (i.e., "mirror writing"), your tendency will be to slant your *l*'s backward (or make them upside-down) because the arc of your wrist is no longer oriented in the plane of the "proper" slant for "mirrored" English script.

Now, continue to make these mirror *l*'s from right to left which are slanting bizarrely backwards, and *while your right hand is writing* take your left hand and gradually turn the paper so that it is slanting to the right rather than to the left. You will find that your *l*'s are now slanting in the "correct" direction. Check it all in a mirror if you can not "see" backwards.

There are several ways that the left-handed noninverted writers might accommodate for the lack of wrist mobility in writing from left to right. They can choose to slant the writing backward, which gives them some use of the wrist. They can write small and move their entire arm by using the shoulder, the process that mechanically seems to take advantage of the loose fit of the skin at whatever part of the hand rests on the paper. There is a certain amount of play that can be obtained, even if elbow, wrist, and fingers are immobilized, by simply pushing and pulling the whole arm from the shoulder.

Another method of compensation is to somewhat revise the nature of the script by dropping as many of the diagonal strokes as possible. Printing does not require the same continuous diagonal stroke; it consists more of separated segments of "down" or "pulling" strokes. A left-handed noninverter may prefer printing altogether or may combine printing and script by making **r** instead of *h* or **s** instead of *l*, or *t* instead of *t* . (Similarly, languages that are written from right to left have fewer diagonal "up" strokes and more disconnected "down" strokes, which may make them easier for the right-hander to write without resorting to inverted posture.)

It is interesting to observe the writing in those left-handers who can use either posture. I have recorded some examples of writing of two left-handers who prefer inverted posture for script and report that the noninverted posture seems efficient for them, only if they *print*. Quite by accident, I noted that this posture might be more efficient for them for spelling as well.

Both of these subjects are normal adults, one a college graduate, the other in college. However, they both complain that they make inadvertent errors when writing script with inverted posture. In fact, M. H. is quite dysgraphic. His handwriting is practically illegible (see Figure 10.3-b). He makes frequent spelling errors (spelling phonetically) and neglects to pay attention to details like crossing t's and dotting i's. This neglect of details seems specific to writing as he is an excellent artist and draftsman and pays meticulous attention to detail when drawing. He started printing more consistently only in high school, although he had experimented with other postures and styles earlier. Printing "seemed easier" in the noninverted posture (perhaps because of the "down" or "pulling" strokes mentioned earlier).

Curious about his choice of the noninverted posture for printing, I asked him to print something so I could watch him. He produced Figure 10.3-A. There were no errors in spelling. I then asked him to write something in his normal handwriting. He wrote Figure 10.3-B. He did not notice the spelling error in "skipt" but he did notice errors in "faster," "using," and "printing." I asked him to write in script again but this time in the noninverted position. He found it difficult but wrote Figure 10.3-C. He did not realize that

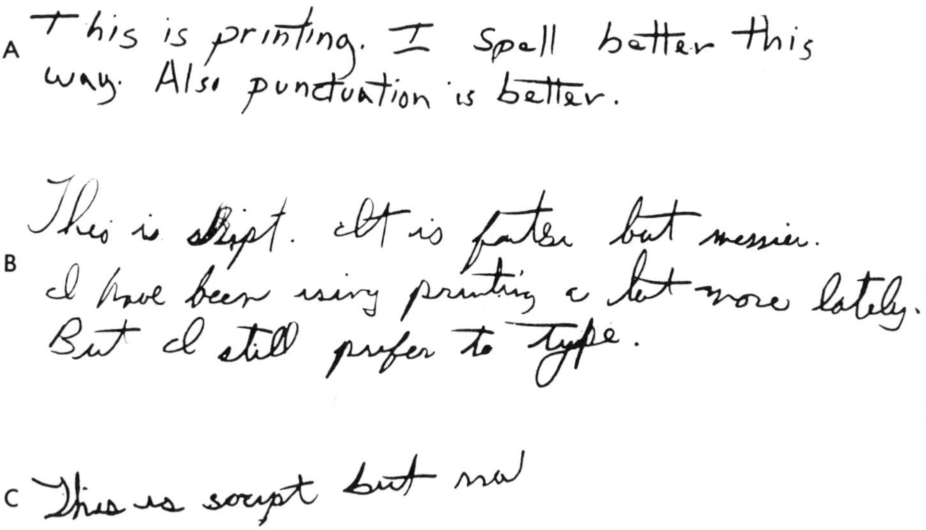

Figure 10.3   Examples of writing from left-handed subject M.H.   A. Printing with the noninverted hand posture.   B. Writing with his usual inverted hand posture.   C. Attempting to write with the noninverted hand posture.

he wrote "script" correctly. I was surprised that changing styles produced changes in the number of errors and that "skipt" had changed to "script" seemingly unconsciously.

A similar thing occurred with the other left-handed subject (P.L.) who wrote an address for me in her usual inverted posture (Figure 10.4–A). I noticed the dropping of the c in "director" and the omission of the a in "Chicago." I wondered whether she would make the same errors if she printed the address. Without telling her what I was doing, I asked her to sit down at a desk and print what I dictated. I dictated the same address. Her response is Figure 10.4–B. This time, there were no errors. Like M. H., she also adopted the noninverted posture for printing. I asked her to maintain the noninverted posture and write the same thing in script. Again there were no errors (Figure 10.4–C). Thinking that she might just be paying

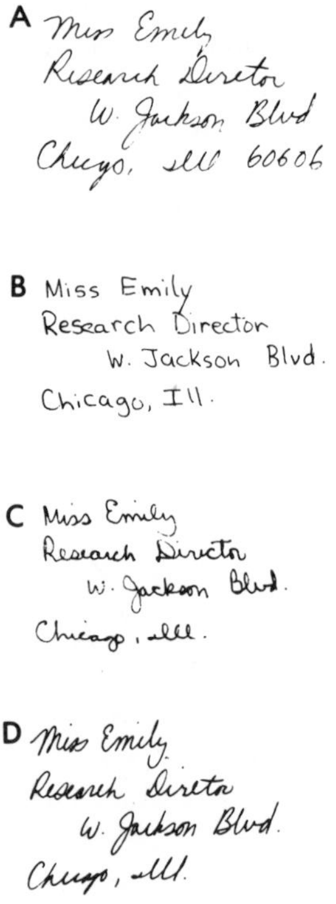

Figure 10.4 Examples of writing and printing from left-handed subject, P.L., in sequence. A. Writing with her usual inverted hand posture. B. Printing to dictation with noninverted hand posture. C. Attempting to write to dictation with noninverted hand posture. D. Repetition of A. Writing to dictation with inverted hand posture.

more attention because I was asking her to do an unusual thing, I asked her to write the address again in her normal handwriting (Figure 10.4–D). She did spell "Chicago" correctly but again she left the c out of "director." When I explained what I was doing she was surprised to see the errors in Figures 10.4–A and D, as she had not observed them herself. It was interesting that although she had just written "director" twice correctly, she made the same error when she returned to her usual inverted writing posture.

It was as if different neural subsystems were being used in the two different situations. Thinking that perhaps she was changing the writing activity from one half of visual space to the other when she changed posture, I watched the way she slanted her head while she wrote inverted and printed inverted. Right-handers generally position their paper with the top of the paper slanted to the left, and tilt their heads to the left, thereby emphasizing the right side of their visual space. This subject also tilted her paper to the left for the inverted posture, but tilted her head to the *right*, thereby emphasizing the *left* side of visual space. She was emphasizing the left eye or the left side in *both* postures. She was also left eye dominant in a pointing task.

Although these anecdotal observations did not provide serious data pertinent to our original questions, they raised more research issues and led us to examine the paper position and the head tilt of left-handed writers in our EEG handedness experiment. Although we had already begun the experiment, we obtained this information for the remaining 31 of our left-handed writers, 23 of whom were inverters and 8 noninverters. Nineteen of the 23 inverters positioned their paper straight or to the left, but unlike the right-handers, they positioned their heads straight or to the *right*, not to the left. (None used straight paper-straight head position.) Of the four exceptions (all ambi-handers) two used a left paper–left head position, and two used right paper–right head positions. Of the eight noninverters, six positioned their paper straight or to the right and positioned their head to the right as predicted. The two exceptions (again, both ambi-handers) positioned the paper to the left and the head tilted to the right.

It seems that left-handers, regardless of hand posture, most frequently position their head and paper to emphasize the left half of visual space, whereas right-handers prefer the right half of visual space. Manual performance may be most efficient when the visual feedback comes to the hemisphere where the output is generated. Sussman and MacNeilage (1975) found that in an eye-tracking paradigm, the optimal condition occurred when the cursor signal (feedback from the tracking hand) was presented in the visual half-field on the same side as the hand (e.g., right hand–right visual half-field). Kinsbourne (1972) has found that right-handed subjects tend to shift their eyes to the right during both overt and covert verbal activity. Furthermore, manipulating the direction of the attention can degrade the verbal performance (Kinsbourne, 1975). He says, "It is, of course, possible to overcome or even reverse that rightward attentional shift while speaking, but apparently only at the price of some proportion of the mental capacity available for the main task [Kinsbourne, 1979]." One might predict then that for any cognitive behavior like writing, performance will be optimal when all the elements (motor/kinesthetic, visual feedback, and visual–verbal processes) are processed in the same hemisphere, especially if callosal transfer between hemispheres is at all inefficient.

In summary, the left-hander who uses the inverted posture may have a pattern of neural organization that requires integration of complex processes across the corpus callosum while writing. If the transcallosal verbal signal is degraded, the precise control of fingers and thumb for the verbal task might be affected. The more simple extension and flexion of the wrist might then be an easier way to accomplish the writing.

The issue concerning the use of the ipsilateral or contralateral pathways is an important one. In the unlikely event that it became established that inverters really have fewer motor fibers crossing at the decussation of the pyramids, and more fibers remaining on the same side, it would still not be clear why the use of ipsilateral pathways might influence the adoption of the inverted posture. Although Egyptologists claim that great secrets lie in the pyramids, I would venture to suggest that the secret of inverted hand posture does not lie in the pyramids, but in the functional organization of the two, differently specialized, cerebral hemispheres.

REFERENCES

Annett, M. The binominal distribution of right, mixed, and left-handedness. *Quarterly Journal of Experimental Psychology*, 1967, *19*, 327–333.
Bryden, M. P. *Neuropsychologia*, Tachistoscopic recognition, handedness and cerebral dominance, 1965, *3*, 1–8.
Corballis, M. Personal communication, 1978.
Curry, F. K. W. A comparison of left-handed and right-handed subjects on verbal and nonverbal dichotic listening tasks, *Cortex*, 1967, *3*, 343.
Davidson, R. J. & Schwartz, G. E. The influence of musical training on patterns of EEG asymmetry during musical and non-musical self-generation. *Psychophysiology*, 1977, *14*, 58–63.
Dee, H. L. Auditory asymmetry and strength of manual preferences, *Cortex*, 1971, *7*, 236–245.
Doyle, J., Ornstein, R. E., & Galin, D. Lateral specialization of cognitive mode: II EEG frequency analysis. *Psychophysiology*, 1974, *11*, 567–578.

Ehrlichman, H. Hemispheric functioning and individual differences in cognitive abilities. Doctoral Dissertation, New School for Social Research. Diss. Abstracts Int. 33: 2319 B, (University Microfilms No. 72-27, 869), 1971.

Ehrlichman, H. & Weiner, M. S. Consistency of task-related EEG asymmetries. Paper presented to American Psychological Association Annual Meeting, S. F., August of 1977.

Ettlinger, G., Jackson, C. V. & Zangwill, O. Cerebral dominance in sinistrals. *Brain*, 1956, *79*, 569–588.

Fennell, E., Bowers, D., & Satz, P. Within-modal and cross-modal reliabilities of two laterality tests. *Brain and Language*, 1977, *4*, 63–69.

Fennel, E., Satz, P., Van Den Abell, T., Bowers, D. & Thomas, R. Visuo-spatial competency, handedness, and cerebral dominance. *Brain and Language*, 1978, *5*, 206–214.

Galin, D., Johnstone, J., & Herron, J. Effects of task difficulty on EEG measures of cerebral engagement. *Neuropsychologia*, 1978, *16*, 461–472.

Galin, D., Johnstone, J., Nakell, L., & Herron, J. Development of the capacity for tactile information transfer between hemispheres in normal children. *Science*, 1979, *204*, 1330–1332.

Galin, D., & Ornstein, R. E. Lateral specialization of cognitive mode: An EEG study. *Psychophysiology*, 1972, *9*, 412–418.

Galin, D., Ornstein, R. E., Herron, J., & Johnstone, J. Sex and handedness differences in EEG measures of hemispheric specialization. In preparation.

Gloning, K., & Quatember, R. Statistical evidence of neurophysiological syndrome in left-handed and ambidexterous patients. *Cortex*, 1966, *2*, 484–488.

Gloning, I., Gloning, K., Haub, G. & Quatember, R. Comparison of verbal behavior in right-handed and non-right-handed patients with anatomically verified lesion of one hemisphere. *Cortex*, 1969, *5*, 41–52.

Goodglass, H. & Quadfasel, F. A. Language laterality in left-handed aphasics. *Brain*, 1954, *88*, 753–762.

Hécaen & Ajuriaguerra, J. *Left handedness*. New York: Grune & Stratton, 1964.

Hécaen & Sauget, J. Cerebral dominance in left-handed subjects. *Cortex*, 1971, *7*, 19–48.

Heilman, K. M., Coyle, J. M., Gonyea, E. F., & Geschwind, N. *Brain* 1973, *96*, 21.

Herron, J., Galin, D., Johnstone, J., & Ornstein, R. E. Cerebral specialization writing posture and motor control of writing in left-handers. *Science*, in press.

Hines, D. & Satz, P. Cross-modal asymmetries in perception related to asymmetry in cerebral function. *Neuropsychologia*, 1974, *12*, 239–247.

Johnstone, J., Galin, D., & Herron, J. Choice of handedness measures in studies of hemispheric specialization. The *International Journal of Neuroscience*, 1979, *9(2)*, 71–80.

Kimura, D. Cerebral dominance and the perception of verbal stimuli. *Canadian Journal of Psychology*, 1961, *15*, 166–171.

Kinsbourne, M. Eye and head turning indicate cerebral lateralization. *Science*, 1972, *176*, 539–541.

Kinsbourne, M. The mechanism of hemispheric control of the lateral gradient of attention. In R. Rabbit & S. Dornic (Eds.). *Attention and performance*, vol. V, New York: Academic Press, 1979.

Kinsbourne, M. (Ed.). Language evolution and lateral action. In *Asymmetrical function of the human brain*, Cambridge: Cambridge Univ. Press, 1978.

Knox, A. W. & Boone, D. R. Auditory laterality and tested handedness. *Cortex*, 1970, *7*, 164–173.

Lansdell, H. The effect of neurosurgery on a test of proverbs. *American Psychology*, 1961, *16*, 488.

Lansdell, H. A sex difference in effect of temporal lobe neurosurgery design preference. *Nature*, 1962, *194*, 852–854.

Lansdell, H. Effect of extent of temporal lobe ablations on two lateralized deficits. *Physiology and Behavior,* 1968, *3,* 271–273.

Leissner, P., Lindhom, L. E., & Peterson, I. Alpha amplitude dependence on skull thickness as measured by ultra sound technique. *Electroencephalography and Clinical Neurophysiology Journal, 1970, 29,* 392–399.

Levy, J. & Reid, M. L. Variations in writing posture and cerebral organization. *Science,* 1976, *194,* 337.

Levy, J. & Reid, M. L. Variations in cerebral organization as a function of handedness, hand posture in writing, and sex. *Journal of Experimental Psychology,* 1978, *107* (2), 119–144.

McGlone, J. & Kertesz, A. Sex differences in cerebral processing of visuospatial tasks. *Cortex,* 1973, *9,* 313–320.

McKee, G, Humphrey, B, & McAdam, D. W. Scaled lateralization of alpha activity during linguistic and musical tasks. *Psychophysiology,* 1973, *10,* 441–443.

McKeever, W. F. & VanDeventer, A. D. *Neuropsychologia,* in press.

Moscovitch, M. & Smith, L. C. Differences in Neural Organization Between Individuals with Inverted and Noninverted Handwriting Postures. *Science,* 1979, *205,* 710–713.

Satz, P. Achenbach, K., & Fennel, E. Correlations between assessed manual laterality and predicted speech laterality in a normal population. *Neuropsychologia,* 1967, *5,* 292–310.

Shankweiler, D. & Studdert-Kennedy, M. A continuum of lateralization for speech perception? *Brain and Language,* 1975, *2,* 212–215.

Subirana, A., P. J. Vinken & G. W. Bruyn (Eds.) In *Handbook of clinical neurology.* Amsterdam: North Holland Publishing Co., 1969.

Wada, J. A., Clark, R. & Hamm, A. Cerebral hemispheric asymmetry in humans: cortical speech zones in 100 adult and 100 infant brains. *Archives of Neurology,* 1975, *32,* 239–246.

Zurif, E. & Bryden, M. P. Familial handedness and left-right differences in auditory and visual perception. *Neuropsychologia,* 1969, *7,* 179–188.

III

SINISTRAL ABILITIES

11

Handedness and Memory for Tonal Pitch[1]

DIANA DEUTSCH

INTRODUCTION

There are certain well-known relationships between handedness and
mode of brain organization. For instance, the large majority of right-
handers have speech represented in the left cerebral hemisphere; however,
of the left-handed population, about two-thirds have speech represented in
the left hemisphere and about one-third in the right. Furthermore, whereas
right-handers tend to show a clear-cut dominance of the left hemisphere for
speech, a significant proportion of left-handers have some speech
represented in both cerebral hemispheres. Therefore, left-handers as a
group differ from right-handers, and are also more heterogeneous than
right-handers, both in terms of direction of cerebral dominance and also in
terms of degree of dominance (Goodglass & Quadfasel, 1954; Hécaen & de
Ajureaguerra, 1964; Hécaen & Piercy, 1956; Hécaen & Sauget, 1971;
Milner, Branch, & Rasmussen, 1966; Subirana, 1969; Zangwill, 1960).

Recently, interest has developed in the possibility that such neurological
differences might be reflected in ability differences of various types. Thus,
some investigators have argued for a relationship between left- or mixed-
handedness and reading disability (Ginsburg & Hartwick, 1971; Satz &
Sparrow, 1970; Shearer, 1968; Wold, 1968; Wussler & Barclay, 1970; Zurif

[1] This work was supported by USPHS Grant No. MH–21001. Special thanks are due to Sam
Hickey and George Wargo for their assistance in data collection; and to Jeff Miller, Nancy
Walton, and Wayne Wickelgren for valuable discussions.

NEUROPSYCHOLOGY
OF LEFT-HANDEDNESS

& Carson, 1970; but see also Applebee, 1971; Hartlag & Green, 1971). Others have presented evidence that left-handers or mixed-handers perform more poorly than right-handers on visuospatial tasks (Levy, 1969; Miller, 1971; Silverman, Adevai, & McGough, 1966; but also see Newcombe & Ratliff, 1973). In both cases, explanations have been advanced in terms of a more bilateral representation of speech and related functions in the mixed or left-handed groups. The present study demonstrates that left-handers with mixed hand preference show enhanced performance on certain auditory tasks, and it is hypothesized that this superiority also reflects a bilateral representation of function. It is further suggested that some of the discrepancies in the literature may be due to the heterogeneity of the left-handed and mixed-handed groups; and that a four-way classification of handedness based on hand used in writing and on consistency of hand preference would produce more homogeneous results.

EXPERIMENT 1

The first experiment was prompted by the observation that a group of subjects who had been selected for high performance on a pitch memory task contained an unexpectedly large proportion of left-handed writers. The experiment was therefore undertaken to determine whether left-handers and right-handers differ statistically in terms of their ability to make such pitch memory judgments.

The following task was employed. A test tone was presented followed by a sequence of six interpolated tones, and then by a second test tone. The test tones were either identical in pitch or they differed by a semitone, and subjects were instructed to judge whether they were the same or different. The tones were produced at equal amplitude by a Wavetek oscillator controlled by PDP–8 computer, and were recorded on tape. They were played to subjects through speakers on a high quality tape recorder. All tones were 200 msec in duration, and separated by 300-msec pauses, except that a 2-sec pause occurred between the last interpolated tone and the second test tone. The tones were sine waves, and their frequencies were taken from an equal-tempered scale (International Pitch; A = 435Hz) ranging over an octave from Middle C (259 Hz) to the B above (488 Hz). The interpolated tones were chosen at random from this range, with the exception that no interpolated sequence contained repeated tones, or tones that were identical in pitch to either of the test tones. Twenty-four sequences were presented, and these were in two groups of 12, with 10-sec pauses between sequences within a group and 2-min pauses between the groups. Before the experiment began, the procedure was explained to the subjects and they were given four practice sequences.

The subjects were 76 right-handed and 53 left-handed university under-graduates. Handedness was assessed by the short form of the Edinburgh Handedness Inventory (Oldfield, 1971). *Right-handers* were defined as those with positive laterality quotients and *left-handers* as those with negative laterality quotients. In both handedness groups the ratio of male to female subjects was 1 to 1.3. The right-handers had had an average of 3.64 years of musical training (this included self-training and school choir) and the left-handers an average of 3.77 years.

The right-handed group produced an average error rate of 38.1%, and the left-handed group an error rate of 32.5%. Applying a median test, the difference between the two groups was found to be highly significant $(\chi^2 = 8.03, df = 1, p < .01)$. No significant difference based on sex was obtained. Further, the variance in error rate for the lefthanders was found to be significantly larger than for the righthanders $(p < .05)$. Given this larger variance, it was hypothesized that a difference might emerge be-tween people who were strongly left-handed and those with mixed hand preference, as individuals in this latter group would be expected to have more bilateral representation of function (Gillies, MacSweeney, & Zangwill, 1960; Hécaen & Sauget, 1971; Zangwill, 1960). So each handedness population was divided into two on the basis of strength of manual preference. Pure right-handers were defined as those with laterality quotients between +60 and +100, and mixed right-handers those with quotients between +1 and +59. Pure left-handers were defined as those with laterality quotients between −60 and −100, and mixed left-handers those with quotients between −1 and −59. Table 11.1 shows the average error rates in each of the four handedness categories. Applying a median test, an overall significant difference between these groups was obtained $(\chi^2 = 12.33, df = 3, p, < .01)$. Furthermore, the performance level of the mixed left-handers was significantly higher than that of any of the other three groups (mixed left-handers versus pure right-handers, $\chi^2 = 10.02$, $df = 1$, $p < .01$; mixed left-handers versus mixed right-handers, $\chi^2 = 9.65, df = 1, p < .01$; mixed left-handers versus pure left-handers, $\chi^2 = 4.45, df = 1, p < .05$). The other groups did not differ significantly

Table 11.1
Error Rates for the Four Handedness Populations in
Experiment 1

Handedness category	Percentage average error
Pure right-handers ($N = 52$)	36.9
Mixed right-handers ($N = 24$)	41.0
Pure left-handers ($N = 30$)	35.3
Mixed left-handers ($N = 23$)	29.0

from each other. It was concluded that the type of brain organization characteristic of mixed left-handers is associated with enhanced levels of performance on this task.

EXPERIMENT 2

This experiment was undertaken to test the generality of the findings obtained in Experiment 1. A different pitch recognition task was used. Subjects were presented with a standard five-tone sequence, and then, after a pause, with a probe tone. They were required to judge whether or not a tone of the same pitch as the probe had been included in the sequence. On half of the sequences such a tone was included, and on the other half it was not. The included tones occurred an equal number of times at each of the first four serial positions of the sequence, and the pitches of these tones were strictly counterbalanced across serial position. As before, all tones were 200 msec in duration, and separated by 300-msec pauses, except that a 2-sec pause intervened before presentation of the probe tone. Forty-eight of these sequences were presented, in 4 groups of 12; and the experimental session was preceded by 8 practice sequences.

This experiment employed 74 right-handers and 30 left-handers. As it could be argued that equating for years of musical training is a rather arbitrary procedure, this time only subjects with three years or less of musical training were selected. The right-handers had had an average of 1.0 year of training, and the left-handers an average of 1.1 years. In both handedness groups the ratio of male to female subjects was 1 to 1.1.

The right-handers produced an average error rate of 41.5% and the left-handers a rate of 36.5%. This difference in performance was found to be statistically significant ($\chi^2 = 4.08$, $df = 1$, $p < .05$). As in the previous experiment, there was no significant effect of sex.

Table 11.2 shows the error rates in the four handedness populations, categorized as before. It was again found that the mixed left-handers

Table 11.2
Error Rates for the Four Handedness Populations in
Experiment 2

Handedness category	Percentage average error
Pure right-handers ($N = 54$)	41.2
Mixed right-handers ($N = 20$)	42.2
Pure left-handers ($N = 22$)	39.5
Mixed left-handers ($N = 8$)	28.4

significantly outperformed all other three groups (mixed left-handers versus pure right-handers, $p = .01$; mixed left-handers versus mixed right-handers, $p < .01$; mixed left-handers versus strong left-handers, $p < .05$, on Fisher Exact Probability tests).

When we look at serial position functions, a further difference between the handedness populations emerges. Figure 11.1 A shows the percentage correct recognitions of the probe tone as a function of its serial position. This function is plotted separately for the mixed left-handers and for the two right-handed groups combined. (Pure left-handers were excluded from this analysis as there was no good rationale for combining them with either group.) It can be seen that the mixed left-handers produced the expected bow-shaped serial position curve, with lowest error rates at the earliest and latest positions, and highest error rates at the middle positions. Yet, the right-handers did not produce this function. It might be argued that the error rates for the right-handers were so high that this difference between the two groups could have been due simply to a ceiling effect. To examine this possibility, serial position functions were again plotted for these two groups, but taking only those subjects whose overall error rates did not exceed 33%. These comprised 6 mixed left-handers and 10 right-handers. As shown on Figure 11.1 B, both subgroups now produced the expected bow-

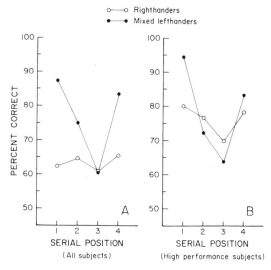

Figure 11.1. Percentage correct recognitions of the probe tone as a function of its serial position (Experiment 2). This function is plotted separately for the mixed left-handers and for the two right-handed groups combined.
A. Plot for all subjects.
B. Plot for those subjects whose overall error rates did not exceed 33%.

shaped curve; however the curve for the mixed left-handers was considerably steeper than that for the right-handers. They made fewer errors at the end positions, but more errors at the middle positions. Although the overall difference between the slopes of the curves for these two subgroups did not reach statistical significance, these results strongly suggest that the substantial difference found overall was not due simply to a ceiling effect. However, a larger study on such selected subjects would have to be performed before we can establish this difference with confidence.

DISCUSSION

In this study, mixed left-handers have been found to outperform other handedness groups in making pitch recognition judgments, and this occurred for two different types of task. These findings suggest an explanation in terms of a duplication of storage of pitch information in the case of mixed left-handers. Assuming that the efficiency of storage and retrieval at one locus is identical for all handedness populations, then the retrieval of this information from two separate loci should significantly increase the overall probability of correct judgment. Such a duplication of storage could also produce an exaggeration in the slope of the serial position curve; for there should be a greater increase in the probability of correct judgment where the strength of the trace at each locus is greater, since such probabilities would be expected to cumulate.

We can therefore hypothesize that such duplication of storage occurs in parallel to the duplication of representation of speech functions in the two hemispheres. However, we cannot at present specify whether the pitch information is retained in the dominant or the nondominant hemisphere in the case of people where a more completely unilateral storage is hypothesized (Critchley & Henson, 1977; Deutsch, 1978; Milner, 1962).

As the performance of mixed left-handers was found to differ from that of mixed right-handers, pure left-handers, and pure righthanders, we should consider the way in which these handedness groups were defined. Subjects were asked to complete the short form of the Edinburgh Handedness Inventory (Oldfield, 1971). They were classified as right-handers if they obtained a positive laterality quotient and as left-handers if they obtained a negative laterality quotient. Such a classification correlates highly with hand used in writing. Indeed, when the data were reanalyzed using this criterion alone, the same pattern of results was obtained, though slightly attenuated. The second basis for classification was consistency of hand preference.

Such a classification accords well with Annett's (1970) conclusions. She performed an association analysis of responses to a handedness questionnaire by university undergraduates. Although preferring to regard variations in hand usage as continuous rather than discrete, Annett concluded that the best criterion for differentiating handedness groups is that of hand used in writing (with the possible exception of hammering). She also concluded that the best criterion for distinguishing subgroups within the right-handed and left-handed populations is consistency of hand usage.

It is interesting that in both the present experiment and that of Annett the subjects had been taught to write within the last 25 years. This means that they would have been permitted to write in accordance with their spontaneous hand preference. However, subjects in earlier studies would have had pressure applied by their teachers to write with their right hand. This would also be true of older patient groups in more recent studies. The hand of writing reported in such studies, therefore, would not reflect basic hand preference in the same way as in experiments using recently educated subjects.

It remains to be determined to what extent the superiority of mixed left-handers found here generalizes to other musical memory tasks. However, the author has found that other left-handers, selected for experiments on the basis of high performance on pitch memory tasks, also did very well on further tasks involving musical memory, including transposition of melodic sequences. Such subjects might also be expected to perform unusually well on tests of memory for speech sounds.

In this context, an experiment by Byrne (1974) should be cited. He compared the performance of a group of pure right-handers with a group of mixed handers on a variant of the Seashore tone memory test, and found no difference between the groups. Using the short form of the Edinburgh Handedness Inventory, he defined right-handers as those with laterality quotients of over +50, and mixed handers as those with laterality quotients between ±50, inclusive. Pure left-handers were excluded from this study. However, this classification combines mixed right-handers and mixed left-handers into a single group, so the lack of effect found by Byrne is not surprising. Had these two groups been combined in the present study, no significant differences would have emerged either. Furthermore, if Byrne's mixed-handers had been sampled at random we would expect the mixed right-handers to form the majority of this group (Oldfield, 1971).

The present findings also raise the issue of a possible overrepresentation of mixed left-handers among musicians as compared to other occupational groups. Oldfield (1969) used the long form of the Edinburgh Handedness Inventory to compare the handedness distribution of members of a school of music with that of a group of psychology undergraduates, and found no differences. He considered this interesting, as most musical instruments are designed for right-handed use, and so are relatively cumbersome for left-handers to manipulate. Thus, left-handed violinists and guitarists sometimes "remake" their instruments so that they can be played in reverse. One famous example here is Charlie Chaplin, who shifted the bar and soundpost and restrung his violin for that purpose (Chaplin, 1964). With other instruments such as the piano, such remaking is not practicable. (The case of the violin is rather interesting, because when played in the normal "right-handed" manner, the left hand actually does the more intricate work; however, the right hand produces the sound by bowing. So what seems to be important is which hand is the "executor.") At all events, the design of most musical instruments is such as to place left-handers at a disadvantage.

In the more recent study by Byrne (1974) cited above, the short form of the Edinburgh Handedness Inventory was administered to a group of students in a music conservatory, and also to a group of unselected university students. Byrne then computed the proportions of pure right-handers and of mixed handers in these two groups, and found that the mixed handers were significantly overrepresented among the musicians. Unfortunately, we cannot tell from this study how much this overrepresentation was due to mixed right-handers and how much to mixed left-handers. A study is currently underway to examine this issue further.

The present finding of handedness differences in the retention of pitch information follows on several earlier studies demonstrating differences at the perceptual level in the processing of tonal sequences (Deutsch, 1974; 1975a, 1975b). It would appear that there are substantial variations between handedness populations in the way music is processed.

REFERENCES

Annett, M. A classification of hand preference by association analysis. *British Journal of Psychology*, 1970, *61*, 303–321.

Applebee, A. A. Research in reading retardation: Two critical problems. *Journal of Child Psychiatry*, 1971, *12*, 91–113.

Byrne, B. Handedness and musical ability. *British Journal of Psychology*, 1974, *65*, 279–281.

Chaplin, C. *My autobiography*. London: Rodley Head, 1964.

Critchley, M., and Henson, R. A. (Eds.) *Music and the Brain*. Heinemann: London, 1977.

Deutsch, D. An auditory illusion. *Nature*, 1974, *251*, 307–309.

Deutsch, D. Two-channel listening to musical scales. *Journal of the Acoustical Society of America*, 1975a, *57*, 1156–1160.

Deutsch, D. Musical illusions. *Scientific American*, 1975b, *233(4)*, 92–104.

Deutsch, D. The psychology of music. In E. C. Carterette and M. P. Friedman (Eds.), *Handbook of perception*, Vol. X Academic Press: New York, 1978.

Gillies, S. M., MacSweeney, D. A., & Zangwill, O. L. A note on some unusual handedness patterns. *Quarterly Journal of Experimental Psychology*, 1960, *12*, 113–116.

Ginsburg, G. P., & Hartwick, A. Directional confusion as a sign of dyslexia. *Perception and Motor Skills*, 1971, *32*, 535–543.

Goodglass, H., & Quadfasal, F. A. Language laterality in left handed aphasics. *Brain*, 1954, *77*, 521–543.

Hartlage, L. C., & Green, J. B. EEG differences in children's reading and arithmetic abilities. *Perception and Motor Skills*, 1971, *32*, 133–134.

Hécaen, H., & Ajuriaguerra, J. de *Left handedness*. Grune and Stratten: New York, 1964.

Hécaen, H., & Piercy, M. Paroxysmal dysphasia and the problem of cerebral dominance. *Journal of Neurology and Neurological Psychiatry*, 1956, *19*, 194–201.

Hécaen, H., & Sauget, J. Cerebral dominance in lefthanded subjects. *Cortex*, 1971, *7*, 19–48.

Levy, J. Possible basis for evolution of lateral specialization of the human brain. *Nature*, 1969, *224*, 614–615.

Miller, E. Handedness and the pattern of human ability. *British Journal of Psychology*, 1971, *62*, 111–112.

Milner, B. Laterality effects in audition. In V. B. Mountcastle (Eds.) *Inter-hemispheric relations and cerebral dominance*. Baltimore: Johns Hopkins Press, 1962, 177–195.

Milner, B., Branch, C., & Rasmussen, T. Evidence for bilateral speech representation in some nonrighthanders. *Transactions of the American Neurological Association*, 1966, *91*, 306–308.

Newcombe, F., & Ratliff. Handedness, speech lateralization and ability. *Neuropsychologia*, 1973, *11*, 399–407.

Oldfield, R. C. Handedness in musicians. *British Journal of Psychology*, 1969, *60*, 91–99.

Oldfield, R. C. The assessment and analysis of handedness: The Edinburgh inventory. *Neuropsychologia*, 1971, *9*, 97–113.

Satz, P., & Sparrow, S. S. Specific developmental dyslexia: A theoretical formulation. In D. J. Bakker, & P. Satz, (Eds.) *Specific reading disability*. Rotterdam University Press: Rotterdam, 1970.

Shearer, E. Physical skills and reading backwardness. *Educational Research*, 1968, *10*, 197–206.

Silverman, A. J., Adevai, G., & McGough, W. I. Some relationships between handedness and perception. *Journal of Psychosomatic Research*, 1966, *10*, 151–158.

Subirana, A. Handedness and cerebral dominance. In P. J. Vinken, and G. W. Bruyn, (Eds.), *Handbook of clinical neurology*, 1969, *4*, 248–272.

Wold, R. M. Dominance—fact of fantasy: Its significance to learning disabilities. *Journal of the American Optometric Association*, 1968, *39*, 908–916.

Wussler, M., and Barclay, A. Cerebral dominance, psycholinguistic skills and reading disability. *Perception and Motor Skills*, 1970, *31*, 419–425.

Zangwill, O. L. *Cerebral dominance and its relation to psychological function*, 1960. Oliver and Boyd: Edinburgh.

Zurif, E. B., and Carson, G. Dyslexia in relation to cerebral dominance and temporal analysis. *Neuropsychologia*, 1970, *8*, 351–361.

12

Handedness in Artists

CAROLYN J. MEBERT
GEORGE F. MICHEL

INTRODUCTION

Handedness and its relationship to a variety of cognitive capabilities and to hemispheric specialization has found a prominent place in the brain–behavior literature. More specifically, handedness has been related to language functions and several theories have been proposed with respect to this relationship (Gazzaniga, 1970; Levy, 1969; Levy & Nagylaki, 1972; Steffen, 1975). Although the major portion of the population (often estimated at approximately 90%) is right-handed and has language functions located in the left hemisphere, the remainder is either left-handed or ambidextrous, and shows a less clear relationship between handedness and hemispheric specialization of function for language (Milner, 1974; Zurif & Bryden, 1969). Not only is the cerebral location of language function less clear for left-handers, but the whole picture of hemispheric specialization for this group is similarly equivocal.

Much of the evidence available suggests that the right hemisphere is specialized for nonverbal, visuo-spatial, and visuo-constructive functions and the processing of nonsequential input (Bryden, 1964; Levy, 1969; Levy & Sperry, 1968). This is assumed to be the case for both left- and right-handers. In the case of left-handers, however, because of the possibility of bilateral representation of language functions, it has been predicted that intrahemisphere competition between language and visuospatial functions would occur, resulting in a decrement in performance on tasks requiring

273

NEUROPSYCHOLOGY
OF LEFT-HANDEDNESS

visuospatial abilities. This prediction has been supported by Levy (1969) and Miller (1971) who found that left-handers and mixed-handers performed at a lower level than their right-handed counterparts on the performance scale of the Wechsler Adult Intelligence Scale (WAIS) and on the NIIP Form Relations Test. The verbal performance of Levy's left-handers and Miller's mixed-handers was apparently unimpaired, suggesting that no matter where or how they are located, language functions will predominate. However, as Marshall (1973) points out, the validity of this hypothesis and its supports rests on the assumption that left-, right-, and mixed-handers form relatively homogeneous groups with regard to both handedness and cerebral organization. It is unlikely that this is the case. Annett (1972) has shown that handedness is continuously distributed, and, through association analysis, has described at least eight categories of handedness. Additionally, the literature is inconsistent with respect to whether strongly or weakly left-handed people would be the ones to show bilateral or right-hemispheric specialization for language.

In any event, a competition hypothesis would suggest another pattern of performance in left-handers. That is, the competition between language and visuospatial functions could lead to a decrease in performance on language-related tasks. This view has also received support in studies of children with reading and other language-related disabilities (Annett & Turner, 1974; Harris, 1957).

Following from this, it might be expected that some left-handers may show a high level of performance on tasks requiring those functions presumably located in the right hemisphere. This final alternative does not necessarily entail the notion of a decrease in language performance in left-handers. Rather, it suggests that because their preferred hand is under control of the hemisphere involved in visuospatial, visuoconstructive functions, some left-handers may be at an advantage in terms of their ability to perform tasks requiring those functions. This alternative has received support from Peterson and Lansky (1974) who found a higher than normal frequency of left-handers in a sample of architecture students. In addition, there appeared to be a relationship between the number of years in this specialized training and handedness, with more left-handers found among the advanced students. Peterson and Lansky's assessment of handedness, however, was somewhat less than rigorous. Subjects were presented with three statements: "I am totally right-handed," "I use either hand equally," "I am totally left-handed," and were asked to check one. The group of left-handers was made up of those subjects who checked either of the last two statements. No distinction was made between mixed- and left-handed individuals.

The present study was preliminary to a large scale study of handedness in relation to career preferences and was primarily demographic in nature. The question we asked was whether there would be a difference in the distribution of handedness between two populations differing in their career orientations as indicated by college major. Based on information suggesting a relationship between hand preference and hemispheric specialization of function, we hypothesized that there would be more left-handers oriented toward a career requiring visuospatial abilities (e.g., art) than toward one which does not.

METHOD

Subjects

The subjects were 101 Boston University, liberal arts, undergraduates (49 males, 52 females) who had less than two years of art training, and 103 students from the Massachusetts College of Art and Boston University School of Fine Arts (45 males, 58 females).

Procedure

Annett's (1967) handedness questionnaire was used to assess the handedness of the subjects. These questionnaires were given out at the beginning of several classes at the two colleges. At the time they were competing the form, the students were uninformed as to the hypothesis under study. In addition to items pertaining to hand use, questions were asked about years of art training and birth order.

RESULTS

Table 12.1 shows the total number of "right," "left," and "either(hand)" responses given by the art students and nonart students for each of the 12 items on the questionnaire. The distribution of "left" and "right" responses differed significantly between the two groups ($U = 3$, $p < .001$ and $U = 20$, $p < .01$, respectively), whereas the "either" responses did not.

To obtain individual measures of laterality the formulae used by Lederer (1939), Satz, Achenbach, & Fennell (1967) and Oldfield (1971) were applied to the present data. The scores obtained in this way yielded comparable results in terms of the distribution curves for the two samples, although the

Table 12.1

Handedness Responses of Artists and Nonartists to Questionnaire Items

	Right[a]		Left[b]		Either	
	Art	Nonart	Art	Nonart	Art	Nonart
Write a letter	72	91	30	9	1	1
Throw a ball	69	93	28	7	6	1
Hold a racket	73	92	23	8	7	1
Strike a match	66	85	26	8	11	8
Scissors	85	88	12	5	6	8
Thread a needle	61	80	28	13	14	8
Top of broom	35	58	32	17	36	26
Top of shovel	46	76	26	9	31	16
Deal cards	71	87	29	10	3	4
Hammer	72	89	27	7	4	5
Toothbrush	71	80	27	9	5	11
Unscrew a jar	48	65	23	17	32	19

[a] Differences in distribution of right responses between artists and non-artists significant ($U = 20$, $p = .01$).

[b] Distribution of left responses differed significantly between the two groups. ($U = 3$, $p < .001$).

Oldfield formula was the only one to include "either" (or both) responses in the computation. Correlations between the scores obtained through each formula ranged from .96 to .99.

The Oldfield scores were used to differentiate between left-handed ($-51 - -100$), mixed-handed ($-50 - +50$), and right-handed ($+50 - +100$) subjects. The numbers of artists and nonartists falling into these three categories differed significantly ($\chi^2 = 15.61$; $df = 2$; $p < .001$). The actual numbers are: (a) 21 artists and 7 nonartists were left-handed; (b) 28 artists and 15 nonartists were mixed-handed; and (c) 54 artists and 79 nonartists were right-handed. These scores were then transformed in order to eliminate negative values and were used in an analysis of variance. This analysis revealed a significant difference between the scores of the artists and nonartists ($F = 18.08$; $df = 1$, 200; $p < .001$), no significant sex-related differences ($F = 2.36$; $df = 1$, 200, n.s.) and no interaction ($F = 0.31$, $df = 1$, 200, n.s.). Additionally, there were no significant differences between the birth order of left- and right-handers in either the artist or the nonartist groups ($\chi^2 = .388$, $df = 3$, n.s., and $\chi^2 = .67$, $df = 3$, n.s., respectively). Furthermore, there were no differences in birth order between left- and right-handers when the data from the two samples were combined ($\chi^2 = .344$, $df = 3$, n.s.), and the birth order of artists compared with nonartists did not differ ($\chi^2 = 1.312$, $df = 3$, n.s.). For these analyses, left-handed was defined as any negative score.

DISCUSSION

The results appear to indicate that the artist group forms a particular subset of the population with respect to hand use. This could be explained, at least in part, as a function of experience. Artists engage in many activities that require a certain amount of skill and proficiency with both hands. The picture might be somewhat different if young children just beginning art training were studied, as it has been shown that experience can influence skilled hand use even after handedness has become established (Provins, 1956). Consequently, although the numbers of right- and left-handers in younger sample populations may not differ from the adults reported on here, it is conceivable that the distribution of hand use might. What we may be seeing in the artist group is a shift in the distribution of handedness toward the expected normal curve, rather than so strongly toward the right as is seen in "normal" populations (Annett, 1972). This shift may be seen as a function of the stimulation and activity experienced by individuals who will eventually make up the artistic subgroup of the population and differing from that experienced by people who go into more verbally oriented fields.

Although information regarding preferred hand use provides no direct evidence about hemispheric specialization, several explanations are possible with respect to the relationship of hand preference and cerebral organization among the artists. The competition hypothesis of Levy and Sperry (1968) may be appropriate for some groups of left-handers. For such groups lower performance on visuospatial tasks of the type found on standardized tests need not interfere with their normal activities. It is unlikely that artists would be found within such a sample as presumably their work requires well-developed visuospatial, visuoconstructive abilities.

Annett (1964) had suggested that the intrahemispheric competition could be manifested in superior visuospatial abilities at the expense of language functions. The left-handed artist group may fit this pattern, although it is not possible to say without a measure of their verbal performance.

The notion that language functions will be those represented in both hemispheres is based on the fact that we are a highly verbal society. Therefore, language is seen as the more important of the two basic functions in question, and the one that is more closely related to skilled hand use. It may, however, be misleading to assume that this is always the case. It could be that visuospatial functions are located in the two hemispheres in proportions equal to those for bilateral representation of language functions. More individuals with this pattern of cerebral organization may be left- or mixed-handed and may find that endeavors requiring a high degree of visuospatial skill would be easier and more rewarding than more verbal endeavors.

A final alternative explanation is that the artist group is among the approximately 60% of left-handers reported by several investigators (Milner, 1974; Satz *et al.*, 1967; Warrington & Pratt, 1973) to have the typical pattern of hemispheric specialization (i.e., language in the left hemisphere and visuospatial functions in the right). In this way there would be nothing interfering with the right hemisphere's control of those left-handed functions required to transform three-dimensional experiences into two-dimensional representations. In addition, it may be that such left-handed artists would differ from right-handed artists in some aspects of their work—either the type of art work they do, or the ways in which they do it.

The data obtained in the present investigation do not provide enough information to enable us to choose from among the available alternatives. A better understanding of the *development* of skilled hand use and hemispheric specialization would help to clarify this issue. Finally, the examination of career preferences in relation to various measures and indicators of lateralized cerebral functioning appears to be a profitable way of exploring the relevance of neuropsychological studies of functional asymmetry to the real world activities of people.

REFERENCES

Annett, M. A model of the inheritance of handedness and cerebral dominance. *Nature*, 1964, *204*, 59–60.

Annett, M. The binomial distribution of right, mixed and left handedness. *Quarterly Journal of Experimental Psychology*, 1967, *19*, 327–333.

Annett, M. The distribution of manual asymmetry. *British Journal of Psychology*, 1972, *63*, 343–358.

Annett, M. & Turner, A. Laterality and the growth of intellectual abilities. *British Journal of Educational Psychology*, 1974, *44*, 37–46.

Bryden, M. P. Tachistoscopic recognition and cerebral dominance. *Perceptual & Motor Skills*, 1964, *19*, 686.

Gazzaniga, M. S. *The bisected brain.* New York: Appleton-Century-Crofts, 1970.

Harris, A. J. Lateral dominance, directional confusion, and reading disability. *Journal of Psychology*, 1957, *44*, 283–294.

Lederer, R. K. An exploratory investigation of handed status in the first two years of life. *University of Iowa Studies in Infant Behavior*, Vol. 16, 1939.

Levy, J. Possible basis for the evolution of lateral specialization of the human brain. *Nature*, 1969, *224*, 614–615.

Levy, J. & Nagylaki, T. A. A model for the genetics of handedness. *Genetics*, 1972, *72*, 117–128.

Levy, J. & Sperry, R. W. Differential perceptual capacities in major and minor hemispheres. *Proceedings of the National Academy of Sciences*, 1968, *61*, 1151.

Marshall, J. C. Some problems and paradoxes associated with recent accounts of hemispheric specialization. *Neuropsychologia*, 1973, *11*, 463-470.

Miller, E. Handedness and the pattern of human ability. *British Journal of Psychology*, 1971, *62*, 111-112.

Milner, B. Hemispheric specialization: Scope and limits. In F. O. Schmitt & F. G. Worden (eds.), *The Neurosciences: Third Study Program.* Cambridge: M.I.T. Press, 1974.

Oldfield, R. C. The assessment and analysis of handedness: The Edinburgh inventory. *Neuropsychologia*, 1971, *9*, 97-113.

Peterson, J. M. & Lansky, L. M. Left-handedness among architects: Some facts and speculation. *Perceptual and Motor Skills*, 1974, *38*, 547-550.

Provins, K. A. "Handedness" and skill. *Quarterly Journal of Experimental Psychology*, 1956, *8*, 79-95.

Satz, P., Achenbach, K. & Fennell, E. Correlations between assessed manual laterality and predicted speech laterality in a normal population. *Neuropsychologia*, 1967, *5*, 295-310.

Steffen, H. Cerebral dominance: The development of handedness and speech. *Acta Paedopsychiatrica*, 1975, *41*, 223-235.

Warrington, E. K. & Pratt, R. T. C. Language laterality in left handers assessed by unilateral E.C.T. *Neuropsychologia*, 1973, *11*, 423-428.

Zurif, E. B. & Bryden, M. P. Familial handedness and left-right differences in auditory and visual perception. *Neuropsychologia*, 1969, *7*, 179-187.

13

Cognitive Deficit
and Left-Handedness:
A Cautionary Note

JAMES M. SWANSON
MARCEL KINSBOURNE
JOSEPH M. HORN

Interest in comparing the intellectual skills of the right-handed and the non-right-handed sections of the general population has been revived by recent suggestions that the non-right-handers include a disproportionate number of individuals with abnormal lateralization of cerebral function (Goodglass & Quadfasal, 1954; Hécaen, & Sanguet, 1971; Zangwell, 1960), and brain damage (Bakan, Dibbs, & Reed, 1973; Gordon, 1920; Satz, 1973). Dividing the non-right-handers into those with other non-right-handers in the immediate family (FS +) and those without (FS –), Satz (1973) has selectively incriminated the latter group as deviant in cerebral organization due to brain damage, whereas Bakan *et al.* (1973) have assumed that all non-right-handers are brain damaged. Others (e.g., Hicks & Kinsbourne, 1977) have discussed the genetics of handedness.

When early left-hemispheric brain damage neutralizes or reverses a right hand (RH) preference, it may also cause language representation to extend to the right hemisphere (Gardner, Karnobi, McClure, & Gardner, 1955). Thus, some left-handers may differ from the norm in the nature of their right-hemispheric specialization for pathological (Bakan *et al.*, 1973; Gardner *et al.*, 1955; Gordon, 1920; Satz, 1973; Subirana, 1969) rather than genetic reasons (Levy, 1969). Levy (1969, 1974) suggested that when verbal and spatial processes both lay claim to right hemisphere territory, the verbal processing prevails. (Recent persuasive evidence to the contrary arises from the infant hemispherectomy findings of Kohn and Dennis, 1975.) Therefore, Levy (1969) predicted a selective deficit of spatial thought

NEUROPSYCHOLOGY
OF LEFT-HANDEDNESS

associated with left-handedness: Left-handers should match right-handers with respect to verbal skills, but be inferior in spatial skills. Levy (1969) and Miller (1971) reported IQ data from college population supporting this prediction. But other studies based on IQ measures have failed to confirm the dissociation between the outcomes of verbal and spatial testing.

Several recent large sample, cross-sectional studies on handedness have been reported. Hardyck, Petrinovich, and Goldman (1976) found that left- and right-handed school children ($N = 7688$) had the same level and pattern of IQs. Roberts and Engle (1974) report data on 7119 children between the ages of 6 and 11 years, who were tested as part of a National Health Survey and constitute a representative sample of the United States population between those ages. There were no differences between left-handers ($N = 762$) and right-handers ($N = 6350$) on the WISC Vocabulary and Block Design tests. Newcombe and Ratcliffe (1973) reported similar results for 823 unselected adult subjects in England.

In recent studies utilizing smaller sample sizes, similar results also have been reported. Ledlow, Swanson, and Carter (1972) found no evidence for an IQ difference between left- and right-handed college students, even though differences in performance on a physical versus name reaction-time task were obtained. Fagan-Dubin (1974) found no difference between left- and right-handed 5–6 year-old children in verbal versus performance IQ difference. Briggs, Nebes, and Kinsbourne (1976) found a small, reliable, but equal, inferiority of non-right-handed adults on *both* verbal and spatial tests.

All reports reviewed implicitly assume that once the discrepancies between different studies (probably due to biased sampling) are solved, a stable and definitive characterization of the intellectual profile of the non-right-hander will emerge. This report weakens this expectation as it shows that a non-right-handed group of individuals, studied longitudinally, can at one stage in their life span exhibit intellectual abilities different from population norms, but at another stage exhibit no such differences. An important difference between mixed left-handers and pure left-handers also complicates the evaluation of the intellectual profile of non-right-handers.

METHOD

Because a biased sample is often obtained when group members are selected by identification rather than selected at random, a population was chosen for which overall group norms were available. The population satisfying this condition consisted of the full complement of elementary school students in the Catholic School System of Austin, Texas—a system in which the Primary Mental Abilities Tests (PMA) is given yearly to all students in fourth and seventh grade. This allows the groups, scores for selected groups of right- and left-handers to be compared to the overall population norms.

Left-handers were identified in 1972 from information provided by "homeroom" teachers in two of the five elementary schools in the system. Teachers were asked to identify the left-handed students in their classes, and then they were requested to indicate which hand those students used for both writing and throwing. Due to a strict agreement with school officials, personal or parental contact was not allowed, nor was more detailed questioning concerning handedness.

In 1972, and again in 1974, the obtained list of left-handers was taken to the central office of the schools, system and PMA IQ scores were obtained from class records. The classes surveyed had a total of 310 students; those students not identified as left-handers were assumed to be right-handers. As records of previous tests are maintained, longitudinal information was available for many of the students in the school system in 1974.

RESULTS

Out of the 310 students in the classes surveyed, 30 left-handers (9.7%) were reported by the teachers. Ten of the left-handers were female. Additionally, 3 of the female left-handers and 4 of the male left-handers were Mexican-Americans; the rest were Anglo-Americans.

Complete longitudinal data (fourth- and seventh-grade PMA Scores) were obtained for 18 of the 30 identified left-handers. A right-hander was chosen to match, on the basis of sex and ethnic group classification each left-hander for whom longitudinal data was available. This was done by finding the left-hander's name and score on the class record of the PMA test, and then selecting from the records a student in the same class who most closely matched on the stated criteria (age, sex, ethnic group) but was not on the teacher's list of left-handers.

All of the data collected for the 30 left-handed students are shown in Table 13.1 along with the complete school system averages for the year 1971. The school norms are based on 541 fourth graders and 373 seventh graders. The 30 left-handers contributed 24 scores for the seventh-grade testing and 25 scores for the fourth-grade testing. As shown in Table 13.1, the left-handers in the sample averaged 1.8 points higher than the school norm at the fourth-grade testing (103.8 versus 102). This indicates that the group of left-handers obtained by the method described earlier were very close to "normal" on the basis of testing with the PMA in the fourth-grade.

Table 13.1
School Norms and the Group Averages for Identified Non-Right-Handers Based on Primary Mental Abilities Test Scores

	Fourth grade	Seventh grade
1971 norms	102.0 (N = 541)	107.0 (N = 373)
Non-right-handers	103.8 (N = 25)	98.4 (N = 24)

The comparison of the school norms and the average of the left-handed group at seventh-grade testing yields a different result. The left-handers averaged 98.4 on the PMA at seventh-grade testing, whereas the school norm was 107. The difference (8.6 points) is statistically significant ($t(23)$ = 2.6, p < .01).

The data presented in Table 13.1 raise several issues. First, there is a rise in IQ and a drop in sample size from the fourth to the seventh grade for the entire school sample. This rise may be real or owing to a selective attrition of poor students. Also, a comparison of the fourth- and seventh-grade left-handers is difficult to interpret as only 18 of the left-handers in the sample at one grade level are represented in the sample at the other grade level. A more decisive analysis can be made of the scores available for the 18 left-handers at both the fourth- and seventh-grade testing, along with the scores for the 18 matched right-handers also available from the sampling procedure described earlier. A split-plot analysis of variance with handedness as a between-subject variable and grade as a within-subject variable was used to resolve the problems outlined above.

The mean scores are shown in Table 13.2. Neither the handedness nor the grade main effects were significant in the analysis, but the handedness times grade interaction was significant (p < .025; $F(1, 34)$ = 6.73). The 6.6 point drop in IQ for this group of left-handers between fourth-grade and seventh-grade testing is significant, $t(17)$ = 2.78, p < .01. The rise in IQ for right-handers is still apparent in this longitudinal analysis as it is in the school norms, but in this sample it is smaller (now only 2.5 points) and not statistically significant. Therefore, the significant interaction may be interpreted as a reflection of different developmental trends for the right- and non-right-handers: The non-right-handed group manifests a decline whereas the right-handed group remains the same.

A nonparametric analysis of these data supports the statistical analyses just mentioned. Of the 18 left-handers, 13 declined in IQ from the fourth- to the seventh-grade testing, but only 6 of the 18 right-handers declined ($\chi^2 (1)$ = 5.43, p < .025). However, a conditional analysis showed that, given a decline, the average decline was the same for the 13 left-handers (10.3 IQ points) and the 6 right-handers (10.2 IQ points). Thus the significant drop in IQ in the left-handed group was not owing to a subset of the sample that showed an abnormal drop in IQ, but rather was due to a larger number of left-handers than right-handers who showed a drop in IQ of comparable magnitude.

As the group data show in Table 13.2, the score for right-handers increased for each subtest of the PMA except the Reasoning subtest, and the average score for left-handers dropped for each subtest except for Reasoning. It appears that the decline in IQ of the left-handers was not contributed by a particular mental ability, but involved multiple aspects of intellect.

Annett (1964, 1970) recommends separating the data from "pure" and "mixed" left-handers for analysis. As information on only two activities was gathered in this study by "homeroom" teachers, Annett's (1964) binomial proportions should not be expected, but the identified left-handers can still be classified as "pure" or "mixed" on the basis of writing and throwing. Of the 18 non-right-handers, 11 used the left hand for writing and throwing ("pure" lefthanders). Of the remaining 7 ("mixed" left-handers), 4 used the right hand for writing and the left for throwing, and the remaining 3 did the reverse. The longitudinal data for pure and mixed left-handers are shown in Figure 13.1. The "pure" left-handers at first testing averaged 111.00 on PMA IQ, which is a significant 9.0 points above the average of the school population at the fourth-grade testing (t (10) = 2.2, $p < .05$). At second testing, the average PMA IQ of the 11

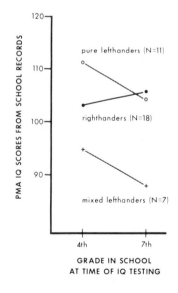

Figure 13.1 Profiles for the handedness by grade interaction.

Table 13.2
Longitudinal Data for 18 Right-Handers and 18 Non-Right-Handers from Primary Mental Abilities Subtests

	Grade	Verbal	Numerical	Reasoning	Spatial	Performance	Total
Right-handers (*N* = 18)	7	107.6	106.1	106.2	104.6	—	105.6
	4	104.6	99.9	106.3	102.6	102.8	103.1
Difference		3.0	4.2	−.1	2.0		2.5
Left-handers (*N* = 18)	7	101.2	101.8	100.7	99.2	—	98.1
	4	102.3	104.1	100.3	101.2	106.7	104.7
Difference		−1.1	−2.3	.4	−2.0		−6.6

"pure" left-handers had dropped 6.5 points to 104.5, a value slightly lower but not significantly different from the mean IQ (107) of the school population at the seventh-grade testing. The 7 "mixed" left-handers averaged 94.86 on the PMA at first testing, which is a significant 13.14 points below the fourth-grade population average (t (6) $= 4.3$, $p < .005$). At second testing, the average IQ of the 7 "mixed" left-handers had dropped 6.7 points to 88.14, and thus was 18.86 points below the seventh-grade population average. The obtained inferiority of mixed left-handers replicates and extends the findings of Annett (1970). The four "mixed" left-handers who wrote with the right hand were among the lowest scoring individuals of all those tested. All four declined substantially in measured IQ between the fourth- and seventh-grade testing. These could have been "shifted sinistrals" who had succumbed to social pressures to write with the right hand. The other three "mixed" left-handers who wrote with the left hand averaged 97 on the PMA at the fourth-grade testing and 95 at the seventh-grade testing.

Despite an overall difference in IQ of more than 16 points between the "pure" and the "mixed" left-handers, both groups suffered a similar drop of about 6.5 IQ points between the fourth- and seventh-grade testing. Orthogonal decomposition of a handedness times grade interaction obtained in an unweighted means analysis indicates that the statistical significance is due to the component comparing left-handers (pure and mixed) to right-handers by grade (F (1,33) $= 8.8$, $p < .01$). The component of the interaction comparing the decline in IQ across grade for pure versus mixed left-handers is not significant (F (1,33) < 1.0).

DISCUSSION

The results at the first and second testing in our longitudinal study are each consistent with several previous claims, but not necessarily the same ones in each case. Overall, our data indicate that left-handers and right-handers do not differ in IQ as measured by the PMA. However, as longitudinal information and mixed handedness (which are data that are often unavailable or ignored in large studies) are considered, then interesting differences are indicated and will be discussed.

At the first testing, given in the fourth grade, right-handers and non-right-handers did not differ in overall intelligence test scores, confirming Newcombe and Ratcliff (1973), Ledlow, Swanson, and Carter (1972), and Roberts and Engle (1974). Among the non-right-handers, the mixed left-handers scored lower and the pure left-handers scored higher than the right-handers, confirming Annett (1970). Non-right-handers showed neither an overall lower score (Briggs, *et al.* 1976) nor a selectively lower spatial score (Levy, 1969; Levy, 1974; Miller, 1971) at the first testing.

At the second testing, given in the seventh grade, non-right-handers were found to score lower than right-handers in overall intelligence, confirming Briggs *et al.* (1976). Within the non-right-handers at the seventh-grade testing, "mixed" handers scored lower than and "pure" left-handers scored equal to right-handers, confirming one of Annett's (1970) two claims, but not the other. The results of the second testing conflict with the findings of Newcombe and Ratcliff (1973), Ledlow *et al.* (1972) and Roberts and Engle (1974), as the non-right-handed group averaged significantly lower in IQ than the right-handed group. Additionally, the data again contradict Levy (1969) and Miller (1971) because no selective spatial deficit was obtained.

In the present study, the main effect of "handedness" must be interpreted with reference to the interaction between age and handedness. This showed non-right-handers as a group to be slipping relative to right-handers with respect to IQ scores. This was equally the case for the pure left-handers who happened to start off higher than the right-handers and the mixed-handers who started off significantly lower. The main effects in question may not be free from an undetermined sampling bias, but the interaction, affecting equally as it does such different subgroups as the pure left-handers and mixed-handers in the same sample, calls for an explanation.

An evaluation of the pathological left-handedness explanation (Bakan, *et al.* 1973; Gordon, 1920; Satz, 1973) is not possible because family information could not be obtained for these children. This was because of a strict agreement with school officials that no personal or family contact would be made with the students for whom IQ information was obtained. However, as a group "mixed" left-handers are more suspect of minimal undetected brain damage than "pure" left-handers, and the large difference in IQ between these two subgroups is in accord with the pathological theory of left-handedness. However, the similar developmental trend of a drop in IQ for bright ("pure") and dull ("mixed") non-right-handers weakens any explanation of this decline based on the pathological origin of left-handedness. In fact, by reversing the logic on which the pathological theory of left-handedness is based (Satz, 1973), one might argue that the high IQ scores for pure left-handers in the fourth grade precludes brain damage as a determining factor of handedness for this group, and that the drop in IQ detected at the seventh-grade testing of this group suggest that environmental discrimination suffered by these left-handers accounts for the decline.

Usually, individual differences in measured intelligence are explained in both environmental and biologic terms and so it is here. It is possible that environmental discrimination or dwindling motivation affected the non-right-handers between fourth and seventh grade, though whether it did and if so, why, is obscure. There is, however, a plausible biologic alternative to consider. This phenomenon may represent a lag in, or premature termination of, higher cognitive developmental sequences in the non-right-handed group (Kinsbourne, 1973). Although the simpler mental operations unfold comparably, at the same rate in both groups, in so far as they are adequately tested by the instruments used in the early (fourth grade) test, in the right-handed and non-right-handed groups, the more advanced operations may be less developed in the non-right-handers at the older of the two ages tested. Only further sampling could distinguish a temporary from a permanent lag.

A comparable situation appears to obtain after early hemispherectomy (Kohn & Dennis, 1974). The isolated residual hemisphere, whether left or right, is indifferently able to support verbal and spatial cognitive processes up to a certain level. However, during the most sophisticated problem solving in those modes, the residual right hemisphere reveals its spatial bent and the residual left hemisphere, its verbal aptitude.

The present study shows that the characteristic of hand preference may be a marker for individual differences in the acquisition of cognitive processes underlying intelligence test performance. It does not follow that the trends prevailing in our sample accurately reflected comparable trends in the population at large. Indeed, the much larger cross-sectional studies that fail to find differences between left- and right-handed populations cast doubt on any such assumption.

A comparison of our limited longitudinal data to the most impressive set of cross-sectional data available (Roberts & Engle, 1974) does provide some consistency if the three classes of handedness are considered: pure left-handers, mixed-handers (or ambidextrous), and right-handers. In our data, the main effects of these three levels of handedness is significant, with mixed-handers scoring significantly lower (91.5) on the PMA test than pure left-handers (107.8) or right-handers (104.4). This pattern is also reflected in the cross-sectional data: Left-handers are slightly higher in IQ than right-handers (99.1 versus 99.0), but ambidextrous children are significantly lower (90.6). A major discrepancy between these two studies is apparent when the incidence of the three classes is considered. In the HEW study by Roberts and Engle (1974) only .1% of the children tested were ambidextrous, but in our study 3.7% of the children were mixed-handers. This discrepancy probably is due to a different definition of ambidextrous or mixed handedness.

Hardyck, Petrinovich, and Goldman (1976) report a large cross-sectional study ($N = 7688$) of school children in grades 1–6 in California. They found no evidence of a cognitive deficit associated with left-handedness at any grade, which means their cross-sectional study conflicts with the present longitudinal study. Surprisingly, they also found very few "mixed" left-handers, even though they used three indices (writing, cutting, and sighting) of handedness, and they did not report separately the data for the few mixed-handers that were identified.

Annett (1970) found that mixed-left-handers scored lower than right-handers on the Peabody picture vocabulary test. However, her incidence figures indicated that more left-handers were "mixed" (25.6%) than were "pure" (6.7%), which directly opposes the pattern obtained in the HEW study (Roberts & Engle, 1974) and by Hardyck et al. (1976). Consistent with Annett (1970) and the present study, Kovac (1973) reported that subjects with "nonpronounced" lateral preference score less well than subjects with "pronounced" lateral preference on verbal and spatial intelligence tests.

These studies illustrate the necessity of separating "pure" and "mixed" left-handers, as Annett (1970) emphasized. However, differences in procedures used to classify subjects as having a "mixed," "ambidextrous," or a "nonpronounced" lateral preference differ widely across these studies making any cross-experiment comparison difficult. For example, we used only two important and frequently used motor tasks to determine manual preference: writing (requiring fine motor control) and throwing (requiring gross motor control). Diluting the definition of mixed handedness with other measures of manual preference (e.g. shuffling cards) or dominance e.g. sighting) may result in a large but uninterpretable group of mixed left-handers. Yet, it is clear that ignoring the class of mixed handedness will also produce a heterogeneous group of left-handers. However, one must conclude that the data show that pure left-handers as a group have no cognitive deficit as measured by IQ tests. The large-scale cross-sectional studies and literature reviews (e.g. Hardyck & Petrinovich, 1977; Hicks & Kinsbourne, 1977) are clear on this point, and the data presented here support that hypothesis *if mixed-handers are excluded.*

An intriguing finding of our study is that both "pure" and "mixed" left-handers drop in IQ from the fourth to the seventh grade. Even though the pure left-handers do not show a deficit with respect to the population during this period, their decline is as important as that of the mixed left-handers who showed a cognitive deficit at both tests with respect to the group norms. To put the drop in IQ in perspective, consider the ages at which the children were tested. The first test, at the fourth grade, occurred when the children were about 10-years-old. The second test, at the seventh grade, occurred when the children were about 13-years-old. Piaget (1970) has noted that this time in the life span is characterized by a transition from concrete operations to formal operations in cognitive functioning. Palermo and Molfese (1972) have reviewed the literature and similarly indicated that between 10 and 13 years, children exhibit unstable linguistic performance. Perhaps our reported decline in the IQ of left-handers is related to, or isolated in, this stage of development.

A final caution must be stated forcefully. For reasons unknown to us, our sample (or population) might have been unrepresentative in some manner as any relatively small sample is open to that possibility. The dangers of relying on small samples to speculate on aspects of individual differences are clear, and is even emphasized in many introductory textbooks. However, this warning is often ignored (e.g. Levy, 1969). We realize the short-coming of our study; the sample size is too small. However, we meet the requirements of sound experimental investigation, and our data present (and renew) some interesting questions that remain unanswered. Still, we must confine ourselves to the one conclusion that follows inescapably from our data: Only a large-scale, longitudinal study will finally resolve the question of whether the rate of acquisition of intellectual abilities in the population at large in any way differ in relation to variations in handedness. We also must emphasize that it may be necessary to consider several classes of non-right-handers, not a heterogeneous group of "left-handers," in order to evaluate the relationship between handedness and IQ.

REFERENCES

Annett, M. A. Handedness, cerebral dominance, and the growth of intelligence, In D. J. Bakher & P. Satz (Eds.) *Specific reading disability: Advances in theory and method.* Rotterdam: University Press, 1970.

Annett, M. A. A model of the inheritance of handedness and cerebral dominance. *Nature,* 1964, *204,* 59–60.

Bakan, P., Dibbs, G. & Reed, P. Handedness and birth stress. *Neuropsychologia,* 1973, *11,* 363–366.

Briggs, C. Nebes, & Kinsbourne, M. Intellectual differences in relation to personal and family handedness. *Quarterly Journal of Experimental Psychology,* 1976, *28,* 591–602.

Fagan-Dubin, L. Lateral dominance and development of cerebral specialization. *Cortex,* 1974, *10,* 69–74.

Gardner, W. J., Karnobi, L. J., McClure, C. C. & Gardner, A. K. Residual functions following hemispherectomy for tumor and for infantile hemiplegia. *Brain,* 1955, *78,* 487–502.

Goodglass, H., & Quadfasal, F. A. Language laterality in left-handed aphasics. *Brain,* 1954, 77, 521–548.

Gordon, H. Left-handedness and mirror-writing especially among deflective children. *Brain,* 1920, *43,* 313–368.

Hardyck, C. & Petrinovich, L. F. Left-handedness. *Psychological Bulletin,* 1977, *84,* 385–404.

Hardyck, C., Petrinovich, L. F., & Coldman, R. D. Left-handedness and cognitive deficit. *Cortex,* 1976, *12,* 266–279.

Hicks, R. E. & Kinsbourne, M. Handedness Differences: Human Handedness. In M. Kinsbourne (Ed.), *The asymmetrical function of the brain*. New York: Cambridge University Press, 1977.

Hécaen, H. & Sauguet, J. Cerebral dominance in left-handed subjects. *Cortex*, 1971, *7*, 19–48.

Kinsbourne, M. Minimal brain dysfunction as a neurodevelopmental lag. *Annals of the New York Academy of Sciences*, 1973, *205*, 268–273.

Kohn, B. & Dennis, M. Patterns of hemispheric specialization after hemidicortication for infantile hemiplegia. In M. Kinsbourne & W. L. Smith, (Eds.), *Hemispheric disconnection and cerebral function*. Springfield, Ill.: C. C. Thomas, 1974.

Kovac, D. Pairedness, an open problem in information processing. *Organismische Informationsverarbeitung* (Proceeding of Symposium at Berlin, September, 1973) 210–223.

Ledlow, A., Swanson, J. & Carter, B. Specialization of cerebral hemisphere for physical and associational memory confusion. Paper presented at the Midwestern Psychological Association meeting, Cleveland, Ohio, 1972.

Levy, J. Possible basis for the evolution of lateral specialization of the human brain. *Nature*, 1969, *224*, 614–615.

Levy, J. Psychobiological implications of bilateral asymmetry. In S. J. Diamond, & J. G. Beaumont, (Eds.) *Hemispheric function in the human brain*, Elek Science, London, 1974.

Miller, E. Handedness and the pattern of human ability. *British Journal of Psychology*, 1971, *62*, 111–112.

Newcombe, F. & Ratcliff, G. Handedness, speech lateralization and ability. *Neuropsychologica*, 1973, *11*, 339–407.

Palermo, D. S. & Molfese, D. L. Language acquisition from age five onward. *Psychological Bulletin*, 1972, Vol. 78, p. 409–428.

Piaget, J. Piaget's theory. In P. H. Mussan (Ed.). *Carmichael's manual of child psychology*. New York: Wiley, 1970.

Roberts, J. & Engle, A. Family background, early development, and intelligence of children 6–11 years. (*National Center for Health Statistics. Data from the National Health Survey, series 11, No. 142*) (DHEW publication No. (HRA) 75–1624). Washington, D.C.: U.S. Government Printing Office, 1974.

Satz, P. Left-handedness and early brain insult: An explanation. *Neuropsychologic*, 1973, *11*, 115–117.

Subirana, S. Handedness and cerebral dominance. In P. J. Vurpec & G. W. Bruyn, (Eds.), *Handbook of clinical neurology, Vol. 14*, Amsterdam: North Holland Publishing Co., 1969.

Zangwill, O. Cerebral dominance and its relationship to psychological function. Springfield, Ill.: C. C. Thomas, 1960.

14

Age-Related Changes
in Cognitive Abilities
and Hemispheric Specialization

KATHERINE M. KOCEL

INTRODUCTION

This book offers a variety of perspectives on the origins of sinistrality and the relationship between handedness and hemispheric specialization. Rather than being intended as a demonstration of the inherent or learned strengths and weaknesses of the left-handed, the majority of the research reported here might be said to be directed toward revealing the nature of brain–behavior relationships. Once it had been established that the left- and right-handed frequently show different patterns of cerebral lateralization (Dimond & Beaumont, 1974; Galin, Ornstein, Kocel & Merrin, 1971; Kimura, 1961), the cognitive abilities of handedness groups acquired a special significance for brain research.

The study of handedness and sex-related variations in the central theme of hemispheric specialization, as a means of revealing essential elements in the differentiation of the two sides of the human brain, continues to receive increasing attention. A variety of methods have been used to determine that different types of left-handers (Dee, 1971; Hécaen & Sauguet, 1971; Lake & Bryden, 1976) and the left- and right-handed (Bryden, 1975; Goodglass & Quadfasel, 1954; Hécaen & Sauguet, 1971) differ with respect to cerebral lateralization. In addition, evidence that males and females frequently show different patterns of hemispheric differentiation is accumulating (Harshman & Remington, 1975; Lansdell, 1964). Studies of groups that differ in hemispheric specialization may reveal the etiology of

NEUROPSYCHOLOGY
OF LEFT-HANDEDNESS

cerebral differentiation and aid in understanding its development. When demonstrated differences in the cortical organization of females and males and left- and right-handers are successfully related to gender and handedness group differences in human behavior, new light may be shed on the struggle to comprehend brain–behavior relationships.

The relevance of neurophysiological and psychological differences between gender and handedness groups to efforts to increase understanding of human behavior, does not depend upon the assumption that such differences are inevitable or inherited. For present purposes, it is assumed that hereditary and environmental influences interact to determine both neurophysiological and behavioral differences between males and females, and left- and right-handers. Within such a context, an attempt to understand developmental changes in sex-related and handedness differences in cognitive abilities may reveal some of the factors influential at various stages in the development of hemispheric specialization. Consideration of long-term developmental changes in the cognitive abilities of left- and right-handed females and males offers a new approach to the processes operative in the lateralization of cognitive functions.

HEMISPHERIC DEVELOPMENT

Two conflicting views of the development of hemispheric specialization have been offered. Analysis of the auditory evoked responses of human infants, children, and young adults led Molfese, Freeman, and Palermo (1975) to conclude that the lateralization of verbal and nonverbal stimuli decreases with age. Brown and Jaffe (1975) reviewed clinical and experimental evidence to develop the hypothesis that the lateralization of language is a process that continues throughout life. If the cognitive abilities of groups that differ with respect to hemispheric specialization develop differently with age, then it might be inferred that hemispheric specialization also changes with age. Evidence that the cognitive abilities of right- and left-handed males and females do change differently with age will be presented and then long-term developmental changes in hemispheric specialization will be discussed.

It seems appropriate to note that data on the cognitive abilities of parents and offspring may be especially valuable to the study of developmental changes in hemispheric specialization. Such a selection of subjects allows for the control or minimization of certain sources of error that have plagued cross-sectional studies of cognitive development. Perhaps the most significant of these is that the two generations are similar with respect to the genetic determinants of cognitive abilities. Innumerable environmental variables (e.g., sources of nutrition, availability of reading materials, and recreational interests) likewise exert comparable influences on members of the same families. In addition, attitudinal variables affecting test-taking behaviors are likely to be analogous in close relatives.

COGNITIVE ABILITIES

Investigators of the University of Hawaii and the University of Colorado collaborated in a large-scale study of genetic and environmental factors affecting cognitive abilities. For present purposes the completed sample consists of 926 Caucasian families who were paid to take 15 cognitive tests and provide information on their environmental experiences. Responding to the two handedness questions 3251 subjects, ranging in age from 14 to 65 years, answer "right" or "left" to both "Which hand do you write with?" and "Which hand do you use most of the time?" Factor analyses of scores on the 15 cognitive tests produced 4 interpretable, orthogonal factors: a verbal factor, a spatial factor, a perceptual-speed factor, and a memory factor. Details on test reliabilities, procedures, and factor analyses are available in Wilson, DeFries, McClearn, Vandenberg, Johnson, and Rashad (1975). Table 14.1 shows the names of the tests, the test times, and the primary factors each test loaded on.

Three-way analyses of variance of performance on the four cognitive factors were done with sex, generation, and handedness as the independent variables. There were significant two-way interactions between sex and generation on the verbal and spatial factors. On the perceptual-speed factor there were significant two-way interactions between generation and hand preference ($p < .01$) and generation and gender ($p < .01$). These interactions are displayed in Figure 14.1.

No significant differences were found between left- and right-handed males or left- and right-handed females. Right-handed males and females differed significantly on all of the factors and all of the tests. Right-handed females showed an advantage on the verbal, perceptual-speed and memory factors, whereas right-handed males showed an advantage on the spatial factor. On the other hand, left-handed males and females differed significantly in the same directions on only the spatial and perceptual-speed factors.

As previously reported (Kocel, 1977), comparing parent and offspring groups separately revealed a left-handed offspring superiority on the perceptual-speed factor ($p < .01$) and a left-handed parent superiority on the verbal factor ($p < .02$). Comparisons of all left- and right-handers on the 4 cognitive factors and the 15 cognitive tests revealed no significant differences between the left-handed group of 246 subjects and the right-handed group of 3005 subjects.

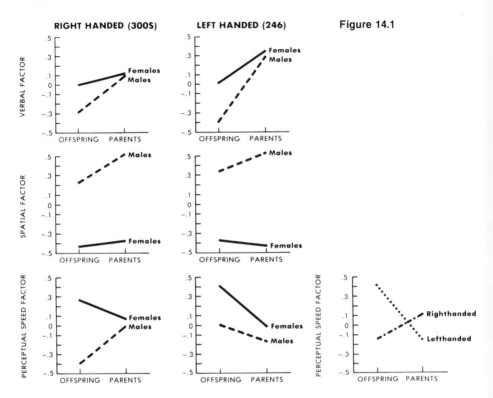

Figure 14.1

Table 14.1
Cognitive Tests, Test Times and Factors Loading .40

Test	Time	Factor
Vocabulary (PMA)	3 min	Verbal
Word Beginnings and Endings (ETS)	3 min each	Verbal
Things: Red & Metal	2 parts/3 min each	Verbal
Whiteman Test of Social Perception	10 min	Verbal
Mental Rotations (by Vandenberg)	10 min	Spatial
Hidden Patterns (ETS)	2 parts/2 min each	Spatial
Card Rotations (ETS)	2 parts/3 min each	Spatial
Elithorn Mazes	5 min	Spatial
Raven's Progressive Matrices (modified)	20 min	Spatial
Paper Form Board	3 min	Spatial
Visual Memory (immediate)	1 min learn/recall	Memory
Visual Memory (delayed)	1 min	Memory
Number Comparisons	2 parts/1.5 min each	Speed
Subtraction and Multiplication	2 min each	Speed
Pedigrees (PMA)	4 min	Speed

IMPLICATIONS OF COGNITIVE DIFFERENCES

What do the cognitive differences between handedness groups, males and females, and parents and offspring suggest about the role of hemispheric specialization in the development of cognitive functions? First, let us consider what might be inferred about the influence of handedness, sex, and age on cognitive abilities and attempt to relate this information to contemporary understanding of hemispheric specialization. Then, having developed something of a perspective from which to approach the reported interactions, an attempt will be made to discover what the study of the development of cognitive abilities in groups believed to differ in cerebral organization may tell us about the development of inter- and intrahemispheric specialization.

In Figure 14.1 the interaction between sex and generation on the verbal, spatial, and perceptual-speed factors are displayed for the right- and left-handed subjects separately. Changes between offspring and parent groups in the spatial abilities of left- and right-handed males and females are fairly similar. There is a significant interaction between handedness and generation in the perceptual-speed factor. When the interactions between sex and generation in the two handedness groups on the perceptual-speed factor are displayed separately, it becomes clear that the left-handed of both sexes, and right-handed women, show a different pattern of apparent change with age in perceptual-speed abilities than right-handed men. The interactions between gender–generation and handedness–generation are remarkably similar.

The reported differences between females and males (Wilson *et al.*, 1975) are apparent here. Females show an advantage on the verbal and perceptual-speed factors, whereas males show an advantage on the spatial factor. The greater apparent increase in the abilities of males between offspring and parent groups might be attributed to the much higher rate of employment in the male subjects. However, the fact remains that women do appear to increase their verbal abilities, and decline with respect to perceptual-speed abilities.

Assuming that the displayed differences between parent and offspring groups do reflect the relationship between age and cognitive abilities, what might be observed about the development of cognitive abilities in the left- and right-handed? Verbal abilities seem to continue to improve in both handedness groups, with the increase in the verbal abilities of the left-handed especially dramatic. When results for both sexes are combined, the perceptual-speed abilities of the right-handed increase whereas the same skills in the left-handed decline.

The described differences in the cognitive abilities of groups differentiated by their handedness, gender, and generation can be discussed in terms of differences in the cerebral organization of these groups. Sinistral offspring have an advantage on tests of perceptual-speed. An argument can be made that the tests of number comparisons and pedigrees each provide more of an opportunity to use both verbal and spatial abilities simultaneously than the other tests used in this study. Subjects can approach the number comparisons test by comparing sets of numbers as assortments of different forms, with labeling reserved only for discrepancies. Finding family members on the family tree provided for reference in the pedigrees test is a spatial task, whereas discovering the meaning of the questions requires verbal analysis. Perhaps the hemispheric specialization of left-handers facilitates coordinating verbal and spatial processing. With age, however, it appears that the left-handed experience a loss in perceptual speed.

Females also scored higher in the perceptual-speed factor as well as in the verbal factor. It would seem that females and left-handers have similar cerebral organization, except that there is no sinistral spatial deficit corresponding to the apparent female spatial deficit. Consideration of processing demands posed by the spatial tests used in this study may lend insight into the hemispheric specialization of females. Proficiency in dealing with hundreds of similar meaningless forms, such as those presented in the card rotations, hidden patterns, and mental rotations tests, may rest more upon a preference for processing similar stimuli in the same manner, or the ability to take a very single-minded approach to simple problems, than upon spatial ability. Of the spatial tests used in this study, the test that used the most complex and varied forms and resembled real life tasks the most, showed the least sex-related differences. I am suggesting that it was not spatial synthetic abilities that were being measured, but rather a preference for taking a single-minded approach repetitiously. More complex spatial tasks, such as some of those in the performance section of the Weschler Adult Intelligence Scale (WAIS), do not show spatial deficits for the female population. A study involving a spatial test that requires the synthesis of fragments into recognizable wholes has shown urban females to score higher than males (Bogen, DeZure, TenHouten, & Marsh, 1972). A spatial task involving the location of dots in the visual field (Kimura, 1969) showed no sex-related difference. That females do well on the perceptual-speed tests that seem to require hemispheric interaction, on spatial-synthetic tasks, and on tests of creativity (Maccoby & Jacklin, 1974) and poorly on tasks that might seem to require unihemispheric activation suggests that females may be intra- and interhemispherically integrated.

Assuming for the moment that the difference in the spatial performance of females and left-handers can be attributed to differences in hemispheric specialization, what differentiates the cerebral organization of females and left-handers so that females but not left-handers have a spatial deficit? The hemispheric specialization of left-handers might be described as involving intrahemispheric coordination of verbal and spatial abilities with the potential for activating only one mode of processing or hemisphere at a time. This arrangement would allow enough cooperation to facilitate perceptual-speed tasks while permitting the kind of single mindedness required for proficiency on the hidden patterns, card rotations, and mental rotations tests. The hemispheric specialization of females might be seen as involving both intra- and interhemispheric integration, which could facilitate perceptual-speed tasks and the performance of complex spatial tasks. By giving females ready access to the mnemonic device described by Bowers (1970), this same interaction may contribute to the female verbal and memory factor advantages mentioned earlier.

As parents, both left-handers and females fail to show the same advantage in perceptual-speed skills seen in these groups as offspring. The interaction between handedness and generation reveals that, as the left-handed decline in perceptual-speed abilities, the right-handed improve. What age-related changes in hemispheric specialization might contribute to this shift as well as other developmental changes in cognitive abilities reported here and elsewhere?

AGE-ASSOCIATED CHANGES IN COGNITIVE ABILITIES AND HEMISPHERIC SPECIALIZATION

Let us consider some evidence for the suggestion that communication between the two hemispheres increases with age, and, like two people in constant contact, the hemispheres become more similar as time passes. Two complimentary mechanisms may be seen as contributing to this development. First, there is evidence of a relatively greater decline with increasing age in right-hemisphere abilities, if the performance section of the WAIS (Brown & Jaffe, 1975) and Cattell (1971) and Horn's (1970) "fluid" dimension of intelligence are seen as reflecting right hemisphere functions. Horn and Donaldson (1977) observed that fluid abilities are most sensitive to the influence of degeneration of the neurophysiological substratum. Additional evidence for this approach might be found in Reitan's (1957) report of a relatively greater decline with increasing age in performance on those measures of spatial functions most sensitive to the organic condition of the brain.

Second, there appears to be increasing reliance with age on left-hemisphere strategies, either in response to, or provoking right-hemisphere decline. The data supporting the idea that the right-hemisphere deteriorates with increasing age comes from studies, like this one, of the normal population of the United States. Technologically advanced countries might be said to attach great value to verbal-analytic approaches to problem solving and, by doing so, to encourage the development of left-hemisphere strategies. Whether the reported age-related decline in measures of performance and fluid intelligence is a result of a relatively greater deterioration of the right hemisphere from disuse, a product of left-hemisphere development, or a dysfunction related to the differential effect of age upon the neuronal substrate of the right hemisphere, remains to be seen.

Whatever the source of the reported eventual decline in those abilities related to the right hemisphere, I propose that communication between the two hemispheres increases with age, as does the contribution of the left hemisphere. No decline is apparent in the spatial abilities measured between parent and offspring groups (probably because the parent group is not advanced in age). Increases in the verbal abilities of all groups and the perceptual-speed abilities of right-handed males are evident. This pattern of change might suggest that the development of interhemispheric communication precedes (and perhaps precipitates) right-hemisphere decline. The previously noted parallel between the sex–generation and handedness–generation interactions on the perceptual-speed measure would suggest that the left-handed and females are similarly vulnerable to the effects of age, the latter less than the former.

It has been posited that the left-handed and females have an initial advantage on perceptual-speed tasks due to their more frequent representation of verbal and spatial abilities within both hemispheres, or greater intrahemispheric cooperation. How would the assumed age-related increase in interhemispheric communication result in a decrease in perceptual-speed abilities in the left-handed and females, and an increase in perceptual-speed abilities in right-handed males? In males, increasing interhemispheric communication may facilitate the coordination of verbal and spatial skills necessary to perceptual-speed performance. In left-handers and females, this same rise in communication may result in a decline in perceptual-speed abilities simply because additional unnecessary interhemispheric interactions take longer.

An attempt has been made to understand the complex age-related changes in cognitive abilities described here in terms of the development of hemispheric specialization. It was assumed that adolescents of both sexes and left- and right-handers do not have the same hemispheric specialization, and that age does not affect them in the same way. Based on reports of sex-related differences in cognitive abilities and the results of research utilizing more direct measures of hemispheric specialization (Dimond & Beaumont, 1974), males were assumed to have greater cerebral lateralization of cognitive abilities, and females and sinistrals were assumed to each show a cerebral organization characterized by less cognitive specialization. Given these sex and handedness group differences and a reanalysis of demands imposed by the tasks from which each factor was derived, it was concluded that there are long-term changes in hemispheric specialization. Describing these changes in terms of an increase in interhemispheric communication seems the most efficient way of accounting for the diverse effects reported.

Additional research is needed to answer questions centering around the etiology of developmental changes in cognitive abilities. Some of the cultural factors entering into the proposed relationship between the age-related changes in cognitive abilities and the inferred developmental changes in hemispheric specialization have already been mentioned. Additional sociocultural factors may also exert a substantial influence upon early development of hemispheric specialization. Demonstration of hemispheric specialization in newborns (Witelson & Pallie, 1973) does not preclude the possibility of a significant environmental contribution to the cerebral organization of even adolescents. An early sex-related difference in the degree of specialization for dichoptic spatial tasks (Witelson, 1976) might be the product of a culturally imposed lack of requisite stimulation during an early critical period. The later development of hemispheric specialization in both males and females may be greatly influenced by the cognitive demands placed upon them by their chosen occupations. People who are engaged in occupations requiring continued use of right-hemispheric functions may not manifest the patterns of development of cognitive abilities and hemispheric specialization described here.

The fact that the cognitive abilities of groups known to differ with respect to hemispheric specialization appear to change with age in different ways has been taken as support for the idea that the development of hemispheric specialization continues throughout a lifetime, and that its development differentially affects these groups. Questions have been raised about the role of sociocultural variables in the development of the initial between-group differences in hemispheric specialization and the development of hemispheric specialization within each group over time. The resolution of such questions will have bearing on the issue of how developmental changes in hemispheric specialization are related to developmental changes in cognitive abilities.

REFERENCES

Bogen, J. E., DeZure, R., TenHouten, & W. D., Marsh, J. F. The other side of the brain IV: The A/P ratio. *Bulletin of the Los Angeles Neurological Societies* 1972, *34*:191-220.
Bower, G. H. Analysis of a mnemonic device. *American Scientist*, 1970, *58*:496-510.
Brown, J. W. & Jaffe, J. Hypothesis on cerebral dominance. *Neuropsychologia*, 1975, *13*, 107-110.
Bryden, M. P. Speech lateralization in families: A preliminary study using dichotic listening. *Brain and Language*, 1975, *2*, 201-211.

Cattell, R. B. *Abilities, their structure, growth and action.* Boston, Mass.: Houghton Mifflin, 1971.

Dee, H. L. Auditory asymmetry and strength of manual preference. *Cortex,* 1971, 7, 236–245.

Dimond, S. J. & Beaumont, J. Experimental Studies of Hemisphere function in the human brain. In S. J. Dimond & J. Beaumont, (Eds.), *Hemisphere function in the human brain.* New York: Wiley, 1974.

Galin, D., Ornstein, R., Kocel, K., & Merrin E. Hemispheric localization of cognitive mode by EEG. *Psychophysiology,* 1971, 8(2), 246–247.

Goodglass, H. & Quadfasel, F. Language laterality in left-handed aphasics. *Brain,* 1954, 77, 248–251.

Harshman, R. & Remington, R. Sex, language and the brain, part I: A review of the literature on adult sex differences in lateralization. Unpublished manuscript, UCLA, 1975.

Hécaen, H. & Sauguet, J. Cerebral dominance in left handed subjects. *Cortex,* 1971, 7, 19–48.

Horn, J. L. & Donaldson, G. Faith is not enough. A response to the Baltes-Schaie claim that intelligence does not wane. *American Psychologist,* 1977, 32(5) 369–373.

Horn, J. L. Organization of data on life span development of human abilities. In L. R. Goulet, & P. B. Baltes (Eds.), *Life span developmental psychology: theory and research,* New York: Academic Press, 1970.

Kimura, D. Cerebral dominance and the perception of verbal stimuli. *Canadian Journal of Psychology,* 1961, 15, 166–171.

Kimura, D. Spatial localization in left and right visual fields. *Canadian Journal Psychology,* 1969, 23, 445–458.

Kocel, K. M. 1977. Cognitive abilities: Handedness, familial sinistrality and sex. *Annals of the New York Academy of Sciences,* 1977, 299, 233–243.

Lake, D. A. & Bryden, M. P. Handedness and sex differences in hemispheric asymmetry. *Brain and Language,* 1976, 3, 266–282.

Lansdell, H. Sex differences in hemispheric asymmetries of the human brain. *Nature,* 1964, 203, 550.

Molfese, D. L., Freeman, R. B., & Palermo, D. S. The ontogeny of brain lateralization for speech and nonspeech stimuli. *Brain and Language,* 1975, 2, 356–368.

Maccoby, E. E. & Jacklin, C. M. *The psychology of sex differences.* Stanford, Calif.: Stanford University Press, 1974.

Reitan, R. M. Differential reaction of various psychological tests to age. *Proceedings of the Fourth Congress of the International Association of Gerontology.* 1957, 4, 158–165.

Wilson, J. R., DeFries, J. C., McClearn, G. E., Vandenberg, S. G., Johnson, R. C., & Rashad, M. N. Cognitive abilities: Use of family data as a control to assess sex and age differences in two ethnic groups. *International Journal of Aging and Human Development.* 1975, 6(3), 261–276.

Witelson, S. F. Sex and the single hemisphere: specialization of the right hemisphere for spatial processing. *Science,* 1976, 193, 425–427.

Witelson, S. F. & Pallie, W. Left hemisphere specialization for language in the newborn: Anatomical evidence for asymmetry. *Brain,* 96,, 641–646.

15

Which Hand Is the "Eye" of the Blind?— A New Look at an Old Question[1]

LAUREN JULIUS HARRIS

INTRODUCTION

Long before braille was invented, alphabets for the blind typically consisted of embossed characters, exemplifying different simplications of print
letters. In early nineteenth-century France, the system in widest use was
one devised by Valentin Hauy, a pioneer in education for the blind. This
was the system favored at the Paris School for the Blind (founded by Hauy)
when Louis Braille first enrolled there as a student in 1819. Braille was then
10-years-old, and blind since an accident 6 years earlier. Like other pupils,
Braille found Hauy's system cumbersome and difficult. To be readable, the
single letters had to be so large that each was embossed on a separate card,
making the letters so far apart in the composition that the blind "reader"
could not do much more than spell out the words. Even setting up the letter
cards took so long that most blind people refused to use them.

Some years before Braille came to Paris, an engineer and cavalry officer

[1] Expanded text of a paper presented at a symposium, "The sinistral mind," J. Herron, Chm.
San Francisco, Calif., March 3–4, 1977. Portions of the research results reported here also
were presented by the author and by Nancy M. Wagner and Jean Wilkinson at the Fourth An-
nual Meeting of the International Neuropsychology Society, Toronto, 4 Feb., 1976, and at the
XXIst International Congress on Psychology, Paris, 20 July, 1976, and, with the further col-
laboration of Richard Feinberg, at the 17th Annual Meeting of the Psychonomic Society, St.
Louis, Mo., 12 Nov., 1976. The research reported in this chapter was supported, in part, by
All-University grants from Michigan State University and by the National Institute of Mental
Health (grant 5T32MH14622).

NEUROPSYCHOLOGY
OF LEFT-HANDEDNESS

by the name of Charles Barbier (1767–1841) had made what was to be, for Braille, a critical discovery. Barbier, a veteran of the Napoleonic wars, did not have the needs of the blind in mind. He wanted instead to design a ciphering code to be used in the dark of the battlefield for the transmission of secret intelligence. A tactual code was the obvious choice, and among all the embossed script systems available at the time, square letters seemed to be the simplest forms. Barbier thought to retain only the characteristic corner points of the square letters, to separate these points more widely, and to omit the nonessential middle points. The letters now looked so different that, according to one account (Ross, 1951, pp. 127–128), Barbier saw that the conventional letters could be replaced by arbitrary combinations of 12 points, or dots, in a cluster. In this way, Barbier developed what he called "ecriture nocturne," or "night-script." He described his system in 1808 and at the same time introduced the slate and stylus, which are still in use today.

By 1815, after the war, Barbier's dots found a popular new use in Paris as a kind of parlor game. Then in 1820, at the suggestion of teachers of the blind, Barbier tried his system at the Paris School for the Blind. Evidently only Louis Braille, now 11 years old, was impressed with its possibilities. Later, while still in his teens and now a teacher at the school, he tried it with his own students and observed how much better a medium for touch the dot was over the embossed print system of Hauy's.

Braille brilliantly recognized and corrected several problems: Barbier's system required the use of a cipher (a bad complication for the blind), was phonetic rather than alphabetic, and took up far too much space when written. However, the major fault was that the basic grouping of 12 dots was too large for the span of the finger tips, and Braille finally devised the simple arithmetical arrangement used today—combinations of one to five dots within an array of six equally spaced positions, three high by two wide, called the braille cell. By 1834, Braille had worked out his system in detail and had proved its usefulness to other domains including music and mathematics.

The new alphabet did not win instant approval. For instance, sighted teachers of the blind objected that they themselves would have to learn braille, either visually or tactually (Foulke, 1974). Resistance finally broke down, and braille rapidly gained in popularity, after it was first shown, in the 1860s, that braille not only could be read far more easily than embossed letters, but that the latter could scarcely be read at all. Sadly, Louis Braille died in 1852, too early to see his alphabet come into wide use.

However superior braille is to the older systems, it is far slower than the *visual* reading of print. An experienced, high-school braille reader can read about 100 words/min. as compared with rates of 250–300 words/min. for sighted students. Consequently, from Braille's own time to the current day, there have been attempts to improve the efficiency of braille. For example, fast and slow readers have been compared in hopes of identifying important differences in style; the braille patterns have been analyzed for legibility; new "contracted" spellings have been devised; and new more efficient ways to display braille have been studied. In 1929, an American psychologist, Josephine M. Smith, addressed the question of increasing the speed of braille reading in yet another way, one of special interest for the psychology of handedness. In reading braille, should the child use the two hands together or one hand in preference to another? Or as Smith asked, "Which hand is the 'eye' of the blind?"

To Smith's contemporaries, the answer to her question probably seemed obvious at first consideration. They knew that in right-handers, then, as now, constituting about 90% of the population, the right hand (RH) is the master hand, and that the left hand (LH), by comparison, is ineffectual. The left hand's lesser status was even promoted as a social goal. In Europe in the early 1900s it was believed, as a writer of that time remarked, that "One of the signs which distinguish a well-brought-up child is that its left hand has become incapable of any independent action [Hertz, 1973, p. 5]." (Also see Harris, Chapter 1 of this volume.)

By the 1920s, the reason for RH dominance was widely accepted as neurological, notwithstanding the implication in the quotation above that LH skill is actively suppressed. The reason is that in both medical and educational circles, the left hemisphere of the brain was recognized as dominant for the important intellectual functions, including speech and language. Furthermore, a strong relationship between handedness and cerebral specialization was acknowledged after Broca, in 1865, had identified an anatomical structure in the left frontal lobe that he believed underlay speech functions. For braille, then, it is understandable, as Graseman (1917) noted, that "the right index finger was traditionally regarded as the reading finger, whereas the left was presumed to have only the function of looking for the following line at the proper time, in order to avoid an interruption of the reading at the transition to the next line [p. 67]."[2]

HAND ASYMMETRIES IN BRAILLE READING: EARLY STUDIES

Although there would have been every reason for early investigators to have considered the question of hand dominance for braille in neuropsychological terms, the fact is they did not. One reason may be that from

[2] I am grateful to Suzanne Corkin (Department of Psychology, Massachusetts Institute of Technology) for providing a translation of parts of this paper.

the outset, anecdotal reports and empirical studies challenged the conventional wisdom by suggesting that the LH did more than just "look for the following line at the proper time." For instance, a German investigator proposed a more nearly equal division of labor, with each hand having its own function—the LH for slow, analyzing exploration, the RH to furnish the picture of the whole word or phrase (Heller, 1904; cited in Smith, 1929, p. 220). Harmon, an English surgeon, noted an important LH role during writing and reading:

> The writing is done from right to left; the right hand holds the tool which impresses the paper, whilst the left hand guides the point into the marks on the guiding frame; when the writing is complete the writer withdraws the paper, reverses it, and reads the embossed characters, feeling with both hands from left to right. Often I have noticed the left hand running on to the beginning of the succeeding line whilst the right hand was feeling out the finish of the line above. Was bimanual division of labour ever more surprising! [1905, p. 16]

Other early writers went a radical step further, hinting that the LH role, rather than being secondary or even equal to the right, was actually primary. A blind writer (Javel, 1904, cited in Critchley, 1953) commented on the effects of prolonged reading sessions on changes in the sensitivity of his finger-tips, saying that "when I have read much, the dots feel like wool to the right index finger, but, on the contrary, like points to the left [p. 26]." Chlumetzky, another blind reader, also was aware of a hand difference but discounted it:

> It is true that my left index finger, when carried over whole phrases, is able to perceive these more rapidly and more easily than the right finger; however, the degree of this difference is very insignificant. Further, the right finger also is suitable for the recognition of single letters. But the distinction between the use of the two hands is never of any practical value with me . . . I value my reading fingers equally [1918; quoted in Smith, 1929, p. 220].

The strongest challenge to the notion of a right-handed superiority came in German research in the 1920s. These studies indicated that although two-hand braille reading was fastest, usually less additional time was needed for the LH alone than for the RH alone. One researcher concluded that "the right index finger can by no means be regarded as the proper reading finger, but rather the left," and therefore declared that "the teacher should, especially in the beginning of reading instruction, put the left forefinger on the script [Grasemann, quoted in Smith, 1929, p. 221]."

Notwithstanding the aforementioned reports, the early evidence was far from conclusive, and even seemed to divide along national lines: Villey, in 1931, contrasted the German studies that supported the superiority of the

LH with studies in the United States showing that most *good* readers used the RH, and suggested that the differences may be the result of differences in method of instruction rather than in hand dominance as such. If teachers of the blind were aware of any of these reports, they evidently came out on the side of caution, either favoring the use of both hands or the RH alone (Smith, 1929, 1933). The view is mostly the same today (Lowenfeld, Abel, & Hatlen, 1969).

In 1953, the possibility of LH superiority was raised again, now evidently for the first time by a neurologist. McDonald Critchley (1953) wrote that "in many blind persons, the master finger is exclusively one-sided, though well-taught braillists should be able to read with either index finger. Even so, there is always a manual preference, the hand of choice reading faster than the other [p. 21]." Critchley went on to report that "in nearly three quarters of bi-manual braille readers, the left hand is the one preferred [p. 21]." Two cases were mentioned: a 31-year-old-man, blind since the age of 5, who was a "particularly skilled and rapid braillist, who always used the left hand for reading [p. 31]"; and a 45-year-old man, blind since the age of 7, who when he used his "right or unaccustomed forefinger . . ." read a line in 40 sec compared to 12 sec for the left forefinger. Critchley himself recognized that the LH superiority was incompatible with neuropsychological evidence, and therefore said only that "most blind persons . . . prefer to use the one hand rather than another for braille reading, and this has little to do with the question of ordinary cerebral dominance [1953, p. 26]."

Early Explanations

If Critchley saw the neuropsychological evidence as irrelevant to the question of hand asymmetries in braille reading, there nevertheless were other attempts to explain the apparent reversal in hand skill. For example, many supposed that the LH is preferred for reading braille because, as Smith (1929) put it, it is free "from the toughness which characterizes the more frequently used right hand. . . . The left hands of most right-handed persons are more delicate—less callous—than the right hands [p. 279]." Except that if this were so, as Villey (1931) pointed out, the calloused fingers of basket weavers and other manual workers should be less suitable for tactile reading than the fingers of "intellectuals"—and they were not. Most writers therefore accepted Smith's (1933) conclusion that, "the reading finger of the blind person becomes toughened but does not lose its sensitiveness because of this fact [p. 280]."

Still other explanations were suggested. Smith summarized the views of German investigators. They proposed that, because braille is read from left to right, the left hand becomes the follower, and so it "might have been better trained in making final decisions [Smith, 1929, p. 223]," whereas, the RH "skims" ahead, since its progress is never obstructed by the LH (Smith, 1929). The LH also would gain practice because of the distribution of work during braille writing with the slate and stylus. Harmon (1905), quoted earlier, described how, when the writing is complete, the writer reads the characters with both hands. My students and I also have noticed that *before* the writing is complete, the progress of the work often is checked with the LH alone so that the stylus, held in the RH, need not be put down.

Smith proposed that the hand difference had little to do with practice or the presence of calluses, but lay in a more fundamental asymmetry in hand function: The LH was better at sensory functions, the RH at motor functions. To support this position, she cited a report by Bowman (1928), who, speaking of the operation of putting pegs on a board, said that in most right-handers, the RH is more "skillful in feeding." Smith explained that the phrase, "skillful in feeding," is the equivalent of "skillful as a sensory organ."

> In the operation of pegging, the work is so divided that while the right hand is doing the actual pegging on the board—motor activity—the left hand is holding the pegs and handing them to the right hand just where they are needed—sensory activity. The fact that in the "feeding" movement the left hand of the right-handed person is, according to Miss Bowman, more skillful than the right hand, indicates that the left hand is naturally more readily used for sensory activity, the right hand being needed for the motor activity of the real pegging, which is *controlled by the visual sense* [Smith, 1929, p. 244, emphasis in original].[3]

Smith offered further support for this interpretation in studies of hand specialization in formboard manipulation (1933, 1934). Here she made an important new point that, as we shall see, comes close to a contemporary analysis:

> The most probable explanation for the preference of the nonpreferred motor hand in sensory functions is that whatever causes handedness in the sense of motor preference also causes handedness in the sense of sensory preference. The sensory preference is not the result of motor preference . . . but is a concurrent and causally independent phenomenon [1933, pp. 281–282].

[3] Many years before, E. H. Weber, in his classic *Der Tastsinn und das Gemeingefühl* [On the sense of touch and common sensibility] (1846), had observed that things lifted with the LH seemed heavier, and that sensory discriminations (especially tactile) were finer on the left side of the body. Wilhelm Wundt, among others, spoke of the left side as passive and sensory, the right side as active and motor (cited in Hall & Hartwell, 1884, p. 94).

Recent Research

After Critchley's (1953) paper, the question of hand differences in braille reading was not raised again until 1971. At this time, a letter was published in *Nature* by Beata Hermelin and Neal O'Connor (1971a), two psychologists engaged in research on perceptually handicapped children. In the course of their work, they chanced to observe a right-handed blind boy who had hurt his left hand, which he called his "reading hand." He said he could not read with his RH and indeed could not when put to test.[4] Curious and skeptical, Hermelin and O'Connor tested 16 more children, all blind from birth. Fourteen were right-handed, and two were apparently bidextrous. Each child was asked to read simple sentences with the index finger and middle finger separately, for each hand. For the group, LH scores were significantly faster than RH scores. Only two children, both right-handers, read faster with their RH fingers.

When the measure was number of errors, the over-all hand differences were not significant, though marginally so for the middle finger, perhaps because it was the less-practiced finger. In certain cases, the difference in accuracy was striking: Some children, although fluent LH readers, could produce only gibberish when they read with the RH. Because of the possible confounding influences of the direction of reading and of writing practices, Hermelin and O'Connor (1971b) carried out a new test with random orderings of braille alphabet letters arranged vertically and read from top to bottom. The subjects were 15 blind adults, 25–65-years-old. Again, significantly fewer errors were made with the LH.

BRAILLE READING AND
RIGHT-HEMISPHERE FUNCTIONS

Like Critchley (1953) before them, Hermelin and O'Connor saw the inconsistency between their findings and the prediction of RH superiority based on the neuropsychological evidence. But where Critchley had implied that the asymmetry found was not explicable in terms of cerebral specialization, Hermelin and O'Connor suggested a different characterization of braille reading, putting emphasis this time on the right hemisphere instead of the left.

Where the left hemisphere is important for language and sequential

---

[4] A recent magazine story reports another and poignant instance: Hal Krents, a blind lawyer who was the subject of the Broadway play and film, "Butterflies are free," was reported to have contracted encephalitis, "triggering a stroke . . . that partially paralyzed his left side, including his Braille-reading hand" [Ward, 1977, p. 52]. The story did not mention, however, whether Krents is left- or right-handed.

analytic processing, the right hemisphere is specialized for nonlinguistic, spatial, wholistic processing. For example, tachistoscopically projected Roman letters are better discriminated by adult subjects when projected to the right visual hemifield (left cerebral hemisphere), whereas random dot patterns are better discriminated when projected to the left hemifield, or right cerebral hemisphere (Kimura, 1966). In this demonstration, Hermelin and O'Connor saw a clue. Noting the similarity of these spatially and numerically arranged permutations of dots to braille, they proposed that braille characters, though symbols of alphabet letters, nevertheless are treated "as spatial items, to be analyzed by the right hemisphere before or while verbal coding of the material takes place in the left [Hermelin & O'Connor, 1971b, p. 434]." Hermelin and O'Connor are not more explicit than this, but presumably, they mean that when the LH feels the braille characters, the spatial information is directly accessible to the right hemisphere which analyzes it (efficiently), and then the information is transferred to the left hemisphere where it is named. But when the RH feels the braille characters, the spatial information is directly accessible only to the left hemisphere which analyzes it less efficiently. The right hemisphere comes in only through the weaker ipsilateral connections, or after the information is passed across the corpus callosum. In either case, the information obtained by the RH is processed less efficiently than the information obtained by the LH.

Why had an explanation like this not occurred to earlier researchers? (As we saw, Josephine Smith came close, though she never put her analysis in neurological terms.) I think the reason is that even as late as the 1940s and early 1950s, the prevailing view of cerebral specialization gave to the left hemisphere not just language but *all* the important intellectual functions. The right hemisphere was regarded as merely a mute, less competent version of the left, with no special functions of its own. The few early dissenting voices, pre-eminently that of the English neurologist J. Hughlings Jackson (1874, 1876), were hardly noticed amid the clamor of interest in left-brain dominance (Benton, 1972; Harris, 1975). So on neurological grounds, an inferior status for the LH would have been implied for practically all important tasks, and the reported LH superiority might well have seemed paradoxical even as late as 1953 when Critchley's paper appeared. Hermelin and O'Connor's explanation, therefore, is attractive because it incorporates a more contemporary understanding of lateral cerebral functions. Nevertheless, other questions remain to be addressed. In the remainder of this chapter, I shall summarize the results of new experiments that students and I have carried out since 1976 at Michigan State University.

EXPERIMENT 1: BLIND SUBJECTS

First, we were sufficiently impressed with Hermelin and O'Connor's report, particularly the dramatic mention of children who could produce only "gibberish" when required to read with the RH, that we wanted to see for ourselves whether similar cases would appear in a new sample of blind individuals. The first experiment was conducted by Jean Wilkinson (1978). The subjects were 27 blind students, 10- to 20-years-old (14 boys, 13 girls), at the Lansing (Michigan) School for the Blind. Most had been premature babies and blind from early infancy, the result of retrolental fibroplasia from pure-oxygen environments. For most students, braille instruction began at 6- to 8-years-of-age. Teaching methods varied, but no emphasis evidently had been placed on either hand, contrary to what reportedly is recent practice (Lowenfeld *et al.*, 1969). All the students were right-handed according to a questionnaire based on the Edinburgh Inventory.

Before administering the reading tests, Wilkinson tried to learn whether the students themselves were aware of having a hand preference for reading irrespective of their handedness. The students therefore were asked to read a *column* of randomly ordered letters however they thought they could do it most efficiently. Five students used both hands (i.e., both index fingers), 10 used the right index finger, and 12 used the left. So here already was an indication that the "reading finger" was not always the right for these right-handed students.

All the students normally used their index fingers, sometimes alone and sometimes with the middle fingers assuming a secondary role. Therefore, the reading test was conducted with the left and right *middle* fingers alone to help control for previous practice. The test required reading 24 brief paragraphs from fifth-grade reading comprehension tests used in the school. A 300-sec maximum time was allowed for each paragraph. The fifth-grade test was chosen so that it would not be beyond the level of the youngest child (a 10-year-old fifth-grader.)

The paragraphs were presented in left-finger–right-finger alternation by groups of three paragraphs. Half the paragraphs were read aloud, the remaining paragraphs silently. Each paragraph asked a question about its contents that the student answered aloud in each case. All students were highly accurate, provided they could read the paragraphs in the time allotted. The hand asymmetries noted were primarily in speed scores, so only these scores will be reported.

The data are presented graphically in Figure 15.1 for each reading condition. The left half of the figure shows mean reading-time scores for the first half (6 paragraphs, 3 per hand) of each condition. Note that those 12

BLIND STUDENTS

READING SILENTLY

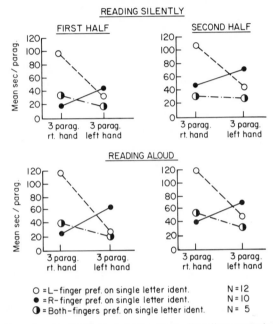

O = L–finger pref. on single letter ident.   N = 12
● = R– finger pref. on single letter ident.   N = 10
◑ = Both–fingers pref. on single letter ident.   N = 5

Figure 15.1 Experiment 1, blind right-handers. Reading speeds on paragraphs shown according to subjects' preferred finger on single-letter identification pretest (Wilkinson, 1978).

students who preferred to use their left index finger on the single-letter identification task now averaged nearly 100 sec per paragraph on the three paragraphs read with the middle finger of the RH, and only 40 sec per paragraph for the three paragraphs read with the LH—and roughly the same magnitude difference during the second half, and in both parts of the reading-aloud condition. The differences were statistically significant in all instances ($p < .0006$). Of these students, several were not simply slower with the right finger, but, like some of Hermelin and O'Connor's subjects, almost incapable of reading at all. The right-finger-preferrers also read faster with their RH than with their LH, but the difference was smaller and not significant (averaging across both halves of the two conditions, $p = .258$). Finally, the five students who preferred both fingers for single-letter identification read about equally as fast with either hand on the paragraphs tests, averaging across both halves of the two conditions. Wilkinson also had the students read columns of random sequences of individual alphabet letters. The results were consistent with the paragraph-reading test.

These results, therefore, suggest a qualification to Hermelin and O'Connor's findings, namely, that among right-handed blind students, the LH advantage is clearest among those whose preferred finger (for reading individual letters) is the *left* index finger. However, hand advantage is not merely a product of initial finger preference, since there was not an equally strong RH advantage for students whose preferred finger was the right index finger.

HAND ASYMMETRIES IN SIGHTED SUBJECTS

If the results so far support an interpretation in terms of hemispheric specialization, we cannot rule out the possible role of a blind reader's experience with a left-to-right directed alphabet. Even the tests of the less-practiced middle finger on vertical, random orderings of alphabet letters could only have diminished, but not eliminated, the effect of any LH advantage that may accrue from prior experience because such an advantage surely could generalize to new testing situations. A more convincing test would be to see whether the same kind of hand difference appears when braille is taught to sighted subjects who are unfamiliar with braille. Smith (1929) carried out such a test. The subject was a female (of unspecified age and handedness) who was asked to learn sequences of braille letters and two- and three-letter words, in both left-to-right and right-to-left directions. The result was that the LH was superior over-all, although the direction of scan also played a role in that the over-all left-to-right scores were superior to the right-to-left scores.

Little, of course, can be concluded from a demonstration with one subject. More recently, however, Rudel, Denckla, and Spalten (1974) tested 80 7–14-year-old right-handed children. Each child had to learn six braille letters with one hand and six different letters with the other, in a paired associates procedure. Half the children were trained to use the LH first, half the RH. A LH advantage was found, but this depended on the age and sex of the children. At ages 7–8, boys did equally well with either hand, whereas the girls' RH scores were superior. The LH advantage was significant by age 11 for boys but only by age 13 for girls. Furthermore, the girls did about as well with their RH whether it was tested first or second, but their LH scores far exceeded the RH scores when the LH was tested second, and were much worse than the RH scores when tested first. The boys' LH performance was more stable and fluctuated less than RH performance over the two testing orders.

If braille symbols are first encoded as spatial configurations so as to bestow a LH advantage, as Hermelin and O'Connor propose, then the

Rudel *et al.* results suggest that this kind of spatial-configurational processing comes into play earlier and more reliably in boys than girls. Rudel *et al.*
suggest two reasons: Girls develop more slowly than boys in the performance of right-hemispheric-dependent tasks, or girls depend more than
boys on language (i.e., left-hemisphere) strategies in complex discrimination–learning tasks. With respect to the hand–testing-order interaction for
girls, Rudel *et al.*, therefore, suggested that prior training with the RH
helped or "prepared" the LH because RH use activates verbal strategies.[5]
There is indeed evidence that verbal strategies are more likely to be relied
on by females than by males in complex spatial discrimination tasks (see
review by Harris, 1978) and that females have an advantage in using verbally encoded material in information-processing tasks (Majeres, 1977).

Because of the Rudel *et al.* results, Wilkinson checked for sex-related differences in his study of blind subjects. The margin of LH superiority did
prove to be greater in the males than in the females, but the difference was
not statistically significant and, in any case, was confounded with subject
age and initial hand preference.

EXPERIMENT 2: SIGHTED SUBJECTS,
MASSED LEFT-RIGHT TRIALS

The hand–sex interaction in the Rudel *et al.* study with sighted subjects
indicated that a further test of sighted subjects was needed, but over a
larger age range than Rudel *et al.* had used. This was necessary so that we
could see whether the results with children would stabilize in adults. To do
this, Nancy Wagner (1977) tested 96 normal, sighted children, an equal
number of boys and girls from third grade, fifth grade, and eighth grade.
She also tested 32 college students—16 men and 16 women. All were right

---

[5] This proposal is consistent with Kinsbourne's (1970, 1973) model for the analysis of
laterality effects in terms of "attentional sets" induced by the nature of the task or response
method. Lateral asymmetries usually are explained as direct manifestations of better
discrimination of linguistic and nonlinguistic stimuli by the left and right hemispheres, respectively (e.g., Kimura, 1973). Kinsbourne suggests, instead, that the effects are an indirect product of postexposural lateral shifts of attention in a direction contralateral to the hemisphere activated in solution of the problem—that is, to the left when a spatial stimulus has been
presented and to the right for linguistic stimuli. Therefore, when the task or response method
favors processing in one hemisphere, that hemisphere is activated, turning attention to the opposite side, and, at the same time, inhibiting activation of the other hemisphere. In a braille-
learning task, it therefore might be easier initially to establish a left-hemispheric "verbal set,"
but once the verbal aspects of the tasks are mastered, a right-hemispheric spatial set would be
more effective. The implication is that the RH first testing order would be the more advantageous.

handed as determined by a questionnaire.[6] Each subject had to learn the names of 6 2- to 4-dot letters with each hand (for third-graders, this number was reduced to 4 in an attempt to make the tasks of roughly equivalent difficulty across the subject groups). The design was a Latin square, counter-balancing for school grade, sex of subject, particular subsets of letters assigned to each hand, and hand testing order. Following the procedure of Rudel et al. (1974), half the subjects had all the LH trials first, the remaining subjects had all the RH trials first. The third-graders had 40 trials per hand and the older subjects had 60 trials per hand (longer sessions proved arduous for the younger children).

Letter names were assigned to subsets so as to obtain a fairly even distribution of the first (possibly overlearned) letters of the alphabet, to avoid acoustically similar names in the same subset, and to have an equal number of 2-, 3-, and 4-dot letters in each subset. (To meet these criteria, most of the letters had to be changed slightly in design so that, strictly speaking, they were braille-like, not braille, letters.) The braille letters were typed, with a braille typewriter, on ordinary playing cards. The cards were placed into metal slots, close enough so that the subject's left and right *index* fingers—the fingers used in the experiment—were each, respectively, about 7.6 cm to the left and right of body midline. The subject could see neither his hands nor the cards. The children were given 4 sec, the college students 3 sec, to feel each pattern, after which the experimenter called for the letter name, using a standard correction procedure (i.e., the experimenter gave the correct name after every trial, whatever the subject's response).

Multivariate ANOVA of the mean percentage of correct responses per trial block for the four school grades disclosed significant improvement across trials for all grades ($p < .001$). The performance of older subjects was better over-all than younger subjects ($p < .06$), and there was significantly better performance by the LH ($p < .0002$) across all school grades. The margin of LH superiority, however, was very small—for the third-grade, fifth-grade, eighth-grade, and college groups, it was 13.1%, 2.6%, 4.2%, and 14.4%, respectively. The hand effect, however, varied depending on whether the LH trials preceded or followed the RH trials, as Rudel et al. (1974) found. This interaction ($p < .0001$) is illustrated in Figure 15.2. In nearly all groups, performance was better for the second hand tested, suggesting a "learning to learn" effect, and this effect was

[6] The third- and fifty-graders were called right-handed if they performed at least four of five common actions with the RH (pointing to a picture, drawing a circle, cutting a piece of paper, throwing a ball, and screwing the lid of a jar; Annett, 1970 a), as well as by teacher's designation. Handedness of the eighth-graders and college students was determined by a 12-item questionnaire (Annett, 1970 b).

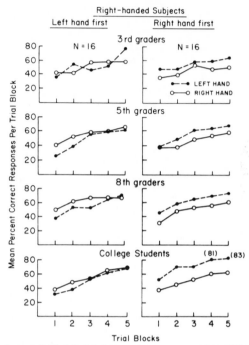

Figure 15.2 Experiment 2. Sighted right-handers, massed LH, RH trials. Mean percent correct responses per trial block for each hand according to school grade and hand testing order (Wagner, 1977).

strongly and significantly asymmetrical. The left side of Figure 15.2 shows the scores, for each hand, for those subjects in each grade whose LH trials came first. Except for the third-graders, for whom the LH remained slightly (4.1%) better over-all, in every case the RH was barely and not significantly superior (ranging from 13.3% for first-graders, to 12.8% for eighth-graders, to 8.5% for college students). Note, too, that for the fifth- and eighth-graders, the LH and RH were equal by the end of training.

On the right side of Figure 15.2 are the scores for those subjects whose LH trials came after the RH trials. Here, the LH scores were significantly and substantially better by margins for the youngest to oldest groups of 23.6%, 19.2%, 23.9%, and 37.3%, respectively.

With respect to the question of sex-related differences, the analyses disclosed no main effects of sex ($F = 1.02$), and in contrast to the Rudel *et al.* (1974) results, no interactions involving sex (all $Fs \leq 1.1$) were found. The previously described test order–hand interaction is the same for both males and females for the four age groups combined (see Figure 15.3). These, however, are *group* results. When Wagner considered individual subjects, she found that LH superiority was more frequent for boys than girls among the *youngest* subjects (i.e., 8-year-olds). Of the 16 8-year-old

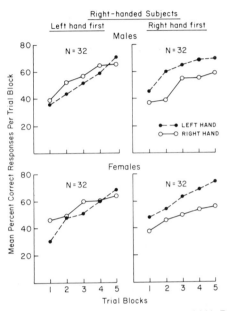

Figure 15.3 Experiment 2. Sighted right-handers, massed LH, RH trials. Mean percent correct responses per trial block for each hand according to sex-of-subject and hand testing order (Wagner, 1977).

boys, 12 had higher LH scores, two were even, and 2 had higher RH scores. Of the 16 girls, only 6 had higher LH scores, 1 was even, and 9 had higher RH scores. As a further check, Wagner computed a mean laterality coefficient for each grade–sex group that was designed to be independent of overall accuracy (Marshall, Caplan, & Holmes, 1975). With testing orders combined, the coefficients for males indicated a strong LH superiority for the third-graders, a slight RH superiority for the fifth-graders, and LH superiority of increasing strength from the eighth-grade to college level. In contrast, a LH superiority for females was clearly evident only among the college students. So these differences, although not strong enough to yield the implied sex–hand–age interaction in the analysis of variance, are at least weakly consistent with the Rudel *et al.* (1974) findings.

EXPERIMENT 3: SIGHTED SUBJECTS, ALTERNATING LEFT-RIGHT TRIALS

The finding that for the group scores, LH superiority appeared only when the LH trials followed the RH trials, suggests that LH superiority depends on prior, massed RH practice. Will the LH advantage appear only under these conditions? To find out, Wagner and I performed a third experiment with 40 different right-handed college students. Each received a different 4-letter subset to each hand, but this time we alternated the LH and RH tests trial-by-trial. The results are summarized in Figure 15.4.

Analysis of variance for repeated measures again disclosed a significant main effect of trial block ($p < .001$), and also a significant hand effect ($p < .001$). For both men and women, LH performance was superior, at least by the beginning of the second trial block and thereafter. The trial block effect merely reflects the improvement across trials. The only interaction was sex–trial block ($p < .001$), apparently resulting from slight differences in the shapes of the acquisition curves. But at least from Trial Block 2 on, the margin of LH superiority was approximately equal in each trial block for both sexes. These results show that the laterality effect is not tied to the massing of LH and RH trials with the presumptive establishment of an attentional bias (see Footnote 6, p. 314). Some kind of direct, "structural" explanation, taking account of the preferential access of the LH to the right hemisphere, also must be considered (Kimura, 1973).

EXPERIMENT 4: LEFT-HANDERS, MASSED LEFT-RIGHT TRIALS

Our results thus far largely agree with earlier reports in indicating that the LH is not only capable of independent action but, for certain intellec-

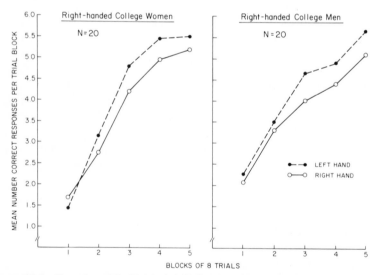

Figure 15.4 Experiment 3. Sighted right-handers, alternating LH, RH trials. Mean percent correct responses per trial block for each hand according to sex of subject.

tual skills, is the right hand's superior. This much can be said for the right-handed person. But what about that 10% of the population whose LH is the dominant hand? In fact, left-handers can provide a further check on the Hermelin and O'Connor hypothesis inasmuch as left-handers are known to represent a variation from the "standard" lateral specialization pattern. The variation once was believed to be simply a mirror-reversal of the typical ($\approx$ 98%) right-hander's pattern of left-hemispheric dominance for language (see Harris, Chapter 1 of this volume). In that case we might expect left-handers to learn braille letters more quickly with the RH than with the LH, and by about the same margin as the LH margin found in right-handers. The current view of left-handers, however, is that about two-thirds of them are left-dominant for language, but that the extent of lateral separation of functions is less in the individual case (Goodglass & Quadfasel, 1954). This, presumably, is why in a variety of both clinical and experimental neuropsychological tests, left-handers usually show smaller lateral asymmetry effects than right-handers show. We therefore might expect left-handers to show absolutely smaller hand differences in braille learning, or even no hand difference at all.

Another earlier belief about left-handers is that they were intellectually inferior to right-handers; for example, the incidence of left-handedness was found to be raised in various clinical populations (see Harris, Chapter 1 of this volume). Current research, however, finds no evidence of intellectual inferiority in left-handers compared with right-handers when nonclinical populations are sampled (cf. Hardwyck, Petrinovich, & Goldman, 1976; Harris, Thompson, & Crano, in preparation). We therefore were interested in comparing left-handers and right-handers in overall performance on the braille-learning task.

The literature on braille, for the most part, has ignored the question of handedness, and what hints there are about handedness differences are inconclusive. For instance, in the survey mentioned earlier (Lowenfeld et al., 1969), more than half the teachers of the blind reported giving consideration to left-handed pupils when encouraging hand usage for braille reading, though what this actually means in practice is not clear from the report. As for tests of sighted subjects, at least two investigators have taken handedness into account. Merry (1931) gave two sighted college students a few hours of practice in learning braille, allowing them to use "any finger or fingers for reading which they chose, the only restriction being that they adhere to a certain method once it was adopted [p. 408]." One of the students was left-handed, the other right-handed, but both students used the left forefinger alone for reading, the right-hander saying that his LH was "more sensitive" (Merry, 1931, p. 408).

Smith (1934) also repeated her 1929 test with two sighted adults, one left-handed, one right-handed. In contrast to Merry's finding, in both subjects the *non*preferred hand was superior. In neither case was the margin of hand difference considered.

To measure handedness differences in sighted subjects unfamiliar with braille, Wagner and I tested 48 left-handed undergraduates—24 men and 24 women. The procedure was identical to Wagner's original study, with half the subjects receiving the LH trials first, and half the RH trials first. The results are shown in Figure 15.5

Consistent with the performance of left-handers in other tests of lateral asymmetry, our left-handed subjects, as a group, showed no over-all hand superiority. Like the right-handers, however, there was a significant hand testing-order effect, with performance better for the second hand tested, although as the absence of an overall hand difference implies, the interaction was symmetrical. That is, the RH profited as much from following the LH (LH-first condition) as the LH profited from following the RH (RH-first condition), and this was equally true for both sexes. If the interpretation of the hand testing order effect suggested earlier is correct, then in these left-handers, strategies were equally strongly activated by prior training with

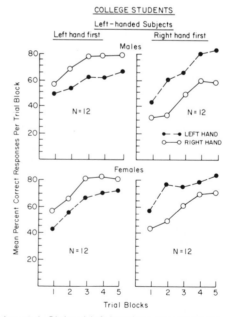

Figure 15.5 Experiment 4. Sighted left-handers, massed trials. Mean percent correct responses per trial block according to sex of subject LH, RH.

either hand. We also found no differences in over-all performance between the left-handers and the right-handed adults in the earlier studies.

EXPERIMENT 5: LEFT-HANDERS, ALTERNATING LEFT-RIGHT TRIALS

Again, because of the hand–testing-order effect, we wondered what would happen with trial-by-trial LH–RH alternation. In Figure 15.6, the results for 24 additional left-handed university students (12 men and 12 women) are compared with a new group of 24 right-handers. These are data collected by Richard Feinberg (1979).

Of the right-handers, both sexes again did significantly better with the LH, but this time the hand difference emerged only at the fourth trial block. (In the men, the RH actually led through the third trial block, though not significantly.) For the left-handers, the figure shows the predicted *absence* of hand difference, but this time only for the men. The left-handed women showed overall RH superiority, with the hand difference appearing only in

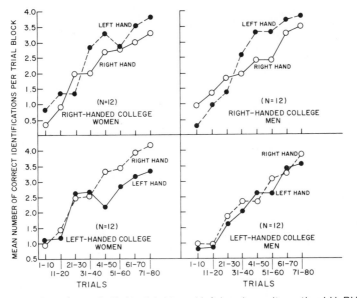

Figure 15.6 Experiment 5. Sighted right- and left-handers, alternating LH, RH trials. Mean percent correct responses per trial block according to sex of subject (Feinberg, 1979).

the latter trials, as it had for the right-handers. However, with no indication of a similar sex-related difference in our first study of left-handers, and
with only 12 left-handed women tested in this second study, we are not
ready to conclude that there is a sex-related difference among left-handers
in "reverse cerebral dominance."[7] Again, there was no difference in over-all
performance by left-handers and right-handers.

SUMMARY AND CONCLUSIONS

In summary, most right-handed blind subjects read faster or more accurately with the LH (i.e., the middle finger of the left hand) than with the
RH, although there are large individual differences that depend importantly on initial hand preferences. We also find that sighted right-handed
children and young adults who are unfamiliar with braille learn braille-like
patterns more quickly with the left index finger than the right (although
again there are several exceptions) whereas sighted left-handers either show
no hand difference or, among young women in one study, superior RH
learning. For right-handers, the results therefore appear to support
Hermelin and O'Connor's hypothesis that braille dot patterns, though they
are symbols of alphabet letters, nevertheless are analyzed more efficiently
by the right hemisphere than by the left because of their spatial-
configurational design. Notwithstanding this apparent support, I would
like to suggest a different explanation of these results.[8]

Role of Sensory Modality

In 1973 Brooks reported finding a small, consistent left-field (i.e., right-
hemispheric) superiority for adults' recognition of tachistoscopically projected *handwritten* words. Bryden and Allard (1976) went on to see
whether the same effects would be obtained with individual letters in a
variety of both cursive and print typefaces. The result was that college
students showed superior right-visual-field (RVF) recognition of Roman

[7] In our first study of left-handers, however, we did find that most of the males wrote with
their hand above the line, whereas most of the females wrote in the conventional position. The
proportions in each case were close to those found by Levy (personal communication). If
above-the-line position reflects ipsilateral motor control, as Levy and Reid (1976) have proposed, then our findings suggest that among left-handers, contralateral motor control for
hand-writing—the "standard" neurological design—is more typical of females than males
(Harris, Wagner, & Mellen, in preparation).

[8] The general form, if not the specific points, of this analysis was outlined in earlier reports
(Harris & Witelson, 1977; Witelson & Harris, 1977). A more extensive theoretical and empirical analysis has been developed by Wagner (1979).

alphabet letters that appeared in more printlike typefaces (which also are simpler and more familiar), and superior left-visual-field (LVF) recognition of more scriptlike (also more complex, less familiar) typefaces. In other words, there was no simple, uniform RVF, or left hemispheric, advantage, for these linguistic stimuli, contrary to what would be expected from the usual characterization of left-hemispheric specialization. Bryden and Allard's explanation was that the direction and extent of the laterality effect *in vision* varies widely depending on the relative degree of involvement of right-hemisphere "preprocessing," and that scriptlike typefaces require more such preprocessing than printlike typefaces. By "preprocessing" they mean, for example, those operations that normalize the stimulus by segregating the relevant components of visual input, "cleaning up" the initial representation, and eliminating irrelevant detail—all operations that process-oriented theories of cerebral specialization (e.g. Levy, 1972) ascribe to the right hemisphere.

The analysis to this point looks compatible with Hermelin and O'Connor's analysis of laterality effects for the reading of braille. We would say that braille patterns, like the more scriptlike typefaces, require relatively more right-hemispheric preprocessing, and that is why the LH (in right-handers) is superior. It is the stimulus pattern that counts—the fact that braille consists of spatial configurations to which meaning must be attached. It follows that tactile stimuli that are more like *printlike* letters also would require relatively little preprocessing and therefore would be better recognized with the RH. So far the analysis seems reasonable, though the further implication appears to be that braille dot configurations are even more spatial-configurational in nature than the combination of lines, curves, and circles that constitute the printed Roman alphabet, which seems unlikely. Moreover, braille patterns, unlike scriptlike typefaces, contain no "irrelevant detail" and no stimulus to be "normalized," and, in these respects, seem to be more like idealized print letters. In any event, taking this emphasis on stimulus characteristics at face value, one might expect superior RH accuracy for the *tactual* discrimination of, for example, Roman block letters by sighted persons who are familiar with the Roman alphabet, since we already know from Bryden and Allard's and others' work that Roman block letters (or words or syllables formed from them) are better and faster recognized in the right visual hemifield (left hemisphere). The little available evidence, however, is equivocal or to the contrary. Gardner (1942) had blindfolded, right-handed adults tactually identify nonsense syllables made up of letters that could be read in either direction (e.g., A, H, T). The letters were made of cord on cardboard which then appeared in embossed form. Performance was faster and more accurate with the LH, regardless of reading direction. Witelson (1974) had 6–14-year-old boys identify dichhaptically presented cut-outs of Roman letters, and found no overall hand differences. (See also Labreche, Manning, Goble, & Markman, 1977.) Witelson (1974) suggested that "tactually presented linguistic stimuli are initially analyzed in a spatial code by the right hemisphere [p. 14]."

These findings suggest that an explanation of lateralization effects in perceptual discrimination that emphasizes only stimulus characteristics is incomplete. What is missing, I believe, is some consideration of another factor—the sensory modality, or, following James Gibson (1966), the "perceptual system."

As we have seen, Bryden and Allard (1976) propose that the contribution of right-hemispheric processing to visual recognition ranges widely, from low to high, and that consequently the direction and extent of laterality effects range widely. For tactile perception, however, the evidence implies that the range of the contribution of right-hemispheric processing is biased toward the high processing end of the scale. This implies a greater likelihood of LH advantage in right-handers for the discrimination of tactile stimuli, whether they are simple or complex, than the likelihood of a left visual field advantage for visual recognition of stimuli of the same range of complexity of design. In other words, what may be most important about braille dot patterns is *not* their physical similarity to dot patterns used in tachistoscopic recognition tests, but that they must be perceived by touch rather than by sight.

This emphasis on perceptual system, or modality, is not new. Indeed, sensory modalities once were so identified with a certain kind of hemispheric specialization that the left and right cerebral hemispheres were called the "auditory-linguistic" hemisphere and the "visuospatial" hemisphere, respectively. More recently, though, neuropsychologists have stressed the absence of hemispheric "material specificity" (e.g., Bogen & Vogel, 1975; cited in Rudel, Denckla, & Hirsch, 1977) and instead propose *functional* descriptions to which we already have referred (see pp. 309, 323). The results of Bryden and Allard's (1976) experiment are compatible with this more recent view. Nevertheless, vestiges of the old view remain. For example, if Bogen and Vogel (1975) stressed the lack of hemispheric "material specificity," they also proposed that the right hemisphere is "relatively more kinesthetic than visual [p. 261]"; and Rudel et al. (1977) wrote, "It is indeed paradoxical that much of the lateralization evidence for the right, so-called visual-spatial hemisphere comes from experiments where vision is excluded . . . [p. 164]" To propose now that the perceptual system be reconsidered is not, of course, to urge a return to the view that identified each hemisphere uniquely with a particular modality. It is only to suggest that the kind of processing for which the right hemisphere is specialized is more likely to be brought into play in one kind of perceptual task (tactual, kinesthetic) than another (visual).

How, then, can the paradox to which Rudel *et al.* alluded be resolved? Why should right-hemispheric engagement be greater during tactual discrimination than during visual discrimination of the same stimulus? The answer may lie in certain fundamental differences between touch and vision as sensory and perceptual *systems* (i.e., as ways of registering, extracting, organizing, and processing information in the world).

Some Differences Between Skin and Sight

First, the skin is much inferior in temporal resolving power to the ear or eye (e.g., it takes more than 1 sec for a tactile stimulus to produce its full subjective sensation, compared to .02 sec for the ear, Békésy, 1959). Similarly, it takes longer for a tactile sensation to disappear after stimulus offset.

The skin's spatial resolution, manifested as simultaneous masking, also is much poorer than the eye's (e.g., Békésy, 1959; Geldard, 1968; Kirman, 1973). This implies that it is more difficult to build and sustain the simultaneous "picture" of a stimulus necessary for recognition tactually than visually. This is one reason why object perception is absolutely more difficult tactually than visually. However, to the extent that the right hemisphere is more capable of gestaltlike processing (e.g., inferring a part from a whole), or—in Broadbent's (1974) phrase, sustaining the continuing representation of the environment as one moves through it—then the right hemisphere (through the LH) should be more capable than the left hemisphere of compensating for the skin's limited spatial resolving power.

Another difference between tactual and visual perception is in the extent to which they require integration from separate points in time and space. As Gibson (1962) said, visual perception is based on "the simultaneous registering of the whole contour [Gibson, p. 488]" whereas the unity of tactual perception must depend on "cutaneously separate impressions or on successive impressions [Gibson, p. 488]." Tactual perception thus becomes spatiotemporal, requiring the integration of separate points in time and space.

Yet another difference is in speed of information-gathering. Notwithstanding the magician's dictum that the hand is quicker than the eye, the research evidence indicates the opposite—the hand generally is slower. The slower tempo, combined with the serial nature of tactual exploration, makes tactual perception still more spatiotemporal in comparison to visual perception, creating still a greater need for the integration of separate points in time and space.

Finally, possibly because of differences in how the hand and eye detect information, particularly in how they "sample" object properties, the spatial position or orientation of an object seems to be more salient to the hand. For example, when children compare standard forms with their left–right and up–down reversals, they judge the forms to be very different when the comparison is made tactually, but essentially the same if judged visually (Goodnow, 1969). To the extent that object-orientation is more effectively processed by the right than left hemisphere, the haptic perceptual system is predisposed to be "right-hemispheric" or spatial, in turn predisposing LH superiority in tactual perception.

All these considerations suggest new experiments. For instance, Wagner is carrying out a study employing tactile and visual stimuli varying along continua of complexity, familiarity, and similarity to script in hopes of clarifying at what point, if any, a stimulus perceived tactually is more efficiently processed by the left hemisphere, and whether such points are reached at different times by subjects of different ages and different handedness. In addition, direct studies of hand differences in temporal and spatial resolution and spatial integration are needed, in both right- and left-handed individuals and in children and adults.

All these many complications and further questions notwithstanding, one conclusion seems justified. In the tactual discrimination of braille letters and words, and perhaps for a great variety of other designs as well, the "master hand" is not always master. If there is a more deserving candidate for "eye" of the blind, it is not the right hand but the long-maligned left hand. At least this is so for right-handed people, whether in the blind or in sighted people when they shut their eyes. For left-handers, however, both hands appear to be more nearly equal in skill, although the data are less clear. As usual, the left-hander is more difficult to understand.

REFERENCES

Annett, M. A classification of hand preference by association analysis. *British Journal of Psychology,* 1970, *61,* 303–321 (a).

Annett, M. The growth of manual preference and speed. *British Journal of Psychology,* 1970, *61,* 545–558 (b).

Békésy, G. V. Similarities between hearing and skin sensation. *Psychological Review,* 1959, *66,* 1–22.

Benton, A. L. The 'minor' hemisphere. *Journal of the History of Medicine and Allied Sciences.* 1972, *27* (1), 5–14.

Bogen, J. E. & Vogel, P. J. Neurologic status in the long term following complete cerebral commissurotomy. In F. Michel & B. Scholt, Eds., *Les syndromes des disconnexion calleuse chez l'homme.* Lyon, France: Hop. Neurol., 1975.

Bowman, H. The effect of practice on different dextral types. *American Journal of Psychology,* 1928, *40,* 117–120.

Broadbent, D. E. Division of function and integration of behavior. In F. O. Schmitt & F. G. Worden (Eds.), *The neurosciences: Third study program.* Cambridge, Mass.: MIT Press, 1974.

Broca, P. Sur le siége de la faculté du langage articulé. *Bulletins de la Société d'Anthropologie de Paris*, 1865, *6*, 377–393.

Brooks, L. R. Treating verbal stimuli in a novel manner. In M. P. Bryden (Chm), Recent work on perceptual asymmetry and its relation to hemispheric organization. Symposium presented at meetings of the Eastern Psychological Association, Washington, D.C., 1973.

Bryden, M. P. & Allard, F. Visual hemifield differences depend on typeface. *Brain and Language*, 1976, *3*, 191–200.

Chlumetzky, H. *Kritische Betrachtungen uber das Tastlesen*. Brunn, 1918.

Critchley, M. Tactile thought, with special reference to the blind. *Brain*, 1953, *76*, 19–35.

Feinberg, R. The relationship of subject sex and handedness to hand differences in performance on a braille paired-associates learning task. Unpublished Ph.D. dissertation, Michigan State University, 1979.

Foulke, E. The perception of braille. Paper presented at Annual Meeting of the American Psychological Association, 31 Aug. 1974, New Orleans, La. Mimeo, 57 pp.

Gardner, L. P. Experimental data on the problem of sensory lateral dominance in feet and hands. *Psychological Record*, 1942, *5*, 65–124.

Geldard, F. A. Pattern perception by the skin. In D. R. Kenshalo (Ed.), *The skin senses*. Springfield, Ill.: C. Thomas, 1968.

Gibson, J. J. Observations on active touch. *Psychological Review*, 1962, *69*, 477–491.

Gibson, J. J. *The senses considered as perceptual systems*. Boston: Houghton Mifflin Co., 1966.

Goodglass, H. & Quadfasel, F. A. Language laterality in left-handed aphasics. *Brain*, 1954, *77*, 521–548.

Goodnow, J. J. Eye and hand: Differential sampling of form and orientation properties. *Neuropsychologia*, 1969, *7*, 365–373.

Grasemann, P. Eine Untersuchung uber das Lesen der Blinden. In *Beiheft zur Ztschr. f. ang. Psych.*, Leipzig, 1917, *16*, 67–72.

Hall, G. S. & Hartwell, E. M. Research and discussion, bilateral asymmetry of function. *Mind*, 1884, *9*, 93–109.

Hardyck, C., Petrinovich, L. F., and Goldman, R. D. Left-handedness and cognitive deficit. *Cortex*, 1976, *12*, 266–279.

Harmon, N. B. Ambidexterity. *British Medical Journal*, 1905, *1*, 14–16.

Harris, L. J. Neurophysiological factors in the development of spatial skills. In J. Eliot & N. Salkind, Eds., *Children's spatial development*. Springfield, Ill.: C. Thomas, Publ., 1975, 5–55.

Harris, L. J. Sex differences in spatial ability: possible environmental, genetic, and neurological factors. In M. Kinsbourne (Ed.), *Asymmetrical function of the brain*. Cambridge, England: Cambridge University Press, 1978, 405–522.

Harris, L. J., Thompson, E., and Crano, W. Academic achievement and teachers' ratings of left- and right-handed British school children: A longitudinal study. In preparation.

Harris, L. J., Wagner, N. M., & Mellen, G. Side of language lateralization in left-handers as indexed by hand-writing posture: Evidence for a sex difference. In preparation.

Harris, L. J. & Witelson, S. F. The analysis of cognitive processes in children through the study of hemisphere specialization in different perceptual systems. Paper presented for a symposium, "Towards a developmental neuropsychology," Bienniel Meetings of the Society for Research in Child Development, New Orleans, La., March, 1977; and Witelson, S. F. and Harris, L. J., Meetings of the International Neuropsychology Society, Santa Fe, N. M., Feb., 1977.

Heller, T. *Blinden-Psychologie*. Leipzig: Engelmann, 1904.

Hermelin, B. & O'Connor, N. Right and left handed reading of braille. *Nature*, 1971, *231*, 470 (a).

Hermelin, B. & O'Connor, N. Functional asymmetry in the reading of braille. *Neuropsychologia*, 1971, *9*, 431–435 (b).

Hertz, R. The pre-eminence of the right hand: a study in religious polarity. ("La prééminence de la main droite: étude sur la polarité religieuse," *Revue Philosophique*, 1909, *68*, 553–580). In R. Needham, (Ed.) *Right & left: Essays on dual symbolic classification.* Chicago and London: The University of Chicago Press, 1973.

Jackson, J. H. On the nature of the duality of the brain. *Medical Press Circular*, 1874, *17*, 19, 41, 63 (reprinted in *Brain*, 1915, *38*, 80–103).

Jackson, J. H. Case of large cerebral tumour without optic neuritis and with left hemiplegia and imperception. *Royal London Ophthamology Hospital Reports*, 1876, *8*, 434–444.

Javal, E. *Der Blinde und seine Welt.* Hamburg-Leipzig, Voss, 1904.

Kimura, D. Dual functional specialization of the brain in visual perception. *Neuropsychologia*, 1966, *4*, 275–285.

Kimura, D. The asymmetry of the human brain. *Scientific American*, 1973, *228*, 70–80.

Kinsbourne, M. The cerebral basis of lateral asymmetries in attention. *Acta Psychologica*, 1970, *55*, 193–201.

Kinsbourne, M. The control of attention by interaction between the cerebral hemispheres. In S. Kornblum (Ed.), *Attention and performance, Vol. 4.* New York: Academic Press, 1973.

Kirman, J. H. Tactile communication of speech: a review and an analysis. *Psychological Bulletin*, 1973, *80*, 54–74.

LaBreche, T. M., Manning, A. A. Goble, W., & Markman, R. Hemispheric specialization for linguistic and nonlinguistic tactual perception in a congenitally deaf population. *Cortex*, 1977, *13*, 184–194.

Levy, J. Lateral specialization of the human brain: behavioral manifestations and possible evolutionary basis. In J. A. Kiger (Ed.), *The biology of behavior.* Corvallis: Oregon State University Press, 1972.

Levy, J. & Reid, M. Variations in writing posture and cerebral organization. *Science*, 1976, *194*, 337–339.

Lowenfeld, B., Abel, G., & Hatlen, P. *Blind children learn to read.* Springfield, Ill.: C. Thomas, 1969.

Majeres, R. L. Sex differences in clerical speed: perceptual encoding vs. verbal encoding. *Memory & Cognition*, 1977, *5*, 468–476.

Marshall, J. C., Caplan, D., & Holmes, J. M. The measure of laterality. *Neuropsychologia*, 1975, *13*, 315–321.

Merry, R. V. An experiment in teaching tactual reading to seeing subjects. *Pedagogical Seminary and Journal of Genetic Psychology*, 1931, *39*, 407–413.

Ross, I. *Journey into light, the story of the education of the blind.* New York: Appleton-Century-Crofts, 1951.

Rudel, R. G., Denckla, M. B., & Hirsch, S. The development of left-hand superiority for discriminating braille configurations. *Neurology*, 1977, *27*, 160–164.

Rudel, R. G., Denckla, M. B., & Spalten, E. The functional asymmetry of braille letter learning in normal, sighted children. *Neurology, Minneapolis*, 1974, *24*, 733–738.

Smith, J. M. Which hand is the eye of the blind? *Genetic Psychology Monographs*, 1929, *5*, 213–252.

Smith, J. M. The sensory function of the non-preferred hand. *Journal of Experimental Psychology*, 1933, *16*, 271–282.

Smith, J. M. The sensory function of the non-preferred hand. *Journal of Experimental Psychology*, 1934, *17*, 154–159.

Villey, P. Psychologie de la lecture. tactile. *Journal de Psychologie*, 1931, *28*, 214–249.

Wagner, N. M. Hand differences in braille letter learning in sighted children and adults. Unpublished M. A. thesis, Michigan State University, 1977.

Wagner, N. M. A developmental analysis of hand and visual hemifield differences for letter identification: effects of modality of presentation and letter typeface characteristics. Ph.D. dissertation, Michigan State University, 1979.

Ward, P. Butterflies may be free, but blind Hal Krents finds new evidence of the price of life. *People,* 6 June, 1977, 7, (2), 51–52.

Weber, E. H. Der Tastsinn und das Gemeingefühl. In R. Wagner (Ed.) *Hand-Wörterbuch der Physiologie.* Brunswick, 1846, Vol. III, Part 2, 481–588.

Wilkinson, J. M. The functional hand asymmetry of braille-reading in blind braille readers. Unpublished M. A. thesis, Michigan State University, 1978.

Witelson, S. F. Hemispheric specialization for linguistic and nonlinguistic tactual perception using a dichotomous stimulation technique. *Cortex,* 1974, *10,* 3–17.

less difference between the hands in sinistrals and in RD children. In t. kind of study the inference was that "nonverbal tactile-temporal process are right-cerebrally mediated [Bakker, p. 82]." The inference also is made that older normal children show greater lateralization, and that this is a noteworthy developmental factor.

A second method of evaluating tactile discrimination skills is to consider what underlying mechanisms might be affected as a result of extended tactile training at one body location. What happens, for example, when children are trained in tactile letter discrimination on one hand, and are then tested on both hands? If both hands perform equally well, transfer of learning from the trained to the untrained body location has occurred. Interhemispheric functions are presumably intact, and the child is able to learn tactile information bilaterally. If, however, both hands do not perform equally well, the object would be examine possible factors influencing irregular bilateral transfer.

The research described in this chapter is based on the second approach; that is, the comparison of performance on two body locations after training and stimulation only on one area. If the cumulative evidence of the tactile research showed a consistent pattern of regular bilateral tendencies for the RD right-handers, and of irregular bilateral processing for the RD left-hander, then the findings would suggest that there may be a difference in neurological organization between RD dextrals and sinistrals. While the main purpose was to investigate the effect of handedness on bilateral transfer and learning within disabled reading groups, a secondary purpose was to examine the problem within normal reading groups.

Research about the transfer of learning from the trained to the untrained hand would be easier if we could assume that there was a consistent pattern of lateral dominance in both left- and right-handed individuals. Many studies have shown that each hemisphere has an independent and distinctive capacity for learning. The left hemisphere in normal dextrals is dominant for language processing, whereas the right hemisphere specializes in spatial analysis, the perception of geometric patterns, and the Gestalt image of an entire pattern. Assuming that the crossed anatomical connections between the hand and brain affect tactile learning, training given to one hand is initially transmitted to the contralateral hemisphere. Animal and human studies (Beaumont & Dimond, 1973; Hamilton, 1977) have suggested that memories are stored bilaterally, and that transfer and cross-integration normally occur. The transfer may not be so clearly defined, however, for left-handers. Instead of a consistent contralateral relationship between the preferred hand and the speech dominant hemisphere, left-handed and ambidextrous individuals may have speech represented in either or both hemispheres, without necessarily relating to handedness (Levy, 1974).

16

Tactile Learning, Handedness, and Reading Disability[1]

HELEN SHANER SCHEVILL

INTRODUCTION

The nature of hemispheric specialization in children with reading disabilities (RD) is frequently discussed, but the relationship of handedness to interhemispheric transfer has not been so thoroughly researched. This chapter deals specifically with tactile discrimination skills in normal and RD children. It is the purpose of the study to propose one theoretical orientation about the variability in tactile performance in RD sinistrals, particularly in interhemispheric transfer skills of tactile information. The extent to which left- and right-handed RD children differ in transfer skills may be one basis for understanding cerebral organization in different learning styles, and for evaluating learning strategies in terms of individual needs. Furthermore, subtle differences in learning patterns between left- and right-handers might suggest which sensory mechanisms lend themselves to modifications of cortical asymmetries.

Tactile performance in left- and right-handed RD children can be evaluated in more than one way. One approach is to compare the two sub groups of children in tactile performance before any specific extended tactile training has taken place. Bakker (1972), for example, used a temporal series of slight tactile sensations on the surface of three fingers on each hand separately. He found a tendency for left hand superiority in dextrals, and

[1] This work has been supported by a grant from the National Science Foundation, R/ APR 75–16202 A05, and by a grant from the Smith-Kettlewell Eye Research Foundation

It has also been hypothesized that the brain of the normal non-right-hander is less clearly lateralized than it is for the normal right-hander (Bryden, 1965; Levy, 1969; Zangwill, 1962). Levy has suggested that as a consequence of this poor lateralization, speech is represented in both hemispheres, a condition that diminishes the capacity of the right hemisphere for spatial-perceptual processing. Buffery and Gray (1972) qualify the hypothesis by conjecturing that the visuospatial function may also be represented in both hemispheres in non-right-handed individuals.

If the brain of the normal sinistral is less clearly lateralized than for his dextral peer, the problem may become even more complex when the sinistral has a reading problem. That is to say, the problem of storing and transferring tactile skin writing images bilaterally may be especially difficult for left-handed RD children because of inadequate lateralization of the spatial function. Dependence on dominant hemispheric processes, therefore, may be even more pronounced for the left-handed within an RD group than within a normal reading group.

The left-hander's greater propensity for dominant hemispheric functioning may be indirectly inferred from the research by Efron (1963b). He found that left-handed subjects require a shorter interval of time to transmit information from their right sentient field to their left than right-handers require to transmit information from left to right. Efron (1963a) also found that the conscious comparison of the time of occurrence of any two sensory stimuli requires the activation of dominant hemispheric processes. If tactile stimulation consisted of a series of temporal components, and if the stimulation were applied to the subject's nonpreferred hand, the inference here would be that for left-handers the untrained hand might be more sensitive than the trained hand, and tactile performance would be more accurate on the left than the right hand. By contrast, right-handers might be as sensitive to tactile stimulation on the trained as on the untrained hand.

MECHANICAL TACTILE STIMULATION

The present study describes the findings of a research program using one specific form of tactile stimulation applied to the surface of the skin. Differences that are noted between left- and right-handed children in tactile discrimination skills are described only in this contextual framework. The tactile modality was selected for investigation not only because of theoretical considerations, but also as a possible source of information of what to anticipate in the event that left- and right-handed RD subjects would be trained in tactile reading as part of an intervention program in the schools.

One approach that educators sometimes use in RD classes is to finger trace alphabet letters on the child's back. The teacher may finger trace individual letters or a whole word. The child may give an oral response or point to the matching visual representation. This kind of gamelike practice places emphasis on a multisensory approach to sound-symbol association.

The form of tactile stimulation described in this chapter was devised expressly for experimental use with RD children. A special tactile letter decoding system was constructed for the research, first by Kwatny and Schevill (1974), and later by Electronics Associated Incorporated in New Jersey. The tactile system was generated by a computerized stimulus generator. Instead of the finger tracing method, the tactile stimulation consisted of a series of dotted impulses occurring mechanically at a regular predetermined rate. Depending on the experiment, the tactile stimulation occurred either on the chest area or on the palm of the hand. When the tactile stimulation occurred on the chest, the child held the small $3\frac{1}{2} \times 3\frac{1}{2}$ inch matrix against his t-shirt or blouse above the waistline and felt the tactile sensations of a series of "dots" or points touch his body at an even predetermined rate. The "dots" were tiny lucite rods projecting one at a time a sixteenth of an inch beyond the surface of the box. When tactile stimulation occurred on the palm of the hand, the child placed his hand on the surface of the matrix and felt the dotted impulses on the palm and fingers.

The stimulus generator was programmed to produce dotted linear movement in the form of lowercase alphabet letters at a regulated rate of presentation, duration, pressure, and spatial arrangement. The surface of the tactile matrix had a series of indentations (7 columns and 7 rows). When the tactile system was activated, each dotted letter was traced with the same directionality and form generally used in manual drawing of lowercase letters (Figure 16.1). The time interval between each individual point was set at 60 msec., and the time interval was set at 200 msec. between line segments. The concept of this type of tactile instrument was derived from the tactile visual sensory substitution system for the blind, used originally at Smith-Kettlewell Institute of Visual Sciences (Bach-y-Rita, 1972).

Tactile skin reading with the tactile mechanical system is a complex task by itself. It requires complete attention from the subject in following the series of dotted impulses, converting them to a Gestalt image, and associating a symbolic label to the spatial form. The main question asked is whether the hemispheres are equally ready to receive and interpret the tactile stimulation that occurs at one body location, and to transfer the information bilaterally. It was anticipated that the main difference between dextrals and sinistrals would be in the relative consistency of the former and the relative variability of the latter subjects in interhemispheric transfer skills with the kind of tactile information used in this study.

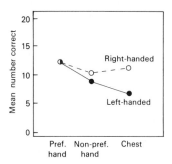

Figure 16.1 Schematic representation of three lower-case letters, *b, i, t,* as they would appear one-by-one on the tactile matrix. The circled dots indicate the pegs that are activated in succession, with a 60 millisecond time interval between each dot. The directionality of each letter agrees with the way the children are taught to draw the letters. Thus, the motion descends for the first segment of *b,* and is then completed by the semicircle descending. The *i* first has the descending motion and then is completed with the dot. The *t* has first the descending motion and then the cross bar from left to right. As soon as one peg appears, the pressure of the palm against the tactile matrix forces the peg to recede. Thus, only one peg protrudes at a time.

EXPERIMENT 1: INTERHEMISPHERIC TRANSFER
FROM THE CHEST AREA TO THE HANDS

The purpose of the first experiment was to show that extended tactile instruction on the center chest area with the mechanical tactile instrumentation might influence tactile letter decoding facility not only on the chest area, but also on the palm of the hands where no previous tactile training had taken place. That is, the objective was to explore the assumption that training on the chest area might be transferred bilaterally and stored in cerebral mechanisms subserving each hand.

The ability to decode tactile letters involves a keen analysis of the spatial dimensions and movement of the tactile impulses, and the ability to ascribe a symbolic label to the form. These two complementary skills represent the integration of bilateral mechanisms in spatial and verbal processing. It was assumed that the center chest area, crossing the midline, was a strategic body location to engage bilateral processes. Research has indicated (Schevill, 1979b) that the center chest location in RD and normal dextrals is more receptive to tactile stimulation than either the left or right chest area. Whereas the left side is least sensitive, especially when the rate of tactile movement is slow, the center chest area is as sensitive to the mechanical form of tactile stimulation at slow as at fast rate of scanning movement. Another study (Schevill, 1979c) showed no difference in performance between normal dextrals and sinistrals at the center chest location, but significantly greater variability at the sides than the center for the sinistrals. Their performance at the sides was relatively inaccurate at both fast and slow rates of movement.

If the center chest was such a strong receptive area and a location connecting to bilateral mechanisms, it was anticipated that information received at this area could be transferred bilaterally to neurological areas subserving each hand. That is, the child would be able eventually to identify tactile letters on the hand after receiving specific training on the chest.

Method

Subjects

The children in this sample were between 7 and 9 years old. Of the 23 children in the sample, 14 were boys and 9 were girls. An informal test of hand preference containing 9 tasks showed that only 5 of the subjects were left-handed. None were ambidextrous.

The children were recommended for the tactile program by the school's reading specialist. All were one year below grade level in Tests 1 and 5 of the Stanford Achievement Test (1964). Three of the children had repeated first grade, 17 were in the second grade even though they were reading at first grade level, and 3 were in the third grade. They attended a private school in suburban Philadelphia, and received individualized reading instruction from their classroom teacher and from the reading specialist in the school. One year after the tactile experiment took place, a follow-up of the children's reading indicated that 15 children had achieved grade level in reading. All of the left-handers, however, were still below grade level in reading scores. Essentially the whole group could be considered "slow bloomers" with a small percentage of mildly disabled readers. The mean average in the full scale score of the Wechsler Intelligence Scale for Children (WISC) (Wechsler, 1949) for the group was 106.

Training and Posttesting

The tactile training period, extending over a period of 3½ months, was administered only on the chest area. The children came in pairs to the tactile reading laboratory and received 20-min lessons twice weekly. The total time of tactile practice amounted to 11 or 12 hours. During the training period the children learned to recognize 15 lowercase alphabet letters and to decode and spell simple words with the tactile method.

At the conclusion of the training period each child was individually tested in oral labelling of letters felt on the chest and on each hand. If the child named the tactile letter at first trial, he received 2 points. He had 2 trials for each letter at each body location. If he named the letter at second trial, he received 1 point. The letters that each child was required to identify were *c, l, o, s, t, d, m, p, h,* and *r.*

During the training period there was enough irregularity among the left-handers' performance to suggest that this form of sensory stimulation was extremely difficult. In fact, the left-handers as a group were so inaccurate during training on the chest that we were quite surprised to find in post-testing that they could identify letters tactilely with their left hands even though no training whatsoever had taken place on the hands. During post-testing one of the left-handers received only 6 points for chest performance, but 18 out of 20 on his left hand! Another child, ambidextrous, showed a similar discrepancy between hand and chest scores. The third child could not distinguish her left hand from her right hand and could only analyze directionality in tactile dot reading on her left palm. The fourth child was inaccurate on all three body locations, and the fifth was the only one who was almost as accurate on the chest as the right-handers.

Results

A mixed analysis of variance was carried out with one between factor, Handedness, and one within factor, Body Location. The results supported the assumption of irregular bilateral transfer for the left-handers. Table 16.1 and Figure 16.2 summarize the results. No significant Handedness effect was found, which suggests that sinistrals did not differ from dextrals in their total performance. The variable, Body Location, was a significant main effect ($p < .001$). This main effect was qualified by the significant interaction effect, Handedness by Body Location ($p < .05$). Further analysis using the Duncan Multiple Range Tests (Duncan, 1955) showed no differences between chest and hands for dextrals. There was a significant difference, however, between hands for this group. Their right hand was more accurate than their left ($p < .05$). For sinistrals the analysis showed that the left hand was significantly more accurate than the chest ($p < .01$), and significantly more accurate than the right hand ($p < .05$).

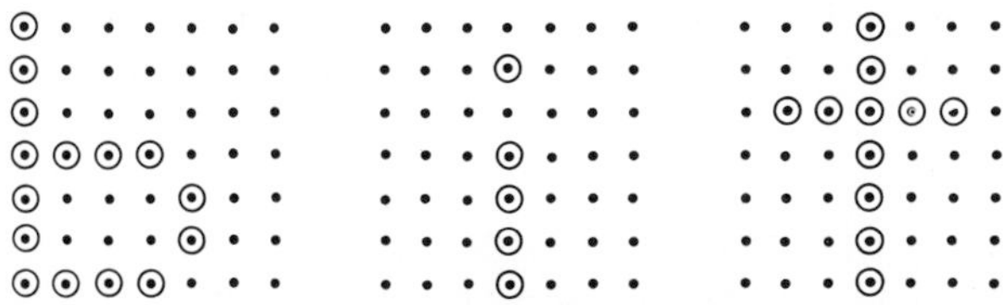

Figure 16.2 Mean accuracy scores by handedness and body location in slow learners after tactile instruction on the chest

Table 16.1
Main Effects and Mean Accuracy Scores by Handedness and
Body Location in Slow Learners after Tactile Instruction on the
Chest

	Summary of analysis of variance			
	Significant main effects			
Body Location	$F = 9.49$	$df = 2/42$		$p < .001$
	Interaction effects			
Handedness by Body Location	$F = 4.06$	$df = 2/42$		$p < .05$
	Mean accuracy scores			
	Right-handed (N = 18)		Left-handed (N = 5)	
Body Location	Mean	SD	Mean	SD
Chest	11.33	2.76	7.00	1.41
Preferred hand	12.28	3.70	12.40	4.15
Nonpreferred hand	10.44	3.11	9.00	5.43

These results imply a different kind of cerebral organization for dextrals than for sinistrals. The dextrals had better spatial and directional skills on their chests. They could decode letters tactilely on the chest and transfer the learning bilaterally. The sinistrals had poor decoding ability on the trained area, the chest, but were nonetheless learning from the training. They were absorbing the information at the cerebral level and using coding processes relating to the area directly subserving their left hands. This finding infers a distinct bias in one hemisphere for spatial linguistic synthesis, and a partial disregard of these processes in the other hemisphere.

The fact that the response in the tactile testing was verbal may have influenced to some extent the preferred hand superiority over the nonpreferred hand for both dextrals and sinistrals. Seamon (1974) hypothesized that if subjects use a verbal code, as opposed to a visual code, this should influence the hemispheric bias. In the present experiment the stronger transfer to the preferred hand suggests the influence of laterality bias resulting from the verbal coding strategies the children were using.

EXPERIMENT 2: INTERHEMISPHERIC TRANSFER FROM THE NONPREFERRED TO THE PREFERRED HAND

Experiment 2 assessed RD and normal readers' tactile discrimination skills on both palms of the hand after specific instruction had taken place only on the nonpreferred palm. A more complex design is used here than in Experiment 1 to assess bilateral transfer with various conditions. By administering pre- and posttests, we could explore more thoroughly the strength of bilateral connections and the effect of training. By using both a verbal and a visual response condition, we could explore the influence of the nature of the response in bilateral transfer and hemispheric bias. By using levels of visual memory ability as one of the main factors, we could investigate the relative influence of this factor in bilateral transfer as it interacts with handedness.

The objective of Experiment 2 was to investigate the extent that bilateral transfer occurred in RD right- and left-handed children after training was administered only on the nonpreferred hand. Specifically, we were investigating the possibility that:

1. RD sinistrals may be more sensitive on their left hands than RD dextrals on their right hands in tactile skills requiring an oral naming response.
2. There may be no consistent pattern, however, for RD sinistrals in the performance of tactile skills requiring a visual matching response. One means of clarifying the issue may be to introduce visual memory skills as a factor in the design.

Training on the Nonpreferred Hand

Tactile letter decoding only on the nonpreferred hand may seem unusual to the reader. We justify the procedure on grounds that this form of tactile stimulation on the nonpreferred hand might be beneficial in different ways for different subjects. If it proved to be ineffective, at least we felt that no real harm could be inflicted on the child from a total of only 12 hours instruction extending over a period of 3½ months.

Witelson (1976) hypothesized that RD dextrals may have bilateral superiority of the right hemispheric spatial function. If this hypothesis applied to behavior in tactile decoding, the rationale would be that the RD child can learn through his stronger hemisphere (the right), and then integrate the information with his weaker hemisphere (the left). Tactile stimulation on the nonpreferred hand would first be interpreted in a spatial context and then integrated with language associations.

By contrast, another rationale was to focus on the child's cognitive deficits as opposed to his cognitive strengths. Approximately 40% of the dextral and 66% of the sinistral RD subjects were deficient in visual memory skills in this particular population. As spatial conceptualization is a right hemisphere process, we rationalized that specific training on the nonpreferred hand might possibly affect visual imagery in the tactile tasks for those deficient in this respect.

Before the second experiment began, we had already trained one left-handed RD child with the tactile system. This boy, 9 years old, was an extreme case of uneven development in interhemispheric integration. He had cerebral palsy on his right side, had poor motor control, and was deficient in visual memory skills on the Benton Visual Retention Test (Benton, 1974). He was unable to program movements for handwriting skills, and his classroom teacher refrained from giving him instruction in this subject.

Jon received the tactile letter decoding training for one school term on his right hand only. Before the training began, his error scores on the preferred and nonpreferred hand were 8 and 9, respectively, out of a possible 10 letters. In the pretest he was required to give a verbal response for each tactile form felt on the palm. After the 3½-month training period his error scores for the left and right hands were 4 and 8, respectively, from a possible error score of 10. The training had occurred only on the right hand, and yet at the conclusion of the experiment Jon was able to identify more than half of the tactile letters by name on his untrained left hand.

Deficient visual memory skills, however, must have hindered his performance in the tactile–visual matching task. Research (Schevill, 1979a) has indicated that this task is significantly easier than the tactile–verbal task. Yet Jon was exceedingly poor in making a visual match after the training experiment. He made 7 errors on each hand from a possible 10 errors. The findings implied that specific training on the nonpreferred hand with the tactile system did not necessarily facilitate the desired spatial frame of reference. He was using the memory codes from his stronger hemisphere to interpret the spatial–verbal task, and the memory codes seemed to be more verbal than spatial in bias.

There were positive aspects to the experiment. Jon could now program movements in handwriting skills, and did not distort or reverse letter forms. The other positive aspect to the experiment was that a partially paralyzed child could receive tactile information on the weaker side of the body and could transfer it to the stronger side for active use. We anticipated that if transfer could occur in such an extreme case, it could also occur for RD sinistrals and dextrals who did not have organic damage.

VISUAL MEMORY

In this experiment every child was given the Benton Test of Visual Retention, Form C (Benton, 1974) as a means of evaluating whether this factor was significant in interhemispheric transfer. Those with "critical" scores (Benton, p. 48) were compared to those with adequate scores. It is noteworthy that so many of the RD children were deficient in this respect. By contrast, not even one normal reader was deficient in visual memory.

In a study dealing only with the right-handed RD population (Schevill,

1979a), the findings indicated a significant main effect ($p < .01$) for the Visual Memory factor only on the left hand. The specific task was the tactile–visual matching test used in the present experiment. There was no significant effect, however, in the verbal response condition, or in the visual response condition with the right hand. The results can be interpreted to infer that for the dextral RD subjects deficient in visual memory skills, it was difficult to use a right-hemisphere bias. Hence, they were inadequate in matching the tactile letters that were felt on the left hand. From the finding one can infer that the same stimuli can be interpreted with either a visual or a verbal coding system. Dextral RD children who are deficient in visual memory skills are also lacking in adequate visual coding competency.

The objective of using the Benton Visual Retention Test in the present experiment as an independent variable was to investigate any interaction effects between handedness and visual memory in both the verbal and visual responses to the same tactile letters.

Method

Subjects

Seventy-five reading-disabled children between the ages of $7\frac{1}{2}$ and $9\frac{1}{2}$ were randomly selected from a larger population of 200 subjects in reading disabilities classes in the public schools in Philadelphia. Approximately half of the sample came from the Cornman Diagnostic Center, which caters only to the learning-disabled, and the other half came from two satellite schools in which special classes for learning disabilities had been formed. Most of the children had either perceptual–motor or expressive language deficiencies. Their reading would have been at least 2 years below grade-level had they been in normal classes for children of their own age. Even the oldest of the subjects were still reading at a first grade level, and many of the 7-year-olds were not reading at all. The mean Performance intelligence quotient on the WISC for the whole group was 96, with a range from 85 to 115. Not all of the children were tested on the Verbal scores of the WISC. Each child in the sample had been previously screened and diagnosed as learning-disabled by a competent staff of psychologists and neurologists at the Cornman Diagnostic Center. Children with primary neurological problems (such as cerebral palsy) or primary emotional problems were excluded from the sample.

Approximately one-fourth of the sample population could be considered "long-term" candidates for special education, whereas the remainder of the sample, it was hoped, could eventually be mainstreamed into regular classrooms with possibly only a year lag in reading skills.

The comparison group consisted of 40 normal subjects, matched in age to the RD group, who came from two public schools in Philadelphia. The normal reading group represented the same socioeconomic level as that of the subjects from the RD group. The normal children were randomly selected from second to fourth grades. All subjects were within grade level in reading and had no history of difficulty in learning to read. There were 17 girls and 58 boys within the RD sample, and 17 girls and 23 boys within the normal sample.

Handedness

Each child was assessed in hand preference by an informal test consisting of 9 tasks. The preferred hand for writing received a weighted score of 2 points, and each of the other skills, such as cutting with a scissors, throwing a ball, eating with a spoon, shoveling, throwing a ball, unscrewing a bottle cap, tracing a circular figure, and picking up small objects, received 1 point. The total sample included 60 right-handed and 15 left-handed RD subjects. Of these RD subjects, 3 sinistrals were ambidextrous. The total sample of normal subjects included 33 dextrals and 7 sinistrals. None of the children in the normal sample happened to be ambidextrous.

It was unfortunate that the left-handed sample was so small. The small percentage of sinistrals is consistent with other studies that assess left- and right-handed children with reading disabilities (Belmont & Birch, 1965). When the evidence from the first experiment in this study is combined with that of the second experiment, we have a consistent tendency for a total of 20 sinistral children below grade level in reading. The findings even with this small number of children probably represent the behavior of non-right-handed RD children if a larger population could be tested.

Tactile Training

During the $3\frac{1}{2}$ month period between the pre- and posttests, the tactile training was done only on each child's nonpreferred palm. Children were tutored in pairs for two 20-min sessions per week in the tactile laboratory set up in each school, and received a total of 11 to 12 hours of specific training. All lessons were mimeographed for standardization of procedure.

The training consisted of the following types of testlike exercises:

1. Subjects either named the alphabet letters or pointed to cards with visual representations of the letters after an individual letter or a sequence was presented tactilely. If sequences of letters were used, such as *c l; c l c,* or *c l c c,* the child would wait until each sequence of 2, 3, or 4 letters was completed before responding.

2. The subjects identified by oral response or by visual selection the first or last part of a specified word. For example, if the child had a "ma" visual pattern in front of him, he felt on the tactile box one of the following letters for word completion: *n, t, p*. As soon as he felt each letter, he selected an appropriate card to make the word *man, mat,* or *map.*
3. The subjects identified a whole word by visual selection after feeling each letter on the tactile box.

Tactile Testing: The Task with the Verbal Response

In this task 10 tactile letters were given as the stimulus (i.e., *l, o, c, m, h, n, p, s, t, and d*). If the child identified the letter on first trial, he received 2 points. A correct answer on second trial received 1 point. In all tests, half of the children were tested first on their preferred hand, and the other half were tested first on their nonpreferred hand. This test was first given as a pretest. At the conclusion of the extended training period, each child was once more given the same 10-letter tactile-verbal test. In addition, another posttest was administered to each child.

The Task with the Visual Matching Response

The second posttest was a tactile–visual matching task. With the exception of one substitution (*r* instead of *h*), the same 10 letters were used in this version as in the verbal version. The child felt a letter from the movement of the dotted impulses on the tactile box. He then selected an appropriate visual representation from a visual array consisting of three choices. He selected the specific letter that he thought matched the tactile scanning he had just felt. The child did not name the letter he selected. He received only one chance per letter for the tactile–visual matching task. Each hand was tested separately.

Thus, the posttests consisted of 20 letter presentations to each hand with 2 response conditions: an oral identification of letter name, and a matching of a visual representation without any verbal labeling. Two trials for each response were allowed in the verbal labeling task, and one trial for each letter was allowed in the visual matching task.

Results

Pre- and Posttests in the Tactile-Verbal Task

Within the RD group two analyses of variance were carried out for the tactile–verbal condition. One analysis was performed for the pretest, and

the other for the posttest. In each one the significant main effects of
Handedness, Side (preferred and nonpreferred hands), and Visual Memory
were assessed in a mixed design with two between factors, Handedness and
Visual Memory, and one within factor, Side.

In the pretest no significant main effects were found. This was an exceedingly difficult task, and both dextrals and sinistrals were unable to
identify at least 7 of the 10 letters before specific extended training on the
nonpreferred hand. There were no differences for Handedness, Side, or for
Visual Memory in this test. In the posttest, however, for the same RD
children the results indicated significant effects. Table 16.2 summarizes the
findings for the RD group in both the pre- and the posttests (see Figure 16.3
also). In the posttest there was no significant main effect for Visual
Memory. There was a significant main effect for Handedness ($p < .05$),
and a significant interaction effect for Handedness by Side ($p < .05$). The
interaction effect qualified the main effect; namely that sinistrals were more
accurate than dextrals on the untrained preferred hand.

The change in significant effects between the pre- and posttest scores can
be interpreted to infer that the effect of training was significantly more
focused for the sinistrals on memory codes serving their untrained than

Table 16.2

Main Effects and Mean Error Scores by
Handedness and Side in the Tactile–Verbal Tests
for Disabled Readers

Mean error scores in the pretest

Right-handed subjects (N = 60)			Left-handed subjects (N = 15)		
Side	Mean	SD	Side	Mean	SD
Right	.72	.18	Left	.74	.22
Left	.72	.18	Right	.77	.16

Summary of analysis of variance in the posttest

Significance of interaction effects
Handedness by Side $F = 5.04$ $df = 1/71$ $p < .05$

Mean error scores in the posttest

Right-handed subjects (N = 60)			Left-handed subjects (N = 15)		
Side	Mean	SD	Side	Mean	SD
Right	.49	.23	Left	.41	.19
Left	.48	.23	Right	.50	.17

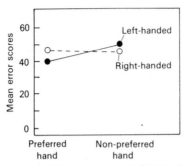

Figure 16.3 Mean error scores by Handedness and Side in the factile-verbal posttest for disabled readers

trained hand. Beaumont (1974) suggests that relatively complex tasks may show greater laterality differences for non-right-handers. This experiment qualifies Beaumont's hypothesis. Here we can infer that the complex cognitive operations in verbal and tactile decoding over a period of time caused the greater laterality differences for non-right-handed RD subjects. Mechanisms subserving their preferred hand were more activated than those subserving their trained nonpreferred hand.

Within the normal reading group two analyses of variance were also performed, one for the pretest and the other for the posttest in the tactile–verbal task. In each case the design was a mixed analysis of variance, Handedness by Side, with Handedness as the between factor and Side as the within factor. As all of the normal readers had adequate visual retention scores, that variable was not included in the analysis of variance design for this group.

Results indicated no significant main effects for either the pre- or the posttest scores in the tactile–verbal scores. That is, there were no significant differences for Handedness or Side either in the pre- or the posttest scores. The scores indicated fewer than 2 errors in the posttest condition, as opposed to almost 5 errors in the pretest condition. Thus, normal sinistrals learned and stored the tactile–verbal images bilaterally. In this respect they differed from their RD peers. Table 16.3 summarizes the mean error scores in the tactile–verbal task for normal readers.

Posttest in Tactile-Visual Matching

The tactile–visual matching task was used as a second method of evaluating how the two factors, visual memory and handedness might influence bilateral integration and transfer after the extended training period on the nonpreferred hand. In contrast to the verbal naming task, it was

Table 16.3
Mean Error Scores by Handedness and Side in
Tactile–Verbal Tests for Normal Readers

Mean error scores in the pretest					
Right-handed subjects (N = 32)			Left-handed subjects (N = 7)		
Side	Mean	SD	Side	Mean	SD
Right	.49	.21	Left	.50	.29
Left	.47	.26	Right	.48	.36

Mean error scores in the posttest					
Right-handed subjects (N = 32)			Left-handed subjects (N = 7)		
Side	Mean	SD	Side	Mean	SD
Right	.19	.18	Left	.11	.09
Left	.17	.17	Right	.14	.11

possible in the visual matching task to bypass the language processes, and to make a correspondence of tactile image with visual form. The question was whether the RD sinistral population generally would still use a dominant hemispheric bias for a response that probably engaged greater activation of the right hemispheric processes. Another question asked was whether children with deficient visual memory would have as much difficulty in this task as Jon did. A third question asked was whether RD left-handed children who are adequate in visual memory are necessarily well lateralized in tactile–visual skills.

Within the RD group a mixed analysis of variance was carried out with two between factors, Visual Memory and Handedness, and one within factor, Side. Table 16.4 and Figure 16.4 summarize the results. Findings indicated that in this task Visual Memory was a significant main effect ($p < .01$). The interaction effect, Side by Handedness by Visual Memory was significant ($p < .05$). An analysis was also done to examine the interaction of Handedness by Side within levels of Visual Memory. The results indicated a significant effect for sinistrals who were adequate in visual memory ($F = 4.52$; $df = 1/71$; $p < .05$). No significance was found for sinistrals with deficient visual memory. That is, RD sinistrals with adequate visual memory were significantly more accurate on the untrained preferred hand, whereas RD sinistrals with deficient visual memory were equally inaccurate on both hands. The dextrals with adequate and deficient visual memory skills transferred the tactile-visual information bilaterally in this experimental design.

Table 16.4
Main Effects and Mean Error Scores by Handedness, Side, and Visual Memory in the Tactile–Visual Posttest for Disabled Readers

Summary of analysis of variance				
	Significant main effects			
Visual Memory	$F = 14.60$ $df = 1/71$ $p < .01$			
Side by Handedness	*Interaction effects*			
by Visual Memory	$F = 5.52$ $df = 1/71$ $p < .05$			

Mean Error Scores				
Side	*Visual Memory*	*N*	*Mean*	*SD*
Right-handed subjects				
Right	Deficient	26	.39	.16
Left	Deficient		.41	.21
Right	Adequate	34	.32	.20
Left	Adequate		.26	.18
Left-handed subjects				
Left	Deficient	10	.52	.12
Right	Deficient		.47	.17
Left	Adequate	5	.18	.16
Right	Adequate		.28	.19

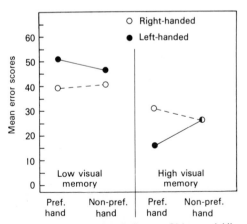

Figure 16.4 Mean error scores by Handedness, Side, and Visual Memory in the tactile-visual posttest for disabled readers

Table 16.5 summarizes the mean error scores for the normal readers. The results of an analysis of variance, Handedness by Side, yielded no significant effects in the tactile–visual task. Inspection of the scores in this task and in the tactile–verbal tasks indicate that sinistrals are even more astute than dextrals in tactile performance, even though there is no significant difference between the subgroups of children. Within the normal sample, left-handedness by itself in no way affected successful bilateral transfer of information or the quality of performance in tactile discrimination.

DISCUSSION

Irregular Transfer for Left-Handed Reading-Disabled Children

This study has analyzed several sets of tactile tasks for dextrals and sinistrals within the RD and normal samples. In each experiment the comparison included handedness and the transfer of abilities from one body location, such as the chest or the nonpreferred hand, to the preferred hand. In each analysis handedness by itself was not a significant factor. Handedness was always qualified by an interaction with body location. In fact, variability between body locations in tactile sensitivity was the noteworthy factor for RD sinistrals. The variability manifested itself only after specific extended instruction on a body location other than the left hand. The findings imply that for these children interhemispheric transfer is irregular and is dependent primarily on dominant hemispheric coding.

The contributing factor to the unilateral transfer was the specific response variable, namely the factor of a verbal or a visual matching response. The verbal response condition, more than the visual, generally called attention to the dominant hemispheric function for RD sinistrals. With the visual response condition, only a small proportion of RD sinistrals showed the unilateral bias, namely those with adequate visual memory skills. It is noteworthy that these few RD sinistrals ($N = 5$)

Table 16.5
Mean Error Scores by Handedness and Side in the Tactile–Visual Posttest for Normal Readers

Right-handed subjects (N = 32)			Left-handed subjects (N = 7)		
Side	Mean	SD	Side	Mean	SD
Right	.12	.10	Left	.09	.12
Left	.10	.13	Right	.06	.05

showed the same unilateral bias for verbal and visual coding strategies. That is, their left hand was more accurate for both the tactile–verbal and the tactile–visual processing.

The bilateral storage and interhemispheric transfer occurred in a more regular pattern for sinistrals without reading problems, and for both normal and RD dextrals. These findings infer that whatever irregularities in lateralization normal left-handers or RD right-handers may have, these did not show up in tasks of bilateral transfer of tactile information in the present design.

Theoretical Implications

The findings of this experiment form the basis for the following hypotheses:

1. Reading-disabled sinistrals tend to use a greater degree of dominant hemispheric bias in processing tactile–verbal information than do RD dextrals.
2. The brain in the RD child is capable of transmitting information from a less active to a more active cerebral area.
3. Specific tactile training develops intersensory skills through the child's cognitive strengths. The RD sinistral's cognitive strengths center primarily in the dominant hemisphere.
4. Reading-disabled sinistrals with adequate visual memory tend to use the same hemispheric bias for verbal and visual coding strategies. Reading-disabled sinistrals with deficient visual memory show a diffuse tendency in selecting a visual code for a visual matching response, since neither hand is accurate in response. Nevertheless, RD sinistrals with deficient visual memory show a unilateral bias for verbal coding strategies.
5. Dextral and sinistral RD children can arrive at the same degree of proficiency by using different mechanisms and pathways for the same task.

The findings also give rise to questions that require further research. The children in the present study were between 7 and 9 years old. Does the RD left-hander become more spatially lateralized as he grows older and as reading-related tasks become easier? Is there a greater relationship between coding strategies and accuracy on a particular hand for older subjects? Is the unilateral bias after tactile training singular with this form of stimulation, or would it occur for sinistrals in other kinds of training experiments as well? What kind of bilateral organization would have occurred if tactile instruction had been given only on the preferred hand?

SUMMARY

Two experiments of within-group comparisons were carried out between right- and left-handed children in tactile letter decoding skills. The populations selected were normal readers, slow readers, and severely disabled readers. In each comparison, results showed qualitative differences between left- and right-handed children. Findings indicated a significant degree of variability in performance for the left-handed slow and disabled reading samples. In each instance the untrained left hand was more accurate than either the trained chest or the trained right hand. Findings suggest that these left-handers may be using a unilateral bias for coding, transfer, and interhemisphere integration.

A second issue addressed in the studies was whether visual memory skills corresponded with spatial lateralization in left-handed disabled readers. Findings indicated that the reading disabled with adequate visual memory may be using the same unilateral bias for visual as for verbal coding processes, but that those with deficient visual memory may be using a unilateral bias primarily for verbal processing and are analyzing spatial dimensions as well as they can from a verbally dominant frame of reference.

In the first experiment bilateral transfer was studied in a tactile–verbal task after training took place only on the chest. In the second experiment bilateral transfer was studied in a tactile–verbal task both before and after training took place on the nonpreferred hand. Also in this experiment bilateral transfer was studied in a tactile–visual matching task. Levels of visual memory affected only the response dimension for the visual matching task, suggesting the close relationship of internal coding systems and laterality bias. The findings suggest that whether slightly or severely reading disabled, left-handed children may be partially disregarding the nondominant spatial function and using a dominant bias for both spatial and verbal processing.

ACKNOWLEDGMENTS

My appreciation is extended to the staff and children of the schools in which Experiments 1 and 2 were implemented. For Experiment 1 special thanks is extended to Principal Sam Jackson of the Lower School of Germantown Academy. His fine cooperation with the testing and training program made it possible to work with the children over a school term. For Experiment 2 special thanks is extended to the Philadelphia Public School District for allowing me to carry out the research. My appreciation is extended to Dr. Irving Farber, Director of Research, and to Dr. Win Tillery, Director of Special Education, for their complete cooperation in allowing me to implement the research in the schools. Special thanks is also extended to Principal Harriet Grass of the Cornman Diagnostic Center, Principal Ellen Wholey of the Franklin Elementary School, and Principal Ethel Rubin of the Solis–Cohen School for their splendid cooperation in allowing the research to be carried out during the course of a school year.

REFERENCES

Bach-y-Rita, P. *Brain mechanisms in sensory substitution.* New York: Academic Press, 1972.

Bakker, D. *Temporal order in disturbed reading.* Rotterdam: Rotterdam University Press, 1972.

Beaumont, J. Handedness and hemisphere function. In S. Dimond & J. Beaumont (Eds.), *Hemisphere function in the human brain.* New York: Wiley, 1974.

Beaumont, J. & Dimond, S. Transfer between the cerebral hemispheres in human learning. *Acta Psychologica,* 1973, *37,* 87–91.

Belmont, L. & Birch, H. G. Lateral dominance, lateral awareness and reading disability. *Child Development,* 1965, *36,* 57–71.

Benton, A. Benton Revised Visual Retention Test (manual), 4th ed. New York: The Psychological Corporation, 1974.

Bryden, M. Tachistoscopic recognition, handedness, and cerebral dominance. *Neuropsychologia,* 1965, *3,* 1–8.

Buffery, A. & Gray, J. Sex differences in the development of spatial and linguistic skills. In C. Ounsted & D. Taylor, (Eds.), *Gender differences: Their ontogeny and significance* London: Churchill Livingstone, 1972.

Duncan, D. Multiple range and multiple F. tests. *Biometrics,* 1955, 11, 1–42.

Efron, R. Temporal perception, aphasia, and deja vu. *Brain,* 1963a, *86,* 403–423.

Efron, R. The effect of handedness on the perception of simultaneity and temporal order. *Brain,* 1963b, *86,* 261–284.

Hamilton, C. Investigations of perceptual and mnemonic lateralization in monkeys. In S. Harnod, R. Doty, L. Goldstein, J. Jaynes, & G. Krauthamer, (Eds.), *Lateralization in the nervous system.* New York: Academic Press, 1977.

Kwatny, E. & Schevill, H. A tactile-visual sensory aid system for dyslexic children. Twenty-seventh ACEMB, Krusen Research Center, Temple University School of Medicine, Philadelphia, 1974.

Levy, J. Possible basis for the evolution of lateral specialization of the human brain. *Nature,* 1965, *224,* 614–615.

Levy, J. Psychological implications of bilateral asymmetry. In S. Dimond & J. Beaumont, (Eds.), *Hemisphere function in the human brain.* New York: Wiley, 1974.

Schevill, H. Tactile learning and reading failure. In H. Myklebust (Ed.), *Progress in learning disabilities,* vol. IV. New York: Grune & Stratton, 1979a.

Schevill, H. Reading disability and tactile performance in temporal ordering and information processing skills. In press, 1979b.

Schevill, H. Unpublished data on tactile discrimination and handedness, 1979c.

Seamon, J. Coding and retrieval processes and the hemispheres of the brain. In S. Dimond & J. Beaumont, (Eds.), *Hemisphere function in the human brain.* New York: Wiley, 1974.

Stanford Achievement Test (Primary II Battery, Form X). New York: Harcourt, Brace & World, 1964.

Wechsler, D. Wechsler Intelligence Scale for Children (Manual), New York: The Psychological Corporation, 1949.

Witelson, S. Abnormal right-hemisphere specialization in developmental dyslexia. In R. Knights and D. Bakker, (Eds.), *The neuropsychology of learning disorders.* Baltimore: University Park Press, 1976.

Zangwill, O. Handedness and dominance. In J. Money, (Ed.), *Reading disabilities.* Baltimore: Johns Hopkins Press, 1962.

Index